Scientists and Inventors

MACMILLAN
PROFILES

Scientists and Inventors

MACMILLAN LIBRARY REFERENCE USA
New York

Produced and designed by Miller Williams Design Associates, Lake Villa, IL

Macmillan Library Reference USA
1633 Broadway
New York, New York 10019

Manufactured in the United States of America

Printing number
1 2 3 4 5 6 7 8 9 10

Library of Congress Cataloging-in-Publication Data

Scientists and inventors / [editor Judy Culligan].
        p.   cm. — (Macmillan profiles ; 1)
    Includes index.
    Summary: Alphabetical articles profile the life and work of notable sci-entists and inventors from antiquity to the present, beginning with Jean Louis Rodolphe Agassiz and concluding with the Wright Brothers.
    ISBN 0-02-864983-4
1. Scientists—Biography—Encyclopedias, Juvenile. 2. Inventors—Biography—Encyclopedias, Juvenile. [1. Scientists—Encyclopedias. 2. Inventors—Encyclopedias] I. Culligan, Judy. II. Series.
Q141.S294 1998
509.2 ′ 2—dc21
[B]   98–28744
                                                                     CIP
                                                                      AC

Front cover clockwise from top: Thomas Edison (UPI/Corbis-Bettman), Marie Curie (Corbis-Bettman), George Washington Carver (Corbis-Bettman), Albert Einstein (Corbis-Bettman)
Cover design by George Berrian

This paper meets the requirements of ANSI/NISO A39.48-1992 (Permanence of Paper).

Contents

Macmillan **Profiles:** *Scientists and Inventors* is a unique reference featuring over 100 profiles of notable scientists and inventors from antiquity to the present. The articles describe the life and times of anthropologists, biologists, chemists, geologists, mathematicians, psychologists, physicians, and physicists, as well as the inventors of everything from the printing press to dynamite to the geodesic dome.

Macmillan Library Reference has published a wide array of award winning reference materials for libraries across the world. It is likely that several of the encyclopedias on the shelves in this library were published by Macmillan Reference or Charles Scribner's Sons.

Librarians, teachers, and parents continue to seek reliable, accurate, and accessible biographies of notable figures in science and history. The Macmillan Profiles Series is a collection of biographical volumes featuring carefully selected biographies from distinguished Macmillan sources. In some cases, original biographies were commissioned to supplement entries from original sources. All biographies have been recast and tailored for a younger audience by a team of experienced writers and editors.

Our goal is to present an exciting introduction to the life and times of important figures in history and science. The article list was based on the following criteria: relevance to the curriculum, importance to history, name recognition for students, and representation of as broad a cultural range as possible. The article list was refined and expanded in response to advice from a lively and generous team of high school teachers and librarians (names listed below, in Acknowledgments). The result is a balanced, curriculum-related work that brings these historical figures to life.

FEATURES

Scientists & Inventors is the inaugural volume in the **Profiles Series**. To add visual appeal and enhance the usefulness of the volume, the page format was designed to include the following helpful features:

- ■ **Time lines:** Found throughout the text in the margins, time lines provide a quick reference source for dates and important accomplishments in the life and times of these scientists and inventors.

- **Notable Quotations:** Found throughout the text in the margins, these thought-provoking quotations are drawn from interviews, speeches, and writings of the scientist or inventor covered in the article. Such quotations give readers a special insight into the distinctive personalities of these great men and women.

- **Definitions and Glossary:** Brief definitions of important technical terms in the main text can be found in the margin. A glossary at the end of the book provides students with an even broader list of definitions.

- **Sidebars:** Appearing in shaded boxes throughout the volume, these provocative asides relate to and amplify topics.

- **Suggested Reading:** An extensive list of books and articles about the scientists and inventors covered in the volume will help students who want to do further research.

- **Index:** A thorough index provides thousands of additional points of entry into the work.

ACKNOWLEDGMENTS

We thank our colleagues who publish the *Merriam Webster's Collegiate® Dictionary*. Definitions used in the margins and many of the glossary terms come from the distinguished *Webster's Collegiate® Dictionary*, Tenth Edition, 1996.

We are also grateful for the contributions of the following inimitable team of teachers and librarians who helped compile the article list. Their experience and insight were invaluable: Kathy Conway, Gary Fritz, Mike Hickey, Marie Lackey, Neil McLoughlin, Bernadette Meisenheimer, Sally Pilcher.

The biographies herein were written by leading authorities at work in the fields of biology; chemistry; earth sciences; medicine; psychology; physics; and American, European, and world history. *Scientists & Inventors* contains 80 photographs. Acknowledgments of sources for the illustrations can be found on page 328.

This work would not have been possible without the hardwork and creativity of our staff. We offer our sincere thanks to all who helped create this marvelous work.

Macmillan Library Reference

Agassiz, Jean Louis Rodolphe

1807–1873 ● NATURAL HISTORY, GEOLOGY, & PALEONTOLOGY

"One naturally asks, what was the use of this great engine set at work ages ago to grind, furrow, and knead over, as it were, the surface of the earth? We have our answer in the fertile soil which spreads over the temperate regions of the globe. The glacier was God's great plow."

— Jean Louis Agassiz

A descendant of a Huguenot family that had moved to Switzerland, Agassiz was born in Motiers, Canton de Fribourg, on 28 May 1807. He studied at Bienne, Lausanne, Zurich, Heidelberg, and Munich, receiving a degree in medicine from the University of Heidelberg in 1830. From early childhood Louis Agassiz had a strong interest in natural history, and after receiving his medical degree he went to Paris to study under the great comparative anatomist and founder of **vertebrate paleontology**, Georges Cuvier. In 1832 Agassiz was appointed a professor of natural history at the College of Neuchâtel, where he remained until 1846. In that year he was invited to give a series of lectures at the Lowell Institute in Boston. The success of these lectures, plus Agassiz's interest in the natural history of the United States, resulted in a permanent move to America. In 1848 he was made professor of natural history at the Lawrence Scientific School at Harvard University. Though he traveled extensively during the latter part of his career, he remained at Harvard

verteberate paleontology: a science dealing with animals with backbones that lived during past geological periods.

until his death. This lifelong residence was made despite the fact that he was offered, among other honors, the professorship of paleontology at the Museum of Natural History in Paris in 1859. At Harvard in 1859–1860 Agassiz founded the Museum of Comparative Zoology and also served as its first director. In 1863 Agassiz helped to found the National Academy of Sciences in Washington, DC.

Agassiz is perhaps best known for his work on fossil fishes; his work on **glaciers**, which resulted in the concept of the "Ice Age"; his contributions to general natural history (particularly of North America); and his opposition to Darwin's theory of evolution by natural selection.

glaciers: large bodies of ice moving slowly down a slope or valley and spreading outward.

Relatively early in his career Agassiz established his reputation with a massive, five-volume study of fossil fishes, *Recherches sur les poissons fossiles* (1833–1844); in addition he published *Monographie des poissons fossiles du vieux grès rouge ou système dévonien des Iles Britanniques et de Russie* (1844). Agassiz also had a general interest in zoological nomenclature and classification, publishing *Nomenclator Zoologicus* (1842–1846).

While pursuing the above-mentioned studies Agassiz also became interested in problems of glacial geology, building on the work of earlier geologists (especially Johann H. Charpentier [1786–1855]). Beginning about 1836 he began investigating the modern glaciers of the Swiss Alps. Agassiz demonstrated that glaciers move or flow. One demonstration of this characteristic was that a cabin built on a glacier in 1827 moved about a mile from its original site in a dozen years. Agassiz also performed experiments on glaciers, such as driving a straight line of stakes across a glacier and then returning several years later to find that the middle stakes had moved downhill, forming a "U" shape. Agassiz also documented the physical effects of glacial movement on the land's surface. He noted grooves and scourings on rock surfaces over which glaciers had moved, as well as various rock accumulations that formed on the sides and ends of glaciers (lateral and terminal moraines, erratic boulders, and so forth). Finding similar features in northern Europe and North America, Agassiz established that glaciers had once (in the relatively recent geological past) covered a much more extensive area than they do today. This fact established the concept of an Ice Age. Among Agassiz's important works on glacial geology are

1829 Agassiz publishes *Fishes of Brazil.*

1833 Agassiz publishes the first part of his pioneering history of fossil fishes.

1836 Agassiz begins investigating glaciers.

1840 Agassiz publishes *Studies on Glaciers,* establishing the concept of an Ice Age.

1848 Agassiz becomes professor of natural history at Harvard University.

Études sur les glaciers (1840), *Système glaciaire* (1846), and *Nouvelles études et expérences sur les glaciers actuels* (1847).

In North America, Agassiz continued his studies of natural history, publishing such works as *Contributions to the Natural History of the United States* (1857–1862), a work that was never completed although four volumes were published, *The Structure of Animal Life* (1862), *Methods of Study in Natural History* (1863), *A Journal in Brazil* (1868), based on his travels to that country, and *Geological Sketches* (two volumes, 1866-1876). During this time he also traveled widely, including journeys to Florida and the western United States, Europe, Brazil, and a trip around Cape Horn to the Pacific.

Throughout his life Agassiz opposed the concept of evolution, both as formulated by Charles Darwin and by Jean-Baptiste Lamarck and his followers. Agassiz acknowledged (indeed, helped to elucidate) the progression of fossil forms that outlined the history of life through geological time. But, like Cuvier, he did not interpret this history as being the result of evolution. Rather, Agassiz approached the fossil record from what has been considered an "idealist" and "embryological" point of view. Agassiz viewed the development of a human **embryo** as being a process in which the organism goes through a progressive hierarchy of levels of organization—fish, amphibian, reptile, mammal, and so forth—as it approaches a certain perfection of being in the final adult form. Embryological development is a goal-directed process. Likewise, according to Agassiz, the history of different species and biotas through geological time is also a developmental series representing progress toward the highest organic beings, namely humans (*Homo sapiens*). These concepts of Agassiz and of like-minded thinkers of the nineteenth century (such as the Scottish geologist Hugh Miller [1802–1856]) might seem to approach evolutionary thinking, but they were actually far from it. Agassiz was convinced that the history of life on Earth was a series of discontinuous stages, and each stage of fauna and flora had been catastrophically destroyed and replaced with a new stage. The driving force behind the history of life was a supernatural Deity who regularly intervened to miraculously produce new suites of species. Agassiz believed that any particular species, once created, was fixed and incapable of change or evolution.

Despite his opposition to evolution, Agassiz is generally

Agassiz believed that any particular species, once created, was fixed and incapable of change or evolution.

embryo: a vertebrate organism at any stage of development prior to birth or hatching.

acknowledged as one of the great naturalists of the nineteenth century. He was known as an enthusiastic and eloquent teacher, and his lectures were well attended. His son, Alexander Agassiz, was also a well-known naturalist and director of the Museum of Comparative Zoology (1874–1910) after his father's death, in Cambridge, Massachusetts, on 14 December 1873. In 1879 a large **Pleistocene** lake, which covered parts of North Dakota, Minnesota, and Manitoba, was named after Louis Agassiz. Louis Agassiz was elected to the Hall of Fame for Great Americans in 1915. ◆

Ampère, André-Marie

1775–1836 ● ELECTRODYNAMICS

Ampère was the only son of Jean-Jacques Ampère and Jeanne-Antoinette Desutieres-Sarcey, descendants of prosperous silk-merchant families in Lyons, where he was born on January 20, 1775. One of his two sisters died quite young and the other later served him as a housekeeper in Paris. In 1793, when Ampère was eighteen, his father was unjustly executed by **guillotine** during the Reign of Terror, the most violent period of the French Revolution. In 1799

Ampère married Catherine-Antoinette Carron, and in 1800 she gave birth to their son, Jean-Jacques. Her health failed shortly there after, however, and she died in 1803. Ampère's personality took on a permanently melancholy cast following these tragic events of his youth.

Ampère received no formal education whatsoever. His father encouraged him to read extensively, and the young Ampère committed to memory entire articles of the famous *Encyclopedia* edited by Jean Le Rond D'Alembert and Denis Diderot. His parents were devout Catholics; Ampère often was tormented by tensions between his intellectual and spiritual inclinations. One of his earliest scientific interests was botanical classification, and he also developed an early talent for mathematics. Following some teaching and tutoring in Bourg and Lyons, in 1804 Ampère was appointed to teach mathematics at the École Polytechnique, the prestigious institute for scientific education in Paris. He wrote several mathematics memoirs on partial differential equations, and in 1814 he won election to the French Academy of Sciences as a mathematician. During this period, Ampère also kept abreast of developments in chemistry. He proposed a highly geometric conception of molecular structure, developed a classification scheme for the chemical elements, and gave an independent presentation of what is generally referred to as Avogadro's hypothesis.

Ampère did not devote detailed attention to physics until 1820, when he was forty-five years of age. In that year Hans Christian Oersted discovered that an electric current can alter the orientation of a suspended magnet. Ampère immediately followed up Oersted's work by discovering that two linear electric currents either repel or attract each other depending upon their mutual orientation. He then argued that all magnetic phenomena are due to similar forces between tiny molecular circuits within magnets. He discovered a mathematical formula for the force between any two infinitesimally short circuit elements, and he applied this formula to a wide variety of experimental arrangements of electric circuits and magnets, a new branch of physics he called "electrodynamics." In 1822 he came very close to discovering electromagnetic induction, subsequently discovered by Michael Faraday in 1831. Ampère's most creative contributions came during the transition from the electrostatics and

> Ampère was tormented by tensions between his intellectual and spiritual inclinations.

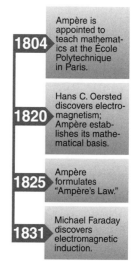

1804 ▸ Ampère is appointed to teach mathematics at the École Polytechnique in Paris.

1820 ▸ Hans C. Oersted discovers electromagnetism; Ampère establishes its mathematical basis.

1825 ▸ Ampère formulates "Ampère's Law."

1831 ▸ Michael Faraday discovers electromagnetic induction.

magnetic theories of the early nineteenth century to the electrodynamic field theory that subsequently became a major component of classical physics. His experimental and theoretical ingenuity earned him recognition from the famous English physicist James Clerk Maxwell as the "Newton of electricity." In 1881 his name was commemorated as the unit of electric current.

Ampère died at Marseilles, France, June 10, 1836. In addition to his contributions to mathematics, chemistry, and physics, Ampère also maintained an interest in philosophy, particularly scientific methodology and classification schemes. ◆

Archimedes

C. 287–212 BCE
MATHEMATICS & INVENTOR

"Eureka!"
(Greek for "I
have found it!")
— Archimedes

lever: a rigid bar used to exert a pressure or sustain a weight at one point of its length by the application of a force at second and turning on a third by a fulcrum.

Archimedes was one of the greatest mathematicians of all times, both for his contributions to theoretical mathematics, which anticipated many modern discoveries, and for his mechanical inventions, among them the **lever**. Son of the astronomer Pheidias, he was born in Syracuse, Sicily, and educated in Alexandria. Although he spent time in Egypt he lived most of his life in the vicinity of Syracuse and was a friend of the Syracusan king Hieron II.

A popular story is related about Archimedes's discovery of the law of hydrostatics (the principle of Archimedes), which states that a body immersed in a fluid is buoyed up with a force equal to the weight of the fluid displaced. Hieron had asked Archimedes to verify whether his crown was indeed made of pure gold. While taking a bath Archimedes noticed the bath water overflowing and suddenly perceived that the volume of water displaced was equal to the volume of his body submerged inside the bath. He then realized that if he put the crown into a vessel filled with water and weighed the water that overflowed and then did the same with a piece of pure gold the weight of the crown, the weight of the water that overflowed would be equal only if the crown also were of pure gold. Without stopping to dress he ran through the streets of the city shouting, *Eureka!* ("I have found it!")

He invented the spiral pump, which raised water from a lower to a higher level by winding a tube around an inclined axis. His discovery of the principle of compounded pulleys was responsible for his famous remark, "Give me a firm spot on which to stand, and I will move the earth." He showed Hieron how little force was needed to move a ship with pulleys. Although he devoted most of his energy to his studies and was little involved in public life, when the Romans besieged Syracuse he put his skills to work for the defense of his native city. He invented such mechanical devices as catapults and a system of concave mirrors, which used the rays of the sun to ignite the sails of the Roman ships. Nevertheless, the city fell in 212 BCE and Archimedes was killed by a Roman soldier who came upon him while he was working on a problem of geometry in the sand. According to the story he was so involved in his work that all he said to the soldier was "Do not disturb my diagrams."

Archimedes was responsible for creating the fields of hydrostatics and statics in mechanics. Although he wrote works on geometry, mathematics, optics, astronomy, and mechanics, he did not write about his inventions. His extant works include: *On Quadrature of the Parabola; On the Sphere and Cylinder; On Spirals; On Conoids and Spheroids, Measurement of the Circle; Book of Lemmas, On the Heptagon; On Equilibrium of Planes;* and *On Floating Bodies.* He requested that his best-known works—on the sphere and the cylinder—be inscribed on his tombstone. ◆

275 BCE ▸ Completion of Colossus of Rhodes and Lighthouse of Pharos in Alexandria, Egypt.

264 BCE ▸ First public gladiator fights in Rome.

239 BCE ▸ Introduction of the leap year into the Egyptian calendar.

212 BCE ▸ Romans conquer and sack Syracuse, killing Archimedes.

Aristotle

384–322 BCE
PHYSICS & BIOLOGY

*"Every science and every inquiry, and
similarly every activity and pursuit, is
thought to aim at some good."*
— Aristotle, *Nicomachean Ethics*

chronology: the sci-
ence that deals with the
measuring of time in
regular divisions and
that assigns to events
their proper dates.

ristotle, who is best known as a Greek philosopher,
was once a student of Plato, but his works cover
almost every conceivable topic including logic, philosophy of science, physics, astronomy, meteorology, biology,
psychology, metaphysics, ethics, politics, rhetoric, and theory of poetry. He had an encyclopedic mind and though he
admired and was influenced by Socrates and Plato, in many
ways he went beyond the two in his inquiries. In some of his
writings Aristotle expresses an affinity for Platonic thought
and in others refutes it. One of their differences was on the
subject of ideal forms. While Plato held that there existed
ideal forms that could not be perceived by the senses,
Aristotle maintained that every object has both Form and
Matter that are inseparable and can be studied only in that
object. Aristotle believed that nature was purposeful and did
nothing by accident and that a philosopher's responsibility
was to observe the objects in nature to discover their purposes.

Though scholars have worked out different theories in an
attempt to explain the development of Aristotle's philosophy,
it is almost impossible to know with certainty when Aristotle
developed any one idea as there exists no accurate **chronology** of his writings. What is certain is his influence on east-

ern and western civilizations, and on Christianity, **Islam**, and Judaism.

Aristotle was born in the Greek colony of Stagiros in Macedonia. His father, Nicomachus, was a court physician to King Amyntas III of Macedonia (father of Philip II and grandfather of Alexander the Great). It is likely that as a youth Aristotle studied medicine and biology in the family tradition, and although he did not become a physician, his early studies probably had some influence on his later interest in biology and the natural sciences.

Islam: the religion of Muslims, including belief in Allah as the sole deity with Mohammed as his prophet.

Aristotle's parents died when he was young; at age seventeen he went to Athens and entered Plato's Academy (367 BCE), where he remained for some twenty years lecturing, writing, and researching. His studiousness and intelligence reportedly earned him the nicknames the Mind (from Plato) and the Reader (from his fellow students). At the Academy he wrote dialogues (which now only exist in fragments) and began his work in the natural sciences.

Aristotle left Athens around the time of Plato's death (348/47 BCE). Some suggest that he left because the Academy did not choose him to succeed Plato but others say that it had more to do with the political climate in Athens. After Philip II conquered the Greek city-state of Olynthus, anti-Macedonian feeling spread to Athens and Aristotle might have been subjected to abuse had he stayed. He and a group of followers, including Theophrastus of Eresus (his eventual successor), settled in Assos in Asia Minor, where Aristotle became an adviser to the ruler Hermias. He married Hermias's niece Pythias, with whom he had one daughter, also named Pythias. When Aristotle married he was in his late thirties, which he regarded as the ideal age for men to marry (with eighteen as the ideal age for women). Pythias did not live long and after her death Aristotle took a companion, Hermeias (it is not clear if they were married), with whom he had a son, Nicomachus.

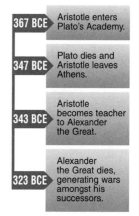

367 BCE — Aristotle enters Plato's Academy.

347 BCE — Plato dies and Aristotle leaves Athens.

343 BCE — Aristotle becomes teacher to Alexander the Great.

323 BCE — Alexander the Great dies, generating wars amongst his successors.

In about 345/44 BCE Aristotle moved to the island of Lesbos, where he and Theophastus established a philosophical circle in the fashion of the Academy. Judging from the many place names from this area in his writings, he conducted much of his biological research during his stay on Lesbos.

A few years later (343/42 BCE), Aristotle went to Pella in response to an an invitation from Philip II to tutor his thir-

Though Aristotle admired Socrates and Plato, in many ways he went beyond the two in his inquiries.

teen-year-old son, the future Alexander the Great. It is not certain how much influence the tutor had on his pupil in the three years they spent together, for many of their ideas are divergent. For one thing, Aristotle told Alexander to completely dominate the barbarians (non-Greeks) and not to intermix with them, to treat them "as beasts or plants," as Plutarch later reported. But Alexander did no such thing and, in fact, actively promoted intermarriage between his soldiers and the people they conquered.

Aristotle returned to Stagiros, where he remained until 335/34 BCE, when he traveled to Athens. There, he founded his own academy, later called the Lyceum, for it was located in a gymnasium attached to the temple of Apollo Lyceus on the outskirts of Athens. The school, which boasted the first large library, differed from Plato's Academy in that it stressed the systematic collection of material and became a leading research center. At the Academy mathematics was the focus of inquiry, but at the Lyceum biology and history were central. In addition, the predominant writing style at the Lyceum became that of expository analysis as opposed to the dialectic style of the Academy. Here Aristotle wrote and organized what later became the largest parts of his corpus of works. Each morning he would walk with his students during their philosophical discussions and eventually the Greek term *peripatetic*, meaning "walking about," became synonymous with Aristotelian philosophy.

impiety: the quality of lacking reverence or proper respect for authority.

The death of Alexander the Great in 323 BCE signaled the revolt of many of the Greek city-states, including Athens. Anti-Macedonian feelings ran high and Aristotle was charged with **impiety**, as Socrates had been. "Proof" of his crime was a poem he had written twenty years before as a **eulogy** to King Hermias that compared him to the gods. He left the city for Chalcis (now Khalkis) on the Strait of Evripos. In a letter to Antipater, a deputy of Alexander, he wrote that he would not allow Athens to sin twice against philosophy, a reference to the sentence imposed on Socrates. He died the following year, reportedly from a stomach illness.

eulogy: a speech or written work that gives high praise to another person.

Copies of busts of Aristotle exist and give the impression of a handsome man with noble features. Written descriptions report that he was thin-legged, had small eyes, spoke with a lisp, and dressed well. He was said to have had a quick and sharp wit and once, when told someone had insulted him, reportedly said, "He may even scourge me, as long as it is in my absence." Aristotle's kindness has been noted in anecdotes and especially in reference to the kind treatment of slaves and servants he expressed in his will.

There are a number of surviving works (in part or whole) that have been attributed to Aristotle. Scholars believe more than one hundred of his works have not been found.

Aristotle's main works include *Metaphysics*, consisting of fourteen volumes covering a range of philosophical concepts such as the nature of being or substance, causality, God, and nature; *Organon*, a compilation of logical works; *Physics*; *On the Heavens*; *Nicomachean Ethics*; *Politics*, a comparison of over 150 governments; *Rhetoric*; and *Poetics*.

The **extant** works of Aristotle were not written for publication but as teaching aids. His contribution to thought was immense and it was Aristotle who founded the scientific method. In his works on logic he introduced the study of logical propositions and developed the system of syllogisms. In his *Ethics* he expounded the concept of the Golden Mean: human happiness consists in virtue, defined as the mean between two extremes.

extant: not destroyed or lost.

It was said of him that "he set in order all parts of philosophy," and at that time all knowledge was seen as a whole. He laid the foundation for research work and its exposition within the framework of defined branches of science. He established the model for the correct definition of scientific subjects: by definitions and assumptions, by classification and orderly arrangement of the material, and by careful progression from one stage to the next. He laid the foundations for the sciences of zoology, anatomy, and physiology, transforming mere information into science. His works on rhetoric and politics are classics and in his *Poetics* he taught that tragedy is based on imitation and associated with a **catharsis** of fear and pity. One of his chief contributions to philosophy was his division of all things into Matter and Form. God, the Prime Mover, is pure Form or thought. In man, the highest Form is represented by reason.

catharsis: purification or elimination of negative emotions through art.

Aristotle's thought has been studied and expounded since his time. For three centuries after his death his school remained a center of research. The influence of Aristotelianism was paramount in the Middle Ages and was basic in Islamic and Jewish philosophy and Christian scholasticism.

Many of our major concepts—energy, substance and essence, subject and predicate, potential and actual, quantity and quality—can be traced back to the immense contribution and originality of Aristotelian thought. ◆

Babbage, Charles

1791–1871 ● MATHEMATICS & INVENTOR

"Every moment dies a man, every moment one and one sixteenth is born."

— Charles Babbage

harles Babbage was born on December 26, 1791, in Teignmouth, Devonshire, England. From the very beginning, he showed a great desire to inquire into the causes of things that astonish children's minds. On receiving a new toy, Charles would ask, "Mamma, what is inside of it?" Then he would carefully proceed to dissect it and figure out how it was constructed and what made it work. All throughout his career, he continued to have a curious and questioning mind. This curiosity played a significant part in the development of many of his famous ideas.

He was one of the two surviving children of Benjamin Babbage, a wealthy banker, and Betty Plumleigh Teape, both descended from well-known Devonshire families. Babbage's parents were affluent and he had the opportunity to attend private schools.

After a succession of private tutors he entered Trinity College, Cambridge, in 1810. At Trinity College, Babbage's studies led him to a critical examination of the **logarithmic**

logarithmic: relating to the exponent that indicates the power to which a number is raised to produce a given number.

Babbage was
born a hundred
years ahead of
his time.

tables used to make accurate calculations. He was well aware of the difficulty and tediousness of compiling the astronomical and nautical tables and dreamed of a machine that would one day calculate such tables. At Trinity College, he proved to be an undisciplined student, constantly puzzling his tutors. He was often annoyed to find that he knew more than his teachers. But in spite of his outward displays of rebellion, he was already on his way to absorbing the advanced theories of mathematics.

In 1815, Babbage, John Herschel, and other contemporaries founded the Analytic Society. Its purposes were to emphasize the abstract nature of algebra, to bring continental developments in mathematics to England, and to end the state of suspended animation in which British mathematics had remained since the death of Sir Isaac Newton.

After receiving his master of arts degree from Trinity College in 1817, Babbage plunged into a variety of activities and wrote notable papers on the theory of functions and on various topics in applied mathematics.

In 1822, Babbage designed his difference engine, considered to be the first automatic calculating machine. Based on the recommendation of the Royal Society, he was able to obtain a grant from the British government that permitted him to work on this machine. The difference engine was to be a special-purpose device, constructed for the task of preparing

The Computer and the Loom

Although many people contributed to the development of the computer, it was an 18th-century weaver who made one of the greatest contributions. In 1805, French weaver Joseph-Marie Jacquard invented a new type of loom that used a system of punched cards with sprung needles. The needles only lifted threads corresponding to the punched pattern on the cards. By changing the cards and the patterns of holes, it became possible to mechanically weave complex designs into the cloth. About three decades later, Charles Babbage adopted Jacquard's punched card method to encode instructions for his analytical machine. In 1888, Herman Hollerith used Babbage's punched card method to feed data into a machine he designed to tabulate the 1890 U.S. census. Hollerith's machine was one of the first practical computers. By the late 1930s, punched card computers had become well established. Punched cards are now one of numerous methods by which data are fed into a computer.

mathematical tables. After eight years of work, Babbage lost interest and abandoned this machine and turned to the design of the analytical engine.

In 1833, Babbage conceived his analytical engine, the first design for a universal automatic calculator. He worked on it with his own money until his death. Babbage's design had all the elements of a modern general-purpose **digital** computer, namely, memory, control, arithmetic unit, input, and output. The memory was to hold 1,000 words of fifty digits each, all in counting wheels. Control was to be by means of sequences of Jacquard punched cards. The very important ability to modify the course of a calculation according to the intermediate results obtained, now called conditional branching, was to be incorporated in the form of a procedure for skipping forward or backward a specified number of cards. The arithmetic unit, Babbage supposed, would perform addition or subtraction in 1 second while a 50 x 50 multiplication would take about 1 minute. Babbage spent many years developing a mechanical method of achieving simultaneous propagation of carries during addition to eliminate the need for fifty successive carry cycles. Input to the machine was to be by individual punched cards and manual setting of the memory counters. Output was to be punched cards or printed copy. Although Babbage prepared thousands of detailed drawings for his machine, only a few parts were ever completed.

The description of Babbage's ideas would not be adequate without mention of Augusta Ada Byron, Countess of Lovelace, who was acquainted with Babbage and his work. Her writings have helped us understand this work and contain the first descriptions of programming techniques.

An oversensitive and tactless person, Babbage was unpopular with many of his contemporaries. By the end of his life, he was disappointed by his failure to bring his principles within sight of completion; however, Babbage was actually attempting the impossible with the means at his disposal. He was a man born a hundred years ahead of his time. He died in London on October 18, 1871, surrounded by the drawings, cog wheels, and fragments of his hopeless, half-finished dream.

Babbage is thus the grandfather of the modern computer, and although this was not understood by his contemporaries, Babbage himself was probably aware of it. ◆

digital: relating to data in the form of numbers or discrete units.

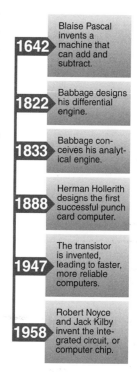

1642 Blaise Pascal invents a machine that can add and subtract.

1822 Babbage designs his differential engine.

1833 Babbage conceives his analytical engine.

1888 Herman Hollerith designs the first successful punch card computer.

1947 The transistor is invented, leading to faster, more reliable computers.

1958 Robert Noyce and Jack Kilby invent the integrated circuit, or computer chip.

Bacon, Francis

1561–1626 ● PHYSICS

> "*I have taken all knowledge to be my province.*"
>
> — Francis Bacon

Bacon has been acclaimed as the father of the scientific method.

Francis Bacon, the great English philosopher, statesman, and writer, was born in London on January 22, 1561. The phrase "Like parents, like son" can be appropriately applied to Bacon as his father, Nicholas, was a man of principle, well versed in law, an able statesman and keeper of the Great Seal. Anne, his mother, was also talented, especially in foreign languages and in theology.

With such a background and home tutoring Francis entered Trinity College, Cambridge, at the age of thirteen. Although he was one of the youngest students at the college, Francis was able to succeed academically during his three years at Cambridge. Apparently these years were not challenging for him, as he felt little more than contempt and scorn for the curriculum, especially the philosophy of Aristotle.

Looking forward to a diplomatic career, Francis and his brother Anthony enrolled in Gray's Inn, a law center, in 1576. Soon thereafter the two brothers went to Paris as part of the English ambassador's staff, but their stay in France was brief due to the death of their father in 1579. Having lost not only a father but also a powerful political influence, Francis was unable to advance his career as hoped. Returning to the study of law with great intensity, he was admitted to the bar in 1582. Three years later Francis gained a seat in Parliament, where he attracted attention as a brilliant orator.

Because of his outstanding abilities, and a bit of political favoritism, Bacon achieved a series of promotions and advancements: knighthood in 1603, solicitor general in 1607, attorney general in 1613, member of the Privy Council in 1616, keeper of the Great Seal in 1617, and Lord Chancellor of England in 1619.

On the darker side Bacon was somewhat vain, usually lived beyond his means, and was placed in debtors' prison in 1598. Worst of all, in 1621 he was charged with accepting bribes, was convicted, fined 40,000 pounds, sentenced to the Tower of London, and barred from the Parliament. However, King James I soon remitted the fine and imprisonment but not the Parliament restriction.

Even without other activities and achievements, the life of Francis Bacon could be considered a very full one. More important than his political career was his tremendous production of essays and other writings. He covered a vast scale and a wide spectrum of topics: marriage and family life, ethics, wealth, gardening, friendship, politics, and science. His *History of Henry II* is considered a classic today.

In the realm of science, Bacon rejected the authority of Aristotle and other ancient scholars. He believed scientists should rely on experiment and observation, not authority. Bacon has been acclaimed the "father of the scientific method" because he advocated a procedure based on **induction**. Bacon advised scientists to proceed from the particular to the general. Scientists could arrive at general conclusions as they accumulated particular facts through experiment and investigation. This method greatly influenced the way later scientists conducted research. In his own investigations, Bacon tended to include far more variables than he needed, leaving little room for judgment. Thus, few scientists have followed his method rigorously. Nevertheless, by his penetrating and powerful essays, Bacon aided others to throw off the yoke of idle speculation and unexamined pronouncements of authority.

One experiment performed by Bacon had a tragic end. Late in the winter of 1626 he bought a freshly dressed fowl and stuffed it with snow to see if that would retard or prevent spoilage. In doing this he became chilled and died on April 9, 1626, of a lung or bronchial infection in London. ◆

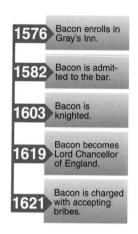

1576 ▶ Bacon enrolls in Gray's Inn.

1582 ▶ Bacon is admitted to the bar.

1603 ▶ Bacon is knighted.

1619 ▶ Bacon becomes Lord Chancellor of England.

1621 ▶ Bacon is charged with accepting bribes.

induction: the act of reasoning by inference of a general conclusion from particular facts or truths.

Banneker, Benjamin

1731–1806 ● ASTRONOMY & MATHEMATICS

"The color of the skin is in no way connected with strength of the mind or intellectual powers."
— Benjamin Banneker

Banneker received no formal schooling except for several weeks' attendance at a nearby Quaker one-room schoolhouse.

Banneker was the first African-American man of science. He was born free in Baltimore County, Maryland, on November 9, 1731, the son of a freed slave from Guinea named Robert, and of Mary Banneky, the daughter of a formerly indentured English servant named Molly Welsh and her husband, Bannka, a freed slave who claimed to be the son of a Gold Coast tribal chieftain.

Raised with three sisters in a log house built by his father on his 100-acre farm near the banks of the Patapsco River, Banneker received no formal schooling except for several weeks' attendance at a nearby Quaker one-room schoolhouse. Taught to read and write from a Bible by his white grandmother, he became a voracious reader, borrowing books when he could. He was skillful in mathematics and enjoyed creating mathematical puzzles and solving others presented to him. At about the age of twenty-two, he successfully constructed a wooden striking clock without ever having seen one. He approached the project as a mathematical problem, working out relationships between toothed wheels and gears, painstakingly carving each from seasoned wood with a pocketknife. The clock continued telling and striking the hours until his death. Banneker cultivated tobacco, first with his parents and then alone until about the age of fifty-nine, when **rheumatism** forced his retirement. He was virtually self-sufficient, growing vegetables and cultivating orchards and bees.

It was during his retirement that Banneker became interested in astronomy after witnessing a neighbor observing the stars with a telescope. With borrowed instruments and texts and without any assistance from others, Banneker taught himself sufficient mathematics and astronomy to make observations and to be able to calculate an **ephemeris** for an almanac. His efforts to sell his calculations for 1791 to a printer were not successful, but he continued his celestial studies nonetheless.

Banneker's opportunity to apply what he had learned came in February 1791, when President Washington commissioned the survey of an area ten miles square in Virginia and Maryland in which to establish the national capital. Unable on such short notice to find an assistant capable of using the sophisticated instruments required, the surveyor Andrew Ellicott selected Banneker to assist him until others became available. During the first three months of the survey, Banneker occupied the field observatory tent, maintaining and correcting the regulator clock each day, and each night making observations of the transit of stars with the zenith sector, recording his nightly observations for Ellicott's use on the next day's surveying. During his leisure, he completed calculations for an ephemeris for 1792. Banneker was employed on the survey site from early February until late April 1791, then returned to his home in Baltimore County. Recently discovered records of the survey state that he was paid $60 for his participation and the costs of his travel.

Shortly after his return home, Banneker sent a handwritten copy of his ephemeris for 1792 to Secretary of State Thomas Jefferson, because, he wrote, Jefferson was considered "measurably friendly and well disposed towards us," the African-American race, "who have long laboured under the abuse and censure of the world. . . have long been looked upon with an eye of contempt, and. . . have long been considered rather as brutish than human, and scarcely capable of mental endowments." He submitted his calculations as evidence to the contrary, and urged that Jefferson work toward bringing an end to slavery. Jefferson responded promptly: "No

rheumatism: a disease characterized by inflammation and pain in the muscles and joints.

ephemeris: a table of the positions of planets and stars for a given interval of time.

1751 Banneker builds an accurate clock.

1791 Banneker becomes assistant to surveyor Andrew Ellicott.

1792 Banneker completes and publishes an ephemeris for 1792.

1797 Banneker writes his last almanac.

Promoted by
the abolitionist
societies of
Pennsylvania
and Maryland,
Banneker's
almanacs were
published by
several printers
and sold widely
in the United
States and
England.

body wished more than I do to see such proofs as you exhibit, that nature has given to our black brethren, talents equal to those of other colors of men, and that the appearance of a want of them is owing merely to the degraded condition of their existence, both in Africa & America. . . . no body wishes more ardently to see a good system commenced for raising the condition of both their body & mind to what it ought to be, as fast as the imbecility of their present existence, and other circumstances which cannot be neglected, will admit." Jefferson sent Banneker's calculations to the Marquis de Condorcet, secretary of the French Academy of Sciences, with an enthusiastic cover letter. There was no reply from Condorcet because at the time of the letter's arrival he was in hiding for having opposed the monarchy and having supported a republican form of government. The two letters, that from Banneker to Jefferson and the statesman's reply, were published in a widely distributed pamphlet and in at least one periodical during the following year.

Banneker's ephemeris for 1792 was published by the Baltimore printer Goddard & Angell with the title *Benjamin Banneker's Pennsylvania, Delaware, Maryland and Virginia Almanack and Ephemeris for the Year of Our Lord 1792.* It was also sold by printers in Philadelphia and Alexandria, Virginia. He continued to calculate ephemerides that were published in almanacs bearing his name for the next five years. Promoted by the abolitionist societies of Pennsylvania and Maryland, Banneker's almanacs were published by several printers and sold widely in the United States and England. Twenty-eight separate editions of his almanacs are known. A recent computerized analysis of Banneker's published ephemerides and those calculated by several contemporaries for the same years, including those by William Waring and Andrew Ellicott, has revealed that Banneker's calculations consistently reflect a high degree of comparative accuracy. Although he continued calculating ephemerides through the year 1802, they remained unpublished.

Banneker died in his sleep following a morning walk on October 9, 1806, one month short of his seventy-fifth birthday. He was buried several days later in the family graveyard within sight of his house. As his body was being lowered into the grave, his house burst into flames, the cause unknown, and all of its contents were destroyed. Fortunately, the books and table he had borrowed, his **commonplace book**, and the astronomical journal in which he had copied all of his ephemerides had been given to his neighbor immediately following his death, and have been preserved. Although he espoused no particular religion or creed, Banneker was a very religious man, attending services and meetings of various denominations held in the region, preferring those of the Society of Friends. ◆

commonplace book: an album for collecting photos, letters, or other memorabilia.

Bell, Alexander Graham

1847–1922 ● INVENTOR

"Mr. Watson, come here; I want you."
— Alexander Graham Bell, to his assistant in the world's first telephone conversation.

Bell was the American scientist and educator of the deaf who invented the telephone. He was born in Edinburgh, Scotland, where he was educated at Edinburgh University and the University of Scotland. In 1865 he moved to London with his father, Alexander Melville Bell, becoming his professional assistant. The elder Bell was a highly regarded scientist in the field of vocal physiology. In the course of his work the senior Bell invented a system of symbols indicating the position of the human vocal cords in speech, known as visible speech. The invention of the telephone by Alexander Graham Bell was a natural outgrowth of his work for the deaf.

As early as 1865 Bell developed the idea that it was possible to transmit speech by electrical waves. While working with his father in London, Bell sought to improve his knowledge in the field by taking courses in anatomy and physiology at University College, London. In 1868 he adapted his father's visible speech system at a school for deaf children in Kensington. By 1869 his father had made him a full partner in his professional work. The elder Bell became familiar with North America in the course of a lecture tour there in 1868 and the family moved to Canada in 1870. While on a lecture tour in the United States, the elder Bell had stimulated interest in his visible speech system. This led to the employment of Alexander Graham Bell at the Boston Day School for the Deaf, where he trained teachers in the use of visible speech in 1871. By October 1872 he was conducting his own private school in Boston to train teachers in this method, for which he developed a system of notations. In 1873 he was appointed a professor of vocal physiology and the mechanics of speech at Boston University.

Bell had been conducting studies of the human ear while he tried to invent a so-called phonautograph. This was to be an instrument that would explain how to make tone vibrations correctly to deaf pupils. The idea was that this could be done by comparing visual representations of the sounds that deaf pupils made with standard records of the same. From this work, he developed the concept of the membrane element in the telephone. By March 10, 1876, the first telephone apparatus had been invented and perfected by Bell. He was able to transmit the first intelligible and audible sentence to his assistant, "Mr. Watson, come here, I want you." Basically, the apparatus made it possible to reproduce the tones and overtones of a steel spring that in turn could yield the tones and overtones of the human voice.

Bell obtained patents for his invention of the telephone. Immediately, other claimants contested Bell's right to his invention. This resulted in what was at the time the most important and prolonged patent **litigation** in U.S. history. Some sixty-six legal cases developed about this invention,

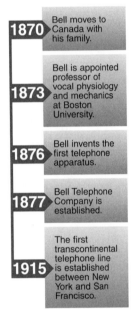

1870 ▶ Bell moves to Canada with his family.

1873 ▶ Bell is appointed professor of vocal physiology and mechanics at Boston University.

1876 ▶ Bell invents the first telephone apparatus.

1877 ▶ Bell Telephone Company is established.

1915 ▶ The first transcontinental telephone line is established between New York and San Francisco.

litigation: the use of the courts to settle a dispute.

culminating in a decision by the U.S. Supreme Court that found Bell to be the inventor of the telephone.

Financing the future development of this invention was not easy. Eventually, Gardiner G. Hubbard, a well-known citizen active in the education of the deaf, gave Bell the assistance he needed for the commercial development of the telephone and other inventions. In 1877 the telephone company trusteeship known as the Bell Telephone Company was established with Hubbard as its first trustee. His daughter, Mabel, who had been deaf from early childhood, married Bell.

In 1880 France awarded Bell the Volta prize of 50,000 francs in recognition of his invention of the telephone. This led to extensive research and invention, especially for the benefit of the deaf, through the establishment of the Volta Laboratory by Bell. There he invented the photophone to transmit speech over a ray of light by means of the variable resistance of silenium to light and shade, as well as the induction balance to locate metallic objects in the human body. Both of these inventions were not patented but were given to the world by Bell. In the Volta Laboratory, Bell invented the audiometer and brought his scientific inventions ever closer to service for the deaf.

Never to be limited to a single direction, Bell became interested in the field of aviation and was one of the first to consider aerial locomotion practicable. He founded the Aerial Experiment Association, under whose auspices the first public flight of a heavier-than-air machine took place in 1908. By 1915 the first transcontinental telephone line was established from New York to San Francisco. In 1920 Bell was recognized by his birthplace and childhood home, Edinburgh, Scotland, which elected him a burger and brother of the city as well as conferring upon him the freedom of the city. ◆

The invention of the telephone by Alexander Graham Bell was a natural outgrowth of his work for the deaf.

Bohr, Niels Henrik David

1885–1962 ● NUCLEAR PHYSICS

> *"An expert is a man who has made all the mistakes, which can be made, in a very narrow field."*
>
> — Niels Bohr

It was Bohr's genius to see that new concepts based on quantum theory could serve to stabilize the atom.

Bohr, who ranks among the most prominent figures in the history of science, was a fifth-generation Dane. He was born in Copenhagen, Denmark, October 7, 1885. Academic distinctions have a long tradition in his family. A brother of Peter Georg Bohr, Niels's great-grandfather, was a member of the Royal Norwegian and Swedish Academies of Sciences. His grandfather was rector of the Westenske Institut, a high school in Copenhagen. Christian Bohr, Niels's father, was a distinguished physiologist, rector of the University of Copenhagen in 1905–1906, and was proposed for a Nobel Prize in 1907 and 1908.

Niels's mother, Ellen, hailed from a prominent wealthy Jewish banker's family. David Adler, her father, was a cofounder of Handelsbanken and Privatbanken, Danish banks that are still flourishing, and a member of Parliament. Niels was born in the Adler mansion at Ved Stranden 14 in Copenhagen. He grew up in a harmonious and stimulating family. He had an older sister, Jenny, and a younger brother, Harald, who became a distinguished mathematician.

From 1891 until he completed high school in 1903, Niels attended Gammelholms *Latin Realskole*. After passing his final exam "with distinction" he enrolled in Copenhagen

University, choosing physics as his major, with astronomy, chemistry, and mathematics as minor subjects. In those years he was goalkeeper for Akademisk Boldklub, a well-known soccer club. In 1907 he was awarded a gold medal by the Royal Danish Academy of Sciences and Letters (KDVS) for his answer to a problem on surface vibrations of liquids. In 1911 he received a Ph.D. for his thesis "Studies on the Electron Theory of Metals." In September of that year he left for Cambridge to study with Joseph J. Thomson. From March to July in 1912 he was in Manchester for further work under Ernest Rutherford, the man who was to become the role model for his scientific and personal style.

The timing of Bohr's arrival in Manchester could not have been more propitious. In 1911 Rutherford had published his new model of the atom, consisting of a heavy central body, the nucleus, around which orbit electrons, very light-weight particles. According to the theories of that time, however, such a system should have been unstable; the electrons would fall into the nucleus. It was Bohr's genius to see that new concepts based on **quantum** theory could serve to stabilize the atom. He made a first rudimentary attempt to do so while still in Manchester, then returned to Denmark, where in August he married Margrethe Nøzlund. They had six sons.

In April 1913 Bohr completed the most important scientific paper of his life, which would make him world famous. It contains his theory of the simplest atom (of hydrogen), and is based on the (for its time) very audacious hypothesis that of all possible electron orbits, then believed to form a continuous set, only a **discrete** subset of "quantum orbits" actually occur in nature. This hypothesis appeared to defy logic, yet had to be correct, since Bohr was able to make successful predictions that could not have been made on the continuum picture. His success caused his career to make rapid strides, from reader in Copenhagen (1913) to associate professor in Manchester (1914) to full professor in Copenhagen (1916), with an office at the *Polytekniske Læreanstalt* (Institute of Technology)—the university did not have a physics institute or laboratory.

It was Bohr himself who in 1917 took the initiative for creating such an institute. He raised the funds in Denmark and America, oversaw its construction and later extensions, and became its first director, giving guidance to the theoreti-

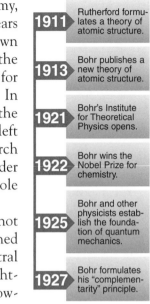

1911 Rutherford formulates a theory of atomic structure.

1913 Bohr publishes a new theory of atomic structure.

1921 Bohr's Institute for Theoretical Physics opens.

1922 Bohr wins the Nobel Prize for chemistry.

1925 Bohr and other physicists establish the foundation of quantum mechanics.

1927 Bohr formulates his "complementarity" principle.

quantum: an extremely small unit of energy.

discrete: consisting of distinct or unconnected units.

cal as well as experimental programs. In 1921, at the official opening of his *Institut for Teoretisk Fysik* (renamed the *Niels Bohr Institutet* in 1965), Bohr stated its main function: "To introduce a constantly renewed number of young people into the results and methods of the sciences"—not just Danes but people from all over the world.

Bohr was not only a creative scientist but the founder, administrator, and leader of an institute that was the world's most important center of theoretical physics.

And that is what indeed happened, on a spectacular scale. Between 1921 and 1961, 444 physicists from thirty-five countries spent at least a month in Copenhagen. Bohr, one of the most inspiring teachers of his time, was forever ready, in fact eager, to discuss their work with them. Some of these young people became leading physicists, for example Paul Adrien Maurice Dirac, Werner Karl Heisenberg (who wrote his paper on the uncertainty relations at Bohr's institute), and Wolfgang Pauli. Furthermore, beginning in 1929 Bohr initiated a series of conferences to which leading physicists of the world flocked. These meetings made the institute the gathering place for the best physics discussions of that period.

During Bohr's life some 1,200 papers were published from Copenhagen. Of these, about 200 were by Bohr himself. In spite of many other duties, he never ceased doing research. One important result of his early work was his development of the theoretical basis for the periodic table of elements (during the period from 1920 to 1922), which made him the founder of quantum chemistry. It also led to the discovery at his institute of a new chemical element named hafnium (after Copenhagen's Latin name).

Thus Bohr was not only a creative scientist but also the founder, administrator, and intellectual leader of an institute that during its first two decades was the world's most important center of theoretical physics.

Bohr was well aware that his early work was based on illogical premises. However, relief came with the discovery of quantum mechanics, a new theory that wiped out all previous paradoxes. This revolutionary development proceeded in two stages. During the first stage (1925–1926), new equations (**matrix** equations, wave equations) were formulated that accounted, now in a logical way, for the earlier work of Bohr and others. The second stage began with a paper by Bohr in 1927, which, put in simplest terms, posed the following question: The new equations are clearly good, but what do they mean? Bohr gave the answer in terms of a new logic, a new

matrix: a rectangular composition of mathematical elements that can be combined to form sums.

philosophy, which he called **complementarity** (and which he considered his most important scientific contribution). In later years Bohr continued to refine these ideas, especially stimulated by objections from Albert Einstein, who could not accept the new logic. However, their intellectual antagonism never diminished their mutual respect and affection.

The next important year in Bohr's career was 1932, when the Bohr family moved into the "Residence of Honor" on the Carlsberg brewery grounds. That year Bohr made an attempt (unsuccessful) to use complementarity in biology and, together with his faithful assistant Léon Rosenfeld, engaged in applying complementarity to the quantum theory of the electromagnetic field. Elsewhere that year, experimental discoveries, notably of the neutron, laid the basis for theoretical nuclear physics. Then, in 1933, came the rise to power of the Nazis, causing many to flee Germany. Bohr took part in providing help, as board member of the Danish committee for support of refugee intellectuals, and especially by raising funds for providing temporary hospitality at his institute. Among those who came was Georg von Hevesy, who in 1935 began the first effort anywhere of applying artificially radioactive isotopes in biology, thus founding the new science of nuclear medicine. That same year Bohr went after funds for building accelerators for use in physics and biology. The result of his efforts was that in late 1938 a high tension generator went into operation, soon followed by one of Europe's first **cyclotrons**.

Meanwhile, during 1936 and 1937 Bohr made important contributions to nuclear theory, dealing with neutron physics, the study of what happens when nuclei are bombarded by neutrons. He worked out a model for these processes based on an analogy with a liquid drop that vibrates when disturbed. This theory could explain many phenomena studied in the Los Alamos atomic bomb laboratory.

Early in 1939 it was reported from Berlin that hitting uranium nuclei with neutrons causes fission, their violent rupture. Within weeks the theory of the process was worked out using Bohr's model. The term "fission" was suggested, in analogy with biological cell division, by a coworker of Hevesy. Bohr took the news in person to America, where (at age fifty-three) he also made the crucial discovery that fission by slow neutrons occurs only for the rare isotope uranium 235.

complementarity: ideas relating to the dual nature of light as both waves and particles.

cyclotron: a particle accelerator in which charged particles are propelled by an alternating electric field in a constant magnetic field.

Bohr was one of the most inspiring teachers of his time.

After the German occupation of Denmark in April 1940, Bohr continued to lead his institute until September 1943, when he was forced to flee to England. He then became adviser to the Anglo-American atomic weapons program.

Bohr was less concerned with the war effort, however, than with the changes the new weapons would create in the postwar world. To forestall competition with the Russians it would be necessary, he emphasized, to inform them at once of the Western effort and offer them full future cooperation. In 1944 he met personally with Winston Churchill and with Franklin D. Roosevelt to urge them to do so, but had no success. Nor did his 1948 meeting with Secretary of State George Marshall help. In 1950, and again in 1956, he repeated his proposal in open letters to the United Nations, again without success. Times were not yet ripe for Bohr's farseeing ideas.

Bohr dutifully accepted social obligations resulting from his stature. From 1939 until his death he was president of the KDVS. Also at one time or other he was president of the Danish Physical Society and of the Society for the Dissemination of Natural Science, chairman of the Danish Atomic Energy Commission, president of the National Association for Combating Cancer, chairman of the governing board of Nordita (the Nordic Institute for theoretical atomic physics), and prime mover in founding the Risø research center, not far from Copenhagen.

On November 18, 1962, Bohr died of heart failure. His ashes rest in the family grave at Assistens Kirkegården in Copenhagen.

The honors bestowed on Bohr during his lifetime were numerous. They include the Nobel Prize (1922) and the first Atoms for Peace Award (1957); many orders of chivalry, including the Elephant Orden (1947), Denmark's highest order; and some thirty honorary degrees. Yet it can be said of him what he himself has said of Rutherford: "In his life all honors imaginable for a man of science came to him, but yet he remained quite simple in all his ways. . . . He created around him a spirit of affection wherever he worked." ◆

Boyle, Robert

1627–1691 ● CHEMISTRY

B orn January 25, 1627, in Lismore Castle, Ireland, Robert Boyle was the fourteenth child and seventh son of the Earl of Cork. A child prodigy, fluent in Latin and Greek, he entered Eton College, a boy's preparatory school founded by King Henry VI, at the age of eight. He was influenced by reading the works of Galileo Galilei and René Descartes. His education by private tutoring rather than in universities, where Aristotle's views of natural philosophy were taught, resulted in his rejection of the ancient Aristotelian beliefs in "principles" and "elements" in favor of a mechanical philosophy postulating that the world is composed of particles of matter in motion.

Returning to England during the Civil War, he lived at Stalbridge in Dorsetshire. He then settled in Oxford (1656–1668), where he constructed an air pump with the help of his assistant Robert Hooke (1635–1703), who later became curator of experiments for the Royal Society. Boyle became a member of the "Invisible College," or Royal Society, a group of natural philosophers promulgating the experimental method espoused earlier by Francis Bacon.

Boyle used his air pump, which created what be came known as a "Boylean vacuum," to carry out experiments to demonstrate the physical properties of air and to show that it is necessary for combustion, respiration, and the transmission of sound. He described this work in his *New Experiments Physio-Mechanicall, Touching the Spring [Pressure] of the Air and Its Effects* (1660). The second edition (1662) contained his 1661 report to the Royal Society on the fundamental relationship that has become known as Boyle's Law: the volume of a gas is inversely proportional to its pressure, i.e., the product of its pressure and volume is constant.

In his book *The Sceptical Chymist* (1661), written in the form of a dialogue, Boyle transformed alchemy into chemistry by attacking Aristotle's theory of the four "elements" (earth, air, fire, and water) and Paracelsus's three "principles" (sulfur, mercury, and salt), and replacing them with a **corpuscular** theory of matter. Although he still regarded the different ele-

"He that thoroughly understands the nature of Ferments, and Fermentations, shall probably be much better able than he that ignores them, to give a fair account of divers Phenomena of several diseases."

— Robert Boyle

corpuscular: relating to an elementary particle, such as an electron or a isolated cell.

ments as being composed of some primary matter, he defined them as "certain primitive and simple, or perfectly unmingled bodies; which not being made of any other bodies, or of one another, are the ingredients of which all those perfectly mixed bodies are immediately compounded, and into which they are ultimately resolved," a view that had great influence on chemical thinking at the time.

In 1668, Boyle moved to London and set up a laboratory. He described general properties of acids and bases, and differentiated acids, bases, and salts by means of chemical indicators. He carried out quantitative experiments on combustion and calcination. In the latter (1673), he described the increase in weight of metals in air but mistakenly ascribed this increase to "particles of fire." He recognized the difficulties inherent in analysis by fire (dry distillation) and used the method sparingly, only when confirmed by synthesis. He described a number of chemical tests and can be considered one of the founders of Qualitative Analysis. In 1680, he prepared phosphorus from urine; although his discovery was antedated in 1669-1675 by Hennig Brand, Boyle described many important properties and reactions of this element. His writings were numerous, and Dutch chemist Hermann Boerhaave considered him one of the first to "treat of chemistry with a view to natural philosophy." Boyle has been called the founder of modern chemistry because he recognized chemistry as a science worthy of study for its own sake, introducing the experimental method to the new science while rejecting on experimental grounds Aristotle's four elements and Paracelsus's three principles, and because he clearly defined the element in the modern sense. ◆

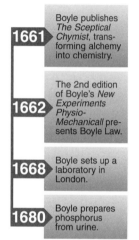

1661 Boyle publishes *The Sceptical Chymist*, transforming alchemy into chemistry.

1662 The 2nd edition of Boyle's *New Experiments Physio-Mechanicall* presents Boyle Law.

1668 Boyle sets up a laboratory in London.

1680 Boyle prepares phosphorus from urine.

Brahe, Tycho

1546–1601 ● ASTRONOMY

"Last year, in the month of November, on the eleventh day of the month, in the evening, after sunset, when, according to my habit, I was contemplating the stars in a clear sky, I noticed that a new and unusual star, surpassing the other stars in brilliancy, was shining almost directly above my head."

— Tycho Brahe

Tycho Brahe was the second child of an old and noble Danish family. He was raised by a childless paternal uncle. His uncle wanted Brahe to become a statesman and provided him with an excellent Latin education, sending him to the University of Copenhagen when he was thirteen years old.

The solar eclipse of 1560 aroused Brahe's interest in astronomy and he devoted himself to its study until his uncle sent him to the University of Leipzig, employing a tutor to ensure that he studied law, not science. Nevertheless, Brahe continued studying astronomy in secret and came to realize that his books (mostly derived from classical authorities) presented a different picture of the heavens than that revealed by his observations. Deciding that the books were wrong, he concluded that the movement of the planets and stars could only be understood through systematic, continual observation.

Although Brahe's family disapproved of his scientific interests, his careful observations of a new star that appeared in 1572 attracted the attention of Denmark's King Frederick II, who offered him the island of Hveen and generous financial grants so that he could conduct his observations in peace. Brahe accepted Frederick's offer and moved to Hveen with his

1560 Brahe observes a solar eclipse that arouses his curiosity.

1572 Brahe observes a new star.

1599 Brahe moves into a castle in Bohemia.

1600 Kepler becomes Brahe's assistant.

Brahe concluded that the movement of the planets and stars could only be understood through systematic, continual observation.

family (he had formed a relationship with a woman with whom he lived unmarried for twenty-eight years and had eight children). He built an elegant and extensive compound there, which he called Uraniborg, since his work was that of studying the heavens.

The years in Hveen (1576-1597) were happy, active, and productive. Brahe invented instruments with which he made detailed observations of 777 stars. He was aware of Nicholaus Copernicus's theory that the Earth revolved around the Sun, but did not accept it since his own observations revealed inaccuracies in Copernicus's calculations. Instead, Brahe developed his own theory explaining the movement of the planets claiming that while the planets orbited the Sun, the Sun and the planets orbited a stationary Earth. Word of Brahe's methods and discoveries spread, Uraniborg frequently had visitors, astronomy students were eager to assist him, and Frederick increased his endowments.

The adulation made Brahe haughty, and he offended powerful people. He willingly accepted royal endowments of estates but refused to fulfill his legal obligations and was involved in several law cases over his mistreatment of tenants. His behavior was overlooked during Frederick's lifetime but Frederick's son refused to tolerate it and confiscated the estates. Insulted and angry, Brahe left Denmark in search of a more appreciative patron.

Brahe made only sporadic observations before becoming reestablished with his family and instruments in Bohemia in 1599, where Emperor Rudolph II provided him with a castle and promised him a generous annual grant. However, Brahe's work in Bohemia was limited by lack of assistants, Rudolph's empty treasury, inferior facilities, and a feud with another astronomer. However, it was in Bavaria that Johannes Kepler became Brahe's assistant, and Kepler's laws of planetary motion—the basis for modern planetary astronomy—were derived from Brahe's work, which ended with his death just two years after his move to Bohemia. ◆

Browning, John Moses

1855–1926 ● INVENTOR

Recognized as "the greatest firearms inventor the world has ever known," John Moses Browning (1855–1926) was among the foremost contributors to America's national defense in the twentieth century.

Browning was born in Ogden in the Utah Territory. His talent for firearms design was fostered by his father, a frontier gunsmith who supplied arms to Brigham Young's Mormon immigrants. As a young man, Browning augmented his limited education with the rudiments of gunsmithing at his father's shop, but his genius in arms design was innate and self-taught.

Browning designed his first practical gun, a single shot, breech-loading rifle, in 1878 for the commercial market. With brothers Matthew, Edward, Samuel, and George, and gunsmith Frank Rushton, he established the Browning Brothers Factory in 1880 to manufacture the new rifle and service the Western trade.

In 1883, the Winchester Repeating Arms Company purchased manufacturing rights to the single-shot rifle and inaugurated a twenty-year relationship in which Browning sold the firm all his designs for sporting longarms. The famed Winchester repeating rifles, Models 1886, 1892, 1894, and 1895, were all Browning creations.

During the 1890s, Browning designed semiautomatic and automatic actions for pistols and machine guns and worked with Colt's Patent Fire Arms Manufacturing Company. He also developed the first semiautomatic shotgun, manufactured by Fabrique Nationale of Belgium and later by Remington Arms Company. He received little public acclaim for his inventiveness because all his sporting arms were produced by others under their marque.

Browning's genius finally was manifested during two world wars and in later American conflicts. His military contributions included the regulation Model 1911 Colt Automatic Pistol, the Browning Automatic Rifle (BAR), and all the

> Browning has been called the greatest firearms inventor the world has ever known.

1878 ▶ Browning designs his first practical gun.

1880 ▶ Browning establishes the Browning Brothers Factory to manufacture rifles.

1883 ▶ Winchester Repeating Arms Company purchases rights to Browning's rifle.

1911 ▶ Browning designs the regulation Model 1911 Colt Automatic Pistol.

1980 ▶ More than 24 million Browning-designed arms have been manufactured.

light and heavy machine guns used by U.S. forces in the field or mounted on tanks, ships, or planes.

In all, Browning received 128 patents for eighty distinct firearm mechanisms. By 1980, more than twenty-four million Browning arms of sporting and military design had been manufactured; many patterns remain in production. ◆

Carnot, Nicolas-Léonard-Sadi

1796–1832 ● THERMODYNAMICS

Carnot was born at Paris, France, June 1, 1796. He was the elder of two sons in a distinguished Burgundian family. His father (Lazare Carnot) was a leading military figure who had served with distinction in the early years of the revolutionary wars of France and wielded great political power as a member of the five-man Directory that governed the country from November 1795, until Napoleon Bonaparte's coup d'état in September 1797. Carnot's education was governed until 1812 by his father, who was also a notable mathematician. In that year, after a brief period of preparation at the Lycée Charlemagne in Paris, Carnot entered the Ecole Polytechnique. Despite the disruption of his studies during the defense of Paris in the spring of 1814, he graduated and proceeded in January 1815 to the Ecole de l'Artillerie et du Génie at Metz. He was commissioned as a military engineer in April 1817, but his army career was undistinguished and unhappy, and in January 1819 he went on the reserve list, where he remained until he resigned his commission in 1828.

From 1819 until his death during the **cholera** epidemic of 1832, Carnot lived a quiet, studious life in Paris. In these years, his only significant academic contact was with Nicolas Clément, professor of industrial chemistry at the Conservatoire Royal des Arts et Métiers. Nevertheless, supporting himself modestly by inherited family money and his reduced military pay, Carnot wrote his 118-page *Réflexions sur la Puissance Motrice du Feu* (*Reflections on the Motive Power of Fire*), a work that the Scottish physicist William Thomson

> *"Nothing in the whole range of Natural Philosophy is more remarkable than the establishment of general laws by such a process of reasoning."*
> — Lord Kelvin, describing Carnot's *Réflexions*

cholera: an serious intestinal disease caused by bacteria.

35

(later Lord Kelvin) was one of the first to recognize as a masterpiece, though long after its publication in 1824. "Nothing in the whole range of Natural Philosophy," Thomson wrote of the book in 1849, "is more remarkable than the establishment of general laws by such a process of reasoning." In the *Réflexions*, Carnot laid some of the most important foundations of modern thermodynamics, using an argument that possessed rigor and elegance, despite being constructed almost entirely without the use of mathematics.

Although the results were above all of theoretical significance, the problem that Carnot tackled in the *Réflexions* had its origins in the practical world of power technology. Like many engineers and physicists of his day, Carnot was intrigued by the economy of a generation of medium- and high-pressure steam engines that had been developed in Britain during the Napoleonic Wars and only became known in France after 1814. The most notable of these engines was that of the Cornish engineer Arthur Woolf, which applied a technique, patented by James Watt but not seriously exploited by him, for enhancing the amount of work that could be obtained from steam. The technique consisted in avoiding unnecessary waste by allowing the steam to expand in the cylinder of an engine until its pressure was no longer sufficient to move the piston.

Attempts to explain the economy of the "expansive" engine had yielded little agreement by the time Carnot turned to the question, probably about 1820. His treatment, as presented in the *Réflexions*, was a highly abstract one. It was based on the **caloric** theory, which treated heat as an invisible, weightless fluid whose accumulation in a body was manifested as a rise in temperature. In Carnot's ideal engine, heat entered the working substance (usually steam, although the theory could be applied equally well to air or any other elastic fluid) at the high temperature of the boiler. Then, after the working substance had yielded its work, expanding and cooling in the process, the heat would pass from it to the condenser as the steam condensed. Essentially, therefore, heat had "fallen" from the higher temperature of the boiler to the lower temperature of the condenser, and it was this "fall" that, in Carnot's theory, yielded work or, as he called it, motive power.

There was a close analogy between Carnot's conception of the source of work in a heat engine and the operation of a

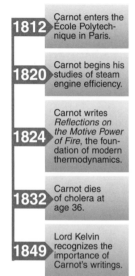

1812 Carnot enters the École Polytechnique in Paris.

1820 Carnot begins his studies of steam engine efficiency.

1824 Carnot writes *Reflections on the Motive Power of Fire*, the foundation of modern thermodynamics.

1832 Carnot dies of cholera at age 36.

1849 Lord Kelvin recognizes the importance of Carnot's writings.

caloric: relating to calorie, the amount of heat required to raise the temperature of one kilogram of water one degree Celsius.

water wheel. In both cases, a substance (heat or water) passed from a higher to a lower "level," producing work without being consumed. In this conception of an ideal engine, the influence of Lazare's theoretical investigation of the work produced by a water-powered engine is unmistakable, and there can be little doubt that both the general approach and certain key details of the *Réflexions* owe much to this earlier work. Apart from the fundamental notion of the "fall" of heat, Carnot was able to draw from his father's analysis the core of what he developed in the *Réflexions* as the concepts of reversibility and the closed cycle of operations.

Using these concepts, Carnot presented what can be regarded as a form of the second law of thermodynamics. By insisting that the production of work required the presence of both a hot and a cold source and the passage of heat between these sources, he was breaking totally new ground. Also novel was his insistence that, in calculating the work produced by an ideal heat engine, the working substance had to be restored to its original conditions; in other words, the cycle of operations—the "Carnot cycle" of modern thermodynamics—had to be completed. Carnot's cycle was reversible, and by an ingenious and subtle argument, he proved that the "Carnot engine" was the most efficient of all engines that could operate between the same two temperature intervals. The unfamiliarity of such ideas probably mystified the few contemporaries who read the *Réflexions*. At all events, the book was largely ignored, with only the engineer Emile Clapeyron (in 1834) making any significant use of its argument until it was finally recovered, independently and almost simultaneously, by Rudolf Clausius and William Thomson, a quarter of a century after its publication.

Perceiving the fundamental error of Carnot's assumption that work could be produced without some heat being consumed, Clausius and Thomson showed how the essentials of his argument could be reconciled with the newly discovered principle of the conservation of energy (or first law of thermodynamics). In their version of Carnot's theory, the amount of heat leaving the system at the lower temperature was less than the amount entering at the higher temperature by an amount proportional to the quantity of work produced. Although this reconciliation between the first and second laws of thermodynamics moved Carnot's theory

In the Réflexions, Carnot laid some of the most important foundations of modern thermodynamics.

definitively into the main stream of modern physics, it was only in 1878 that the full extent of Carnot's achievement became apparent. It was then that his brother Hippolyte presented to the *Académie des Sciences* a set of manuscript notes that had remained in his possession since Carnot's death. These notes showed that at some time between the publication of the *Réflexions* in 1824 and his death eight years later, in Paris, on August 24, 1832, Carnot himself had reached the conclusion that work could only be produced if a corresponding amount of heat was consumed; he had even calculated a remarkably accurate value for the mechanical equivalent of heat. The **posthumous** recognition was generous, and Carnot's reputation has remained undimmed ever since. ◆

posthumous: occurring after death.

Carson, Rachel

1907–1964 ● NATURAL & ENVIRONMENTAL SCIENCES

"For the first time in the history of the world, every human being is now subjected to contact with dangerous chemicals, from the moment of conception until death."
— Rachel Carson, *Silent Spring*

Rachel Carson was a pioneer of the modern environmental movement in the United States. She was born in Springdale, Pennsylvania, on 27 May 1907 and died in Silver Spring, Maryland, on 14 April 1964. Carson made a career of her fascination with wildlife and concern for the environment, working for the U.S. Bureau of Fisheries and its successor, the U.S. Fish and Wildlife Service, from 1936 to 1952. Her best-known book, *Silent Spring* (1962), provided a **catalyst** that changed the way Americans think about their surroundings and particularly the impact of modern chemicals on the landscape. Rachel Carson played a significant role in the ideological enlightenment that led policy makers to focus on the serious study of environmental issues. The first Earth Day on 22 April 1970 was one outcome of the new environmental awareness, and a second was the creation of the Environmental Protection Agency (EPA) the same year.

catalyst: an agent that provokes significant action.

Rachel Carson attended public schools in Springdale and nearby Parnassus, Pennsylvania. Her mother taught her to enjoy the outdoors and fostered her daughter's interest in wildlife. Carson showed an early talent for writing, and on graduation from Parnassus High School enrolled in Pennsylvania College for Women in Pittsburgh to study English with the intention of becoming a writer. A course in biology rekindled her interest in science and led to a change to a science major. Carson was awarded her bachelor of arts in 1929, and went on to postgraduate studies at Johns Hopkins University. Commencing in 1930, she taught at Johns Hopkins summer schools for seven years. She joined the zoology staff of the University of Maryland in 1931, and obtained a master of arts from Johns Hopkins in 1932.

Carson developed a special interest in the life of the sea and undertook further postgraduate work at the Woods Hole Marine Biological Laboratory in Massachusetts. In 1936 she accepted a position as an aquatic biologist with the U.S. Bureau of Fisheries in Washington, D.C. She became editor in chief at the U.S. Fish and Wildlife Service, the successor to the Bureau, in 1947. During her years with the service Carson practiced her writing skills preparing many leaflets and informational brochures that publicized the central objective of the bureau: "to insure the conservation of the nation's wild birds, mammals, fishes and other forms of wildlife, with a view to preventing the destruction or depletion of these natural resources, and to promote the maximum present use and enjoyment of the wildlife resources that is compatible with their perpetuity."

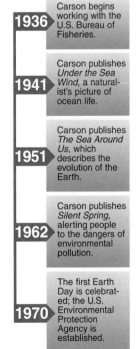

1936 Carson begins working with the U.S. Bureau of Fisheries.

1941 Carson publishes *Under the Sea Wind*, a naturalist's picture of ocean life.

1951 Carson publishes *The Sea Around Us*, which describes the evolution of the Earth.

1962 Carson publishes *Silent Spring*, alerting people to the dangers of environmental pollution.

1970 The first Earth Day is celebrated; the U.S. Environmental Protection Agency is established.

"The sea lies all about us. The commerce of all lands must cross it. The very winds that move over the lands have been cradled on its broad expanse and seek ever to return to it. The continents themselves dissolve and pass to the sea, in grain after grain of eroded land."

— Rachel Carson,
The Sea Around Us

Her first book, *Under the Sea-Wind,* appeared in 1941. The subtitle was "a naturalist's picture of ocean life" and the narrative told the life of the shore, the open sea, and the sea bottom. *Under the Sea-Wind* was well received both for the accuracy of its scientific content and its accessible style. Her second book, *The Sea Around Us* (1951), was delayed both by war work and a painstaking and prolonged period of research and writing. By her own admission, Carson was a slow writer who subjected her work to multiple revisions. As a general rule Carson declined offers from magazines to publish extracts from her books fearing that serialization would detract from the coherence of her arguments. However, before its publication in book form, *The Sea Around Us* was excerpted in the *New Yorker* in the summer of 1951.

When *The Sea Around Us* appeared in book form in July 1951, it was an immediate success. The work was greeted with praise for its literary style, approachability and informative content. In a *New York Herald Tribune Book Review,* Francesca La Monte described Carson's story of the sea as "one of the most beautiful books of our time." Writing in the *New York Times Book Review,* Jonathan Norton Leonard said of *The Sea Around Us*: "Its style and imagination make it a joy to read." *The Sea Around Us* provides a layman's geological guide through time and tide. It begins with an account of the contemporary understanding of the origins of the Earth and Moon, and then proceeds through the geological timetable, mapping the evolution of the planet, the formation of mountains and islands and oceans. Then follows the description of the sea, commencing with the surface and its inhabitants, and descending through lower depths to the sea bottom. Carson reveals the fascination of the hidden world of the oceans to nonscientists, exploring the mystery of the sea, its history and treasures. The book went into nine printings and was at the top of the nonfiction best-seller lists nationwide. It was selected by the Book of the Month Club, condensed for Reader's Digest, and translated into 33 languages. In the year of publication (1951), *The Sea Around Us* received the National Book Award for Non-Fiction.

The success of *The Sea Around Us* wrought major changes in Carson's life. In 1951 she accepted a Guggenheim fellowship that enabled her to take a year's leave of absence from her government job to start work on a third book. Her future secured by success, she resigned her position at the U.S. Fish and Wildlife Service in 1952 to devote herself fulltime to her writing. The result was *The Edge of the Sea*, published in 1955. Conceived as a popular guide to the seashore, studying the ecological relationship of the seashore to animals on the Atlantic Coast of the United States, this work complemented her previous book and evidences Carson's growing interest in the interrelationship of Earth's systems and the **holistic** approach that would mark *Silent Spring*.

Silent Spring opens with a brief account of a fictional town in the American heartland "where all life seemed to live in harmony with its surroundings." Prosperous farms line roadsides alive with wildflowers and ferns. In winter, birds feed on colorful berries above the snowline. Then a blight spreads through the region. Sheep and cattle sicken and die. Chickens become ill. In the spring the hens brood but no chicks are hatched. The birds disappear. Crops fail. The hedgerows wither and die. The cause of this "creeping death" is the widespread use of pesticides. In *Silent Spring*, Carson propounds an eloquent argument for the careful and thorough consideration of both the short- and long-term effects of the use of chemicals for a range of applications. The book documents the negative effects that result from the use of pesticides, chemical fertilizers, and an array of chemical treatments designed to enhance production or simplify the production process.

The information contained in *Silent Spring* was not new. All the issues she covered had been discussed in the scientific journals. Carson's contribution was her presentation of "the overall picture" in a highly readable style. Carson highlighted the fact that while individual chemical products might be viewed as safe because they achieve what they were designed to do, the combined effects of an assortment of chemical products could be deadly. As an example, Carson cites the streams that became chemical soups carrying the outpourings of chemical treatment plants and the runoff from fields treated with pesticides and chemical fertilizers, killing algae, plant life, fish, and animals.

Carson began to awaken the public to the need to think beyond short-term quick chemical fixes and profit taking: "The central problem of our age has become the contamination of man's total environment with substances of incredible

"If we are going to live so intimately with these chemicals—eating and drinking them, taking them into the very marrow of our bones—we had better know something about their nature and their power."
— Rachel Carson, *Silent Spring*

holistic: concerned with complete systems; viewing the relationship of people and the environment as a single system.

potential for harm—substances that accumulate in plants and animals and even penetrate the germ cells to shatter or alter the very material of heredity upon which the shape of the future depends." Carson used her considerable literary skills to bring these scientific concerns to the attention of the general public.

In detailed, well-documented accounts, *Silent Spring* revealed the vested interest of a chemical industry that marketed the effectiveness of a product designed to destroy pests without any reference to the irrevocable changes that would be wrought in the pest habitat. She emphasized that the ecology of the soil had essentially been ignored in the rush to apply chemical solutions to pest problems, as if the soil would remain unaffected by the poisons being poured onto it and channelled into it by affected insects. Carson also noted that it was well documented that some pests could and did develop resilience to the pesticides requiring ever more powerful pesticides resulting in an escalating toxic spiral. "The chemical war is never won, and all life is caught in its violent crossfire," she warned.

On publication, *Silent Spring* received much adverse criticism. The chemical industry united against Carson accusing her of ignorance, sensationalism, and distortion. There was even an attempt to convince her publisher that the book should not be published. More balanced reviews appeared in the scientific press including one in *Scientific American* which suggested that *Silent Spring* "may help us toward a much needed reappraisal of current policies and practices." Acceptance by the establishment was not long delayed. A 1963 report by the President's Science Advisory Committee was reviewed by the journal Science as "a fairly thorough-going **vindication** of Rachel Carson's *Silent Spring* thesis." ◆

vindication: defense or justification against criticism.

Carver, George Washington

C. 1864–1943 ● BIOLOGY & AGRICULTURAL SCIENCE

"I do not deal very much in extreme technical processes as it takes it out of and away from the thing that will help the farmer unless it can be simplified so that he can use it."

— George Washington Carver

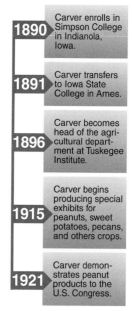

1890 Carver enrolls in Simpson College in Indianola, Iowa.

1891 Carver transfers to Iowa State College in Ames.

1896 Carver becomes head of the agricultural department at Tuskegee Institute.

1915 Carver begins producing special exhibits for peanuts, sweet potatoes, pecans, and others crops.

1921 Carver demonstrates peanut products to the U.S. Congress.

Born in Diamond, Missouri, George Washington Carver did not remember his parents. His father was believed to be a slave killed accidentally before Carver's birth. His mother was Mary Carver, a slave apparently kidnapped by slave raiders soon after he was born. He and his older brother were raised by their mother's former owners, Moses and Susan Carver, on their small, largely self-sufficient farm.

Denied admission to the neighborhood school because of his color, Carver was privately tutored and then moved to nearby Neosho to enter school in the mid-1870s. He soon realized he knew more than the teacher and left with a family moving to Fort Scott, Kansas. After witnessing a lynching there, he left that town and for over a decade roamed around the Midwest seeking an education while supporting himself by cooking, laundering, and homesteading.

In 1890 Carver enrolled in Simpson College in Indianola, Iowa, where he was an art major and the only African-American student. After his teacher convinced him that a black man could not make a living in art, Carver transferred to Iowa State College at Ames in 1891 to major in agriculture. Again the only black student on campus, Carver participated fully (except for dating) in extracurricular activities and compiled such an impressive academic record that he was hired as a botany assistant to pursue postgraduate work. Before he received his master of agriculture degree in 1896, he was placed in charge of the greenhouse and taught freshmen students

An expert in mycology (the study of fungi) and plant cross-fertilization, Carver could have remained at Iowa and probably would have made significant contributions in one or both fields. However, he felt an obligation to share his knowledge with other African Americans and accepted Booker T. Washington's offer to become head of the agricultural department at Tuskegee Normal and Industrial Institute in 1896.

When he arrived at Tuskegee, Carver intended only to stay a few years and then pursue doctoral work. Instead, he spent his remaining forty-six years there. Although he once considered matrimony, he never married and instead "adopted" many Tuskegee students as his "children," to whom he provided loans and guidance. For the first half of his tenure, he worked long hours in administration, teaching, and research. The focus of his work reflected the needs of his constituents rather than his personal talents or interests. As director of the only all-black-staffed agricultural experiment station, he sought answers to the debt problems of small-scale farmers and landless sharecroppers. Thus, in his teaching, extension work (carried on with a wagon equipped as a movable school), and agricultural bulletins, Carver preached the use of available and renewable resources to replace expensive, purchased commodities. He especially advocated the growing of peanuts as a cheap source of protein and published several bulletins with peanut recipes.

After twenty years at Tuskegee, Carver was respected by agricultural researchers but largely unknown to the general public. His rise to fame began with his induction in 1916 into Great Britain's Royal Society for the Arts and the growing realization of his usefulness by the peanut industry. In 1921, a growers' association paid his way to testify at tariff hearings in Congress. There his showmanship in demonstrating peanut products drew national press coverage. Two years later, some Atlanta businessmen founded the Carver Products Company, and Carver won the Spingarn Medal of the NAACP. Although the company failed, it generated publicity. Then in 1933 an Associated Press release exaggerated Carver's success in rehabilitating polio patients with peanut-oil massages.

Soon he was perhaps the best known African American of his generation.

The increasing publicity caught the attention of numerous people who found Carver's rise from slavery and his personality appealing. Articles began to appear describing the flowers in the lapels of his well worn jackets and his rambles in the woods to commune with his "Creator," through which he expressed his devout but **nonsectarian** belief. Because he took no public stand on political or racial matters, many diverse groups could adopt him as a symbol of their causes. Thus he was appropriated by advocates of racial equality, the "New South," religion, the "American Dream," and even segregation. His significant work as an agricultural researcher and educator was obscured by the myth of the "peanut wizard."

Relishing the publicity, Carver did little to correct the public record, aside from general statements of his "unworthiness" of the honors that came with increasing frequency. Some symbolic uses of his life helped to perpetuate white **stereotypes** of African Americans, but most of the publicity had a positive impact on both white and black Americans. Indeed, Carver became a potent tool for racial tolerance after the Commission on Interracial Cooperation and the YMCA began to sponsor his lecture tours of white college campuses in the 1920s and 1930s. On these tours, Carver added dozens of whites to his adopted "family." To them he was no "**token** black" but a trusted father figure to whom they wrote their innermost thoughts. Many, such as white clergyman Howard Kester, became outspoken advocates of racial justice.

Because of his compelling personality, Carver had a profound impact on almost everyone—black or white—who came in contact with him. His "special friends" ranged from white sharecroppers to Henry Ford. Most of his major publicists were true disciples of Carver's vision of the interrelatedness of all human beings and their environment. Because of his extreme frugality, he was also able to leave a substantial legacy by giving about sixty thousand dollars to establish the George Washington Carver Foundation, which continues to support scientific research at Tuskegee University. Although his scientific contributions were meager relative to his fame, and he could not single-handedly save the black family farm, Carver's work and warmth greatly enriched the lives of thousands.

He died on January 5, 1943. ◆

nonsectarian: not affiliated with a particular religious group.

stereotype: a standardized mental picture that represents an oversimplified, often prejudiced, attitude.

token: representing a symbolic effort to avoid discrimination.

Copernicus, Nicolaus (Nikolai Kopernik)

1473–1543 ● ASTRONOMY

> *"Finally we shall place the Sun himself at the center of the Universe. All this is suggested by the systematic procession of events and the harmony of the whole Universe, if only we face the facts, as they say 'with both eyes open.'"*
> —Nicolaus Copernicus

canon law: the body of laws governing a church.

Nicolaus Copernicus was born in Thorn (Torun), Poland (then Prussia); his father was a merchant with some social standing. Copernicus studied mathematics under Wojciech Brudewski at the University of Cracow. His graduation in 1494 coincided with the election of his uncle, Lucas Waczenrode, as bishop of Ermeland, who appointed Copernicus a canon at the cathedral of Frauenburg. Assured of financial support, he was able to continue his education in Italy and devote his life to research. He studied all branches of the sciences, in addition to canon law and Greek, and earned a doctor's degree in **canon law** at Bologna in 1503 and in arts and medicine in 1506. Returning to Frauenburg, he provided medical care for the community's poor and tended to church responsibilities.

Copernicus's primary scholastic interest was in mathematics. His teacher was a follower of the second-century Greek astronomer Ptolemy, but Copernicus's doubts led him to make his own measurements of the movements of planets. He unsuccessfully attempted to fit his observed measurements to Ptolemy's theory that the Earth was stationary and located at the center of the the solar system with the planets and the Sun orbiting around it. Until Copernicus's investigations, Ptolemy's theory had remained unchallenged for 1,400 years. Now Copernicus's measurements cast serious doubt on the Ptolemaic theory. Being able to read recently published ancient Greek books in their original language, Copernicus discovered that other solar system theories abounded at the time of Ptolemy; there were hints of heliocentric hypotheses even then. The thought of the Sun being at the center of the solar system initially seemed absurd to Copernicus, yet when he applied his observations to that hypothesis his mathematical findings and models fit.

By the time Copernicus was thirty-three years old he had formulated his original theory that the Sun was the center of the solar system and that the planets orbited around it. The

Nicolaus Copernicus

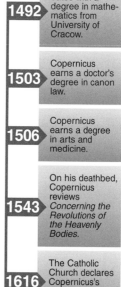

1492 Copernicus graduates with a degree in mathematics from University of Cracow.

1503 Copernicus earns a doctor's degree in canon law.

1506 Copernicus earns a degree in arts and medicine.

1543 On his deathbed, Copernicus reviews *Concerning the Revolutions of the Heavenly Bodies.*

1616 The Catholic Church declares Copernicus's work in conflict with scripture.

Earth rotated daily on its axis, west to east, and also orbited around the Sun beyond the orbits of Mercury and Venus. He dismissed Ptolemy's theory and most of the underlying Aristotelian concepts, although Copernicus retained Aristotle's concept of circular orbits despite the fact that he observed conflicting evidence. To reconcile his findings and theory with Aristotle, he concluded that the Sun was located slightly off center of the planets' circular orbits.

Although he published only excerpts of his theory and gave limited lectures about his work, his reputation was renowned enough for him to be the Lateran Council to express his opinions on questions of calendar reform. He did not disclose much of his theory at the Lateran Council. Pope Clement VII approved of Copernicus's first treatise and requested a complete presentation. A printer's proof copy of his six-volume masterpiece, *De revolutionibus orbium coelestium* (*Concerning the Revolutions of the Heavenly Bodies*), was reviewed by Copernicus on his deathbed; publication followed shortly after his death in 1543.

Proof of his theory could not be made during Copernicus's lifetime as more sophisticated tools, including the telescope, needed to be developed. Accurate measurements of stellar parallaxes and the exact orbits of the planets were necessary to prove his theory. Copernicus knew what was needed but he could only measure angles of ten minutes of arc, whereas measurements in fractions of seconds of arc were required. Nevertheless, he calculated the radii of the planetary orbits within 99 percent of their actual orbits. Copernicus thought that gravity was not an influence of the whole Earth but was a property of its substance. He theorized that gravity extended to the Sun, Moon, and other stars.

Copernicus dismissed Ptolemy's theory and most of the underlying Aristotelian concepts.

Despite the fact that Copernicus's measurements were made with primitive tools, his published tables of planetary movement remained in use more than one hundred years until replaced by the Danish astronomer Tycho Brahe's careful measurements. Johannes Kepler, a German mathematician, worked with Brahe's records and discovered that the planets traveled around the Sun in **elliptical** orbits, thus solving the problem that Copernicus observed when he concluded that the Sun was not located in the center of the planets' orbits. In 1610 Galileo observed through his telescope that Venus changes from a thin crescent into a full circle. Such phenomena proved that Venus revolved about the Sun and that Copernicus's theory was sound. It was Isaac Newton's work on gravity that finally proved Copernicus correct by discovering the law of gravitation, which explains how every body in the universe attracts every other body.

elliptical: having a oval shape.

Copernicus's book was dedicated to Pope Paul III and was financed by a cardinal. The church did not take exception to Copernicus's theory until 1616, when Galileo's work began proving the theory. At that time it was declared false and in conflict with Holy Scripture. ◆

Cousteau, Jacques Yves

1910–1997 ● OCEANOGRAPHY

"Each generation, sharing in the estate and heritage of the earth, has a duty as trustee for future generations to prevent irreversible and irreparable harm to life on earth and to human freedom and dignity."
— Article 2 of The Cousteau Society's Bill of Rights for Future Generations

Jacques Yves Cousteau gave the world a much better understanding of what happens in a place most only get to see on the surface—the ocean.

Cousteau proved himself to be a pioneer is several aspects of oceanography. Not only did Cousteau invent breathing equipment that allowed him to probe the dark undersea depths, he also developed camera equipment to record his travels, allowing them to be witnessed by future generations.

Born near the Bordeaux region of France in St. Andre-de Cubzac on June 11, 1910, Cousteau was a sickly child forced to move often because of his father's work as a lawyer. In an effort to strengthen himself, Cousteau took up swimming at an early age, eventually becoming an avid swimmer.

After graduating from a boarding school in the Alsace region, Cousteau entered the naval academy at Brest. Upon graduation, he entered the French navy as a **midshipman**. It was Cousteau's intention to become a pilot, but in 1936 he accidentally drove his father's car off of a mountain highway, severely injuring his arms.

midshipman: a person in training for a naval officer's commission.

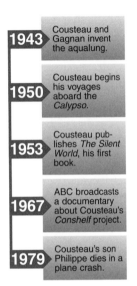

1943 ▷ Cousteau and Gagnan invent the aqualung.

1950 ▷ Cousteau begins his voyages aboard the *Calypso*.

1953 ▷ Cousteau publishes *The Silent World*, his first book.

1967 ▷ ABC broadcasts a documentary about Cousteau's *Conshelf* project.

1979 ▷ Cousteau's son Philippe dies in a plane crash.

bathyscaphe: a submarine for deep sea exploration with a spherical watertight cabin on its underside.

While he eventually healed from the injuries, he would never become a pilot. One reason Cousteau was able to regain the use of his arms was because of his daily swimming in the Mediterranean Sea. About this time, Cousteau began to experiment with a type of underwater diving, commonly referred to as "goggle diving." In 1943, with the help of engineer Emile Gagnan, Cousteau developed the aqualung, which was the first underwater breathing apparatus to be self-contained, hence the acronym SCUBA (self-contained underwater breathing apparatus). Able to dive as deep as 300 feet, the aqualung also served as the perfect cover when Cousteau worked with the French resistance during World War II. Commercial sales of the aqualung began after the war.

Cousteau remained with the French Navy until 1950, when he began the studies that would bring him world fame. Revamping a minesweeper, which he renamed *Calypso*, Cousteau set out to explore the depths of the ocean. As early as his teens, Cousteau was fascinated with the art of photography, especially moving pictures. He wanted to record the underwater images he was seeing. Because normal cameras are not waterproof, Cousteau made modifications that allowed him to film underwater, sometimes as deep as four miles.

In 1953 Cousteau wrote the first of many books describing the universe under the ocean's surface. *The Silent World*, co-authored with Frederic Dumas, became a best-seller in its original English and again after it was translated into several other languages. Three years later Cousteau won the first of three Academy Awards for the film version of *The Silent World*.

Rewarded professionally as well as financially, Cousteau set out for more adventure. He developed a small subsmersible boat known as the **bathyscaphe**. He also attempted to prove a long-held dream that people could survive in an all-underwater community. There were three such projects, all called *Conshelf*.

Cousteau won his third Academy Award for the 1965 documentary, "World Without Sun," which detailed life in *Conshelf II*. He had won a second Academy Award in 1959 for a short film called "The Golden Fish."

Although well-known in many circles by now, his recognizability was bolstered when the American Broadcasting Company televised a film about *Conshelf III* in 1967. Buoyed by the popular appeal of his journeys aboard the *Calypso*, Cousteau received a long-term contract from the network, thus bringing "The Undersea World of Jacques Cousteau" into American homes for the next nine years.

As the international community held the first Earth Day in the early 1970s, Cousteau's attention turned toward environmental matters. His Cousteau Society strove to protect sea-going creatures, although Cousteau was chastised for allegedly harming animals to film his underwater scenes, which he denied.

In addition to the many documentaries and movies he produced, Cousteau also wrote several books, including *The Ocean World* (1985) and *The Living Sea* (1988, coauthored with James Dugan).

Cousteau married in 1937 and had two sons, Philippe and Jean-Michel. A plane crash in 1979 claimed the life of Phillipe, leaving his older brother to struggle with the burden of following in his famous father's footsteps. Deciding he could no longer do so, Jean-Michel eventually resigned from the Cousteau Society.

Yet another blow was dealt to Cousteau when his wife died in 1990. Not long after, the *Calypso* was involved in a collision and sank. While trying to raise money to build a second *Calypso*, Cousteau died in June of 1997 at the age of 87. Cousteau's research, writings, and films not only brought him fame and prestige, they inspired a generation to be more environmentally concerned about the ocean. ◆

> *"The health of the global water system rooted in the ocean is vital to the future welfare of our planet, and is of particular concern to me as an ocean explorer."*
>
> — Jacques Cousteau

Crick, Francis Harry Compton

1916–PRESENT ● MOLECULAR BIOLOGY

Watson, James Dewy

1928–PRESENT ● BIOPHYSICS

"We have discovered the secret of life!"
— Francis Crick, quoted in J. D. Watson's *The Double Helix*.

Francis Crick and James Watson won the Nobel Prize for Physiology or Medicine in 1962 for deducing the structure of the deoxyribonucleic acid (DNA) molecule. Their work was based on earlier research by New Zealand-born biophysicist M.H.F. Wilkins, who shared the award with them. Their model of the DNA molecule, which is considered one of the greatest scientific discoveries of the century, revolutionized science as it revealed the essence of biological life.

Crick was born June 8, 1916, in Northampton, England, the first of two sons belonging to Henry and Annie Elizabeth Crick. He received his elementary education at Northampton Grammar School and Mill Hill School. Afterwards, he attended University School in London, studying physics and mathematics to earn a B.S. degree in 1937.

Studying for his Ph.D. under E.N. Andrade, Crick's education was interrupted by his country's declaration of war on Nazi Germany in 1939. During World War II, Crick became a member of the scientific services team of the British Admiralty, chiefly concentrating on magnetic and acoustic **mines**. He remained with that operation through 1946.

mine: a type of bomb that explodes when disturbed.

The next year, he resumed his doctoral studies in biology, not physics. While working for the British Admiralty, Crick had chanced upon the book, *What Is Life?* by physicist Erwin Schrödinger. Schrödinger predicted that the study of genes would hold the secret of life itself. This idea inspired Crick immensely and influenced his career.

With financial help from the National Research Council and from his family, Crick attended Cambridge University. Taking biology classes by day, he worked evenings at the Strangeways Research Laboratory. Two years later, he joined the Medical Research Council Unit for Molecular Biology

(Cavendish Laboratory) under the direction of M.F. Perutz. At Cavendish in 1951, he met the young American student James Watson. Crick switched to Caius College at Cambridge and received his Ph.D. in 1954. His final two years of college were spent in the United States, in research with the Protein Structure Project of the Polytechnic Institute of Brooklyn, New York.

James Watson was born in Chicago, Illinois, on April 6, 1928. Watson's above-average intelligence was obvious in his early years. At age 15, he was accepted to the University of Chicago where he majored in zoology. Upon graduation, however, both Harvard and CalTech turned him down for graduate studies. Instead, he entered Indiana University. He changed his major from natural history to genetics and biochemistry, being greatly influenced by Nobel laureate Herman Mueller. Upon completion of his doctoral thesis on the effects of X-rays on viruses that kill bacteria, he received his Ph.D. in genetics. He was only 21 years old.

For a brief period, Watson attended the University of Copenhagen (Denmark) as a National Research Council Fellow. Although his work alongside biochemist Herman Kalckar on DNA proved personally unsatisfying, it was in

James Watson (left) and Francis Crick.

helix: spiral in form.

phosphate: an organic compound that permits useful energy to be released.

Copenhagen that Watson first became acquainted with the DNA-related research of Maurice H.F. Wilkins.

Watson traveled to Naples, Italy, to hear Wilkins speak on his work with the DNA molecule. Wilkins had discovered that the molecule had a double **helix** structure, not a single helix structure as was previously thought.

By 1951, when Watson and Crick first met at Cambridge and became intimate friends, interest in DNA was waning in the scientific sphere. Linus Pauling had already theorized that the DNA was a single stranded molecule; Wilkins proved it was a double helix. Rosalind Franklin showed that **phosphate** groups are situated outside the helix; Alexander Todd demonstrated that the acids contain both phosphate and sugar; and Erwin Chargaff indicated that its nucleic acids contain four organic bases.

Wilkins shared his results with Crick and Watson, who sought to build on what was already chemically known about DNA, feeling that the knowledge was incomplete. The model of the DNA molecule they would eventually construct would take 24 months of round-the-clock labor, but would virtually redefine what was understood about the structure and interactions of molecules.

The team believed that the DNA molecule consisted of a double helix (as Wilkins had suggested), comprised of two parallel chains of sugar and phosphate groups linked by pairs of organic bases. They based their work heavily on Wilkins's findings on X-ray diffraction analysis of DNA and, from it, built a series of models—then eventually one inclusive model—that illustrated the three-dimensional DNA molecule. The model displayed the exact arrangements of the molecule's subunits, with all of its physical and chemical properties.

The eventual single Crick-Watson Model (as it came to be known) graphically explained how DNA would replicate and transfer genetic information in the process. This model demonstrated how replication occurred by a parting of the double helix's pair of strands, each then linking with nucleotides, creating two new DNA molecules; each of the new molecules would contain a strand from the original DNA and one new strand.

The thrust of their discovery—what made it dynamic and far-reaching—was that it demonstrated once and for all that

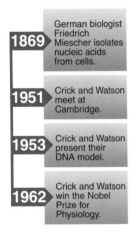

1869 German biologist Friedrich Miescher isolates nucleic acids from cells.

1951 Crick and Watson meet at Cambridge.

1953 Crick and Watson present their DNA model.

1962 Crick and Watson win the Nobel Prize for Physiology.

DNA was the carrier of genetic information for the cell. (Previously, protein was believed to have been the relayer.) In short, Crick and Wilson proved that because genes are known to carry hereditary data from generation to generation, and because genes are essentially DNA molecules, DNA holds the key to heredity.

After the announcement of their findings in 1953, the pair collaborated once more to clarify the basic structure of viruses, again receiving high merits for their work as a scientific team. Both have remained active in their fields since their combined landmark effort.

Crick has lectured around the world, has been inducted into many organizations, such as the Royal Society of London (1959), and has received countless awards. Among these are the Prix Charles Leopold Meyer of the French Academy of Sciences and the Award of Merit of the Gairdner Foundation. He recently received a Fellowship from the Salk Institute for Biological Studies in San Diego. He has authored two books, the highly entertaining *Of Molecules and Men* (1966) and *Life Itself* (1992).

Watson taught at Harvard and CalTech (ironically, the two universities that rejected him as a youth), and from 1989 to 1992 was a principle force on the controversial Human Genome Research Project at the National Health Institute. He currently directs genetic and cancer research at Cold Springs Harbor Laboratory in New York. Having written many scholarly articles, Watson also authored *Molecular Biology of the Gene* (1965) and *The Double Helix*, a lively description of his partnership with Francis Crick.

Both Watson and Crick (along with Maurice Wilkins) received the Lasker Foundation Award in 1960, two years before the Nobel committee cited them. ◆

The Crick-Watson model graphically explained how DNA would replicate and transfer genetic information in the process.

Curie, Marie

1867–1934 ● PHYSICS & RADIOLOGY

"All my life through, the new sights of Nature made me rejoice like a child."
— Marie Curie

progressivism: the policy of making use of new ideas, findings, opportunities.

clericalism: the policy of maintaining or increasing the power of a religious authority.

B orn as Maria Sklodowska in Warsaw, Poland, on November 7, 1867, Maria, who was known by the affectionate nickname of Manya, was the daughter of a secondary school science teacher. In high school she excelled in Russian, but poor health caused her to go to live with her uncle in a more rural setting in Skalbmierz, where her health was soon restored.

From an early age, Maria was politically active in progressive movements advocating Polish freedom from Russian domination. She became fluent in French, German, Polish, and Russian and became a strong advocate of scientific **progressivism** over and against a **clericalism** that she regarded as outmoded.

In 1886 Maria became a governess in the house of M. Zorawski in a small town north of Warsaw. She served there for three years, immersing herself in the Zorawskis' extensive scientific and literary library. While she was there, the Zorawskis' eldest son fell in love with her, but staunch family opposition to their marriage led to a breakup.

In 1891 she went to Paris to live with her married sister Bronia, a medical doctor. Marie received a scholarship to study science and mathematics, and her abilities were quickly apparent to her professors.

In April 1894 Maria met Pierre Curie. They were strongly drawn to each other, and Pierre soon proposed marriage to her. After months of indecision, she accepted in October, although the marriage did not take place until the following year.

In the meantime she completed her first scientific paper under the guidance of Le Châtelier and her husband-to-be. After her marriage, inspired by Roentgen's recent discovery of what later became known as X-rays and by Henri Becquerel's discovery that uranium salts emitted a similar sort of invisible radiation, she decided to conduct a series of experiments to determine if there were still other elements or compounds that emitted such radiation. Using sensitive instruments provided by her husband and his brother Jacques, she carefully analyzed a variety of ores. She even coined the term *radioactive* to describe the kinds of substances she was looking for. In July 1898 she detected a new element that she named polonium after her native land. Further tests followed, and in November she and those working with her reported that a second, much more strongly radioactive substance had been discovered—the element radium—but she struggled for several years before successfully isolating a sample of pure radium, which allowed her to calculate its atomic weight.

In 1903 she was appointed as a lecturer in physics at the École Normale Supérieure in Sèvres. That same year she, her husband, and Henri Becquerel received a joint Nobel Prize for physics for their discovery of radioactivity. Ill health and the birth of their daughter Eve in December 1904 prevented the Curies from traveling to Stockholm to accept the award until 1905. Receipt of the prize brought them a level of public recognition that they found rather burdensome. They sought neither fame nor fortune and refused outright to accept royalties for their discoveries despite lucrative offers.

In April 1906 Pierre Curie died. Marie was devastated but vowed not only to continue caring for their daughters but to continue her research, though from then on her personality became ever more reserved.

She declined the offer of a pension from the French Ministry of Education but accepted a subsequent offer to take over her husband's chair at the Sorbonne—she was the first woman to teach there—beginning in November 1906. From 1910 to 1914 she published a series of papers on the phenom-

In 1911, Marie Curie became the first scientist ever to receive a second Nobel Prize.

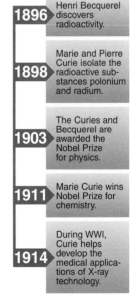

1896 Henri Becquerel discovers radioactivity.

1898 Marie and Pierre Curie isolate the radioactive substances polonium and radium.

1903 The Curies and Becquerel are awarded the Nobel Prize for physics.

1911 Marie Curie wins Nobel Prize for chemistry.

1914 During WWI, Curie helps develop the medical applications of X-ray technology.

enon of radioactivity. In 1911 she became the first scientist ever to receive a second Nobel Prize, this time for her discovery of the elements radium and polonium.

During World War I, she served on the front lines with the radiological service of the French Red Cross. In 1918 she joined the Radium Institute, which was later renamed in her honor. In declining health from 1923 onward, she suffered from recurrent eye problems and from lesions of her fingers that were the result of years of handling radium. (In the early years it was not fully understood that exposure to radiation could be extremely harmful.) Entering a Paris nursing home in early June of 1934, she was soon transferred to a **sanitarium** in the French Alps, where she died on June 29, 1934. ◆

sanitarium: an institution for rest and recuperation, and for treating the chronically ill.

Daguerre, Louis-Jacques-Mande

1789–1851 ● INVENTOR

> *"I have seized the light! I have arrested its flight! In the future the Sun itself shall draw my pictures!"*
> — Louis Daguerre

Frenchman Louis-Jacques-Mande Daguerre was the inventor of the daguerrotype, an early form of photography. After the Napoleonic War, Daguerre was apprenticed to an architect, but he was more interested in painting landscapes and portraits than architectural drawings and, overcoming his father's opposition, he went to Paris to be an artist.

At sixteen, Daguerre began studying theater design at the Paris Opera and at nineteen was made assistant to the panorama painter, Pierre Prévost. His skills as an innovator in theatrical design were revealed in the **diorama** exhibitions he began in 1822; he placed on stage large transparent and opaque painted screens depicting views, using a *camera obscura* to insure perfect accuracy. By varying the light falling on these screens, he created the illusion of twilight or daybreak.

diorama: a scenic representation in which sculpted figures are displayed with a realistic painted background.

From the *Camera Obscura* to the Kodak Box Camera

The first camera, the *camera obscura*, consisted of a huge box with an opening on one side that admitted light. On the opposite side of the box, the light formed an inverted image of the scene outside. The *camera obscura* was chiefly a tool for artists, who would trace the outline of the image. In the early 19th century, Joseph Niepce and Louis Daguerre learned how to capture and fix the *camera obscura's* image using silvered copper plates treated with light sensitive chemicals. These early photographs had to be developed immediately and required an exposure of 10 or 15 minutes for each shot. In the following decades, inventors and scientists improved the photographic process and the design of the camera. These improvements allowed many copies to be made from a single negative, unlike Daguerre's method, which only produced one print. About mid-century, people began to experiment with the artistic possibilities of photography and it was extremely popular by the time of the American Civil War.

At first, photography was limited to people who could afford and knew how to use the cumbersome, complicated, and costly equipment. Then, in 1888, George Eastman introduced the Kodak box camera. It was lightweight, inexpensive, and easy to use. The box camera led to a tremendous rise in the popularity of amateur photography. Today, photography has been firmly established as an art form, a hobby, and an essential tool for scientists, historians, and journalists.

These lifelike scenes brought him fame in Paris, and in 1823 he took the diorama to London's Regents Park, where his show was an outstanding technical triumph and financial success.

Daguerre was excited by the possibilities of recording permanently his *camera obscura* images. He was aware of the work of his countryman J. N. Niepce, who since 1814 had been trying to obtain permanent pictures from the action of sunlight on **bitumen**-coated pewter or glass plates. Daguerre began a correspondence with him in 1825 but Niepce was unwilling to share the secrets of his process until 1829, when the two made an agreement to carry out research together.

bitumen: a hydrocarbon substance such as tar.

The two attempted to find a substance more light sensitive than bitumen, which reacted too slowly for the process today called photography. Niepce died in 1833 with the search still unsuccessful.

Two years later, Daguerre discovered that silver iodine was what he had been looking for. He had put an unsuccessful photographic plate away in the cupboard with the intention of re-coating it for future use; when he came to take it out after a few days, he found a strong image registered on it. Careful investigation of the bottles in the cupboard showed that mercury from a broken thermometer had acted as the developing agent on the silver iodine coated plate. In his excitement he exclaimed, "I have seized the light! I have arrested its flight! In the future the Sun itself shall draw my pictures!"

Daguerre, along with Niepce's son, agreed to sell the invention while preserving the secret of the method; it was a thankless task trying to get people to invest in an unknown process. Daguerre then tried to sell the invention to businessmen and politicians, even starting a rumor that it might be lost to France if he could not find a buyer. He eventually found an advocate in the Chamber of Deputies who convinced the government that both he and Niepce had made an outstanding contribution to the nation's artistic heritage with their invention, soon to be known as the daguerreotype. In 1839 Daguerre and Niepce were voted lifetime pensions, an award which could not have come at a better time for Daguerre—his diorama exhibition burned down that year. Nevertheless, although he was appointed an officer in the Legion of Honor, he died in relative poverty; his skill as inventor and promoter brought him no fortune.

The daguerreotype had many shortcomings; the subject had to remain still for a long period and bright sunlight was needed to register the image. Moreover, there was no way of reproducing the picture except by making another daguerreotype of it. Nevertheless, daguerreotypes for the first time allowed people of modest means to have their photograph taken. ◆

1805 Daguerre begins studying theater design at the Paris Opera.

1822 Daguerre creates diorama paintings illuminated in a dark room to give illusion of reality.

1829 Daguerre begins working with J.N. Niepce to find a light sensitive substance for photography.

1835 Daguerre discovers that mercury acts as a developing agent on a plate coated with silver iodine.

1839 The French government gives Daguerre a lifetime pension.

Darwin, Charles

1809–1882 ● GEOLOGY & BIOLOGY

"Man still bears in his bodily frame the indelible stamp of his lowly origins."
— Charles Darwin, *The Descent of Man*

Charles Robert Darwin is regarded by the world as the scientist who provided overwhelming data that evolution of organisms—change through time—occurs, but his contributions to geology have received less attention. Born on 12 February 1809 in Shrewsbury, England, Darwin entered the University of Edinburgh in 1825, where he took a course in geology under Robert Jameson, which he judged to be a dreadful subject. He was a member of both the geological Wernerian Society and the biological Plinian Society. He transferred to Cambridge in January 1828 and became increasingly interested in natural history. His formal field training in geology was a two-week trip with Reverend Adam Sedgwick to Wales in 1831; he may have attended some of Sedgwick's lectures at the university.

By good fortune Darwin became the traveling companion of Captain Robert FitzRoy on HMS *Beagle*. The ship left England 27 December 1831, spending most of the voyage in southern South America preparing Admiralty charts of both coasts and particularly of Tierra del Fuego. The ship continued westward and recrossed the Atlantic to check **chronometers** in eastern South America before docking in England 2 October 1836. Darwin was not the official natural-

chronometers: instruments to measure time.

ist of the voyage, though he soon assumed that role. His note-books contain about four times as much material on geological observations as those on zoology. Darwin explored the Andes, noted fossil evidence of uplifted sedimentary strata, and experienced a dramatic earthquake in Chile where the coastline was raised more than a meter.

Shortly after Darwin's return he was elected to the Council of the Geological Society of London, and in 1838 he was elected one of the secretaries. That year he also presented a formal paper on the Conception, Chile, earthquake that he had witnessed. Darwin was impressed with the concept of change in sea level through time and that year conducted fieldwork on the so-called parallel roads of Glen Roy, Scotland. He interpreted them as beaches formed during higher stands of the sea and presented a paper to the Geological Society in January 1839. With the general acceptance of continental glaciation and allied phenomena, these were reinterpreted in 1847 as former lake levels.

Throughout this period, Darwin was working on both his account of the trip and his views on the origin of coral reefs. During May 1839, only two and one-half years after his return from South America, he published *Narrative of the Surveying Voyages of His Majesty's Ships* Adventure *and* Beagle. . . . This pivotal work remains one of the finest travel books ever written, full of keen geological observations. Darwin married in 1839 and remained in London until September 1842.

In his posthumous autobiography Darwin writes that he thought of the concept of upward growth of corals with rise of sea level while he was still on the coast of South America and had not yet seen a reef. In May 1842, he wrote: "It is very pleasant easy work putting together the framework of a geological theory, but it is just as tough a job collecting & comparing the hard unbending facts." Despite arguments raised by the oceanographer Sir John Murray, Darwin's concept was generally accepted. He concluded that atolls are the result of growth of coral as a volcanic cone became gradually submerged. This theory has been vindicated by drilling through thousands of meters of coral into basalt.

Darwin published *The Structure and Distribution of Coral Reefs* in 1842, and then began writing *Geological Observations on the Volcanic Islands Visited During the Voyage of H.M.S.*

> The general acceptance of evolution has affected humanity's view of its own place within nature.

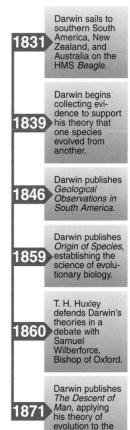

1831 Darwin sails to southern South America, New Zealand, and Australia on the HMS *Beagle.*

1839 Darwin begins collecting evidence to support his theory that one species evolved from another.

1846 Darwin publishes *Geological Observations in South America.*

1859 Darwin publishes *Origin of Species,* establishing the science of evolutionary biology.

1860 T. H. Huxley defends Darwin's theories in a debate with Samuel Wilberforce, Bishop of Oxford.

1871 Darwin publishes *The Descent of Man,* applying his theory of evolution to the human species.

Charles Darwin and Evolution

When Charles Darwin began his five-year journey on the *Beagle* in 1831, most people believed that each species of plant and animal had been individually created and did not change. During the voyage, however, Darwin was struck by the diversity of species he observed, and how species differed from region to region. He became convinced that plants and animals had not always been as they were since creation. In 1859, after accumulating evidence for more than twenty years, Darwin published *On the Origin of Species by Means of Natural Selection*. In this groundbreaking work, Darwin argued that species are constantly changing, with new species evolving from related, preexisting ones. According to Darwin's theory, some individuals within each species have characteristics that make them better suited to life in their environment. These individuals are more likely to survive long enough to reproduce and pass their traits on to the next generation. As the environment changes, the species itself gradually changes to adapt to new conditions. After many generations, this evolution leads to the formation of a new species. The implications of Darwin's theory caused a scientific and philosophical revolution as people were forced to reevaluate long-held beliefs about the origin of species, particularly the human species.

Beagle (published in 1844). Throughout this time, Darwin was also supervising the distribution of natural history specimens and their description by specialists. Darwin's geological investigations were so highly regarded that in 1844 he was elected a vice-president of the Geological Society of London.

The third and final part of the geology of the *Beagle* voyage, *Geological Observations in South America*, was published in 1846, subsidized in part by Darwin himself. By that year, all of the biological specimens had been studied except for a single barnacle. Observation of this specimen would lead to the publication of a monograph of recent and fossil barnacles by the Palaeontographical Society (1881). One school of historians holds that because of this work in systematics, combined with his earlier publications in geology, scientists of the day were prepared to seriously consider Darwin's concept of evolution when it was first presented in 1859.

In *Origin of Species* (1859), Darwin speculated on the length of geologic time and suggested that erosion of the **Cretaceous** chalk Downs of southern England required about 300 million years. This figure upset the physicist William Thomson (Lord Kelvin) and led to Darwin's calculations on

Cretaceous: a geological period beginning about 144 million years ago and ending about 98 million years ago.

the age of Earth and a large body of geologic literature seeking to counter Kelvin's ever shortening concept of geologic time. Darwin removed his estimate from later editions of *Origin of Species* but did not participate in the violent arguments on the age of Earth.

In 1881, Darwin published a work on the formation of vegetable mold through the action of earth worms. This delightful little book may be viewed as a contribution to **geomorphological** processes and soil formation; it shows what a keen mind can do with seemingly prosaic observations.

geomorphological: relating to the form and surface features of the earth.

Charles Darwin died on 19 April 1882, in Down, Kent, England. Darwin's greatest legacy in geology is his work on coral reefs. Despite his observations on the Chilean earthquake, the gradual change in sea level he envisioned provided strong support for Charles Lyell's concept of **uniformitarianism**. More significantly, James D. Dana accepted and amplified Darwin's views on reef formation. The emphasis on vertical movement of land and sea pervaded geologic thought until the more recent shift to the concept of seafloor spreading and lateral movement. Even more important, the general acceptance of evolution (and with it the concept of a great length of geologic time) has affected humanity's view of its own place within nature. ◆

uniformitarianism: the theory that current geological processes are sufficient to account for all past geological change.

da Vinci, Leonardo

1452–1519 ● SCIENTIST

Italian painter, sculptor, architect, scientist, military engineer, and inventor, da Vinci was the embodiment of universal genius known as a Renaissance man. The illegitimate child of a notary and a peasant girl, he was brought up on his father's estate in Vinci, a Tuscan village between Florence and Pisa. As a boy he was talented in writing and music, but painting was his greatest interest, and he was placed in the studio of Andrea del Verrocchio, the Florentine sculptor, whose intellectual curiosity and pursuit of knowledge were inspiring

"Necessity is the theme and the inventress, the eternal curb and law of nature."
— Leonardo da Vinci, *Notebooks*

Leonardo da Vinci

to his young assistant. He worked with Verrocchio until 1478. At twenty da Vinci became a member of the guild of artists. While he was working with Verrocchio he was arraigned on a charge of sodomy and imprisoned for two months, but the case was dismissed because of lack of evidence.

In 1481 he started work on the *Adoration of the Magi* and a *Saint Jerome*, but left for Milan before they were completed. In Milan he applied to Duke Ludovico Sforza for a commission to sculpt an equestrian statue of the duke's father, saying that he was also competent as a military engineer. He received the commission and worked on the statue for sixteen years. Although he had interested himself in the process of casting in bronze, he had never learned the requirements of the process for sculpting. "The Horse" was therefore never cast and the clay model was eventually destroyed by French soldiers.

In addition to designs of canals and artillery pieces for the duke, Leonardo designed pageants and masquerades for the duchess's entertainments. He painted the duke and duchess and many of their courtiers and was rewarded with expensive gifts and a good salary. He also painted the beautiful *Madonna of the Rocks* for the **Confraternity** of the Immaculate Conception, but sued for the return of the painting when they paid him a meager sum. The suit dragged on for years.

confraternity: a society devoted to a religious or charitable cause.

Duke Ludovico ordered the artist to paint the Last Supper on the refectory wall of the convent of Santa Maria della Grazie. The artist worked very slowly, making many studies for the heads of Jesus and the disciples, and spending much time just looking at what he had done before he took up his brushes again. Unfortunately, Leonardo's compulsion to experiment resulted in the use of a medium that was not compatible with the ground. He completed the painting but twenty years later the paint had begun to flake off.

In 1497 the duchess died, and with her death Leonardo's salary stopped. The duke was forced to leave Milan, which shortly afterward was captured by the French; by that time Leonardo had already left.

In the spring of 1500 the painter was in Florence, where he was inspired by the atmosphere. He did more work in his six years in Florence than in all the years he had worked in Milan. It was there that he painted the *Mona Lisa*, one of the world's most famous portraits. He worked on it for four years; it is said that he used a compass to construct the famous "enigmatic" smile. The model was Lisa Gherardini, wife of a wealthy merchant. The critic Giorgio Vasari reported that da Vinci engaged musicians, singers, and jesters to keep her merry "and remove that melancholy which painting usually gives to... portraits." King Francis I of France bought the painting, and it found its home in the Louvre.

He was commissioned to paint an altarpiece for the church of Santissima Annunziata. His first cartoon, on the subject of the Virgin and Child and Saint Anne, was rejected because it was "only beautiful," not instructive. The second, however, showed Saint Anne with the Virgin in her lap, both rising to support the Child, who is reaching for a lamb (the symbol of sacrifice). This version was accepted and the painting was highly acclaimed.

Leonardo left Florence to work on military projects for Caesar Borgia, who was campaigning in the Romagna, but when Borgia ordered the assassination of Leonardo's good

1467 Da Vinci becomes a student of Verrocchio.

1481 Da Vinci starts work on the *Adoration of the Magi* and *Saint Jerome*.

1504 Da Vinci paints the *Mona Lisa*.

1506 Da Vinci moves to Milan.

1509 Da Vinci writes *Trattato de Divina Proportione*.

friend Vitellozzo Vitello, who was one of Caesar's own officers, Leonardo returned to Florence. There he received a commission to make a fresco mural for the Sala di Gran Consiglio in the Palazzo della Signoria. Michelangelo received the commission to do a mural for the opposite wall. The rivalry of these two giants divided the city into two camps. The two cartoons were made and exhibited–much visited and copied. However, neither Leonardo nor Michelangelo finished his fresco. Leonardo, as usual, experimented. The new plaster which he used did not set; he started the work but soon gave up.

In May 1506 he went to Milan for nine months to work for the French king Louis XII and painted the king's portrait. Although he was the official architect and engineer for the French government in Milan, Leonardo spent much time designing pageants and studying various branches of life sciences and geology. In 1509 he wrote his *Trattato de Divina Proportione*, for which he made sixty geometric designs.

Da Vinci met a handsome young artist, Francesco Melzi, and visited him at his family's home in Vaprio for two months. When Giovanni de' Medici became Pope Leo X, Leonardo, with Melzi, went to Rome. The pope's brother,

Leonardo da Vinci as Scientist

When Leonardo da Vinci died, he left behind thousands of pages of uncollected, unpublished, and mostly undated notes and drawings. These pages provide a picture of da Vinci's mind and reveal that vast scope of his scientific inquiry. As a biologist, he explored the structure and development of plants and examined the physiology and anatomy of animals and human beings. He was particularly interested in the structure of the eye, but also studied the action of the heart and the function of the kidney and bladder. As a physicist and mathematician, he addressed the flow of water, the properties of pyramids, and Archimedes' lever. He also probed the relationships of mass, motion, and force, and inquired into the nature of light and vision. Da Vinci entered the realm of geology by exploring the origin and stratification of rocks. He became an engineer when he provided solutions for grinding lenses and practical designs for the construction of canals, buildings, weapons, and military vehicles. In addition, da Vinci proposed designs for such fanciful inventions as flying machines, parachutes, and submarines. Da Vinci's notes covered many other subjects, and explored nearly every branch of science. He was undeniably one of the most creative and original thinkers of all time.

Giuliano de' Medici, Leonardo's patron, arranged for Leonardo to occupy an apartment in the Vatican.

Leonardo was now over sixty years of age and not too pleased with his new situation. His neighbors complained to the pope about him because he studied anatomy by dissecting cadavers. He lived quietly and modestly, tending to be withdrawn and antisocial; his neighbors intruded on his privacy and got on his nerves. Nevertheless, he continued with his studies and writings and completed several paintings.

After Giuliano de' Medici died, Francis I, who had ascended the throne of France the previous year (1515), invited Leonardo to come to live in France, appointing him First Royal Painter, Architect, and Engineer. Francis sincerely admired Leonardo for his artistic genius and his intellect and gave him a liberal pension, as well as the castle of Cloux near the royal residence at Amboise. He appointed Melzi to the position of Gentleman of the Chamber, and often visited Leonardo.

To the great grief of King Francis, Leonardo died at Cloux. He left his manuscripts, his drawings, and his books to Francesco Melzi. None of his writings—several thousand pages, all written in his left-handed "mirror-writing"—had been published. These included his many notebooks, and treatises on the art of painting, on harmony, optics, and aeronautics (he designed a flying machine). There was nothing that did not interest him. If there were phenomena that puzzled him he devised experiments to help him understand—experiments that often resulted in important contributions to the field he was exploring. He also left thousands of pen and ink and chalk sketches on a wide range of subjects.

Leonardo's powerful mind and the diversity of his accomplishments have remained an object of wonder and admiration. He is appreciated as much for his contributions to knowledge and thought as for his artistic genius. ◆

Da Vinci was the embodiment of universal genius known as a Renaissance man.

Davy, Humphry

1778–1829 ● CHEMISTRY

> *"I thank God I was not made a dexterous manipulator; the most important of my discoveries have been suggested to me by my failures."*
>
> — Humphry Davy

Humphry Davy, one of the rare romantics of chemistry, was born in Cornwall, then a remote region of southwest England. Educated at the local grammar school, he was later apprenticed to an apothecary surgeon in Penzance. He was nineteen before he began the study of chemistry by reading Antoine Lavoisier's *Traité Elémentaire* published eight years earlier. Within five years the **neophyte** was to be appointed professor of chemistry at the Royal Institution in London.

Davy's first scientific work was carried out at Dr. Beddoes's Pneumatic Institute. Here he investigated the possible therapeutic value of inhaling various gases, using himself as a guinea pig. Since nitric oxide and carbon monoxide were among the gases studied, it is surprising he survived to write at length on the physiological and psychological effects of nitrous oxide (N_2O), also known as laughing gas.

It was about this time that Davy made the acquaintance of Samuel Taylor Coleridge and William Wordsworth, who both encouraged his lifelong passion for **metaphysics**, art, and poetry. The extraordinary range and intensity of Davy's imagination prompted Coleridge to write:

neophyte: a beginner.

metaphysics: the philosophy concerned with the fundamental nature of reality and being.

Why, Davy could eat them all. There is an energy, an elasticity in his mind which enables him to seize on and analyze all questions, pushing them to their legitimate consequences. Every subject in Davy's mind has the principle of vitality. Living thoughts spring up like turf under his feet.

Versatility may, however, become dilettantism, and Berzelius's description of Davy as a scientist of "brilliant fragments" is not without a sad grain of truth.

At the Royal Institution, Davy exploited the recently discovered voltaic pile to lay the qualitative foundations of electrochemistry. He usually managed to stay a half step ahead of Berzelius and Hisinger in Sweden, as well as Thenard and Gay Lussac in France. In a "capital experiment," elemental potassium was first isolated in 1807. This was soon followed by sodium, barium, calcium, strontium, and magnesium. Since Davy later isolated crude boron and silicon and showed that the green gas first isolated by Scheele was in fact elemental chlorine, he had a hand in the discovery of almost 10 percent of the elements in the periodic table.

Late in 1813, at the height of the Napoleonic Wars (when the emperor had loftily declared, "The sciences are not at war"), Davy set out on an eighteen-month tour of Europe, accompanied by the young Michael Faraday. Although neither then realized it, Davy's star was beginning to set whereas Faraday's was soon to rise. Faraday was to succeed Davy at the Royal Institution. Some have unkindly suggested that Davy's greatest discovery was Michael Faraday. Strictly as a chemist, Davy was the greater of the two. As a natural philosopher, however, Faraday was incomparable.

Davy's last years were rather sad and anticlimactic, even though he served from 1820 to 1827 as president of the Royal Society of London. Brief periods of scientific creativity were interspersed with somewhat aimless travel, salmon fishing, philosophizing, writing, and, toward the end, convalescence from a series of strokes. He died in Geneva on May 29, 1829. ◆

Davy was one of the rare romantics of chemistry.

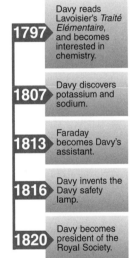

1797 Davy reads Lavoisier's *Traité Elémentaire*, and becomes interested in chemistry.

1807 Davy discovers potassium and sodium.

1813 Faraday becomes Davy's assistant.

1816 Davy invents the Davy safety lamp.

1820 Davy becomes president of the Royal Society.

Descartes, René

1596–1650 ● PHYSICS, MATHEMATICS, & METAPHYSICS

> *"Cogito, ergo sum." (Latin for "I think, therefore I am.")*
> — René Descartes, *Discourse on Method*

Jesuit: A Roman Catholic order of priests devoted to missionary and educational work.

Descartes was the most famous French philosopher, mathematician, and scientist. Through the application of his definitive method of inquiry, he made contributions to theoretical physics, physiology, and astronomy and invented analytical coordinate geometry.

Descartes was born to a noble family at La Haye in Touraine. Both his father and elder brother were councilors in the *parlement* (law court) of Brittany. His formal education began at the age of about ten when he entered the prominent **Jesuit** *collège* (secondary school) at La Flèche. It was during his five years at the *collège* that he became enchanted by the conclusiveness and rigor of mathematics, though somewhat skeptical as to the value of existing methods of inquiry.

Descartes was a sickly child, suffering from a pulmonary complaint inherited from his mother. He was always pale and coughing and his Jesuit masters permitted him to study in bed until late morning. He found these early quiet moments so conducive to meditation and focused inquiry that he became an avowed late riser.

He graduated from La Flèche in 1614 and within another two years had obtained a degree in law from the University of Poitiers, in all likelihood to satisfy his father. This was his last association with any academic institution, either as pupil or teacher.

Wanting to experience the world at large, Descartes chose to pursue a career as a soldier, which was not unusual for younger sons of the upper social classes. To his disappointment, he found the routine mostly unstimulating and mainly an excuse for **debauchery**, though he enjoyed fencing and riding. Indeed he even wrote a text on fencing which, as was his style, examined its theoretical aspects. Then, around 1618, he met and befriended Isaac Beeckman, an eminent mathematician who became his mentor. Descartes ended his military career soon after, evidently never having to draw his sword in battle.

debauchery: extreme indulgence in food, drink, and other sensual pleasures.

Remaining in Germany, Descartes zealously applied himself to elaborating the concepts that he and Beeckman had generated in their discussions. By the winter of 1619, however, he had closeted himself in a small room in Neuburg, emotionally and creatively exhausted by the intensity of his efforts. There, on the eve of Saint Martin's Day (10 November), he had three dreams that he interpreted as reflecting his inner doubts concerning the worth of his life. The dreams, which he believed were divinely cast, resolved his purpose and revealed to him a holistic and methodical science that it was his destiny to create.

Inspired by these visions, for the next nine years Descartes traveled Europe, observing nature, visiting other men of learning on whom he relied for stimulation, and formulating his method. A man of deep religious convictions, while in Italy he visited the shrine of the Virgin Mary in Loreto to satisfy a vow he had made on the night of his three dreams. Although he wrote little during this period, his reputation in scientific circles grew.

Descartes eventually settled in Holland, where he hoped to avoid the distractions of the frivolous French social life. Entirely devoted to perfecting his method, in 1633 he finished his first book, in which he supported contemporary scientific hypotheses such as the circulation of blood in the body and movement of the earth around the sun. The book was nearing publication when, to Descartes's astonishment, Galileo was condemned by the Inquisition for similarly reaffirming the Copernican hypothesis. Descartes prudently withdrew his book from the printers.

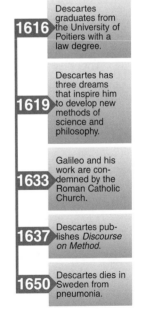

1616 Descartes graduates from the University of Poitiers with a law degree.

1619 Descartes has three dreams that inspire him to develop new methods of science and philosophy.

1633 Galileo and his work are condemned by the Roman Catholic Church.

1637 Descartes publishes *Discourse on Method*.

1650 Descartes dies in Sweden from pneumonia.

After a few years' reflection on his near misadventure, Descartes published anonymously his sensational *Discourse on Method*, taking care to avoid any reference to heretical cosmologies. He wrote with grace and clarity in French rather than Latin, which was the language of learned writing, thereby hoping to make it accessible to all people of intelligence. Over the next decade, Descartes published several other works. To his dismay, however, not all his ideas were welcomed by the religious authorities and they never received the official imprimatur for which he longed. Indeed, most of his writings were eventually proscribed by the church.

In 1649 Descartes was invited to Stockholm by Queen Christina of Sweden to teach her and establish a science academy. At first he was reluctant to live in what he perceived to be a rude and uncivilized society. However, his close friend Pierre Chanut, the French ambassador, eventually persuaded him to accept the invitation. With a sense of foreboding, Descartes tidied up his affairs in Holland and moved north to live with Chanut and his family in the Swedish court. Chanut became ill with pneumonia early in the new year. Descartes, who was weakened by having to

Descartes as Scientist

Though usually classified as a philosopher, Descartes was also one of the first modern scientists. Although many of his scientific speculations were proven erroneous by later scientists, Descartes made the inestimable contribution of demonstrating that the physical world could be investigated objectively, through observation and mathematics. Descartes helped sweep away the mysticism and superstition that had guided, and usually misled, scientific thinkers for centuries. His groundbreaking *Discourse on Method*, published in 1637, included three appendices entitled *Optics, Meteorology,* and *Geometry.* The first appendix is devoted to determining the best shape for telescope lenses and includes an exhaustive analysis of reflection and refraction. In later works, Descartes analyzed the structure of the eye, and described defects in vision and how to correct them. The second appendix, *Meteorology,* contains explanations of various weather phenomena, including rainbows. With this work, Descartes became the first scientist to analyze the weather in purely scientific terms. In the third and most influential appendix, *Geometry,* Descartes created an entirely new system of mathematics, now called coordinate or analytic geometry, by which geometric problems are cast as algebraic equations.

instruct the queen at five o'clock in the morning—a detestable hour for someone accustomed to spending his mornings in bed—soon contracted the illness as well. Nine days later, after a course of bleedings recommended by a court physician, Descartes died.

His remains traveled extensively, as he had in life. They were first buried in Sweden but in 1666 they were taken to Paris and reinterred in the Church of Sainte-Geneviève; in 1819 they were relocated to the Church of Saint-Germain. His skull, however, is held in the Musée de l'Homme in Paris.

Descartes is regarded as the founder of modern philosophy. His system was based on a definite method (known after him as Cartesian) and this mathematical method was a clear recognition of the scientific spirit. He pioneered the modern principles of individuality and subjectivity, with the existence of self as the basis of all constructive thought. He posited that the test of truth is the clearness with which it justifies itself to individual reason and formulated the dualistic principle of body and soul moving along parallel lines, with every event in one accompanied by a corresponding event in the other. By this separation he vindicated the purely mechanical nature of physical processes. The basis of his thought is the undeniability of consciousness, exemplified by his most famous dictum, *Cogito, ergo sum* (I think, therefore I am), which he considered the basic axiom on which to build certainty. He also reached God through the principle of causality: the existence of God must be postulated as the only explanation for the presence in man of the idea of God, which must have been implanted at birth. ◆

"The first precept was never to accept a thing as true until I knew it as such without a single doubt."
— Descartes, *Discourse on Method*

Diesel, Rudolf

1858–1913 ● INVENTOR

1880 Diesel graduates at the top of his class from the Technical University in Munich, Germany.

1892 Diesel applies for a patent for his engine.

1897 Diesel unveils his first diesel engine.

1898 Diesel presents his engine at an exposition.

1913 Diesel disappears while crossing the English Channel.

Rudolf Diesel was an engineer who developed the internal combustion engine that bears his name. Diesel looked for ways to improve the thermal efficiency of the internal combustion engine, which would help lower the cost of running the engines, therefore making them more practical for business use. Using a highly developed background in math and science which came naturally to him, Diesel concluded that if he could design an engine that compressed air at a far greater pressure than previously attempted, the engine would ignite the fuel in the cylinder without the use of a sparking device.

Born in Paris on March 18, 1858, Diesel was the son of German parents who would later move to England. Diesel's childhood was decidedly unhappy; he grew up in poverty with strongly religious and strict parents. The young Diesel took refuge in visiting the museums of Paris, including one that housed a steam wagon developed by Nicolas Cugnot.

When the Franco-Prussian was broke out in 1876, the family was forced to flee to England. Diesel was sent to the Technische Hochschule (Technical University) in Munich, Germany. While at the Technical University, Diesel experienced his first brush with the theory of heat engines.

Carl von Linde was Diesel's teacher. Von Linde had discovered modern refrigeration theory, and his work greatly inspired Diesel. He graduated in 1880 at the top of his class. Moving back to Paris, Diesel worked for a refrigeration company and used his spare time to work on the engine. Building on the work of Carnot, who in 1824 published *Reflections on the Motive Power of Heat*, Diesel experimented for a number of years before successfully building an engine. He applied for patents in 1892 and in 1893; both were granted.

In 1897, Diesel unveiled the engine that he had outlined in his patent applications. The engine eventually exploded, nearly claiming Diesel's life. In its simplest terms, a diesel engine works on the principal that once fuel is sprayed into the cylinder, the air has been compressed so much that a spark can naturally occur. One of the greatest benefits of a diesel engine is that it runs on fuel that is much less refined than the fuel required to operate an engine with a sparking device. A diesel engine also uses less fuel because its inlet air does not have to be throttled.

In order for the engine to work according to Diesel's calculations, the air would have to be compressed to 500 pounds per square inch, creating a temperature of 1,000 degrees Fahrenheit. His first idea was to burn powdered coal, but when that failed, Diesel began to experiment with oil and oil by-products.

When Diesel finally completed a fully operational engine, he took it to an exposition in 1898, where it immediately brought him international attention. Adolphus Busch, a famous American beer brewer, bought a license to manufacture the diesel engine in North America, where it was first used commercially.

While Diesel was a shrewed engineer, he failed miserably when managing finances. He insisted that every engine for which he approved a license be made to his specifications as first outlined in 1893. The diesel engine proved to be unpopular on a wide-scale because it was simply too heavy to be of practical use outside of industry.

Diesel thought he only needed to license the engine to a manufacturer and he could sit back and enjoy the money. However, given the slow nature of his engines, gaining the interest of manufacturers was extremely difficult. He began to promote his engine by sending his published work to various

A diesel engine works on the principle that once fuel is sprayed into the cylinder, the air has been compressed so much that a spark can naturally occur.

professors, which had little effect. Realizing that his engine was not realistic for a large volume commercial environment, Diesel made changes.

franchise: the license granted to an individual or group to market a company's goods in a particular territory.

Despite these setbacks, by 1898 **franchising** fees had made Diesel a very rich man. Diesel's engine was far too impractical to have any applications in the burgeoning automobile industry. Then, in 1910, a diesel engine was placed in a submarine, and it became the predominant type of engine used until nuclear submarines appeared.

The diesel engine was eventually adapted to automobile use, although the gasoline-fire engine remains more popular in passenger cars. Diesel engines are far more common in heavy duty trucks, farming equipment, trains, and other large vehicles.

On 1913, Diesel disappeared while crossing the English Channel on his way to Antwerp. His death has never been satisfactorily explained, with some calling it an accident while others claim it was suicide.

Diesel explained his theories and ideas in two publications: *The Theory and Construction of a Rational Heat Motor* and *The Genesis of Diesel Motors*. ◆

Dirac, Paul Adrien Maurice

1902–1984 ● Physics & Cosmology

D irac was born into a Bristol, England, middle-class family, on August 8, 1902. His mother, Florence Hannah Holten, was British, and his father, Charles Adrien Ladislas Dirac, was an emigre from French Switzerland. The father, a school teacher, was a domineering person who disliked social contacts and brought Paul up in an atmosphere of rigid discipline in which there was no room for social and cultural life. The result was that Paul's early years were unhappy, and he developed into a **taciturn** person for whom mathematical physics became a substitute for a fuller life. In school, Dirac showed a talent for mathematics and

taciturn: disinclined to talk.

"It seems that if one is working from the point of view of getting beauty in one's equations, and if one has really a sound insight, one is on a sure line of progress."
— Paul Dirac

Paul Adrien Maurice Dirac, winner of the 1933 Nobel Prize for physics.

physics, but he did not appreciate the humanistic subjects. From 1918 to 1921 he studied electrical engineering at Bristol University, but in the postwar depression he was unable to find a job. After two years of study in the mathematics department at Bristol University, Dirac entered Cambridge University, where his supervisor was Ralph Fowler, a specialist in statistical physics and atomic theory. Dirac remained in Cambridge for most of his life. When he completed his Ph.D. thesis in 1926, he was already an expert in the new quantum mechanics and recognized as a genius in theoretical physics. Dirac became a Fellow of St. John's College in 1927, and three years later he was elected a Fellow of the Royal Society. In 1932 he was appointed Lucasian Professor at Cambridge, a position he held until his retirement in 1969. He was awarded the Nobel Prize in 1933 for his "discovery of new fertile forms of the theory of atoms and for its applications." After 1969, Dirac went to Florida, where he stayed as a member of the physics department of Florida State University for the rest of his life.

Shortly after Werner Heisenberg had invented quantum mechanics, Dirac developed his own, original version in the fall of 1925. With this version, known as *q*-number algebra, he developed a more general formalism of quantum mechanics that included both Heisenberg's theory and Erwin Schrödinger's wave mechanics of 1926. In 1927 he extended his theory to cover also atoms interacting with electromagnetic fields and showed how to quantize such fields. This work marked the foundation of quantum electrodynamics, a subject to which Dirac contributed throughout his life. The original quantum mechanics of Heisenberg and Schrödinger was non-**relativistic**, that is, only valid for small velocities. The problem of finding a relativistic quantum equation for the electron was solved by Dirac in 1928 in one of the most important works of twentieth-century theoretical physics. Dirac found an equation—known as the Dirac equation—that differed from the ordinary Schrödinger equation, was relativistically invariant, explained electron spin, and predicted the correct fine structure in the spectrum of hydrogen. By analyzing the mathematical properties of the new equation, Dirac predicted the existence of a new particle, the *antielectron* (and also suggested that antiprotons would exist). He pictured this hypothetical particle as a "hole" in the "sea" filled up with unobservable negative-energy electrons that followed from his equation. According to Dirac, the antielectron would have the same mass as an ordinary electron, but with the opposite charge, and might be created, together with an electron, from high-energy electromagnetic radiation. (This process, $y \rightarrow e-$ $+ e+$, is known as pair creation). In 1932 Dirac's prediction was confirmed when Carl D. Anderson detected a positive electron in the cosmic radiation, and later experiments proved that this "positron" was identical with Dirac's *antielectron*. The corresponding prediction of a negatively charged proton was verified in 1955 when the first antiproton was discovered. In 1931, Dirac also concluded that magnetic monopoles—elementary particles with an isolated magnetic charge—might exist according to the laws of quantum mechanics, and he calculated some of their properties. However, although magnetic monopoles are widely believed to exist, and many experiments have been made in order to detect them, they are still hypothetical objects.

Dirac was a rationalist who was strongly attracted by the mathematical structure of physical theories, which, he argued, should be as beautiful as possible. Although he never

relativistic: moving at such a high velocity that there is a change in mass.

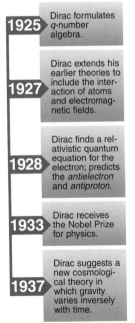

1925 Dirac formulates *q*-number algebra.

1927 Dirac extends his earlier theories to include the interaction of atoms and electromagnetic fields.

1928 Dirac finds a relativistic quantum equation for the electron; predicts the *antielectron* and *antiproton*.

1933 Dirac receives the Nobel Prize for physics.

1937 Dirac suggests a new cosmological theory in which gravity varies inversely with time.

explained what he meant, exactly, by "mathematical beauty," he believed that there is a preestablished harmony between the fundamental laws of nature and the theoretical formulations that can be expressed in mathematically beautiful ways. This "principle of mathematical beauty" was an important inspiration for most of Dirac's work after about 1935. Together with numerological reasoning it led him in 1937 and 1938 to suggest a new cosmological theory in which the gravitational constant G varies inversely with time. As another unorthodox feature, Dirac concluded that the number of particles in the universe would increase in time by some kind of continuous creation of matter (thus violating energy conservation). In the 1970s Dirac returned to cosmology and further developed his varying-G theory. However, the theory was met with skepticism by most astronomers, and experiments in the 1980s showed that the variation in G predicted by Dirac does not exist. In general, most of Dirac's revolutionary work was made between 1925 and 1933, and few of his subsequent contributions had lasting value.

Dirac was an ivory tower physicist who concentrated his intellectual efforts on theoretical physics and had little interest in matters outside physics. Much of his pioneering and highly original work was indebted to an aesthetic view of science and an intuitive philosophy of beautiful mathematics and its manifestations in physics, but Dirac was interested neither in philosophy nor other branches of the humanities. He was a worshiper of mathematical logic and had little appreciation for emotions and what most people would call the human aspects of life. Characteristically, even his view of religion was rationalistic. In 1963, he wrote that "God is a mathematician of a very high order, and He used very advanced mathematics in constructing the universe."

He died on October 20, 1984, in Miami. ◆

> Much of Dirac's original work was indebted to an aesthetic view of science and an intuitive philosophy of beautiful mathematics and its manifestations in physics.

Edison, Thomas Alva

1847–1931 ● INVENTOR

"Genius is one percent inspiration and ninety-nine percent perspiration."
— Thomas Edison

Thomas Alva Edison was born in Milan, Ohio, but financial problems led to the family's moving to Port Huron, Michigan, when Edison was seven years old. His childhood was marked by ill health—a bronchial disorder and an attack of scarlet fever that left its mark in a hearing disability that worsened as he grew older. After briefly attending the local school, his education was left to his mother, who had once worked as a teacher. It was she who seems to have kindled his interest in science by giving him a book detailing basic experiments that a curious child could carry out. The work caught his interest in a manner that must have exceeded all her expectations, for at the age of ten he set up a laboratory in the cellar of their home.

Prompted by a desire to purchase more chemicals for his experiments, Edison got his first job at the age of twelve, selling newspapers and candies on a train. He managed to transfer his primitive laboratory to a baggage car and whenever he had the opportunity he would work there, or read to extend his knowledge.

telegraphy: using a machine to communicate at a distance by electric transfer over wires.

At age sixteen he learned **telegraphy**; the Civil War was at its height then and the new communications system was proving its worth. There was plenty of work for the young and eager operator and Edison began a nomadic existence, traveling between the telegraph offices of the Midwest. His growing mastery of telegraphy and insatiable appetite for knowledge fueled the desire to improve the equipment he was using and make his own contributions to technological progress. His monthly salary of $120 was greatly depleted by his purchase of more laboratory equipment and books, including Michael Faraday's *Experimental Researches in Electricity*, which helped to initiate new directions in his career. Edison received his first patent in 1868 for an electric vote recorder but he did not find a market for it. His big breakthrough came in 1869 when he succeeded in repairing the telegraphic gold indicator at the Stock Exchange in New York. The feat made his name and he was put in charge of the gold indicator at a salary of $300 a month, a small fortune for the time. The Western Union Telegraph Company commissioned him to produce an improved machine and in 1871 he produced the Edison Universal Stock Printer, capable of transmitting 200-300 words per minute. Edison made $40,000 from this invention and used the funds to set up a factory in Newark, New Jersey, employing eminent scientists. At this factory Edison worked on producing improved telegraph instruments and succeeded in making a telegraph that could send two messages in two directions simultaneously.

1868 Edison receives his first patent for an electric vote recorder.

1876 Alexander Graham Bell invents the telephone.

1877 Edison invents the phonograph.

1878 David Hughes invents the microphone.

1880 Edison and Swann independently invent the first practical electric light bulb.

The year 1876 can be summed up by two of Edison's oft-quoted expressions: "There is no substitute for hard work," and "Genius is one percent inspiration and ninety-nine percent perspiration." At Menlo Park, New Jersey, he established an industrial research laboratory where he worked on inventions that were to make dramatic contributions to industry and the home. That year also saw him engaged in making an autographic and a speaking telegraph, an electric pen, an electric dental drill, and a sewing machine, among others. Much of his work was based on improving instruments or processes originated by others–his success lay in changing the device to make it marketable.

In 1876 Alexander Graham Bell invented the **prototype** of the telephone, with the same apparatus used to transmit and receive. In 1877 Edison produced an improved transmitter using the changing resistance of carbon granules to vary the strength of current in the circuit. The basic pattern of a powered circuit—Edison transmitter and Bell receiver—has remained almost unchanged to this day.

prototype: the first full-scale functioning model of a new machine.

Attaching a stylus from an embossing telegraph to a telephone speaker, Edison made what is credited as the most original of his inventions, the phonograph. At first he recorded onto paraffined paper but later found that wax cylinders were more effective. Among the first words in "recorded history" were those of his unique version of a popular nursery rhyme, revealing the inventor's sense of humor: "Mary has a new sheath gown,/ It is too tight by half,/ Who cares a damn for Mary's lamb,/ When they can see her calf!"

The phonograph generated great interest and astonishment; two women fainted when it was demonstrated in 1877 to the National Academy of Sciences.

In 1878 Edison launched himself on the path to even greater fame with pioneering work in electric lighting. Carbon arc lamps had recently come into use for street lighting but their dazzlingly bright light was not suitable for the home. Edison produced an incandescent lamp using a horseshoe shaped carbon filament in an evacuated glass bulb. At the same time, the English inventor Joseph Wilson Swan, working independently, produced a comparable bulb, and together their inventions laid the groundwork for the introduction of electricity for domestic lighting. Edison foresaw electricity replacing gas as the main form of light in the home; and to this end he even worked on the design of light switches, choosing a turning movement in the belief that potential customers would prefer to operate electricity in the same way they had switched gas appliances on and off. In 1882 Edison's first commercial electric power station was opened in New York.

Edison made $4 million from his electric light bulb only to lose it later in an attempt to mine iron ore magnetically. For all his scientific skills he was a poor businessman, losing control of his own Edison Electric Company in 1892 and not realizing the commercial potential of the electricity supply using alternating current developed by his rival, George

1876 saw Edison engaged in making an autographic and speaking telegraph, an electric pen, an electric dental drill, and a sewing machine, among other things.

Westinghouse (Edison utilized direct current). His losses were recovered through increasing sales of his phonograph and the development of the kinetoscope, using principles he had learned from the phonograph to make the prototype film projector. The kinetoscope, a milestone in the creation of cinematography, was basically a peep show, a series of photographic images projected with such speed that it appeared the subject was moving. The discovery in 1883 of the variation in electrical flow that came to be know as the Edison effect, laid the basis for the production of the first radio waves twenty years later, but Edison was unaware of his discovery's significance and did not pursue it since he saw no commercial potential.

In 1887 Edison established a new laboratory at West Orange, New Jersey, employing 120 research assistants. Around the laboratory there developed he world's first science park, with five thousand workers busy turning out the products of Edison's ingenuity. By the 1890s the most dynamic stage of his inventive career was past but he continued working on an impressively wide variety of projects, ranging from motion picture cameras and dictating machines to batteries and cement kilns.

Edison's witticisms, on subjects scientific and otherwise, were treasured. Commenting on tastes in art he once said, "To my mind the old masters are not art; their value is in their scarcity." In 1929 he was honored by Congress with a gold medal; he symbolized the American dream of a man from a poor background who, through great effort, attains success and great wealth. In 1931 he remarked, "I am long on ideas but short on time. I expect to live to be only about 100." He erred on the side of optimism, for he died that year. ◆

Einstein, Albert

1879–1955 ● PHYSICS

> *"When you are courting a nice girl an hour seems like a second. When you sit on a red-hot cinder a second seems like an hour. That's relativity."*
>
> — Albert Einstein

Albert Einstein was born in Ulm, Germany, on March 14, 1879. His ancestors had long lived in small south German towns. The well-to-do family of his mother Pauline, was in the wholesale grain trade, and his father Hermann, was a small businessman. Like many German Jews of their generation, his parents never denied their origins but were nonobservant and culturally quite assimilated. Always independent minded, and rather a "loner," young Albert was close to his sister Maja. A period of childhood religiosity ended at twelve when popular scientific literature made him a free thinker, but a feeling of wonder at the harmony of the universe never left him.

In 1880 the family moved to Munich, the largest south-German city, where Hermann and his brother Jakob, a trained engineer, started one of the city's first electrotechnical firms. Raised in a technological milieu, Albert was originally destined to take over the family business, which at first flourished. In 1894 competition from larger German firms led the brothers to relocate to northern Italy, where further business reverses soon led to the breakup of the partnership. Helped occasionally by Albert, Hermann's small, debt-ridden business ended with his death.

Einstein attended primary and secondary school in Munich. He found much of the curriculum and above all the instructional methods distasteful, later comparing most of his teachers to drill sargeants. His slow but thorough and methodical approach to the subjects in which he was interested earned him good but not outstanding grades. Encouraged by Uncle Jakob, he developed a bent for mathematics, especially geometry and calculus, mainly through self-study; a family friend stimulated a precocious interest in the natural sciences and philosophy. When the family left Munich in 1894, Albert stayed to finish school, but soon left for Italy after clashing with some of his teachers. He continued studying on his own, hoping to be admitted to the Poly (Swiss Federal Polytechnical School, a technical university) in Zurich, which recognized his talent but recommended he finish secondary school at the nearby Aarau Cantonal School. Its more liberal style of teaching and excellent scientific facilities soon changed his attitude toward schooling and made apparent his talent. In 1896 he entered the Poly as a physics student, earning generally good grades; but his independent attitude did not ingratiate him with his teachers. Happily working in the newly equipped physics laboratories, he remedied the dearth of advanced physics courses by self-study of theoretical physics, often joined by fellow physics student Mileva Maric, whom he married in 1903.

Unable to find a university or secondary school position in physics after graduation in 1900, he worked at a variety of temporary jobs until hired as an Examiner at the Swiss Patent Office. While there (1902–1909) he completed studies of the special theory of relativity, Brownian motion, and molecular dimensions (the topic for which he received his doctorate), all in 1905; published his first papers on quantum theory and started work on the general theory of relativity.

Growing recognition of his accomplishments by the physics community soon followed. He was appointed associate professor of physics at the University of Zurich in 1909 and two years later became a full professor in Prague (then part of the Austro Hungarian Empire), but returned to Zurich—now at the Poly—in 1912. He was appointed to the Prussian Academy of Sciences in 1914, a full-time research position in Berlin, where he completed work on the general theory of relativity (1915). Separated from Maric in 1914, he married his cousin Elsa Einstein in 1919.

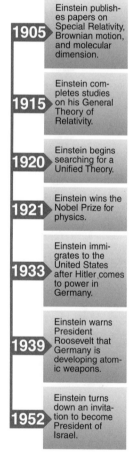

1905 Einstein publishes papers on Special Relativity, Brownian motion, and molecular dimension.

1915 Einstein completes studies on his General Theory of Relativity.

1920 Einstein begins searching for a Unified Theory.

1921 Einstein wins the Nobel Prize for physics.

1933 Einstein immigrates to the United States after Hitler comes to power in Germany.

1939 Einstein warns President Roosevelt that Germany is developing atomic weapons.

1952 Einstein turns down an invitation to become President of Israel.

Einstein remained in Berlin throughout World War I, when his pacifist views set him against the mainstream of academic jingoism, and during the Weimar Republic, when his democratic views made him a hero to defenders of the republic and a target of the growing fascist movement. With Hitler's advent to power in 1933, Einstein left Germany for good and settled in Princeton, New Jersey, at the newly established Institute for Advanced Studies, where he continued to live and work for the rest of his life.

Einstein regarded the special and general theories of relativity and the search for a unified field theory as the central thread of his life's work. The special theory grew out of the problem of reconciling Newtonian mechanics, which implies the equality of all inertial (i.e., nonaccelerated) frames-of reference (principle of relativity), with Maxwell's theory of electromagnetism, which was taken to imply the existence of only one frame (the "ether frame"), in which the speed of light is constant. For the classical law of addition of velocities implies that, with respect to any frame moving through the ether, the velocity of light should depend on that frame's velocity. But all attempts to detect such a variation in the speed of light with respect to Earth as it moves around the Sun had failed. A number of prominent scientists worked on this problem, but Einstein was the first to see clearly that the way out was to give up the classical law of addition of velocities by replacing the Newtonian concept of absolute time, that is, the same for all inertial frames, by that of a time that is relative to each inertial frame. The special theory preserves the equality of all inertial frames, but postulates that the speed of light is absolute, that is, the same in all inertial frames. The failure to detect a variation in the speed of light thus becomes evidence supporting the new relativistic **kinematics**. Such counterintuitive but well-established effects as time **dilatation** and the twin paradox provide further supporting evidence. Physical theories, such as Newtonian mechanics, had to be reviewed and modified to ensure compatibility with relativistic kinematics. Many surprising consequences followed from this review, notably the blending of the previously separate laws of mass and energy conservation into a single law of conservation of mass-energy (often known as the equivalence of mass and energy). The entire modern theory of elementary

"Imagination is more important than knowledge."
— Albert Einstein

kinematics: a branch of physics that deals with motion apart from considerations of mass and force.

dilatation: the action of expanding.

particles is built on the foundations of the special theory, as is the operation of high-energy particle accelerators.

In 1907 Einstein came to the conclusion that a modification of the theory was needed to incorporate gravitation because of a unique feature, already stressed by Galileo: Regardless of their mass, all bodies fall with the same acceleration in a gravitational field. Einstein realized this feature casts doubt on the privileged role of inertial frames because it implies that no mechanical experiment can distinguish between an inertial frame of reference with a uniform downward-acting gravitational field, and an accelerated frame-of-reference with no gravitational field whose upward acceleration is numerically equal to that produced by the gravitational field in the first case. Einstein assumed that there is a complete equivalence between inertial frames with a gravitational field and accelerated frames without a gravitational field, and he made this principle of equivalence the foundation of an eight-year-long search for a relativistic theory of gravitation. In the resulting general theory of relativity, completed in 1915, all frames of reference are equally acceptable. Gravitation is an effect of matter on the structure of space and time, not a force pulling objects off their straight line (inertial) paths in a flat spacetime but a warping of spacetime in which objects attempt to follow the straightest possible paths. The same mathematical object that describes the structure of spacetime, the metric tensor, also characterizes the gravitational field; the very structure of spacetime is now a dynamical field. With the new theory, Einstein was able to explain the hitherto anomalous portion of the **precession** of Mercury's **perihelion** and suggested a number of astronomical tests of his theory, such as the gravitational red shift of stellar spectra, the apparent deflection of light rays passing near a star, and the focusing effect that a concentrated massive object would have on light (gravitational lensing). All of these predictions have been confirmed with increasing accuracy by recent optical and radio wave observations. General relativistic corrections have proved important in the theory of such super-massive objects as neutron stars, and the theory also predicts novel phenomena such as black holes and gravitational waves, which have become the object of recent intense theoretical and observational study.

Starting in the 1920s, Einstein became increasingly

Starting in the 1920s, Einstein became increasingly absorbed by the search for a unified theory of the electromagnetic and gravitational fields.

precession: a gyration of the rotation axis of a spinning body around another line intersecting it.

perihelion: the point in the path of a planet that is nearest the sun.

absorbed by the search for a unified theory of the electromagnetic and gravitational fields. Always fascinated by the discovery of conceptual unity behind apparently different phenomena (Maxwell's unification of electricity, magnetism, and optics provided the outstanding example) and having developed a field theory of gravitation, Einstein felt that some generalization of the metric tensor should encompass the electromagnetic field. In the case of gravitation, the principle of equivalence provided a physical clue that led rather directly to the metric tensor, but Einstein never found a similar physical clue for its generalization, so he continued to explore a large number of mathematical possibilities on the basis of their formal simplicity until the end of his life, without ever really convincing himself or others that he was on the right track.

A major motivation for his decades-long search was the hope that such a unified field theory might have a discrete set of nonsingular solutions, thereby explaining the all-pervasive quantum effects he had been exploring since the turn of the century. Max Planck introduced the quantum of action, but Einstein first took the idea seriously enough to suggest in 1905 that electromagnetic radiation might consist of discrete quanta of energy. He was able thereby to offer simple, quantitative explanations of a number of puzzling phenomena involving the exchange of energy between matter and radiation, notably the **photoelectric effect**, mentioned in his 1921 Nobel Prize citation. Although Einstein continued to develop his concept of the quantum of radiation into that of a full-fledged particle, later named the photon, carrying momentum as well as energy, the idea was not taken seriously by most physicists—including Planck and Niels Bohr—until 1923, when the Compton effect turned the tide. In 1907 Einstein took Planck's idea of quantized material **oscillators** and developed it into the first quantum theory of the solid state, thereby providing an explanation for the anomalous low temperature specific heats of solids. This work, successfully tested almost immediately, was instrumental in making the study of quantum effects a central concern of the physics community. In 1924 Einstein made a major contribution to the development of quantum statistics by showing that the recent derivation of the black body radiation spectrum by Satyendranath Bose, who treated the radiation as a gas of light quanta (pho-

> *"God is subtle, but he is not malicious."*
> — Albert Einstein

photoelectric effect: the emission of free electrons from a metal surface when light strikes it.

oscillator: a device for producing alternating current or radio and audio waves.

tons), was tacitly based on a method of counting particle configurations that differed from the classical one used by Boltzmann. The resulting Bose-Einstein statistics, as it came to be called, was later shown to hold for all particles with integral spins. By applying Bose's method to a gas of material particles, Einstein showed that it would undergo condensation at a certain temperature, thus providing the first theoretical model of a phase transition.

Einstein became the first science "super star," often mobbed during his public appearances.

However, when the new quantum mechanics began to explain a number of quantum phenomena from 1925 on, Einstein found himself out of sympathy with the basic approach of the theory. At first he tried to find flaws in it but soon acknowledged that, within its theoretical framework and when given a statistical interpretation, quantum mechanics is the best explanation that can be given for these phenomena. What he continued to challenge was the theory's alleged completeness—the claim that the theory gave the most complete possible characterization of the state of an individual system—and the assertion that no other theoretical framework could be devised that would avoid what he regarded as objectionable features of quantum mechanics: the introduction of probability as an irreducible feature of reality and the continued entanglement of two quantum systems once they have interacted—no matter how far apart they may subsequently move. He continued to hope that a suitable classical unified field theory, which by its nature would avoid these features, could explain quantum phenomena, a hope shared by few physicists today.

The discovery of the weak and strong nuclear forces made obsolete Einstein's original program of unification confined to gravitation and electromagnetism. On the other hand, it has made the idea of a unification of these four fundamental interactions more attractive. Major successes have been achieved in the unification of the electromagnetic and weak interactions, and then the electroweak and strong forces, although these unifications differ from Einstein's attempts in that they are based on quantum mechanics. But the general theory of relativity has so far resisted all attempts at conventional quantization, let alone its unification with the other fields. It is possible that Einstein was right to the extent that the unique features of gravitation—its character as a space-time structure rather than a force—may require modifications of the quantum-mechanical formalism as well as of general relativity before any unification is possible.

While we have concentrated on those aspects of Einstein's work that go beyond classical physics, he was also a master of the latter, and developed many new applications of its methods. His explanation of Brownian motion and his method of estimating the size of molecules in a solution, both published in 1905, as well as his many studies of fluctuation phenomena over the years, provide outstanding examples.

After the successful testing of Einstein's prediction of the apparent deflection of light rays by two English solar eclipse expeditions in 1919, Einstein's name became well known to the nonscientific public. Indeed, he became the first scientific "super star," often mobbed during his public appearances; as a consequence these became rarer and rarer over the years, especially after his move to the United States. While regarding his notoriety as a personal burden, it offered him a means of disseminating his views on a number of important political and social questions: whatever the great Einstein said was news. Increasingly identifying with the Jewish people as they became ever more frequent targets of anti-Semitic propaganda and physical attacks, first in Weimar Germany and especially after Hitler took power in 1933, he supported the Zionist ideal of a Jewish homeland in Palestine as a way of building up Jewish pride and self-confidence in the face of these attacks, and then as a place of refuge for Jews forced to flee Europe. After the Holocaust, he supported the establishment of Israel to ensure a haven for the remnants of European Jewry.

A convinced antimilitarist, he was first impelled to political action by his opposition to World War I. After the war, he supported the pacifist movement, advocating refusal of military service. When Hitler came to power, Einstein felt that pacifist tactics were powerless again fascism's ruthless threat to peace and democracy, and he advocated rearmament to deter and ultimately defeat aggression in World War II. When the development of nuclear weapons threatened the destruction of humanity, he advocated a world government as the only way to over come national enmities and ensure disarmament. Ironically, he is often credited with—blamed for—playing a major role in the development of the American atomic bomb, although his role was confined to alerting the

> *"Laws alone cannot secure freedom of expression; in order that every man present his views without penalty there must be a spirit of tolerance in the entire population."*
> — Albert Einstein

> *"The unleashed power of the atom has changed everything save our modes of thinking and we thus drift toward unparalleled catastrophe."*
> — Albert Einstein

American government in 1939 to the danger of Germany's doing so.

The economic chaos in Germany in the 1920s, followed by the worldwide economic crisis and collapse in the 1930s, convinced Einstein that the capitalist economic system needed drastic change, and he began to advocate a socialist reorganization of the economy. Well aware of the dictatorial features of the Soviet model, he stressed the need to preserve democratic political rights under socialism.

As may be imagined, Einstein's political and social views were not universally shared, and he became the object of intense personal attacks, often anti-Semitic in nature. He was denounced as unpatriotic for his stand against nationalism and war, and as a "red" for his social and economic views. This was true not only in Germany but also in the United States, especially during the "cold war" period, when he blamed the United States government for a large share of the rising tensions with Russia and urged resistance to all attempts at governmental inquisitions into individual beliefs. His defense of civil liberties in his adopted homeland was an inspiration to many during the McCarthy years.

He died in Princeton, New Jersey, on April 18, 1955. ◆

Euclid

365?–300? BCE ● MATHEMATICS

> *"There is no royal road to geometry."*
> — Euclid

The date and place of Euclid's birth are uncertain and the facts of his life are further obscured by his often being confused by early historians with the Socratic philosopher Eucleides of Megara. The Arabs, who have a long tradition of mathematics, maintain that Euclid was the son of a Greek born in Tyre and living in Damascus. It is known that he founded and taught at a school in Alexandria.

His fame derives mainly from his greatest work, *The Elements*, an elementary geometry text in thirteen books. *The Elements* starts with a list of definitions followed by ten fundamental and self-evident propositions known as the axioms and postulates, from which, it is claimed, all the subsequent theorems contained in the books are logically deduced.

Though credited with the authorship of some of the books, it is believed that Euclid's primary activity was that of editor and compiler, drawing on the body of knowledge developed by his precursors. Nevertheless the design and the organization of the work was enough to merit Euclid's preeminent position in the development of mathematics, for the outstanding feature of *The Elements* is its logical arrangement and systematic approach to reasoning. Until the late nineteenth century, Euclid's work was regarded as the definitive example of deductive theory. However, under the scrutiny of the modern approach to rigorous deductivity, the claim that all theorems in *The Elements* arise logically from the postulates and axioms has been found wanting.

The mathematical quality of *The Elements* is inconsistent, which is a clear indication that it derived from several authors. Euclid as editor, it seems, did not have the mathematical ability to rectify errors in logic and recompose **circumlocutive** passages. He was described by his contemporary Pappus as a modest and unpretentious person, renowned for his consideration of others and his dedication to his pupils. This seems to fit the character of a man whose major work contains no preamble or other form of **self-aggrandizement**. Undoubtedly, though, Euclid was an astute educationalist whose textbook, the oldest surviving Greek mathematical work, was used almost unrevised to teach geometry until the beginning of the twentieth century. *The Elements* so completely overshadowed other mathematical books from that period that none of the others survived. Euclid is also known to have written a number of treatises on optics, astronomy, music and mechanics, but many of them have been lost.

Proculus, a Greek philosopher who wrote about Euclid some 700 years after his death, tells how Ptolemy I once asked Euclid if there was not an easier way to learn the discipline of geometry than through studying *The Elements*. Euclid answered the king's inquiry saying, "There is no royal road to geometry." ◆

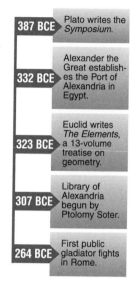

387 BCE Plato writes the *Symposium*.

332 BCE Alexander the Great establishes the Port of Alexandria in Egypt.

323 BCE Euclid writes *The Elements*, a 13-volume treatise on geometry.

307 BCE Library of Alexandria begun by Ptolomy Soter.

264 BCE First public gladiator fights in Rome.

circumlocutive: relating to indirect or roundabout speech.

self-aggrandizement: praise of self.

Faraday, Michael

1791–1867 ● CHEMISTRY & PHYSICS

Faraday was born in Newington near London, England, September 22, 1791, the third of four children and the second son of James Faraday, a blacksmith in ill health, and the former Margaret Hastwell of Yorkshire, who had only recently left their ancestral homes to seek economic security in London.

The Faraday family was brought up within the congregation of a fundamentalist Christian sect known, as Faraday later put it, "if known at all, as the Sandemanians." Sandemanians lived by the letter of the Bible and the words of Jesus. The church stressed love, charity, and sacrifice for one's fellows, rather closely defined as other Sandemanians. It was here that Faraday's character was formed. He learned the rudiments of reading, writing, and **ciphering** in a church school; he learned, as well, that worldly riches were to be shunned and, many years later as one of the most famous scientists in Europe, he still gave most of his income to the needy of his congregation, attended them when they were sick, and

Some have suggested that Humphry Davy's greatest discovery was his assistant, Michael Faraday.

ciphering: the use of symbolic letters in a code or mathematics.

succored them in their troubles. One month after he married Sarah Barnard, the daughter of a Sandemanian elder in June of 1821, he formally became a member of the church and it was to guide him through the rest of his life. These were the two loves of his life. The Faradays had no children, so his natural affection was poured out on his wife, his nieces who spent a good deal of time at the Royal Institution (RI) in London, and his fellow Sandemanians.

Although he said that his religion did not influence his science, it is perfectly clear that it did. It gave him confidence that the cosmos was rational and comprehensible and, more importantly, that God's works were to be seen throughout nature and were **beneficent**. It also made him suspicious of scientific explanations that depended on **subsensible** matter, such as John Dalton's material atoms, which acted solely by ordinary forces, for this implied atheism or, at the very least, the kind of rational deism that many besides Faraday in England felt lay behind the attack on Christianity in the French Revolution.

beneficent: doing or producing good.

subsensible: beyond the reach of the senses.

At the age of twelve, Faraday was apprenticed to a French émigré bookbinder who also loaned out newspapers. Faraday's thirst for learning was partially slaked by being able to read the books that came in for binding. There was, however, no method involved. He read everything from *The Arabian Nights* to the *Encyclopaedia Britannica*, but nothing was wasted; the first stimulated his imagination while the second introduced him to facts of the natural world. He was particularly excited by an article on electricity and promptly constructed an electrostatic machine out of old bottles and other scraps. His passion for science was heightened when, in 1812, one of his master's clients presented him with tickets to the lectures on chemistry given by Sir Humphry Davy at the Royal Institution of Great Britain. Again, he immediately built an electrochemical cell and decomposed water and other compounds. He now desired, above all, to enter the mansion of science but there were absolutely no prospects for him. In October of 1812 his apprenticeship was over and with a heavy heart he entered the world of trade. In that very month, however, fate intervened. Davy was temporarily blinded by an explosion and Faraday was hired as his secretary, a purely temporary position. In February 1813 one of the assistants in the laboratory was fired for brawling, and Davy sent for Faraday.

Faraday read everything from The Arabian Nights to the Encyclopaedia Britannica.

He was hired in March at the RI, an institution in which he was to spend his entire professional life. Faraday's scientific education was now provided for him by his association with Davy, the most eminent chemist in Great Britain. It was Davy who taught him those manipulative skills that made Faraday a superb analytical chemist and it was Davy who introduced him to the theories of matter then current. Davy also introduced Faraday to the larger world. In 1813 Davy was awarded a medal and prize that had been created by Napoleon in honor of Alessandro Volta, the inventor of the voltaic cell and the discoverer of current electricity. Davy immediately set out for France, with Faraday serving somewhat reluctantly as his valet. They traveled through France, Italy, and Switzerland, where Faraday met many of the eminent scientists of the day, learned French and a smattering of Italian, and helped Davy revise his 1812 publication entitled *The Elements of Chemical Philosophy* in which Davy probed deeply the philosophical and metaphysical foundations of the current matter theories. It was undoubtedly during the discussions with Davy on these subjects that Faraday's lifelong interest in and search for an adequate theoretical foundation for the rather unconventional hypotheses that guided his experiments began.

Two basic views dominated Faraday's later thought. One was that "the various forms under which the forces of matter are made manifest have one common origin; . . . or, in other words, as so directly related and mutually dependent, that they are convertible as it were, one into another, and possess equivalents of power in their action." This idea was at the very center of the German eighteenth-century philosophy of nature (*Naturphilosophie*). Davy was exposed to this early in his career when he worked in Bristol for a physician who was intensely interested in *Naturphilosophie*. It was also in Bristol that Davy met and became fast friends with Samuel Taylor Coleridge, the poet and essayist who had just returned from Germany filled with enthusiasm for this new way of looking at nature. The second had to do with the difficulties that followed from Isaac Newton's and John Dalton's views of atoms as infinitesimally small, absolutely hard, completely elastic bodies in empty space. The first objection was that elastic collisions between atoms was ruled out, for elastic rebound depends on deformation and recovery of the colliding bodies

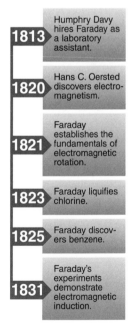

1813 Humphry Davy hires Faraday as a laboratory assistant.

1820 Hans C. Oersted discovers electromagnetism.

1821 Faraday establishes the fundamentals of electromagnetic rotation.

1823 Faraday liquifies chlorine.

1825 Faraday discovers benzene.

1831 Faraday's experiments demonstrate electromagnetic induction.

and, by definition, atoms were perfectly hard and therefore incapable of deformation. The second objection was more theological in nature, for if changes in atomic motions could not be by collisions, they had to be caused by **occult** forces that could, as with the case of Newton, lead dangerously close to pantheism, that is, the supposition that God filled the cosmos. In the *Philosophiae naturalis principia mathernatica*, generally known simply as the *Principia*, Newton had suggested that space was the sensorium of God, thus universalizing the deity.

occult: involving the action or influence of supernatural powers.

There seemed to be only two ways out of this dilemma: either forces acted in some mysterious ways at a distance or all changes of atomic and ordinary motions must be due to impacts. Newton had proven in the *Principia* that impact physics simply did not fit the mathematical laws that he enunciated. Action at a distance violated the old philosophical dictum that bodies could not act where they were not. A "solution" to this difficulty was suggested in the middle of the eighteenth century by a Jesuit, Roger Joseph Boscovich. It involved nothing less than the redefinition of what a body was. Boscovich suggested an atomic theory containing nothing known conventionally as matter, but consisting solely of force. This was to give what philosophers call "**ontological** status" to forces. Boscovich's atoms consisted of mathematical points around which attractive and repulsive forces varied with their distance from the center.

ontological: relating to the branch of philosophy concerned with the nature of being.

Resultant molecules also had a property of great importance for Faraday. They can be "stretched" or, to put it another way, they can undergo strains without decomposing.

It should always be kept in mind that Faraday was a chemist, one of the best chemists of his time. He thought in chemical terms, not in the mathematical formulas of the physicist. Indeed, he was a mathematical illiterate and could not follow the arguments of later physicists like William Thomson or James Clerk Maxwell. By 1819 he was well known as a first-rate analytical chemist, earning money for himself and the RI by analyzing waters from wells and municipal water systems. From 1818 until 1831 he was concerned almost exclusively with matters that could roughly be considered chemical. He worked with a cutler on improving the quality of steel and determined that the properties of steel owed as much to its crystalline structure as it did to its composition. By introducing the practice of examining the structure of polished steel etched by mild acid, Faraday founded the science of metallography. In 1825, at the request of the Royal Society to which he had been recently elected, he began tedious research attempting to produce a clear and dense glass for astronomical purposes. He did succeed but the glass proved useless at that time. It was, however, to play a central part in Faraday's discovery of the action of magnetism on light. From 1820 to 1826 he moved into organic chemistry, discovering a number of organic compounds such as benzene, iso-butene, tetrachloro-ethene, and hexachlorobenzene. He also observed that metals such as mercury were surrounded by their own vapor, thus casting doubt on the existence of a separation between the gaseous, liquid, and solid states. His **liquefaction** of chlorine in 1823 was the first liquefaction of a so called permanent gas. It also could be nicely explained by the continuous Boscovichean curve.

liquefaction: the process of making or becoming a liquid.

Faraday retained his interest in electricity but had little time away from his professional duties to do any active research. From 1820 until 1831 he could only work on this subject sporadically, with one exception. In the summer of 1820, Hans Christian Oersted announced that he had been able to get magnetic effects from a current-carrying wire. This transformation of electricity into magnetism fit in perfectly with the speculations of *Naturphilosophie* and it was no coincidence that Oersted was an ardent adherent of this philosophy. The announcement in Latin in all the leading scientific journals of the day set off a feverish spurt of activity with theories and weird observations turning up almost daily. A friend of Faraday's who edited one such journal asked him if he would check these reports and Faraday agreed. Oersted had noted that a magnetic needle held near a current-carrying wire tended to align itself at an angle to the wire, not parallel to it. In France, André-Marie Ampére had shown that the needle always stood at right angles to the current-carrying wire when the effects of the earth's magnetism were nullified. By careful mapping of needle positions, Faraday discovered, somewhat to his surprise, that the line that the needle followed was a circle with the wire at the center. This discovery was the origin of Faraday's concept of the line of force, which was the foundation of field theory. Except for the works of a very few of those who had published on the subject, Faraday fairly well demolished most of what had been written. His

Faraday thought in chemical terms, not in the mathematical formulas of the physicist.

results were published anonymously in the *Annals of Philosophy* in the autumn of 1821 and winter of 1822. Beyond clarifying the exciting new field of electromagnetism, these papers thrust Faraday deeply into electrical and magnetic phenomena.

Using his discovery of the circular line of force, Faraday then invented a clever demonstration, which was, in fact, the first electric motor.

After 1822, except for occasional forays into electrical matters, Faraday did nothing of much significance in this field until 1831. Then, as he noted in his laboratory journal for August 29, he did an epoch-making experiment. He took a thick iron ring and wound one side with wire connected to a battery. The other he wound and connected to a **galvanometer**. When he threw the switch on the battery, he noted that the galvanometer needle swung—he had created one current by making the iron ring a magnet that then created another current. This induction of a current by magnetism completed the symmetry of Oersted's creation of a magnet by a current. Faraday's paper announcing this discovery was published in 1832 and began the magisterial *Experimental Researches in Electricity* that were to extend for almost thirty years and literally create a new science of electricity and magnetism and firmly establish field theory.

galvanometer: an instrument for measuring a small electric current.

There was one thing that puzzled Faraday in this experiment. When he closed the circuit, the galvanometer needle jumped to the right and then fell back; when he broke the circuit, the needle jumped to the *left*. He hypothesized that closing the circuit threw the secondary wire into a state of strain, which was relieved only when the primary current ceased. It was like pulling on a rope and then suddenly moving the end of the rope up and down: A wave passes down the rope, but the rope is still in tension. When one lets go of the rope, another wave passes as the strain is relieved. Although he could not detect it then (and never could), Faraday named this state the *electrotonic* state. It was to be the unifying idea in his theory of electricity.

Faraday did not stop here. Knowing that magnetism could produce an electric current, he now began to try to find the conditions under which a permanent bar magnet would succeed in doing the same thing. After many trials, he discovered that when a magnet was in motion with respect to a closed circuit so that the wire of the circuit cut the lines of force surrounding the magnet that was made visible by iron filings sprinkled on a piece of paper over the magnet, a current resulted. From here, it was just a short step to producing a continuous current by rotating a copper disk between the poles of a horseshoe magnet and taking leads off the circumference and center of the disk so that the leads cut the lines at different rates. When the arrangement was changed so that the leads provided a current in the wires and the disk, the disk rotated between the magnetic poles. This was the first generator and first real electric motor.

Before continuing this electromagnetic research, Faraday had to meet a challenge that stated that there was more than one kind of electricity. His test was to try all the different kinds—animal from electric fish, static electricity, voltaic electricity, thermal electricity—and see if they caused electrochemical decomposition. Some were just too weak, but static electricity seemed quite capable of proving his case. In the course of these experiments, he was able to cause decomposition, but without any poles or centers of attraction as had been supposed in the voltaic cell. Instead, simply by passing electricity from the static electricity generator through a piece of blotting paper containing sodium iodide (NaI) and starch water as a detector and into the air, he produced free iodine detected by the starch. He was also able to devise what he called a volta-meter that permitted him to compare the current that passed in electrochemical decomposition, either by static or current electricity. This led him to Faraday's first law of electrochemistry: the quantity of decomposition products is directly proportional to the quantity of electricity that passes through the solution. The second law states that the amounts of different substances liberated in an electrochemical process are proportional to their chemical equivalents. Faraday had now successfully refuted the older theories of electrochemistry that depended upon electricity as a material substance, poles and action of the electrical particles on the elements involved at a distance. Instead, he viewed it as the setting up and breaking down of the electrotonic state that occurred when the elements of the compounds involved were separated by the strain and passed along to neighbors who had suffered the same breakdown with electropositive and electronegative particles moving in opposite directions, as in a

Faraday successfully refuted the older theories of electrochemistry that depended upon electricity as a material substance.

square dance, where partners move past one another but are always attached to someone.

To avoid the kinds of theoretical trap that the old language of Newtonian physics had created, Faraday consulted William Whewell and others who were experts in Greek and, with them, created the modern terms of electrochemistry (anode, cathode, anion, cation, electrolysis, etc.).

The specificity of electrochemical action in which the chemical substances all displayed specific "breaking points" that allowed them to move past one another suggested to Faraday that insulators might also have specific capacities for charge before they, too, broke down. Again, with careful experimentation, Faraday was able to show that, indeed, there was a specific inductive capacity for such substances.

> **After eight years of sustained mental effort and clever and accurate experimentation, Faraday possessed the elements for his own theory of electricity.**

After eight years of sustained mental effort and clever and accurate experimentation, Faraday possessed the elements for his own theory of electricity. The electrical force acted on matter by placing the force atoms of which materials were composed under various degrees of strain. Conductors were those substances that could not bear much strain, so that when an electrical force was imposed on them, a strain was momentarily created. However, it broke down rapidly, only to be followed immediately by the reimposition of a strain, and so on. As this wave of strains and relaxations passed down the conductor, it formed the electric current. In electrochemical decomposition, the strain was relieved by the passage of the ions by one another on their way to the electrodes. Insulators could bear much stronger strains and their breakdown was accompanied by a physical and quite perceptible mechanical effect, as when a hole is punched in a glass plate when high voltages are applied to it. In all these operations, the line of force marked the presence of the electrical power.

In 1839 Faraday's line of force ruptured and he suffered a severe mental breakdown forcing him to abandon serious research, seek rest and recreation in places like Switzerland, and generally pull back. From 1839 until his recovery in 1846, little original science emerged from his laboratory. There was, again, one exception. Faraday was called upon unexpectedly and suddenly to fill in for his friend Charles Wheatstone, who was unable to give his scheduled Friday Evening Discourse. Faraday had had no time to prepare, and his lecture only occupied a part of the allotted time. To fill it up, he offered some speculations, later entitled "Thoughts on Ray Vibrations," which were published soon after. In this remarkable little paper of only seven pages, he used Boscovich's concept of matter to suggest that every particle of matter is infinite in extent since the force of gravity extends to infinity. All particles, then, are contiguous and touch each other by their forces, so that the cosmos is an infinite and complex web of forces. Could not this web, he asked, suffice to transmit radiation? Might not the lines of magnetic force, as well as those of gravitation, be quite suitable for the purpose? James Clerk Maxwell, many years later, was to make this speculation scientifically respectable.

The third, and last, of the scientific innovations for Faraday began in 1845 and lasted until his mind failed him in the late 1850s. He was still haunted by the electrotonic state that he had never been able to detect, and for the arch-experimenter who insisted that hypotheses should be backed up by solid experimental evidence, this was intolerable. So he tried once more to reduce this elusive hypothetical strain to measurement. It had long been known that when plane polarized light was passed through transparent substances such as glass under mechanical strain, the light was affected. When he placed a piece of the heavy glass that he had made in the 1820s in as powerful an electric field as he could devise, he still could get no effect when light was passed through it, even though he knew that there must be a strain. It was the young and upcoming physicist William Thomson, later Lord Kelvin, who suggested that he substitute the much more powerful field of the large horseshoe electromagnet at the RI for the electric field. On September 13, 1845, Faraday was successful; the plane of polarization of a light was rotated by passing through the glass placed across the poles of the electromagnet where the field was most intense. This phenomenon later came to be known as the Faraday effect. Further experiments revealed a peculiar situation: objects, such as glass, aligned themselves perpendicular to the magnetic lines of force, rather than parallel to them as is the case with iron. A whole new world of magnetism opened up. Faraday named this transverse magnetism, diamagnetism, and the usual kind, paramagnetism magnetism, or for the more magnetically powerful substances such as iron, nickel, and cobalt, ferromagnetism.

> Faraday suggested that all particles are contiguous and touch each other by their forces, so that the cosmos is an infinite and complex web of forces.

luminiferous: transmitting or yielding light.

ether: an element formerly believed to fill all space and transmit light waves.

colloidal: relating to a substance that consists of particles dispersed throughout another substance.

As Faraday delved ever deeper into the nature of magnetism in general, he made another startling discovery. Unlike the electrical lines of force—electrostatic, electrochemical, and current—all of which had "ends" just like a stretched cord, the magnetic lines of force did not. Nowhere could he find the magnetic equivalent of positive and negative charges that were associated with the termini of the electrical lines of force. The analogy of the stretched cord was not applicable to magnetism for the particles of the cord are distorted by the strain and have "poles" along the line. Hence, he concluded that the magnetic line of force could not be a line of strained particles. This ruled out the **luminiferous ether** that had been invented to account for the wave nature of light. But if the particles were not strained, what was? There was no doubt that the magnetic force did exist in space. Faraday's suggestion was literally unthinkable at the time. Might not space itself be the medium by which the magnetic force was transmitted? With this idea, Faraday was now able to explain both paramagnetism and diamagnetism. Space conducted the lines of paramagnetic force better than did the surrounding medium of material substance and worse for diamagnetics. This was why paramagnetics move into and along the magnetic field and diamagnetics try to move out of it and across the lines. This explanation had few converts at the time, but the general theory of relativity propounded by Albert Einstein in 1916 gave it respectability.

After his work on magnetism, Faraday began to fade both mentally and physically. His last sustained research in the late 1850s was on **colloidal** gold, making him one of the founders of colloidal chemistry. He also attempted again to detect the influence of magnetism on light—a failure that later inspired Peter Zeeman to try it once again and led to the discovery of the Zeeman effect.

From 1859 on, Faraday rapidly lost his intellectual powers until, near the end, he could do little more than sit in his chair and be cared for like an infant. Having turned down a knighthood earlier in his career, he simply remained Mr. Faraday to his death at Hampton Court, Middlesex, England, on August 25, 1867. ◆

Fermi, Enrico

1901–1954 ● NUCLEAR PHYSICS

"Whatever Nature has in store for mankind, unpleasant as it may be, men must accept, for ignorance is never better than knowledge."
— Enrico Fermi, in *Atoms in the Family*
by Laura Fermi

Many people know Fermi as the architect of the atomic age—the scientist who developed the first nuclear chain reaction, the basis for the peaceful uses of atomic energy. However, his contributions to the fundamental theories of atomic physics are of even greater importance. Fermi is an example of that rare type of scientist who is both a superb experimentalist and a brilliant theorist.

Enrico Fermi was born in Rome, Italy, on September 29, 1901. His father, Alberto, was a chief inspector in the Railway Ministry; his mother, Ida de Gattis, was trained as a school teacher and taught in the elementary schools most of her life. Maria, Fermi's older sister, was born in 1898. His brother, Giulio, who was two years older, was his most important playmate and teacher. It was a severe blow to fourteen-year-old Fermi when Giulio died. The children were raised as agnostics. They attended a strictly secular school with other pupils from lower-middle-class families.

Fermi spent a great deal of time studying mathematics and physics from secondhand books and books he borrowed from his father's friend Adolfo Amidie, an engineer. It was Amidie who urged Fermi to compete (successfully) for a fellowship for a free education at the Scuola Normale Superiore in Pisa. While still a student at Pisa, he published a significant paper that established him as the leading expert in Italy on Albert Einstein's general theory of relativity. After being awarded his doctorate magna cum laude from Pisa on July 7, 1922, he received a fellowship to spend a year at Göttingen. He returned to Italy to teach first at Rome in 1923 and then at Florence.

In January 1926, Fermi wrote a paper on one of his most significant theoretical contributions: the Fermi statistics, a method for calculating the behavior and properties of a system of particles that obey the Pauli **exclusion principle**. It was the culmination of two years of effort trying to explain the experimental values of the specific heats of certain (**monatomic**) gases. Several months later, using a very different approach, Paul Dirac derived the same statistical mechanics. Fermi's paper was much more than the announcement of just a theoretical principle, it gave energy and momentum distributions. Almost immediately, Fermi's theory was applied to conduction electrons in metals and provided an understanding of the specific heat of metals. The theoretical foundation for solid-state physics (modern condensed matter physics) is the Fermi-Dirac statistical mechanics. The particles that obey these statistical laws are called fermions. In particle physics, all of the basic building blocks of matter, the quarks and leptons, are fermions.

Another very important theory developed by Fermi was his explanation of the beta decay of nuclei—the radioactive process in which a neutron changes to a proton by creating an electron and a neutrino. Fermi's theory of beta decay introduced a fourth fundamental force, called the weak interaction, to be added to the previously known three: the gravitational force between masses, the electromagnetic force between charges, and the strong force between the particles in nuclei. A new fundamental constant, called the Fermi constant, determines the strength of the weak interaction. In the 1960s the electromagnetic and the weak interactions were combined in a unified theory, and the well measured Fermi constant plays a major role.

A special professorship in theoretical physics was set up for Fermi at the University of Rome in 1927, and at age twen-

exclusion principal: the principal that two similar particals can not have the same position and the same velocity.

monatomic: having one atom per molecule.

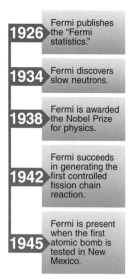

1926 Fermi publishes the "Fermi statistics."

1934 Fermi discovers slow neutrons.

1938 Fermi is awarded the Nobel Prize for physics.

1942 Fermi succeeds in generating the first controlled fission chain reaction.

1945 Fermi is present when the first atomic bomb is tested in New Mexico.

ty-six he became the youngest professor in Italy since Galileo. The following year he married Laura Capon, whose family was Jewish. In 1938, when Mussolini introduced his anti-Semitic laws, Fermi realized he had to leave Italy. The trip to Sweden to receive the Nobel Prize in November 1938 provided the opportunity. On January 2, 1938, Enrico and Laura Fermi and their two children, Nella and Giulio, arrived in New York City.

Fermi followed his achievements in theoretical physics with equally significant discoveries in experimental physics. In 1934 he and a group of young associates in Rome began to produce new artificially radioactive isotopes by bombarding target elements with neutrons. In the course of these experiments, Fermi discovered that neutrons slowed down by collisions with hydrogen nuclei in paraffin or water were more likely than fast neutrons to produce a nuclear reaction. Fermi's discovery of the effect of slow neutrons on nuclear reactions was central to his later work in the development of a nuclear chain reaction. It was also the basis of the Nobel Prize in physics that he received in 1938.

In January 1939, shortly after Fermi had started working at Columbia University, Niels Bohr arrived with the sensational news of the discovery of uranium fission; when a uranium nucleus absorbs a neutron, it splits into lighter nuclei, with the release of enormous amounts of energy. Fermi, Leo Szilard, and others immediately realized the significance of this discovery; if the fission of uranium by neutrons released other neutrons, these in turn could produce additional fissions, leading to a chain reaction of tremendous potential power. Szilard had secretly patented the chain reaction process in 1936. Fermi and Herbert L. Anderson and, independently, Szilard and Walter H. Zinn quickly showed that several neutrons are emitted in the fission process. Anderson, Fermi, Szilard, and Zinn joined forces and worked together first at Columbia and then after April 1942 at the University of Chicago, where studying the feasibility of the chain reaction become a large wartime project. Fermi worked out the detailed theory for the chain reaction in large test assemblies (piles) of uranium and graphite. A total of thirty experimental piles were tested over a two-year period. During the construction of the final pile in November 1942, Fermi gave detailed daily instructions on where to

"If I could remember the names of all these particles, I'd be a botanist."

— Enrico Fermi, *More Random Walks in Science*

place the different materials. From daily measurements during construction, Fermi extrapolated that, on the night of December 1, the pile would allow the control of a self-sustaining nuclear chain reaction at the fifty-seventh layer. On December 2, Fermi made measurements of the neutron intensity over six hours with the control rods at a series of positions to determine the final operating position. At about 3:30 P.M., he instructed that the control rod be set to the calculated position where there would be a self-sustaining chain reaction. After twenty-five minutes of measuring the rising neutron intensity, he stopped the reaction by putting the control rods into the pile. In a very quantitative experiment, Fermi established that man could control nuclear chain reactions.

From 1943 to 1947, using beams of neutrons from nuclear reactors, Fermi established the field of neutron optics as a powerful research tool that is very important in many fields of science. The most expensive National Experimental Research facility planned in the United States, The Advanced Neutron Source, is based on Fermi's pioneering research papers in neutron optics. In the last decade of his life, his experiments used a **synchrocyclotron** for studying the interaction of **mesons**. His theoretical work in astrophysics and cosmic rays included a theory on the origins of cosmic rays.

Fermi's nonphysics activities and fun were mostly in sports such as swimming, skiing, hiking, and tennis. He was very competitive in sports, and he usually was the first one to the top of a hill when hiking. By contrast in physics, he was patiently supportive of his colleagues and a fabulous teacher. For Fermi, and with Fermi, physics was both a challenge and a source of joy. He died in Chicago, Illinois, November 28, 1954. ◆

synchrocyclotron: a type of particle accelerator.

meson: a type of fundamental particle made up of a quark and an antiquark.

Feynman, Richard Phillips

1918–1988 ● THEORETICAL PHYSICS

"If it disagrees with experiment it is wrong. In that simple statement is the key to science." — Richard Feynman

Feynman, one of the greatest and most original physicists of the second half of the twentieth century, was born at Far Rockaway, New York, May 11, 1918, and grew up on Long Island. He attended both junior and senior high school in Far Rockaway, where he was fortunate to have some very competent and talented teachers for his chemistry and mathematics courses. He entered the Massachusetts Institute of Technology in the fall of 1935 and was recognized as an unusually gifted individual by all of his teachers. In 1939 he went to Princeton University as a graduate student in physics and was assigned to be John A. Wheeler's assistant—a propitious event in retrospect. Wheeler, who had just come to Princeton as a twenty-six-year-old assistant professor in the fall of 1938, proved to be an ideal mentor for the young Feynman. Full of bold and original ideas, a man who had the courage to look at any problem, a fearless and intrepid explorer of ideas, Wheeler gave Feynman viewpoints and insights into physics that would prove decisive in later research. In the spring of 1942, Feynman obtained his Ph.D. and immediately thereafter started working on problems related to the development of an atomic bomb. In 1943 he was one of the first physicists to go to Los Alamos. He was quickly recognized by

Feynman disliked pomposity and made fun of pretentious and self-important people.

Hans Bethe, the head of the theoretical division, and by J. Robert Oppenheimer, the director of the laboratory, to be one of the most valuable members of the theoretical division. He was perhaps the most versatile, imaginative, ingenious, and energetic member of that community of outstanding scientists. In 1944 he was made a group leader in charge of the computations for the theoretical division. He introduced punch card computers to Los Alamos and continued to develop his lifelong interest in computing and computers.

While at Los Alamos, Feynman accepted a Cornell University appointment as an assistant professor and joined its department of physics in the fall of 1945. In 1951 he left Cornell to become a member of the faculty of the California Institute of Technology, remaining there until his death of stomach cancer in 1988.

One aspect of Feynman's genius was that he could make explicit what was unclear and obscure to most of his contemporaries. His doctoral dissertation and his 1948 *Reviews of Modern Physics* article, which presented his path integral formulation of nonrelativistic quantum mechanics, helped clarify in a striking manner the assumptions that underlay the usual quantum mechanical description of the dynamics of microscopic entities. In Feynman's approach, a (nonrelativistic) particle in going from the spatial point x_1 at time t_1 to the spatial point x_2 at time t_2 is assumed to be able to take any path that joins x_1 at time t_1 to x_2 at time t_2, and each path is assigned a "probability amplitude." His reformulation of quantum mechanics and his integral over paths may well turn out to be his most profound and enduring contributions. They have deepened understanding of quantum mechanics and have significantly extended the systems that can be quantized. His path integral has enriched mathematics and has provided new in sights into spaces of infinite dimensions.

Feynman was awarded the Nobel Prize for physics in 1965 for his work on quantum electrodynamics (QED). In 1948, simultaneously with Julian Schwinger and Sin-Itiro Tomonaga, he showed that the infinite results that plague the usual formulation of QED could be removed by a redefinition of the parameters that describe the mass and charge of the electron in the theory, a process that is called renormalization. Schwinger and Tomonaga had done this by building on the existing formulation of the theory. Feynman, on the other

1943 Feynman joins the Manhattan Project, the U.S. program to build an atomic bomb.

1953 Feynman develops the quantum mechanical explanation of liquid helium.

1965 Feynman is awarded the Nobel Prize for physics.

1968 Feynman begins working on strong nuclear interactions at Stanford University's Linear Accelerator.

1986 Feynman serves on a commission investigating the explosion of the space shuttle.

hand, invented a completely new diagrammatic approach that allowed the visualization of space-time processes, simplified concepts and calculations enormously, and made possible the exploration of the properties of QED to all orders of **perturbation** theory. Using Feynman's methods it became possible to calculate quantum electrodynamic processes to amazing precision. Thus, the magnetic moment of the electron has been calculated to an accuracy of 1 part in 10^9 and found to be in agreement with an experimental value measured to a similar accuracy.

perturbation: a disturbance of motion, course, arrangement, or state of equilibrium.

In 1953 Feynman developed a quantum mechanical explanation of liquid helium, which justified the earlier phenomenological theories of Lev Landau and Laslo Tisza. Because a ^{4}He atom has zero total spin angular momentum, it behaves as a Bose particle: The wave function describing a system of N helium atoms is unchanged under the exchange of any two helium atoms. The ground state of such a system is described quantum mechanically in terms of a unique function that is everywhere positive. When in this state the system—even when N is of the order 10^{23} and the system is **macroscopic**—behaves as one unit. This is why helium near 0 K is superfluid, acting as if it had no viscosity. Near 0 K, pressure waves are the only excitations possible in the liquid. At somewhat higher temperatures, around 0.5 K, it becomes possible to form small rings of atoms that can circulate without perturbing other atoms; these are the rotons of Landau's theory. With increasing temperature, the number of rotons increases and their interaction with one another gives rise to viscosity. An assembly of rotons behaves like a normal liquid, and this liquid moves independently of the **superfluid**. At a certain point, when the concentration of normal liquid becomes too large, a phase transition occurs and the whole liquid turns normal. This was Feynman's quantum mechanical explanation why at any given temperature helium could be regarded as a mixture of superfluid and normal liquid.

macroscopic: large enough to be observed by the naked eye; relatively large.

superfluid: a state of matter noted only in liquid helium cooled to near absolute zero.

In 1956 T. D. Lee and Chen Ning Yang analyzed the extensive extant data on nuclear beta decay and concluded that mirror (parity) symmetry is not conserved in these interactions. This was soon confirmed experimentally by Chien Wu, Ernest Ambler and Evans Hayward, and others. Subsequent experiments further indicated that the violation of parity is the maximum possible. On the basis of these findings, Robert Marshak and George Sudarshan, and somewhat later and independently Feynman and Murray Gell-Mann, postulated that only the "left handed" part of the wave functions of the particles involved in the reaction enter in the weak interactions. Furthermore, Feynman and Gell-Mann hypothesized that the weak interaction is universal, that is, that all the weak particle interactions have the same strength. This hypothesis was later corroborated by experiments.

In the late 1960s, experiments at the Stanford Linear Accelerator on the scattering of high energy electrons by protons indicated that the cross section for inelastic scattering was very large. Feynman found that he could explain the data if he assumed that the proton was made up of small, point-like entities that interacted elastically with electrons. He called these sub-nuclear entities "partons." The partons were soon identified with the quarks of Gell Mann and George Zweig. The study of quarks and their interactions and, in particular, explaining their confinement inside nucleons and mesons were important components of Feynman's research during the 1980s.

Feynman disliked pomposity and made fun of pretentious and self-important people. He was always direct, forthright, and skeptical. His uncanny ability to get to the heart of a problem—whether in physics, applied physics, mathematics, or biology—was demonstrated repeatedly. Thus, while sitting on the presidential commission that investigated the Challenger disaster, he pinpointed the central problem by dropping a rubber **O-ring** into a glass of ice water to demonstrate its shriveling. In his physics, Feynman always stayed close to experiments and showed little interest in theories that could not be experimentally tested. He imparted these views to undergraduate students through his justly famous *Feynman Lectures on Physics* and to graduate students through his widely disseminated lecture notes for the graduate courses he taught. His writings on physics for the interested general public, *The Character of Physical Laws* and *QED: The Strange Theory of Light and Matter*, convey the same message.

He died at Pasadena, California, February 15, 1988. ◆

O-ring: a ring, usually rubber, used to make a joint fluid-tight.

Fleming, Sir Alexander

1881–1955 ● BACTERIOLOGY

"Surrounded by all those infected wounds, by men who were suffering and dying without our being able to do anything to help them, I was consumed by a desire to discover, after all this struggling and waiting, something which would kill these microbes."   — Sir Alexander Fleming

Fleming was a Scottish bacteriologist who, along with Howard Florey and Ernst B. Chain, discovered and developed penicillin.

Fleming's discovery led to a revolution in contemporary medical practice, paving the way for the treatment of disease with antibiotics.

At thirteen, Fleming was sent to London, where he attended school. He left at fifteen and went to work for a shipping company, but when, in 1900, an uncle left him a legacy, his elder brother, Tom, an ophthalmic surgeon, suggested he use the money to study medicine. Fleming took some preparatory lessons and sat for the entrance exam for medical school, scoring highest of all the United Kingdom candidates.

Fleming studied at Saint Mary's hospital, specializing in surgery, but in 1906 he joined the research team with which he was to remain until his death.

With the outbreak of World War I in 1914 Fleming and several of his colleagues were stationed in Boulogne, France, where they set up a makeshift laboratory and research center in a fencing school. The war wounded were ravaged by infections, largely due to the deep, jagged wounds caused by explosives. Fleming witnessed the ineffectiveness of antiseptics in the treatment of these wounds and conducted experiments to show that not only was it impossible to sterilize war wounds with but that the antiseptics themselves may even have helped to spread infection. Although this research of Fleming's has now been overshadowed by his later discoveries, many experts hold this to have been his most ingenious work.

In 1921, Fleming discovered lys2Olozyme, a substance present in human, animal, and vegetable tissues that dissolves bacteria and is part of the body's natural defense system. Fleming's presentation of his findings to the medical establishment met, however, with an indifferent reception.

Fleming went on to study staphylococci bacteria, which he cultivated in **agar** in petri dishes; often such cultures were accidentally contaminated with airborne spores. As Fleming complained to a colleague one day: "As soon as you uncover a culture dish something tiresome is sure to happen. Things fall out of the air." On saying this, Fleming noticed that on this particular culture, all around the mold that had grown from the spore colonies of staphylococci had dissolved. On further experimentation, Fleming found that this mold inhibited the growth of several bacteria, including diphtheria and anthrax bacteria. He called his mold penicillin.

On presenting his new discovery to the medical world in 1929, Fleming once again met with indifference. He wanted to extract the active ingredient from his mold, but was unable to do so himself and failed to find a chemist who was prepared to, or felt able to extract it. For the next ten years Fleming conducted a series of experiments on penicillin as a local antiseptic, convinced of the importance of his discovery, although few others were. Finally, in 1939, Ernst Boris Chain and Howard Walter Florey in Oxford perfected a method of purifying penicillin, and in World War II this was used on the wounded in Egypt with astonishing results.

When, in August 1942, Fleming successfully treated a meningitis sufferer with penicillin, news of the amazing cure spread throughout the medical world and the national press. The big pharmaceutical companies soon began to manufacture the antibiotic. Fleming was elected a Fellow of the Royal Society in 1943 and knighted a year later, following which, he toured the United States and Europe, receiving the Nobel Prize for physiology of medicine jointly with Chain and Florey in 1945.

agar: a gelatinous substance extracted from red algae.

1914 — World War I breaks out; Fleming and colleagues set up a laboratory in France.

1915 — British chemist James Kendall isolates dysentery bacillus.

1928 — Fleming discovers penicillin.

1939 — World War II begins in Europe; penicillin is used on wounded in Egypt.

1942 — Fleming successfully treats a meningitis patient with penicillin.

1945 — Fleming receives the Nobel Prize for medicine.

In 1946 Fleming took over as principal of the institute, working until 1955. He died later that year and is buried in the crypt of Saint Paul's Cathedral, London. ◆

Ford, Henry

1863–1947 ● INVENTOR

> *"A business that makes nothing but money is a poor kind of business."*
> — Henry Ford

Henry Ford, founder and organizer of the Ford Motor Company, was best known as a pioneer in mass production of automobiles. He was born at Dearborn, Michigan, July 30, 1863.

His earliest interest was in building a successful steam farm tractor but he gave up this idea during the 1890s. Ford was fifteen years old when he left school and moved into Detroit to work as a machinist and repairman on farm equipment. His experience in machine repair and design won him a job as chief engineer for the Edison Illuminating Company in Detroit, where he remained until 1899.

Ford had become interested in the new device of the automobile. He constructed a car by hand—a buggy body, mounted on bicycle wheels with a tiny gasoline engine—as early as 1892. His interest continued so that he left the Edison

Company to organize an auto-making firm. His original financial backers disagreed with his notion of making a cheap automobile instead of an expensive luxury-type vehicle. So, in 1903, Henry Ford organized another firm, the Ford Motor Company.

Ford developed assembly-line techniques, and designed a reliable but inexpensive car, the famous "Model T," which appeared in 1909. The "flivver," as people called the Model T, was relatively easy to repair. It was also the start of a revolution in American habits, for it brought auto ownership within reach of millions of Americans. Ford made other important contributions to the auto industry in its early years. One of these was his stubborn defense in a lawsuit that had been brought, in which the holder of a general patent (the Selden Patent) for a self-powered car claimed that nobody could make any kind of an automobile without paying him royalties. When Ford won that case, other auto manufacturers were free to produce cars.

Ford was a controversial figure in labor relations. He began paying his workers a much higher wage ($5 per day) for a standard eight-hour day than any other manufacturers were offering in 1914; he also introduced a profit-sharing system for his employees. However, Henry Ford stood out strongly against any labor union recognition: he wished to be the undisputed manager of his factories and sales organizations. Ford eventually signed union contracts with the United Auto Workers in 1941 after a long series of disputes with the labor organization.

Henry Ford was a confirmed pacifist, who tried to bring about a peaceful settlement of World War I and who opposed military preparations for World War II. In 1915, he chartered a steamship (*Oscar II*) and sailed to Europe with a boatload of American and other pacifists, hoping to bring the warring powers of Europe together by his action aboard the "Peace Ship." This effort ended in confusion as the many individuals aboard went their separate and sometimes conflicting ways. Before the United States entered World War II, Ford opposed sending military supplies to the European countries (such as France and Great Britain) that eventually became American allies. However, under his direction, the Ford Company then became a leading producer of military equipment ranging from heavy bombers to trucks during the war.

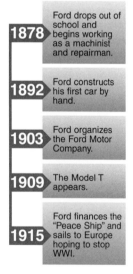

1878 Ford drops out of school and begins working as a machinist and repairman.

1892 Ford constructs his first car by hand.

1903 Ford organizes the Ford Motor Company.

1909 The Model T appears.

1915 Ford finances the "Peace Ship" and sails to Europe hoping to stop WWI.

Ford served as president of his Company from 1903 to 1919, and resumed the presidency in 1943 after his son Edsel Ford died. The older Ford remained in charge of the Ford Company until his own death at Dearborn, April 7, 1947. ◆

Fossey, Dian

1932–1985 ● ZOOLOGY

> *"I shall never forget my first encounter with gorillas. Sound preceded sight. Odor preceded sound in the form of an overwhelming musky-barnyard, humanlike scent."* — Dian Fossey, *Gorillas in the Mist*

Dian Fossey was a zoologist whose investigations of the mountain gorilla advanced knowledge of the great ape and spurred conservation efforts in Africa.

She was born 16 January 1932 in San Francisco, California. After completing high school, Dian began college at the University of California at Davis, majoring in animal husbandry. Two years later, concluding that her science grades were not high enough, Dian transferred to San Jose State University and changed her major to occupational therapy. After her graduation in 1954, she began work at the Kosair Crippled Children's Hospital in Louisville, Kentucky. Shy and reserved, Dian worked well with the children.

Inspired by recent writings of George Schaller, Dian was determined to see gorillas in the wild. Thus, in 1963, she decid-

> *"If mountain gorillas are to survive and propagate, far more active conservation measures urgently need to be undertaken."*
>
> — Dian Fossey, *Gorillas in the Mist*

ed to go to Africa. Borrowing money, she planned a seven-week trip to travel with just a guide. In Africa she saw the gorillas and, in Olduvai Gorge in Tanzania, met Louis Leakey. A Louisville newspaper published several of her stories after she returned. When Leakey, who believed that women were ideal for studying apes, lectured at the University of Louisville in 1966, Dian met with him again and raised the issue of undertaking a study of the mountain gorilla. After some months of negotiations, and while Leakey sought funding for the study, Dian quit her job. She left for Africa in December 1966. By mid-January 1967, she was alone at Kabara in the Virunga Mountains, beginning her investigation.

If Fossey was pleased that her work had begun, she was isolated at the station and could communicate only through an English-speaking tribesman. Enamored by the gorillas, Fossey was uninterested in the tense political situation in newly independent Zaire. As the civil war there became more vicious, most Europeans were attacked or fled then country. Fossey was ordered off the mountain and spent about ten days in detention. She crossed into Uganda under guard but returned to Zaire.

On her return, she was locked in an open cage for two days. During that period she was humiliated, terrorized, and probably sexually assaulted. She never made the extent of her ordeal totally clear, but carried its scars through the rest of her life. Using her need to get additional money and to register her vehicle, she managed to cross again into Uganda.

Despite her recent trauma, Fossey was determined to continue her gorilla studies at Karisoke on the Rwandan side of the border. She set up her new station under conditions that, in some ways, were more difficult than at the one in Zaire; Rwanda was one of the poorest and most densely populated countries in Africa. She had to overcome many problems, such as isolation, lack of funds, and lack of interest on the part of the government of Rwanda.

At Karisoke, Fossey was visited by Alan Root and John Hinde. Root filmed the dramatic sequences of Fossey making physical contact with gorillas; Hinde would become her graduate mentor at Cambridge University. As Fossey's fame spread, more and more students were sent to assist her in her work. In 1973, she began graduate studies at Cambridge; she earned a Ph.D. in 1976. At Karisoke she exhibited increas-

1963 Fossey travels to Africa for the first time.

1967 Fossey begins studying gorillas at Kabara.

1976 Fossey earns a Ph.D. from Cambridge.

1983 *Gorillas in the Mist* is published.

1985 Fossey is murdered in her cabin at Karisoke.

ingly hostile behavior toward Africans, both poachers and the herdsmen who encroached on the park boundaries.

Her major work, *Gorillas in the Mist*, was published in 1983. During these years, Fossey's health suffered and her asthma slowed the pace of her research; relations with others were increasingly strained. She was murdered in her cabin 26 December 1985 at Karisoke; questions remain concerning both her killer and motive. Fossey was buried in the gorilla cemetery she had created at Karisoke.

Fossey's patient, long-term observations of the day to day lives of mountain gorillas enabled her to earn the complete trust of the wild gorillas at Karisoke. Her research revealed many previously unknown aspects of gorilla behavior. Most valuable was her documentation of the slow changes that occur in the animal's social organization from generation to generation. In addition, her research and writings helped focus attention on the plight of mountain gorillas as poachers and loss of habitat threaten their survival. The Dian Fossey Gorilla Fund has continued her research and conservation efforts. ◆

Franklin, Benjamin

1706–1790 ● INVENTOR & SCIENTIST

In his *Autobiography*, Benjamin Franklin notes that his paternal ancestors lived in the village of Ecton in Northamptonshire, England, for more than 300 years as farmers and tradesmen. About 1682, to avoid religious persecution, his father, Josiah, emigrated to New England. Benjamin's mother, Adiah, the second wife of Josiah, was a daughter of Peter Folger, one of the first settlers of New England. Benjamin was born at Boston, Massachusetts, January 17, 1706, the youngest of ten sons and the fifteenth child among seventeen of Josiah, the eighth of Adiah. Benjamin attended school only two years but was an avid,

> *"The greatest monarch on the proudest throne is obliged to sit upon his own arse."*
> — Benjamin Franklin, *Poor Richard's Almanack*

Benjamin Franklin

lifelong student of literature, philosophy, science, and languages. At the age of ten he began assisting his father in his business of candle and soap making. At twelve he was apprenticed to his half brother James, a printer. When James launched a weekly newspaper, Benjamin at sixteen began contributing anonymous articles in which he critiqued many aspects of society under the guise of a poor young widow, "Silence Dogood." Resentful of beatings by his brother, Benjamin at seventeen ran off to Philadelphia. Thus began his extraordinary odyssey.

By dint of industry and thrift, Franklin prospered as a printer. In 1729 he bought a fledgling newspaper, *The Pennsylvania Gazette*; over the next decade his skill as editor and chief reporter enabled it to become the most widely read paper in the colonies. In 1730 he formed a **common-law** marriage with Deborah Read; their family included his son William (mother unknown), their son Francis, and their daughter Sally. From 1732 to 1757 Franklin published *Poor Richard's Almanack*; it was extremely popular and fostered his reputation for wit and wisdom. He also became a bookseller, established a circulating library, organized a debating club that in 1743 developed into the American Philosophical Society, helped to found in 1751 an academy that later became the University of Pennsylvania, and promoted many other civic projects, including a fire company, police force, hospital, and paving and lighting streets. In 1748 Franklin retired from business, turning his print shop over to a partner, and thereafter devoted himself chiefly to scientific research and civic affairs. Among many diplomatic and political roles, Franklin served for years in England as agent for several of the colonies, in France as minister, as a delegate to the Continental Congress, as postmaster general, as a member of the committee to draft the Declaration of Independence, and a delegate to the Constitutional Convention. Franklin crossed the Atlantic eight times, a voyage that took four to six weeks. He lived for a total of twenty five years in London (1724–1726, 1757–1762, and 1764–1773) and Paris (1776–1785), although in America his home remained in Philadelphia until his death.

Franklin was greatly esteemed in his day as a scientist as well as a sage. In the early eighteenth century, electricity was a greater mystery than gravity had been a century earlier. Franklin, almost entirely self-educated and far from any center of learning, solved that mystery. He devised, executed, and correctly interpreted a series of simple, compelling experiments and formulated lucid explanations. Among his several major discoveries, foremost was his concept of electricity as a single fluid, manifest as a positive or negative charge, depending on whether the fluid was present in excess or deficit relative to the neutral condition. He also explained the distinction between insulators and conductors, the role of grounding, the operation of a capacitor such as the Leyden jar, all concepts involved in his most celebrated result, the elucidation and taming of lightning. Franklin introduced into the electrical lexicon terms such as charge, plus or minus, positive or negative, **armature**, battery, and conductor. His book

common-law: the cohabitation of a couple who are not legally married but consider themselves married.

1729	Franklin begins publishing *The Pennsylvania Gazette*.
1732	Franklin publishes the first edition of *Poor Richard's Almanack*.
1745	Franklin begins studying electricity.
1751	Franklin publishes *Experiments and Observations on Electricity*.
1752	Franklin flies a kite in a thunderstorm and invents the lightning rod.
1776	Franklin helps draft the Declaration of Independence.
1791	Franklin's autobiography is published posthumously.

armature: a piece of steel or iron that connects the poles of a magnet or of adjacent magnets.

Experiments and Observations on Electricity, made at Philadelphia in America, consisting of letters he had sent to a colleague in England, was a sensation in Europe; it went through five editions in English (1751–1774) and was translated into French, German, and Italian. It was read not only by scholars but by the literate public, including the clergy and aristocracy. Contemporary scientists often likened Franklin to Isaac Newton.

The link that Franklin made between leaping sparks and lightning bolts was indeed comparable to that Newton made between falling apples and the moon's orbit. Before Franklin, lightning was considered a supernatural phenomenon. If a house was struck by lightning, the fire brigade would douse neighboring structures, but only pray over the struck one, not wanting to intrude on divine punishment. Such views also led to the custom of storing munitions in churches. In 1767 lightning detonated tons of powder in a Venice church; 3,000 people were killed and a large part of the city destroyed.

Despite ample demonstrations of the efficacy of Franklin's lightning rods, he had to weather thunderous attacks for his audacity in stealing a prerogative of the Almighty. He remained unruffled, writing in 1753, "Surely the Thunder of Heaven is no more supernatural than the Rain, Hail or

Franklin's Lightning Rod

For centuries, people believed that lightning was a supernatural phenomenon, sent down from heaven as a punishment. If a building in colonial America was struck by lightning, firefighters would douse neighboring structures, and only pray over the burning one. Numerous buildings burned to the ground as a result of fires started by lightning. When Benjamin Franklin identified lightning as ordinary electricity, he thought of a way to avoid such fires. Franklin's lightning rod was a simple metal pole perched atop a building and attached to conducting cables that connected the rod to the ground. The rod protects the building by intercepting the lightning's electric current and sending it safely through the cables to the ground. Without a rod, lightning is more likely to strike the building. Most buildings are made of nonconducting materials, like wood, which become heated when electric current tries pass through them, leading to fire. At first, people were reluctant to use Franklin's invention because they feared they were stealing the prerogative of the Almighty. But lightning rods soon caught on and began appearing on the roofs of homes and buildings everywhere.

Sunshine of Heaven, against the Inconveniences of which we guard by Roofs & Shades without Scruple."

Like so much else he did, the scope of Franklin's scientific work was remarkable. He wrote major papers on population growth and on meteorology, devised experiments on heat conduction and evaporation, measured ocean temperatures and charted the Gulf Stream, studied bioluminescence and the stilling of water waves by a surface layer of oil, invented a flexible catheter, constructed bifocal eye glasses, and promoted an efficient wood-burning stove. He also advanced arguments in favor of the wave theory of light.

Many high honors were bestowed on Franklin, but perhaps even more telling were what might be termed low honors. His celebrity was immense, particularly in France. His image appeared everywhere on medallions and banners, snuff boxes and inkwells, often with the motto *Eripuit celeo fulmen sceptrumque tyrannis* (He snatched lightning from the sky and the scepter from tyrants). Louis XVI became so annoyed by this veneration that he gave his favorite mistress a chamber pot with a Franklin medallion at the bottom of the bowl. Franklin's popularity aided significantly his efforts to accelerate the vital flow of arms and funds supplied by the French to support the American Revolution.

While Franklin was always alert for practical applications, in his work on electricity and most of his other scientific studies, his style was that of an explorer, eager for adventure and insight rather than profit or utility. During the several years when he was chiefly occupied with his electrical studies, from about 1745 to 1752, Franklin often confessed apologetically to friends that he had become obsessed with his experiments. He called them philosophical amusements, which he pursued despite what seemed then an almost total lack of prospective applications. Three years before he conceived of the lightning rod, Franklin averred that electricity at least "may help to keep a vain man humble."

Benjamin Franklin died in Philadelphia, Pennsylvania, on April 17, 1790. ◆

Franklin wrote papers on meteorology, devised experiments on heat conduction, measured ocean temperatures, charted the Gulf Stream, invented bifocal eye glasses, and promoted an efficient wood-burning stove, among other things.

Freud, Sigmund

1856–1939 ● PSYCHIATRY &
PSYCHOLOGY

*"The poets and philosophers before me dis-
covered the unconscious; what I discovered
was the scientific method by which the
unconscious can be studied."*

— Sigmund Freud

determinist: believing
that everything is
caused or determined
by preceding events or
natural laws.

Sigmund Freud was born in Freiberg, Moravia, but when
he was three the family moved to Vienna to escape anti-
Semitic discrimination. He lived in Vienna for most of
the rest of his life, despite his professed dislike of the city.

A precocious and intellectually gifted child, at the age of
seventeen Freud entered the University of Vienna to study
medicine, motivated primarily by a deep interest in scientific
research, and in his third year he began a study of the central
nervous system with Ernst Brüke, which was to delay the
completion of his degree by three years. Brüke's **determinist**
philosophy was also to inspire and remain with Freud
throughout his life. Even after graduation Freud was reluctant
to practice medicine and would have gladly remained permanently in research, but he was eventually persuaded to join
the staff of Vienna General Hospital.

Freud's interest in what would become the field of psychoanalysis was sparked by his friend Josef Breuer, physician
and physiologist, who in 1884 introduced him to the "talking
cure" by explaining that one of his patients was relieved of
one of her nervous symptoms when she fully recounted the
details of its first appearance. In 1885 Freud received a grant
to spend four and a half months in Paris studying with the

French neurologist Jean Charcot, who was engaged in pioneering treatments of nervous disorders, in particular hysteria, by hypnosis. When Freud returned to Vienna, he opened a private practice in nervous diseases and attempted to introduce Charcot's views on **hysteria** and hypnosis. He met with violent opposition from the medical profession, and there followed a ten-year period of almost complete intellectual isolation during which, although he was personally extremely creative and productive, he received no support from the medical community.

Studies in Hysteria, the outcome of his collaboration with Breuer, was published in 1893. On the assumption that hysteria was caused by undischarged emotional energy, the therapeutic procedure they advocated involved inducing a hypnotic state in which the patient was to recall fully the traumatic experience and thus **cathartically** rid himself of the emotions causing the symptoms. Freud eventually abandoned the hypnotic method when he found that although it could help to break down a patient's resistance to repressed material, it was not always an effective cure. He began to substitute the process of free association. This required careful monitoring of the patient's spontaneous flow of speech and thoughts, which would reveal unconscious mental processes and material. Clues emerging from the analysis of dreams and free association would point to unconscious impulses excluded from awareness because of the anxiety they could cause, yet so powerful that they needed to seek expression and thus emerged as **neurotic** symptoms.

It was during this period that Freud began to find evidence for the mechanisms of repression and resistance; the former was a defense mechanism used to withhold painful or threatening material from the conscious mind; the latter prevented unconscious impulses from coming to awareness and causing anxiety. In 1895 he also undertook self-analysis in order to better understand his own neuroses and improve his ability to understand his patients. He concluded that his own problem, anxiety neurosis, was caused by an accumulation of sexual tension. Much of his analysis was accomplished by consideration of his own dreams. The final product of this intense period of study was the publication of *The Interpretation of Dreams* (1900), in which many of his own dreams were recorded.

hysteria: behavior exhibiting overwhelming fear or emotional excess.

cathartic: serving to eliminate a negative emotion by bringing it to consciousness.

neurotic: relating to a mental or emotional disorder that is less severe than psychosis.

Through the study of free association Freud began to develop his theories on the importance of sexuality and the conviction that all neuroses were based on arrested sexual development. It took some time before he came to the conclusion that sexuality existed even at the infantile stage, and that problems in early sexual development could be responsible for neurotic symptoms. When he first made this discovery he assumed that the victims of neuroses had been molested and traumatized by their elders; only later did he come to the conclusion that many of his patients had fantasized rather than actually experienced such encounters, and that their fantasies had assumed a reality for them because as children they had been unable to distinguish between fact and wish.

His work on sexual development and the related assumption that libido, or sexual drive, is a central human drive at all stages of development, led to his identification of the "Oedipus complex," in which a child develops an erotic attachment toward the parent of the opposite sex, and a consequent hostility toward the same-sex parent. During these years Freud also developed the crucial concept of transference, based on the assumption that during therapy the patient necessarily transfers buried emotional responses originally directed at the parent onto the therapist, and thus confronts the emotions anew.

Freud's emergence from isolation was slow. Public hostility was only exacerbated by his publication of *The Psychopathology of Everyday Life* (1904), in which he traced the slightest errors of speech to unconscious causes (from which the term "a Freudian slip" has passed into the language). Nonetheless, in 1902 he was appointed a professor at the University of Vienna. By 1906 his work was beginning to attract the attention of pupils and followers with similar interests, who eventually began meeting regularly in Freud's waiting room. Among the distinguished analysts participating in these weekly gatherings were Alfred Adler, Wilhelm Stekel, Otto Rank, Abraham Brill, Carl Jung, Sandor Ferenczi, and Ernest Jones. At a later stage Freud was to break with some of these colleagues, both personally and professionally, when their questioning of some of his theories became unacceptable to him. The split with Jung was particularly bitter. Jung complained that for Freud "the brain is viewed as an appendage of the genital glands," while Freud

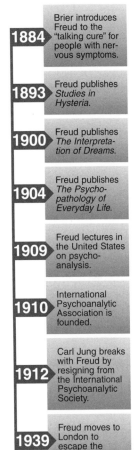

1884 Brier introduces Freud to the "talking cure" for people with nervous symptoms.

1893 Freud publishes *Studies in Hysteria.*

1900 Freud publishes *The Interpretation of Dreams.*

1904 Freud publishes *The Psychopathology of Everyday Life.*

1909 Freud lectures in the United States on psychoanalysis.

1910 International Psychoanalytic Association is founded.

1912 Carl Jung breaks with Freud by resigning from the International Psychoanalytic Society.

1939 Freud moves to London to escape the Nazis in Austria.

felt that Jung's action was a classic case of the son rebelling against the father.

The psychoanalytic movement gradually gained recognition; a first congress was held in 1908, and in 1910 the International Psychoanlytic Association was formed. Although the founding group disintegrated, pschoanalysis continued to grow in importance, and in 1909 Freud was invited to Clark University in the United States to receive an honorary doctorate and to introduce his theories to the American community. After World War I he developed a theory of personality structure based on the id, the ego, and the superego. The id, which corresponds to the unconscious and includes sexual and aggressive instinct, attempts to fulfill the pleasure principle—achievement of maximum pleasure and avoidance of "unpleasure." The ego serves as a mediator between the id and the outside world, controlling the demands of the id in accordance with the exigencies of reality. The superego, or conscience, which develops in childhood as the child internalizes the values of the authoritarian figures in his life, strives for perfection. The burden upon the ego of the triple demands of the id, the superego, and reality may become unbearable, thus leading to the activation of the psychological defense mechanisms by which the ego avoids anxiety.

Freud was a hard worker who did much of his writing at night, after seeing patients all day. He was intensely self-critical, yet intolerant of opinions that differed from his, which led to many bitter defections among his colleagues and disciples. He was sixty-seven when he began to suffer from the cancer of the jaw and palate that would torture him for the next sixteen years, requiring thirty-three operations and the use of a prosthesis. (He nevertheless continued to smoke twenty cigars a day.) Notwithstanding his painful impediment, he continued to write and treat patients until the last months of his life. Several of his later works were attempts to apply his theories to the fields of religion, art, and literature in books such as *Civilization and its Discontents* (1930) and *Moses and Monotheism* (1938). He died one year after moving to London to escape the Nazi invasion of Austria. His collected works fill twenty-three volumes. ◆

> Jung complained that for Freud "the brain is viewed as an appendage of the genital glands."

Fuller, R(ichard) Buckminster, (Jr.)

1895–1983 ● INVENTOR

> *"Nature is trying very hard to make us succeed, but nature does not depend on us. We are not the only experiment."*
> — R. Buckminster Fuller

tetrahedron: a solid geometrical figure with four surfaces.

The second of four children of Richard Buckminster Fuller, a successful Boston tea and leather merchant, and Caroline Wolcott Andrews, a homemaker, R. Buckminster Fuller, Jr., was born in Milton, Mass., July 12, 1895, into a prominent New England family (his forebears included the Transcendentalist social reformer Margaret Fuller and, on the maternal side, the colonial Connecticut governor Roger Wolcott). He was born with such poor vision that his view of the world was shaped by blurred images. Thus, when he received his first glasses at age four, it was an experience that dazzled and stimulated him for life. Two years later, while in kindergarten, he fashioned a **tetrahedron**-shaped device from dried peas and toothpicks that presaged his greatest architectural invention.

Fuller excelled in science and mathematics at Milton Academy but rebelled against traditional teaching methods. Following five generations of Fuller men to Harvard University in 1913, he deviated from the college's social norms by squandering his tuition money and allowance on a extravagant party for the Ziegfeld Follies chorus line in New York City and was promptly expelled. In 1914 his family sent him to work as an apprentice mechanic in a Canadian textile mill, where he so excelled in designing machine parts that he was readmitted to Harvard in 1915, only to be kicked out again for missing classes and other misdeeds.

Fuller's active mind worked best whenever it was challenged. After two years doing menial work for the Armour meatpacking company, in 1917 he obtained an ensign's commission in the U.S. Navy through a ninety-day officer training course in scientific methodology at the U.S. Naval Academy. While assigned to command crash boats for naval aviation trainees at Newport News, Virginia, Fuller invented two devices to expedite air-sea rescues. He returned to Armour in 1919 as an export manager and in 1922 was briefly a national account manager with a trucking firm that soon went bankrupt

Fuller married Anne Hewlett on 12 July 1917; they had a daughter in 1918. With his father-in-law, the prominent architect James Monroe Hewlett, he patented a method of constructing fibrous building blocks invented by Hewlett, and in 1922 they formed Stockade Building System in Chicago to produce them. His daughter suddenly died on her fourth birthday, a crushing blow that drove Fuller to become a workaholic by day and a heavy drinker by night. In 1927, soon after Fuller's second daughter was born, loss of profits forced Hewlett to sell his stocks; the new controlling stockholders blamed Fuller and discharged him. His life in ruins, he contemplated suicide.

Fuller rebounded through a personal transformation in which he vowed to reshape his thinking for the benefit of mankind. Living with his wife and child in a Chicago slum apartment for two years, he cut himself off from the world; for more than a year he spoke to no one, including his family, and he devoted his time and energy to rethinking the human condition and devising solutions to its problems. He stopped drinking, eschewed personal gain, and slept only two hours a night in order to apply his architectural skills to discovering ways for people to do more with less, as he put it. The result was what he later termed a "design-science revolution" of making machines that would liberate people from unnecessary work. Fuller coined the word "dymaxion" from "dynamic" and "maximum" and founded the Dymaxion Corporation in 1932. In 1927 and 1928 he designed a mass-produced, lightweight, hexagonal, 4-D (four dimensional) self-sufficient apartment house and the easily transported single-unit Dymaxion house, suspended from a central mast (to which he added a prefabricated modular bathroom in 1929). The streamlined three-wheeled Dymaxion car, with a rear engine, was his major project from 1933 to 1935, when a fatal accident with a prototype caused such adverse publicity that Fuller had to cancel production after only three prototypes had been built. None of these inventions gained acceptance from the architectural or any other community.

From 1936 to 1938 Fuller was a research and design assistant for the Phelps Dodge Corporation, and from 1938 to 1940 he was a technical consultant for Fortune magazine. In 1940 he designed a steel and fiberglass Dymaxion military igloo that was produced during World War II, when he was

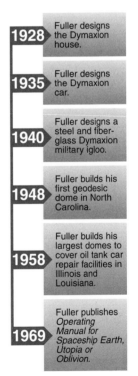

1928 Fuller designs the Dymaxion house.

1935 Fuller designs the Dymaxion car.

1940 Fuller designs a steel and fiberglass Dymaxion military igloo.

1948 Fuller builds his first geodesic dome in North Carolina.

1958 Fuller builds his largest domes to cover oil tank car repair facilities in Illinois and Louisiana.

1969 Fuller publishes *Operating Manual for Spaceship Earth, Utopia or Oblivion.*

chief of mechanical engineering for the Board of Economic Warfare. In 1943 Fuller applied his design principles to create the Dymaxion Air-Ocean World Map, the first projection to depict the entire globe without visible distortion and the first of his designs to attract the interest of scientists. He founded the Dymaxion Dwelling Machines Company in 1944 to mass-produce the prefabricated Wichita House in anticipation of the postwar housing shortage but found no backers.

In 1947 and 1948 Fuller applied mathematics to his geometric use of triangles, tetrahedrons, and circles in his Dymaxion designs to develop the science of geodesics and synergetics, using tensional integrity ("tensegrity"): mutually supporting parts in the three shapes for a dome-shaped building devoid of internal supports. He built the first fifty-foot-diameter geodesic dome at Black Mountain College, in North Carolina, in 1948 and incorporated Geodesics, Inc., in 1949. The Ford Motor Company commissioned Fuller in 1953 to design the ninety-three-foot plastic and aluminum dome for the rotunda of its Dearborn, Michigan, plant, an achievement that brought him international acclaim and more contracts: a helicopter-transported dome hangar for Marine Corps aircraft in 1954; radar enclosures (radomes) for the Air Force Dewline warning system across Alaska and northern Canada in 1955; and storage domes for the Navy in Antarctica in 1956, the same year that a 100-foot dome for an Afghanistan trade fair and subsequent exhibitions stimulated numerous orders.

Fuller founded Plydomes, Inc., in 1957 and the Tetrahelix Corporation in 1959 for further research and development. His largest domes, built in 1958, are the 384-foot structures covering oil tank car repair facilities in Louisiana and Illinois. Kaiser Aluminum had him build a 200-foot golden dome for the American Exchange Exhibition in Moscow in 1959; it dazzled Soviet leaders. His domes ranged from simple houses to immense structures at the 1962 Seattle World's Fair, the pavilion of the 1964 New York World's Fair, and the U.S. pavilion at Montreal's Expo 67 (designed with Shoji Sodao). From 1959 to 1970 Fuller was based at Southern Illinois University as research professor. From 1972 until his death he was World Fellow in residence at the University City Science Center in Philadelphia.

Fuller became a prolific commentator on "human engineering" and a guru of the counterculture with a plethora of

> Fuller held audiences spellbound for hours at a stretch with a nonstop extemporaneous barrage of ideas and insights.

works. Notable are *Ideas and Integrities* (1963); *Nine Chains to the Moon* (written with Robert Marks in 1938 but not acclaimed until it was reissued in 1963); *Operating Manual for Spaceship Earth*, *Utopia or Oblivion*, and his computerized *World Game* (all 1969); *I Seem to be a Verb* (1970); *Synergetics* (with E. J. Applewhite, 1975); *On Education* (1979); and *Critical Path* (1981). Fuller also wrote three volumes of verse, and in the 1961–1962 academic year held a chair of poetry at Harvard University. He lectured widely, received numerous awards, and commanded a widespread cult following as the charismatic "Bucky." He ignored many critics who regarded him as a romantic and was not discouraged when certain of his ideas failed to gain acceptance. He held over 2,000 patents.

A small (five feet, two inches) and humble man with crewcut hair and thick glasses, Fuller held audiences spellbound for up to four hours at a stretch with a nonstop extemporaneous barrage of ideas and insights. A resident of Forest Hills, New York, in later life, he relaxed by sailing at his summer home on Bear Island, Maine.

He died on July 1, 1983, of a heart attack in Los Angeles and was buried in Cambridge, Massachusetts. ◆

R. Buckminster Fuller in front of a geodesic dome.

Galen

129–c. 199 ● ANATOMY & MEDICINE

Galen was a Greek physician and one of the founders of the science of anatomy. Galen's research laid the basis for the development of scientific medicine during the Renaissance. He was born in Pergamon, a provincial capital of the Roman Empire (today in Turkey) renowned for its architectural beauty, where his father was a architect. Exposed to the worship of Asclepius, a healing god whose shrine in Pergamon attracted important personages from throughout the empire, Galen decided to make medicine his vocation. He began his studies at home under the eminent anatomist, Satyros, observing the physician's treatment of injured gladiators who fought at the shrine of Asclepius. He then went to Smyrna where he furthered his knowledge by dissecting animals, since according to Roman law it was forbidden to study human cadavers. In 157 he completed twelve years of medical study in Alexandria, having already written two books on anatomy, now lost.

In 161 Galen cured the well-known philosopher Eudemus in Rome and gained entry into the highest circles of the empire's capital city. He became part of the court of the coemperors Marcus Aurelius and Lucius Verus. His flamboyant pride earned him the resentment of his fellow physicians, who became jealous of his success. Whether it was to escape their ire or the plague that Verus brought to Rome with his returning troops, Galen left the capital suddenly, returning to Pergamon in 166. In 168, after Verus had died, the physician was ordered back to Rome by Marcus Aurelius and entrusted with the care of Commodus, heir to the throne.

His position enabled Galen to study and compose his works on physiology and he wrote his most famous works dur-

"Those things which bring about health where it does not exist are called medicines and remedies, while those which maintain it where it exists are called healthy modes of living."

— Galen

Galen wrote over 300 works on physiology, health, diet, mathematics, ethics, and philosophy.

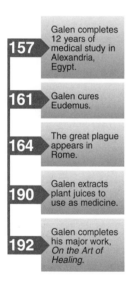

157 Galen completes 12 years of medical study in Alexandria, Egypt.

161 Galen cures Eudemus.

164 The great plague appears in Rome.

190 Galen extracts plant juices to use as medicine.

192 Galen completes his major work, *On the Art of Healing*.

ing this period, including *On the Natural Faculties*, *On the Use of Parts*, and *On Respiration*. When the emperor Commodus died in 192, Galen returned to Pergamon and completed his major work, *On the Art of Healing*.

Galen wrote over 300 works on physiology, health, diet, mathematics, ethics, and philosophy. His works on medicine comprise his commentaries on Hippocrates and attempts to unify medical knowledge within a philosophical framework. His anatomical findings were largely based on the dissection of the Barbary monkey and other lower animals. He assumed the fundamental similarity between primates and humans and based his descriptions of human anatomy on the primates, which he observed with acuity, systematically detailing his findings of muscle and bone structure.

Galen's knowledge of organ function was gained through a series of vivisections. By restricting nerve function he was able to discern the connection of the brain and larynx; by tying the ureters he determined kidney and bladder function, findings unsurpassed for 1,500 years. Through his transaction of the spinal cord he gained knowledge of the musculature. He distinguished between the functions of veins and arteries and established that the arteries carry blood, not air, as traditional sources had held. He also explored the workings of the heart and lungs, correctly understanding the lungs' aeration of the blood. His theory of respiration and combustion as well as liver function represented great strides toward the modem understanding of metabolism.

His theory of health was less creative, being derived from Hippocrates' theory of balancing the four humors—phlegm, black bile, yellow bile, and the blood—with a subtle material substance, pnemena, carried by the blood. But Galen's writings went beyond medicine to include philosophical treatises that sought the significance of every element of the world, adhering to Aristotle's dictum that "Nature does nothing in vain." ◆

Galilei, Galileo

1564–1642 ● P<small>HYSICS</small> & A<small>STRONOMY</small>

"In my studies of astronomy and philosophy I hold this opinion about the universe, that the Sun remains fixed in the center of the circle of heavenly bodies, without changing its place; and the Earth, turning upon itself, moves round the Sun."

— Galileo Galilei

G alileo was born at Pisa, Italy, on February 15, 1564. He was the eldest son of Vincenzio Galilei and Giulia Ammannati and had two brothers, Michelangelo, who became musician to the Grand Duke of Baviera, and Benedetto, who died in infancy, and three sisters, Virginia, Anna, and Livia, and possibly a fourth, Lena. His father was a musician and the author of an influential treatise on music that shows a gift for **polemics** that his son was to develop in his own writings. Galileo was enrolled at the University of Pisa in 1581 but left in 1585 before taking a degree. He studied Euclid and Archimedes and was soon able to tutor students in Florence and Siena. In 1586 he composed a short treatise, *The Little Balance*, in which he reconstructed the reasoning that he believed had led Archimedes to devise a way of detecting whether the goldsmith, who had fashioned King Hero's crown, had substituted a baser metal for gold. Galileo used his newly won insight to construct a **hydrostatical** balance that is the first instance of his interest in applied sciences. He was appointed to the Chair of Mathematics in Pisa in 1589. His notebooks (published only in the twentieth century) show the influence of the professors at the Jesuit College in Rome. The popular notion of Galileo as a hard-headed and thorough-going experimentalist owes much to his first biogra-

polemics: the art or practice of aggressively attacking or refuting the opinions of another.

hydrostatical: relating to fluids at rest and the pressure they exert.

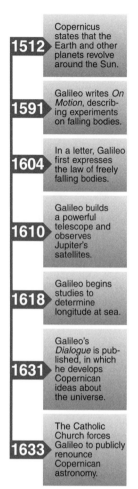

1512 Copernicus states that the Earth and other planets revolve around the Sun.

1591 Galileo writes *On Motion*, describing experiments on falling bodies.

1604 In a letter, Galileo first expresses the law of freely falling bodies.

1610 Galileo builds a powerful telescope and observes Jupiter's satellites.

1618 Galileo begins studies to determine longitude at sea.

1631 Galileo's *Dialogue* is published, in which he develops Copernican ideas about the universe.

1633 The Catholic Church forces Galileo to publicly renounce Copernican astronomy.

heliocentric: having the sun as center.

pher, Vincenzo Viviani, who claimed that Galileo ascended the Leaning Tower of Pisa sometime between 1589 and 1592 to refute Aristotle by showing that bodies fall at the same speed regardless of their weight. In his treatise, *On Motion*, written around 1591, Galileo makes frequent mention of towers, but he does not state that all bodies fall at the same speed but that their speed is proportional to the differences between their specific gravity and the density of the medium through which they descend. In other words, the young Galileo reached the erroneous conclusion that different-size bodies of the same material fall at the same rate while same-size bodies of different materials do not.

In 1592 Galileo was appointed to the Chair of Mathematics in Padua. He lectured on prescribed topics such as Euclid's *Elements*, the *Sphere of Sacrobosco*, Ptolemy's *Almagest*, and the Pseudo-Aristotelian *Mechanics*. Medical students made up the majority of his audience. Galileo gave private lectures on fortifications and military engineering to young noblemen, and he manufactured and sold a mathematical instrument, the military and geometrical compass or sector.

The first indication of Galileo's commitment to Copernicus appeared in a letter that he wrote to his former colleague at Pisa, Jacopo Mazzoni, in May 1597. In August of the same year he received a copy of Kepler's *Mysterium Cosmographicum*, in which the **heliocentric** theory was vindicated on mathematical and symbolic grounds. After reading the preface, Galileo wrote to Kepler to voice his approval of the view that Earth is in motion and to express his fear of making his position known to the public at large.

Galileo never married, but with his common-law wife, Marina Gamba, he had three children: Virginia (born August 13, 1600), Livia (born August 18, 1601), and Vincenzo (born August 21, 1606). For all his children Galileo carefully cast horoscopes.

Around 1602 Galileo began making experiments with falling bodies in conjunction with his study of the motion of pendulums and the problem of the brachistochrone, namely the curve between two points along which a body moves in the shortest time. He first expressed the correct law of freely falling bodies (s is proportional to t^2) in a letter to Paolo Sarpi in 1604, but he claimed to have derived it from the assumption that speed is proportional to distance. (He only realized later that speed is proportional to the square root of the distance.)

In July 1609, when Galileo was in Venice, he heard that a Dutchman had invented a device to make distant objects appear nearer, and he immediately attempted to construct such an instrument himself. Others were at work on similar devices, but by the end of August 1609 Galileo had produced a nine-power telescope that was better than those of his rivals. He returned to Venice where he gave a demonstration of his spying-glass from the top of the Campanile of San Marco. The practical value for sighting ships at a distance impressed the Venetian authorities who confirmed Galileo's appointment for life and raised his salary from 520 to 1,000 florins, an unprecedented sum for a professor of mathematics. Galileo never quite mastered the optics of his combination of a plano-convex objective and a plano-concave eyepiece (our opera glass), but he succeeded in producing a thirty-power telescope, which he turned to the sky in 1610. What he saw is reported in the *Sidereus Nuncius*, which appeared in March 1610. The work was to revolutionize astronomy. The Moon was revealed to be covered with mountains (Galileo was even able to make a rough estimate of their height), the Milky Way dissolved into a multitude of starlets, new stars appeared as if out of nowhere, and, more spectacular still, four satellites were found orbiting Jupiter. This was a particularly important discovery since, if Jupiter revolved around a central body with four attendant planets, it could no longer be objected that Earth could not orbit around the Sun with its moon. Jupiter's satellites did not win the day for Copernicanism, but they removed a major obstacle to having it seriously entertained by astronomers.

In July 1610 Galileo was appointed Mathematician and Philosopher of the Grand Duke of Tuscany. Shortly thereafter he discovered that Venus has phases like the Moon, which was of great significance since it proved that Venus went around the Sun. In the summer of 1611 Galileo debated the cause of floating bodies with **Peripatetic** philosophers. Galileo maintained, along **Archimedean** lines, that the cause of floating was the relative density, against the view of his Aristotelian opponents that it was the shape. In the autumn of that year, Christoph Scheiner, a Jesuit who taught at the

> Galileo wrote to Kepler to voice his belief that the Earth is in motion and to express his fear of making his position known to the public.

Peripatetic: a follower of Aristotle.

Archimedean: following Archimedes.

"Facts which at first seem improbable will, even on scant explanation, drop the cloak which has hidden them and stand forth in naked and simple beauty."

— Galileo

bon mot: good word.

University of Ingoldstadt in Germany, announced that he had discovered spots on the Sun. Galileo took him to task for suggesting that these spots were small satellites orbiting around the Sun and insisted that he had observed the sunspots before Scheiner. In an age conscious of priorities, this was a claim that did not endear him to his rival. It also opened a breach between Galileo and the Jesuits.

In December 1613, theological objections were raised at a dinner at the Court of the Grand Duke in Pisa. Galileo was absent, but his disciple Castelli defended Galileo's views when he was asked his opinion by Christina of Lorraine, the mother of Cosimo II. Galileo felt that the matter was important enough to write a long letter to Castelli, dated December 21, 1613, which he expanded into the *Letter to the Grand Duchess Christina*, his most detailed pronouncement on the relations between science and scripture. Borrowing the **bon mot** of Cardinal Cesare Baronio, "the intention of the Holy Spirit is to teach us how to go to heaven, not how the heavens go," Galileo developed the view that God speaks through the Book of Nature as well as the Book of Scripture. In 1616 the Copernican theory was examined by the Holy Office, the Roman Congregation charged with the defense of Catholic orthodoxy. The result was a ban on the book by Copernicus and all other works containing the same teaching. Galileo himself was not mentioned but an unsigned memorandum found in the proceedings states that Galileo was enjoined not only to relinquish the theory that Earth moved but not to discuss it. (The authenticity of this document has been queried.)

Galileo returned to Florence at the end of May 1616 and turned his mind to a non-controversial topic: the determination of longitudes at sea. He hoped that accurate tables of the periods of revolutions of the satellites of Jupiter would make it possible for seamen to know their location merely by observing the satellites through a telescope, but the tables were never accurate enough for the method to be useful. In the Autumn of 1618 great excitement was generated over the appearance, in rapid succession, of three comets. Galileo thought that comets were merely optical phenomena caused by refraction in the atmosphere, and he criticized the account of Orazio Grassi, the professor of mathematics at the Roman College, who claimed the comets were celestial bodies beyond the sphere of the Moon.

What changed Galileo's Copernican fortune was the election of a Florentine, Urban VIII, to the Roman Pontificate in 1623. Galileo felt that he could now write about Earth's motion. In January 1630 his long awaited *Dialogue on the Two Chief World Systems* was completed. It is divided into four days. In the First Day, Galileo criticizes the Aristotelian division of the universe into two sharply distinct regions, the terrestrial and the celestial. He does this by attacking the apparently natural distinction between **rectilinear** and circular motion upon which Aristotle rested his case and by pointing out similarities between Earth and the Moon. In the Second Day, Galileo argues that the motion of Earth would be imperceptible to its inhabitants, and that the **diurnal** rotation of Earth on its axis is simpler than the daily revolution of all the planets and stars postulated by Ptolemy. In the Third Day, the annual revolution of Earth around the Sun is said to offer a simpler interpretation of the apparent stations and retrogressions of the planets. The Fourth Day makes the ingenious but erroneous claim that the tides are evidence for Earth's motion. The *Dialogue* also contains the correct law of falling bodies and a discussion of the principles of the relativity of motion and the conservation of motion, but Galileo assumed that inertial motion was circular rather than rectilinear.

The *Dialogue* went to press in June 1631. The publisher decided to print a thousand copies, a large edition for the time, and the work was not completed until February 21, 1632. It only reached Rome at the end of March or early April. In the summer of 1632, Urban VIII ordered a Preliminary Commission to investigate the licensing of the *Dialogue*. In the file on Galileo in the Holy Office, the commission found the unsigned memorandum of 1616 that enjoined him not to hold, teach or defend in any way that Earth moves. The Commissioners considered the injunction genuine and concluded that Galileo had **contravened** a formal order of the Holy Office. In the light of this discovery, Galileo was summoned to Rome, arriving, after much delay, on February 13, 1633. Despite his vigorous denial, Galileo was judged by the Holy Office to have contravened the orders of the Church. On the morning of June 22, 1633, he was taken to a hall in the convent of Santa Maria Sopra Minerva in Rome and was made to kneel while the sentence was read; it condemned him to imprisonment. Still kneeling, Galileo formally abjured his error. He was allowed to leave for Siena and later, in

rectilinear: characterized by straight lines.

diurnal: happening every day.

contravene: to oppose or violate.

1634, to return to Florence, where he was confined to his house in Arcetri.

Galileo sought comfort in work, and within two years he completed the *Discourses on Two New Sciences*, the book to which his lasting fame as a scientist is attached. The first of these two new sciences is a novel mathematical treatment of the structure of matter and the strength of materials. Galileo showed that there is a limit to the size of objects made of the same material and maintaining the same proportions. The second science is natural motion, which was discussed, for the first time, in the light of the times-squared law of freely falling bodies and the independent composition of motions. These laws enabled Galileo to show that the path of projectiles is a **parabola**. When he cast about for a publisher, he came up against a new problem: The Church had issued a general prohibition against printing or reprinting any of his books. Galileo's manuscript was sent to Louis Elzevir in Holland, where it appeared in 1638. Although Galileo became blind in that year, he never succeeded in obtaining the pardon he longed for, and he had to remain under house arrest until his death on January 8, 1642, five weeks before his seventy-eighth birthday. ◆

parabola: a bowl-shaped curve.

Gauss, Carl Friedrich

1777–1855 ● MATHEMATICS & ASTRONOMY

"Mathematics is the queen of the sciences, and arithmetic the queen of mathematics."

— Carl Friedrich Gauss

Born in Brunswick, Germany, the son of a bricklayer, by the age of three Gauss demonstrated that he was a mathematical prodigy by finding an error in his father's accounts. The Duke of Brunswick recognized the boy's genius, and over the objection of Gauss's parents sent him to the Collegium Capolinum and later to the University of Göttingen. In college he became known for his unusual intuition in higher mathematics; his diary discloses that the basis of virtually all his theories and discoveries were thought of in his youth. At age nineteen Gauss demonstrated how to divide a circle into seventeen equal arcs with a simple compass and a ruler.

Carl Friedrich Gauss

In 1801 Giuseppe Piazzi accidentally discovered Ceres, the largest asteroid located within the asteroid belt between Mars and Jupiter, but then lost it. Gauss derived a new mathematical procedure that predicted the location of Ceres. Using Gauss's method, other astronomers rediscovered Ceres in 1802. He was appointed the first director of the new observatory at Göttingen in 1807, conducting research and teaching his pupils, the latter not one of his favorite activities. When lecturing he would explain to his students why his right eyebrow was raised higher than the left one. "After all," he would say, "I am an astronomer."

Gauss was conversant with every branch of mathematics. His reputation was established early in his career by his work in the theory of numbers. Among other things he developed a very simple formula to determine the number of prime numbers within a given larger number. From his theory of parallels a new branch of geometry developed. This work was a revolution in the world of mathematics as it ran counter to Euclid's theories. For example, Euclid stated that the sum of the angles of a triangle equals the sum of two right angles. Gauss and his student Janos Bolyai fashioned a triangle in which the sum of its angles was less than the sum of two right

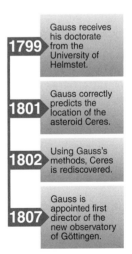

1799 Gauss receives his doctorate from the University of Helmstet.

1801 Gauss correctly predicts the location of the asteroid Ceres.

1802 Using Gauss's methods, Ceres is rediscovered.

1807 Gauss is appointed first director of the new observatory of Göttingen.

angles. Later another of Gauss's students, Friedrich Riemann, constructed a triangle, the sum of whose angles exceeded the sum of two right angles.

Gauss had developed the theory of surfaces with special attention to the curvature and the conditions for one surface to fit another. His theory of parallels was one of several starting points for Albert Einstein's theory of relativity. Additionally Gauss proved the basic theory of algebra (already in his doctoral thesis when he was twenty-two) and made advances in higher trigonometry. He himself said, "Mathematics is the queen of the sciences, and arithmetic the queen of mathematics." ◆

Goodall, Jane

1934–Present ● Zoology

"Often I have gazed into a chimpanzee's eyes and wondered what was going on behind them."
— Jane Goodall, *Through a Window*

Jane Goodall is a zoologist who has spent more than 30 years studying chimpanzees in the wild. Her research has provided the world with a detailed picture of the day-to-day lives of this primate, which scientists say is the human being's closest animal relative. Before Goodall established her observatory in the Gombe Stream Game Reserve (later renamed the Gombe Stream National Park) in 1960, our knowledge of chimpanzees was limited. Goodall's years of observation revealed that chimpanzees, like people, live in communities. Her research also revealed that chimpanzees used tools, which surprised many anthropologists who had believed that only human beings used tools.

Goodall was born in London on April 3, 1934. From an early age, she showed great interest in animals and their habitat. She had a deep yearning to go to Africa, and in 1957, her wish came true. In Africa, Goodall met the famous anthropologist Louis Leakey, who hired her as his secretary at the National Museum of Natural History. She began working in Olduvai Gorge in Tanzania. In 1960 Leakey suggested that Goodall make a long-term study of primates.

Leakey felt that women could better understand primates than men. He used his reputation and name to get funding and Goodall and her mother began the study in July of 1960.

The first major discovery to come from the research at Gombe was that chimpanzees use crude tools. This was revolutionary because, up to that point, most researchers believed that humans were the only species capable to taking an item and using it to accomplish a specific purpose.

The most famous example of the chimpanzees use of tools came when Goodall noticed them taking small twigs and pieces of grass and putting them into termite mounds, pulling out the termites and eating them. Goodall also observed chimpanzees collecting water by using chewed leaves to soak up the liquid from places they normally wouldn't be able to reach.

Goodall met her first husband in 1962 when Hugo van Lawick was sent to Gombe by the National Geographic Society to put her work on film. They were married in 1964 and had a son, Hugo. Their marriage ended in divorce in 1972. Goodall later married Derek Bryceson, who had served as a member of the Tanzanian parliament. He died of cancer in 1980.

Because of Goodall's research on chimpanzees at Gombe, Cambridge University awarded her a Ph.D in ethnology. She was one of only a few students at the prestigious English university given the doctorate without first doing undergraduate work.

As news of Goodall's discoveries spread, she began to attract attention and students from throughout the world to

> *"When I first began to read about human evolution, I learned that one of the hallmarks of our own species was that we, and only we, were capable of making tools."*
> — Jane Goodall,
>   *Through A Window*

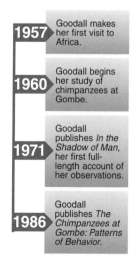

1957 Goodall makes her first visit to Africa.

1960 Goodall begins her study of chimpanzees at Gombe.

1971 Goodall publishes *In the Shadow of Man*, her first full-length account of her observations.

1986 Goodall publishes *The Chimpanzees at Gombe: Patterns of Behavior*.

> *"As long as one looks with gentleness, without arrogance, a chimpanzee will understand, and may even return the look."*
> — Jane Goodall,
> *Through A Window*

help in her research. Often with her son in tow, Goodall continued to study the primates from a long-term perspective. Goodall was eventually able to win the trust of her subjects, who allowed her unprecedented access to their lives.

On May 19, 1975, trouble struck the Gombe Reserve when four researchers were kidnapped. Marxist rebels demanded ransom for the three Americans and one Dutch student, and released them one by one over a period of two months.

Fearing for her safety, the government in Tanzania insisted that Goodall not go near Gombe until the situation was resolved. Afterward, Goodall continued her research, discovering in the late 1970s that chimps often would resort to aggressive and sometimes violent behavior in their communities. Goodall also documented that there were dominant and weak members of the community, and chimpanzees understood and respected those positions.

During her time at Gombe, Goodall realized that she could not only use the work of the reserve to explain the lives of chimpanzees to the world—she could also use it to help save them.

A devoted foe of animal research, Goodall embarked on a public crusade to stop the practice. She founded the Jane Goodall Institute in Ridgefield, Conn., whose mission is to educate people about their environment and what they can do to save it.

Goodall also funded a number of orphanages for chimpanzees who have lost their mothers. While some researchers have criticized Goodall for her compassion to those members of the chimpanzee society, she defends it vigorously.

Goodall used her relationship with the National Geographic Society to bring her research to the public through magazine and films. She also has written several books, including *My Friends the Wild Chimpanzees* (1967), *In The Shadow of Man* (1971), and her comprehensive report of her studies, *The Chimpanzees at Gombe: Patterns of Behavior* (1986). In 1995 Goodall was named a Commander of the British Empire by Queen Elizabeth II. Goodall's research at Gombe continues, making it one of the longest field studies going. ◆

Goodyear, Charles

1800–1860 • INVENTOR

Charles Goodyear gained fame after developing the process that made rubber a beneficial and usable product. Called vulcanization (after Vulcan, the Roman god of fire), Goodyear stumbled on the process after he accidentally dropped some rubber he had treated on a heated stove. Left untreated, the rubber would have quickly melted. With the process he developed, it only charred. Goodyear never saw the wealth normally associated with such a discovery because he was perpetually in debt.

Born on Dec. 29, 1800 in the Connecticut town of New Haven (home to Yale University), Goodyear was the son of a manufacturer and inventor of farm machinery. Amasa Goodyear was good at inventing farm equipment, but his business acumen was not as sharp. When he sent his son to Philadelphia in 1817, Amasa hoped Charles would develop an interest in commerce. When Charles returned to New Haven trained in the ways of merchandising, he and his father immediately established a partnership.

Amasa spent years developing and creating tools and equipment while Charles concerned himself with selling and merchandising. In 1826, two years after Charles married Clarissa Beecher, he moved his young family back to Philadelphia,

On a trip to New York in 1834, Charles Goodyear saw a rubber company's sign and decided to investigate.

where Charles opened a store stocked with his father's tools. Both men found it too easy to provide customers with credit if they couldn't pay. Because of their generosity and kind-heartedness, within five years both were bankrupt.

Instead of declaring bankruptcy, Charles developed a scheme whereby he would pay off his debt by allowing his creditors to receive royalties from any new equipment his father developed. While that satisfied some judgments, the two men's debt had amassed into more than the plan would take care of. His foray into the world of rubber came when he was on a trip to New York in 1834. He saw a rubber company's sign and decided to investigate.

What captured his immediate attention was the air valve of a life preserver, which had been poorly made. Knowing he could create a more efficient one, Goodyear began to experiment. While the shopkeeper wasn't impressed with Goodyear's efforts, he suggested that if Goodyear could find a way to make rubber products usable, it could help to revive an industry that, when it began, was one of the fastest growing in the world. "India Rubber," as it was known in 1834, melted easily during the summer and became cracked and brittle during the winter months, making it unreliable.

Rising to the challenge, Goodyear returned to his home, only to find himself arrested and jailed for not paying his debts. His first experiments with making rubber usable, therefore, were ignobly accomplished in a jail cell. Finding he could get raw rubber for next to nothing, Goodyear tried various concoctions he hoped would make him a fortune. If it weren't for the kindness and generosity of friends, whose patience Goodyear tested time and again, neither he nor his family would have eaten.

Goodyear seemed to be on the brink of yet another failure when he discovered what he thought was the key—mixing nitric acid with a metal, usually copper, then adding it to the rubber. Opening a business that used his composite product, Goodyear set out to make everyday items he thought would be popular. He even made a rubber suit and shoes, and actually wore them.

Finding no one interested in investing capital in his venture, Goodyear again failed. Ignoring pleas that he give up what seemed to many to be another hare-brained scheme, Goodyear moved his family to Roxbury, Massachusetts, which was the birthplace of America's rubber industry.

> Goodyear even made a rubber suit and shoes, and actually wore them.

1826 Goodyear opens a store in Philadelphia to sell the tools his father designed.

1834 Goodyear visits an India rubber factory in New York.

1839 Goodyear accidentally discovers vulcanization.

1844 Goodyear is granted a patent for the vulcanization process.

1860 Goodyear dies deeply in debt.

Finagling his way into an abandoned factory, Goodyear began to produce various items from rubber and hoped for an undisturbed life at last for him and his family. At this time, Goodyear became acquainted with Nathanial M. Hayward, who had discovered that rubber spread with a solution of sulfur and turpentine would prevent it from becoming sticky. Goodyear somehow convinced Hayward to assign his patent to Goodyear. Combining the two seemed to hold promising results, but something still was missing.

That something revealed itself in 1839 when Goodyear, in a fit of rage, accidentally dropped the treated product on a heated stove. Heating the mixture was the answer, although it took Goodyear some time before he found the exact amount of heat necessary. But when he was ready to make the process known, he found no one would take him seriously. After years of experimentation, Goodyear was issued Patent 3,633 for the vulcanization process in 1844.

Because Goodyear was in such deep debt, he was forced to license the product at such a low rate that he barely saw any profit from it. Also, when Goodyear sought to extend his patent internationally, he found that England would not accept it because one of its citizens claimed to have invented the process a year earlier. Goodyear lost the fight in court, but in most other European countries he received honors and several patent extensions.

After a lifetime of struggling and keeping one step ahead of debtor's prison (not always successfully), Goodyear's health began to deteriorate. In 1860, he lost a daughter unexpectedly, which, combined with his general poor health, caused his own death a few days later. When he died, it was discovered that he had left his family several hundred thousand dollars in debt. ◆

> Finagling his way into an abandoned factory, Goodyear began to produce various items from rubber.

Gutenberg, Johannes

C. 1390/1400–1468 ● INVENTOR

guild: a medieval association of merchants or craftsmen.

Gutenberg worked surreptitiously, fully conscious of the potentially historic value of his efforts.

Johannes Gutenburg was a goldsmith who is credited with inventing printing from moveable type. Little is known of his life, and the scant information that is available comes primarily from official records of his financial affairs and litigious struggles. He was born Johannes Gensfleisch in Mainz, but later assumed his mother's family name, Gutenberg. His early career as a goldsmith was cut short when, as a consequence of a prolonged conflict between the craft **guilds** and the gentry of Mainz, he was expelled from the city. Gutenberg reappeared in Strasbourg, where he established himself anew in the gold-smithing business in partnership with several other craftsmen and investors, one of whom was Andreas Dritzehn. It was during this period that Gutenberg began developing his revolutionary printing process. He worked surreptitiously, fully conscious of the potentially historic value of his efforts. Apparently, his secrecy attracted the attention of his partners, who, when they discovered the nature of Gutenberg's work, demanded that their partnership be extended to cover his new activities. He acceded to their wishes and in 1438 a new contract was prepared for the partners which stipulated that should one of them die, his heirs were not entitled to succeed him in the partnership.

When Dritzehn died only months after the contract was signed, his brothers sued Gutenberg, in spite of the explicit contractual agreement. Court records show that Gutenberg won the case. However, evidence presented during the trial indicates that Gutenberg had been working on a number of secret processes that with hindsight can be assumed to be printing from movable type.

Gutenberg had returned to Mainz by 1448. His printing experiments had progressed and he was able to demonstrate to the satisfaction of Johann Fust, a wealthy lawyer, that printing from movable type was practicable. Fust was sufficiently convinced to invest a considerable sum in Gutenberg's enterprise, against which Gutenberg was required to place his printing equipment as collateral.

Gutenberg was sued by Fust for the recovery of his loans in 1455, accusing Gutenberg of not keeping to their agreement. What actually caused their estrangement is open to speculation.

Interestingly, local legend linked Johann Fust with Dr. Faustus, suggesting a more sinister motivation. Nevertheless Gutenberg was ordered to repay the full amount of the outstanding loans plus accrued interest. Unable to do so, he surrendered to Fust his stock and printing works and abandoned all claim to his invention. Fust continued printing, ably assisted by his own son-in-law Peter Schöffer, who, at Fust's insistence, had been taken on as a copyist and calligrapher by Gutenberg.

1448 Gutenberg demonstrates to Johann Fust that printing from moveable type is practicable.

1453 The first Gutenberg (Mazarin) Bible is printed, in Latin.

1455 Gutenberg loses control of his press to Fust.

1462 Gutenberg is exiled from Mainz.

1466 Johann Mentel prints the first German language Bible.

The Progress of Printing

In the 11th century, the Chinese made the first moveable type using clay blocks carved with individual characters. But moveable type was not practicable in China because the language consists of thousands of different characters. Moveable type is better suited to languages written with a limited number of symbols, such as Latin or English. For centuries, monks in Europe spent their lives painstakingly rewriting important books. It was not until the late 14th century that printing from carved wood blocks appeared in Europe. European printers began experimenting with moveable type during the 15th century. In about 1450, Johannes Gutenberg designed a press that used separate pieces of metal type, which he could reassemble and reuse as required. With his new press, Gutenberg could print large numbers of books quickly and inexpensively. Similar presses soon spread throughout Europe. The first printing press in the American colonies was set up by Stephen Daye in 1639 in Cambridge, Massachusetts.

About this time the first copies of the Gutenberg Bible (also called the Mazarin Bible because of its discovery in about 1760 in the library of Cardinal Jules Mazarin) were printed, creating quite a stir. When Fust went to Paris, carrying with him a dozen of these exquisitely executed and immensely valuable works, he was reportedly chased out of the city by the scribes, having been accused by them of doing the devil's work in managing to possess so many identical copies of the Bible.

There are forty-seven known surviving copies of the Gutenberg Bible, of which twelve are printed on **vellum**. They list neither the name of the printer nor the place and date of impression. Consequently historians have been unable to conclusively establish whether or not the Bible was completed before Gutenberg lost control of his press in 1455, although they believe that in all likelihood he was the principal contributor to its production. That being the case, Gutenberg could have averted financial ruin by selling copies of the Bible, and why he did not do so is a mystery. Indeed, the plates for the Bible alone would in all likelihood have been worth considerably more than his debts to Fust. To add to Gutenberg's despair, an exquisite **psalter** on which he had evidently been working became the first book printed with movable type to carry the name of its publishers; it lists Fust and Schöffer.

The tribulations of Gutenberg were not to end there. With the assistance of a Mainz municipal officer Gutenberg reestablished himself in the printing business. What he did during the next few years of his life is unclear but in 1462, while Mainz was in turmoil, this time caused by a feud between its archbishop and a rival claimant, Gutenberg was once again exiled from the city.

Aging and with failing eyesight, by 1465 Gutenberg was destitute. Moved to compassion and possibly contrition, the archbishop allowed Gutenberg to return to his birthplace and gave recognition to his work as an inventor and craftsman by ennobling him. This afforded Gutenberg various privileges and entitled him to a pension, allowing him to see out his last days in comfort and security. ◆

vellum: a fine leather used for writing or printing on or for binding books.

paslter: a collection of Psalms for liturgical or devotional use.

Harvey, William

1578–1657 ● Physiology

> *"Everything is from an egg."*
> — William Harvey

English physician and physiologist William Harvey was the discoverer of the circulation of blood. Son of a successful Folkestone merchant, Harvey was educated at King's School, Cambridge, and in 1593 began studying at Cambridge University. In 1597 he traveled to Padua, Italy, for training in his chosen profession, medicine. Padua was the home of Fabricius of Aquapendente, a leading European anatomist well known for his lectures on the valves in the veins.

Harvey qualified as a physician in 1602 and returned to England, settling in London; in 1604 he married the daughter of Dr. Lancelot Browne, former physician to Elizabeth I. It is possible that through this marriage Harvey now had some influence at the court of the new king, James I. In 1609 James supported Harvey's successful application to become physician at Bartholomew's Hospital, one of the most prestigious medical posts in the capital. In 1615 he was elected Lumleian Lecturer to the Royal College of Physicians, a lifetime appointment.

vivisection: the dissection of an animal for research purposes.

For a number of years Harvey had carried out experiments with the **vivisection** of coldblooded animals and by 1618 had already made his discovery of the circulation of blood, a major landmark in the advancement of medical science. His stay at Padua had coincided with Galileo's tenure there and Harvey was deeply impressed by the Italian's theories. He applied Galileo's science of motion to the biological processes; employing his methods of qualitative calculation of moving objects, Harvey worked out how much blood was pumped by the heart. He calculated that the large amount could only be accounted for if the heart pumped the same blood over and again. He published his conclusions in *On the Motion of the Heart and Blood in Animals,* which can be seen as the foundation of comparative anatomy.

Harvey's opinions were controversial and although by the 1640s some leading scientists had come to agree with him, the majority of doctors opposed his conclusions. Medical practice continued for the rest of the century unaffected by this discovery.

Harvey also became well known as physician to leading noblemen and politicians, including Francis Bacon, the Lord Chancellor. In 1618 he reached the pinnacle of the profession with his appointment as physician to James I, a position he also held under the latter's son, Charles I.

Although Harvey's reputation as an anatomist is unchallenged, his skill as a doctor is open to question. The author John Aubrey, who was well acquainted with him, wrote of Harvey as "an excellent Anatomist, but I never heard of any that admired his therapeutic way." It is also curious that despite his understanding of blood circulation he continued to treat patients by the ancient practice of bleeding, to remove "bad blood."

Charles granted Harvey the wardenship of Merton College, Oxford, in 1646; Harvey was present when the city fell to the Parliamentary forces that same year. Harvey was sixty-eight and happy to escape the turmoil of the times in well-earned retirement. As his wife had predeceased him and they had had no children, he lived his last years with his brothers. A friend who visited him in 1650 recorded his saying that "this obscure life and vacation from public cares which would disgust other minds is the medicine of mine." ◆

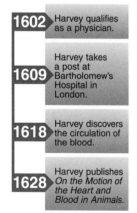

1602 Harvey qualifies as a physician.

1609 Harvey takes a post at Bartholomew's Hospital in London.

1618 Harvey discovers the circulation of the blood.

1628 Harvey publishes *On the Motion of the Heart and Blood in Animals.*

Hawking, Stephen William

1942–PRESENT ● THEORETICAL PHYSICS

"What is the nature of the universe? What is our place in it and where did it and we come from? Why is it the way it is?"
— Stephen Hawking, A *Brief History of Time*

This 20th-century physicist, whose work in cosmology is considered to be as important as the work of predecessors Isaac Newton and Albert Einstein, was born in Oxford, England, on Jan. 8, 1942. Even as a youth attending St. Alban's School near London, Hawking was avidly interested in mathematics and physics, though his father had high aspirations his son would become a doctor. The boy's ambitions won out, however, for in his teens he attended University College, Oxford, where he studied physics and earned a B.A. degree in natural science in 1962.

While at Oxford, Hawking attended a summer course at the Royal Observatory that whetted his appetite for relativity and quantum mechanics (which focuses on matter at the sub-atomic level). This led him to pursue a postgraduate degree as a research student in general relativity at the Cambridge University's Department of Applied Mathematics and Theoretical Physics. He received his doctorate from Cambridge in 1966.

Almost from the beginning of his professional career, Hawking's research concentrated on the concept of "singularities," which deals with objects that have extremely high densities placed into very small volumes. In this realm, crossing beyond the threshold of traditional laws of physics, Hawking

"Does the universe in fact have a beginning or an end?"
— Stephen Hawking, A *Brief History of Time*

determined to link the worlds of quantum mechanics and relativity by developing a quantum theory of gravity. In the late 1960s, he developed a mathematical theory of casuality in curved space and time and demonstrated that a singularity must have occurred at the beginning of the universe.

According to Hawking, at the time of the Big Bang a great deal of mass existed in a tiny space until a huge explosion thrust the contents outward. The universe is still expanding today.

Working with Oxford physicist Roger Penrose, Hawking speculated that the universe was much denser before the Big Bang. At that time, he wrote, all matter would have been a singularity, in which all the laws of physics break down. Therefore, the state of the universe does not depend on anything that happened before the Big Bang; the universe has evolved from the Big Bang independently of what it was like before the Big Bang.

This theory, which contradicted previous Big Bang theories, also emphasized the existence of "black holes." Hawking identified black holes as prime examples of singularities. These theoretical black holes can be no larger than elementary particles with a surface gravity so strong that light cannot escape from within them. Behind them other universes might be concealed. Contrary to earlier assumptions, however, Hawking suggested that black holes emit particles (thermal radiation) that shrink with time and, furthermore, their temperatures rise in doing so. As their temperatures increase, they eventually evaporate with an energy burst.

These "virtual particles," as Hawking calls them, which cannot be observed by particle detectors (but may be detected indirectly), are rampant in empty space, created out of nothing, and can form antiparticle pairs that destroy each other. Over the following decade, Hawking further theorized that when a particle is created near the vicinity of a black hole, half of it disappears into the black hole while the remainder dissolves as thermal energy.

In the early 1970s, Hawking successfully demonstrated the validity of the "no-hair theorem," a hypothesis conceived earlier by John Wheeler. Through mathematics, and with support from peers in the field of cosmology, Hawking determined the only properties of matter inside a black hole are its mass, its momentum, and its electric charge. In the wake,

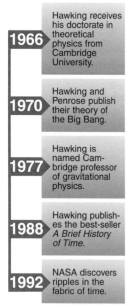

1966 Hawking receives his doctorate in theoretical physics from Cambridge University.

1970 Hawking and Penrose publish their theory of the Big Bang.

1977 Hawking is named Cambridge professor of gravitational physics.

1988 Hawking publishes the best-seller A *Brief History of Time.*

1992 NASA discovers ripples in the fabric of time.

matter loses its shape, its **baryon** number, and its identification as matter or antimatter.

In 1992, NASA announced that its Cosmic Backgrounder satellite had discovered "ripples" in the fabric of space. Hawking proclaimed this find "the discovery of the century, if not all time," for they were, he said, actual remnants of the Big Bang.

Besides his work with black holes and the Big Bang, Hawking is equally known for his "no boundary proposal." This calculation, which he worked out with American physics professor James Hartle during the 1980s, allows physicists to equate the universe contemporary with the time of the Big Bang. The equation flatly rejects earlier beliefs that such a determination is impossible. For this work, the team was awarded the Wolf Foundation Prize in 1988.

The many other honors and professional citations Hawking has received include induction as a Fellow of the Royal Society, as a member of the National Academy of Sciences, and as a Companion of Honor. He holds a dozen honorary degrees. During his illustrious career, he has served as professor of gravitational physics and Lucasian professor of mathematics at Cambridge.

What makes Hawking even more remarkable is the fact that he has been able to accomplish his work from a wheelchair. He is a victim of ALS—amyotrophic lateral sclerosis—commonly known as Lou Gehrig's disease, named after the baseball hall of fame recipient who was first formally diagnosed with the affliction. A crippling degeneration of the nervous system, Hawking was diagnosed with the disease while yet a student at Oxford in his 20s. Because he lost his voice with the removal of his trachea in 1985, he uses an electronic synthesizer, attached to his wheelchair, to communicate. Despite doctors' prognoses of an early death, Hawking has beat the odds. He continues to develop and clarify the origins of what is generically referred to as "space and time."

Hawking is the author and co-author of many articles and books. Among his theses are *General Relativity: An Einstein Centenary Survey* and *The Large-Scale Structure of Spacetime*. Books include the 1998 best-seller, *A Brief History of Time: From the Big Bang to Black Holes*, which simplifies his extremely complex theories for general readers (and which

"Why does the universe go to all the trouble of existing?"
— Stephen Hawking, *A Brief History of Time*

baryon: a class of elementary particles consisting of three quarks each.

was produced as a feature film) and *Black Holes and Baby Universes*, published in 1994.

Best summarizing the results of his professional achievements is a personal quote: "There is no prescribed route to follow to arrive at a new idea. You have to make the intuitive leap. But, the difference is that once you've made the intuitive leap you have to justify it by filling in the intermediate steps." ◆

Heisenberg, Werner Karl

1901–1976 ● THEORETICAL PHYSICS

> *"We have to remember that what we observe is not nature in itself but nature exposed to our method of questioning."*
> — Werner Karl Heisenberg, *Physics and Philosophy*

Heisenberg was born on December 5, 1901, in Würzburg, Germany. He was the younger son of August and Anna Wecklein Heisenberg. The family belonged to the academic upper middle class of Wilhelmian Germany. Heisenberg's father, an authority on the Byzantine empire, taught classical languages at a Würzburg gymnasium (high school) and became professor of Greek philology at the University of Munich. His mother was the daughter of a Munich gymnasium principal. His brother, Erwin, became a chemist in Berlin. In 1937 Heisenberg married Elisabeth

Schumacher, the daughter of a noted Berlin professor of economics. They had seven children.

Heisenberg attended primary schools in Würzburg and Munich before entering his grandfather's gymnasium in 1911. Distinguishing himself in mathematics and classical piano, he graduated at the top of his class and entered the University of Munich in 1920. There he studied theoretical atomic physics and hydrodynamics with Arnold Sommerfeld. After receiving his doctorate in the record time of three years, Heisenberg served as a postdoctoral assistant to Max Born in Göttingen and Niels Bohr in Copenhagen. In 1927 he was appointed Professor of Theoretical Physics at the University of Leipzig, at that time Germany's youngest full professor. In 1942 Heisenberg assumed directorship of the Kaiser Wilhelm Institute for Physics in Berlin, a government sponsored research institute. He remained with the institute thereafter.

Heisenberg is best known for his contributions to quantum mechanics, the new physics of the atom and its interactions with light and other atoms. As a leading member of the small group of mainly European young men who created quantum mechanics during the 1920s, Heisenberg made the initial breakthrough in the field. He relied on laboratory data about the atom to reinterpret the equations of the motion of electrons in atoms as quantum expressions. This led to the use of mathematical entities known as matrices; his new quantum mechanics is still called matrix mechanics. The uniting of matrix mechanics with the alternative wave mechanics developed by Erwin Schrödinger, as well as the introduction of electron spin, resulted in modern quantum mechanics. Heisenberg received the 1932 Nobel Prize for physics for his work on quantum mechanics and its applications to hydrogen molecules.

However successful, the new quantum mechanics of atomic events still required an interpretation or a set of rules for linking the everyday world of the laboratory with the strange world of the atom. In 1927 Heisenberg presented the uncertainty, or in determinacy, principle that, together with Bohr's complementarity principle, formed the so-called Copenhagen interpretation of quantum mechanics. Although debated ever since, it remains the dominant interpretation.

As elaborated by Bohr, the Copenhagen interpretation relies upon the wave-particle **duality**—the notion that, under

1925 ▸ Heisenberg creates a new theory of quantum mechanics called matrix mechanics.

1927 ▸ Heisenberg is appointed Professor of Theoretical Physics at the University of Leipzig.

1927 ▸ Heisenberg formulates the uncertainty, or indeterminacy, principle.

1932 ▸ Heisenberg receives the Nobel Prize for physics.

1942 ▸ Heisenberg heads Germany's effort to construct an atomic bomb.

duality: the condition of consisting of two parts.

certain circumstances, particles can behave as waves and waves as particles. Quantum objects exist as both waves and particles until observed in a laboratory. The act of observation involves choosing one side of the duality, thereby disturbing nature in such a way that Heisenberg's uncertainty principle comes into play. According to this principle, the position and speed (or momentum) of a quantum object at a given instant cannot be measured simultaneously with absolute precision. The more precise the measurement of one variable, the more imprecise, or uncertain, is the other. The same held for the variables of energy and time. Among the many consequences of this principle is the renunciation of strict **causality**, the exact determination of the future on the basis of the present. Since we cannot measure all of the mechanical variables of a quantum object at a given time with absolute precision, we cannot determine its future motion with absolute certainty; we can make only statistical predictions about its probable future motions. As Born showed, the probabilities can be derived from the wave functions of Schrödinger's wave mechanics. A number of physicists, most notably Albert Einstein, objected to the introduction of probabilities and statistics into the foundations of physics. Although Einstein insisted that nature is not statistical, which he expressed by his famous statement that God "does not play dice," he did not succeed in refuting the new physics.

Following the completion of quantum mechanics, Heisenberg worked with Wolfgang Pauli and others to obtain a relativistic form of quantum mechanics for application to high-energy particles and fields. After the discovery of the neutron in 1932, Heisenberg developed the first neutron-proton theory of the nucleus. With the discovery of nuclear forces, Heisenberg intensified his work on relativistic quantum field theories. To the end of his life he searched for a unified theory of elementary particles based upon a unification of all forces, or fields.

Coming of age at the end of World War I, Heisenberg directly experienced the social upheavals of the postwar period in Germany. He became an ardent follower of the German youth movement, developing an unbreakable attachment to Germany. After Adolf Hitler's rise to power in Germany, Heisenberg suffered many indignities but convinced himself that he could help German physics best by remaining at his

causality: the relation between a cause and its effect.

Heisenberg's uncertainty principle relies on the notion that, under certain circumstances, particles behave as waves and waves as particles.

Classical Physics Versus Quantum Physics

The uncertainty principle was formulated by Werner Heisenberg in the 1920s as part of the then new theory of quantum mechanics, which was developed in response to the inability of traditional "classical" physics to explain the properties of atoms and subatomic particles. Classical physics, the physics of Newton and Einstein, deals with the universe of observable objects, such as people and planets, which are made up of many atoms and move through space and time. Quantum physics, on the other hand, deals with individual atoms and subatomic particles, such as quarks, neutrinos, and electrons. Such particles cannot be observed; their existence can only be indirectly detected.

When physicists began investigating the quantum universe, they learned that it seemed to be governed by a different set of rules than the universe of classical physics. Newton and Einstein described objects whose behavior is orderly and predictable. Quantum physics revealed a universe of particles whose behavior is unpredictable and apparently arbitrary. The fundamental uncertainty of quantum theory caused unease among classical physicists. Einstein himself could never fully accept that the universe was governed by chance. He tried to find ways around the uncertainty principle, but never succeeded in refuting it. By the late 20th century, the factual basis of the uncertainly principle had been firmly established and was almost universally accepted. Nonetheless, there remains a gap between our knowledge of the multi-atom universe and our knowledge of the subatomic universe. To date, physicists have failed to completely reconcile classical and quantum physics.

post. His reactions to the Nazis were typical of the non-Jewish cultural elite of Germany. After the discovery of nuclear fission and the out break of World War II, Heisenberg became a leader in German development of nuclear fission. Moving to Berlin in 1942, he headed the main German effort aimed at attaining a sustained chain reaction and, at first, an atomic bomb. The project did not achieve either goal. Although never a Nazi, he traveled as a German cultural representative to Nazi occupied countries and maintained direct access to important government figures. He was greatly criticized after the war for his wartime activities. His aims and motives are still the subject of debate. After the war, Heisenberg again became a leading figure in German science policy, attempting to reestablish international relations and successfully arguing for a West German nuclear reactor program and against West German access to nuclear weapons. He also traveled widely, speaking frequently on the philosophical and cultural significance of quantum mechanics.

He died in Munich, Germany, on February 1, 1976. ◆

Helmholtz, Hermann L. F. von

1821–1894 ● THERMODYNAMICS & ELECTRODYNAMICS

> *"Nature as a whole possesses a store of force which cannot in any way be either increased or diminished."*
> — Hermann L. F. von Helmholtz

ophthalmoscope: an instrument for examining the interior of the eye.

hydrodynamics: the branch of physics that deals with the motion of fluids and with solid bodies immersed in fluids.

Helmholtz was born on August 31, 1821, at Potsdam, Germany, just outside Berlin, the son of a secondary school teacher. He studied medicine and served briefly as an army doctor, then taught anatomy and physiology at the universities of Königsberg, Bonn, and Heidelberg. Easily the most versatile scientist of his age, he formulated the principle of the conservation of energy, invented the **ophthalmoscope**, laid the foundations of modern physiological optics and acoustics, and produced many elegant popular lectures on scientific and philosophical topics. In 1871, amid great political fanfare, Prussia appointed the former physiologist to the prestigious chair of physics at the University of Berlin. In 1887, as the doyen of German natural science, he was named president of the newly created Imperial Institute for Physics and Technology.

Throughout his career Helmholtz sought the underlying principles that unify and govern natural phenomena. He wrote on **hydrodynamic** theory and on the energetics of reaction chemistry, and near the end of his career worked to found scientific laws on the principle of least action and reconcile the second law of thermodynamics with the laws of mechanics. The roots of all these contributions, however, lay in his epic formulation of the principle of the conservation of energy in 1847.

Physicists had traditionally described the living force of a system of moving bodies as the sum of the components' individual masses times the square of their velocities. Because perpetual motion is impossible, the living force can be increased only if work is done on the system. However, engineering tradition agreed that in real systems living force could be lost, through friction or inelastic collisions. Another, more mathematical tradition of analytic mechanics described mechanical systems through mathematical functions known as potentials. Potentials were functions of the spatial position of the objects in the system, and they were known to possess a fixed value for every state of the system, no matter how the state had moved or changed in reaching that state. Sadi Carnot had used this remarkable property indirectly in his famous analysis of heat engines working through closed cycles. In general, however, this tradition attributed no physical significance to the potential, only an abstract, mathematical usefulness.

Helmholtz synthesized these approaches in 1847. He wrote that changes in the living force of a system must be compensated by changes in a mathematical entity possessing the properties both of the work and the potential. He called that entity the tension force in the system. The tension force represented for Helmholtz the total amount of force that is stored in a system and is available to do work in increasing the living force. Living forces and tension forces are interconvertible, but their sum must be constant. Within a few years physicists had renamed Helmholtz's tension force the potential energy of a system; the living force became the kinetic energy; and their sum was the total energy of the system.

Helmholtz recognized that most of the phenomena that interest physicists cannot be analyzed in practice directly in terms of the motions of their ultimate parts. He devoted most of his 1847 paper to discussing how his conservation principle might be applied to apparently non-mechanical phenomena such as optics, frictional electricity, electromagnetism, electric circuits containing voltaic batteries or thermoelectric sources, and heat and the expansion of gases. He defended the mechanical theory of heat, arguing that living force apparently lost through friction or inelastic collisions is actually

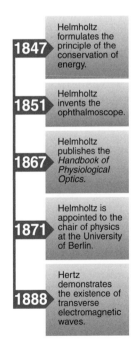

1847 Helmholtz formulates the principle of the conservation of energy.

1851 Helmholtz invents the ophthalmoscope.

1867 Helmholtz publishes the *Handbook of Physiological Optics*.

1871 Helmholtz is appointed to the chair of physics at the University of Berlin.

1888 Hertz demonstrates the existence of transverse electromagnetic waves.

"All that science can hope to achieve is a perfect knowledge and a perfect understanding of the action of natural and moral forces."

— Hermann L. F. von Helmholtz

energetics: the total energy relations and transformations of a physical, chemical, or biological system.

conserved as the vibratory kinetic energy of molecules (free heat) or is converted to tension force. He also discussed the existing experimental data, much of it from James Joule, pointing to fixed conversion equivalents among different forms of energy. Helmholtz also applied energy conservation to living organisms. He argued that animals convert the tension force stored chemically in foodstuffs to heat (in the form of body heat) and work (as muscular exertion) and that they have no other particularly vital source of energy. Physiological issues like this, in particular the origin of the body heat, seem to have motivated Helmholtz's initial interest in the physics of energy conservation.

Energetics guided all Helmholtz's science, including his later contributions to the development of electrodynamics. In the nineteenth century, continental physicists pursued action-at-a-distance approaches to these effects. They sought electrodynamic forces analogous to the force of gravitation, by which a moving charge carrier acts directly across space to influence a similar entity. German physicist Wilhelm Weber derived such a force law in 1846; however, the force that he postulated varied not only with the distance but with the relative velocities and accelerations of the bodies between which the electrodynamic effects acted. In England, Michael Faraday and James Clerk Maxwell conceived electrodynamic phenomena in a very different way. Their field approach envisioned electrodynamic action as propagated across space through contiguous effects in the medium.

Helmholtz introduced Maxwell's field theory to the continent in a form that continental physicists could more readily understand. He believed that forces that vary with velocity cannot conserve energy; therefore, he attacked Weber's theory and sought a more abstract approach to electrodynamics. Helmholtz derived a generalized potential law, from which he claimed that all the various contending theories of electrodynamics, including those of Maxwell and Weber, could be deduced as special cases, depending on the assumptions one made about the medium. Only experiment could decide which special case was actually realized in nature, Helmholtz taught, but he came more and more to favor the Maxwellian limit, in which action-at-a distance effects became negligible. In his laboratory, Helmholtz set his students to experimental tests of the Maxwellian alternative.

In 1888 one of them, Heinrich Hertz, demonstrated the existence of the transverse electromagnetic waves that could be predicted from Maxwell's theory or from Helmholtz's generalized potential. Ironically, Helmholtz's success in popularizing Maxwell's theory on the continent caused his own approach to electrodynamics to be quickly forgotten. Here as elsewhere, however, Helmholtz's insistence on abstraction, synthesis, and ultimate principles powerfully influenced the classical physics of the nineteenth century.

Helmholtz died in Berlin on September 8, 1894. ◆

Henson, Matthew Alexander

1866–1955 ● EXPLORER

Matthew Henson was born on August 8, 1866, in rural Charles County, Maryland, the son of freeborn sharecroppers. At the age of four, Henson and his family moved to Washington, D.C. When he was still a young child both of his parents died, and Henson and his siblings were put under the care of an uncle in Washington. At the age of twelve he left school, traveled to Baltimore, and started his career as a seaman when he was hired as a cabin boy on a ship sailing out of the port city. Henson spent the remainder of his adolescence traveling around the world as a merchant sailor and working menial jobs when back on the East Coast.

At the age of twenty, while working as a clerk in a Baltimore hat store, Henson was hired by U.S. Navy Lt. Robert E. Peary to be Peary's personal servant on a survey expedition for the building of a Central American canal. When the expedition returned to the U.S. in 1888, Henson followed Peary to the League Island Navy Yard, where he worked as a courier.

In 1891 Peary received a commission to explore northern Greenland and again hired Henson as a personal assistant,

> *"The long quest for the North Pole is over and the awful space that separated man from the Ultima Thule has been bridged. There is no more beyond."*
> — Matthew Henson

despite Peary's concern that a "son of the tropics" would not be able to withstand Arctic weather. While surveying Greenland, Henson grew close to the native Inuits, learned the Inuit language, became the expedition's most able dogsled driver, and acted as liaison with the Inuits, who were used as guides and porters by the survey team. Henson and Peary returned to the United States in the summer of 1892 and spent a year touring the country presenting lectures and reenactments of their Greenland expedition. On a second explo-

Matthew Alexander Henson

ration of Greenland, from 1893 to 1895, Peary and Henson led an aborted attempt at reaching the North Pole. For the next eleven years, Peary, with Henson as his chief assistant, led five more unsuccessful attempts at the North Pole, each time succumbing to frostbite or Arctic storms.

In July of 1908, Peary, Henson, and a crew of twenty-seven aboard a specially made icebreaking ship left New York for a final attempt at the pole. In February of 1909, having arrived at Cape Sheridan, between the northern tip of Greenland and the frozen edge of the Arctic Ocean, Peary led a team of twenty two, with Henson as one of his chief lieutenants, across the polar ice cap. On April 6, 1909, Peary, Henson, and four Eskimos became the first people to reach the North Pole.

Upon returning to the mainland, Peary was confronted with the news that Frederick Cook had claimed to have reached the North Pole one year earlier. Thus began a protracted and bitter public controversy over the veracity of each man's claim. By the end of 1910, however, most scientific societies had rejected Cook's account and accepted Peary's.

Though celebrated by African-American leaders for many years, Henson was largely unrecognized by the white public as the co-discoverer of the North Pole. After the historic expedition of 1909, Henson spent the rest of his working life as a messenger in the U.S. Customs House and in the Post Office in New York City. In his later years he finally won some of the honors he deserved. The Explorers Club made Henson its first African-American member in 1937. In 1944 Congress awarded him a medal for his co-discovery of the North Pole. In 1948 he was given the Gold Medal of the Geographical Society of Chicago. In 1950 he was honored at the Pentagon, and in 1954, a year before his death on March 9, 1955, he was received at the White House by President Eisenhower. A U.S. postage stamp commemorating his achievement was issued in 1986. ◆

"If you will get out your geography and turn to the map of the Western Hemisphere you will be able to follow me."

— Matthew Henson

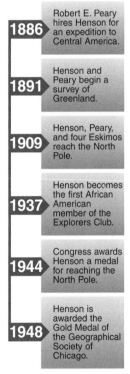

1886 Robert E. Peary hires Henson for an expedition to Central America.

1891 Henson and Peary begin a survey of Greenland.

1909 Henson, Peary, and four Eskimos reach the North Pole.

1937 Henson becomes the first African American member of the Explorers Club.

1944 Congress awards Henson a medal for reaching the North Pole.

1948 Henson is awarded the Gold Medal of the Geographical Society of Chicago.

Herschel, Sir William

1738–1822 ● ASTRONOMY

Herschel, Caroline

1750–1848 ● ASTRONOMY

Herschel, John F. W.

1792–1871 ● ASTRONOMY

"Every student who enters upon a scientific pursuit, especially if at a somewhat advanced period of life, will find not only that he has much to learn, but much also to unlearn."

— John Herschel

reflector: a telescope in which the principal focusing element is a mirror.

Few families have been such prolific contributors to astronomy as were the Herschels: William (originally Frederich Wilhelm), his sister Caroline Lucretia, and William's son John Frederick William. These three astronomers are renowned for the discovery of Uranus, the building of large telescopes, the discovery of comets and moons, the compilation of a catalog of star clusters and nebulae, numerous solar studies, and extensive observations of the southern hemisphere sky, among other accomplishments.

Sir William Herschel was born in Hanover, Germany, on 15 November 1738. His father, Isaac Herschel, was the regimental bandmaster in the Hanover Guards Band, and at age fifteen William joined his father and older brother as a musician in the band. At the start of the Seven Years' War in 1757, William moved to England and held various teaching and musician positions in several English cities over the next twenty-five years. After moving to Bath in 1766, William began an in-depth study of mathematics, optics, and astronomy. He rented a 60 cm focal length Gregorian **reflector** to begin his study of the skies, progressively making several larger telescopes of his own (reflectors of 1.5 m, 3 m, 6 m, 9 m, and 12 m focal lengths as well as over two hundred mirrors of 2.10 m focal length) as his interest in astronomy intensified. Using these telescopes (the best of the day), William began a methodical and ambitious program to survey the heavens in an attempt to determine the three-dimensional structure of the Milky Way. In the course of his observations, he studied over 2,500 nebulae and star clusters, discovered over eight hundred double stars and showed that some of these stars revolved around each other (the first proof that the law of gravitation applied beyond the solar system), and was a pioneer in the new area of stellar **photometry**. William is best known, however, for his observation of a greenish blue disk on the night of 13 March 1781. At first he thought the object was a comet, but he soon realized that it was a planet, the first to be discovered telescopically. William named the object Georgium Sidus (George's Star), after England's King George III, but this name was rejected in favor of Uranus (God of the Heavens). William was elected a fellow of the Royal Society in 1781 and received the Copley Medal that same year in recognition of his discovery of Uranus. He was granted a pension by King George III, which enabled him to retire from his music career and practice astronomy full time. Following his discovery of Uranus, William discovered two of the planet's moons (Titania and Oberon) in 1787 as well as two moons around Saturn (Enceladus and Mimas) in 1789. He was the first to suggest that the Sun moves around the center of the Galaxy, and he discovered the infrared region of the electromagnetic spectrum. He continued an active observing and publishing schedule in spite of declining health. William died in Slough, Buckinghamshire, England, on 25 August 1822.

Caroline Herschel was born 16 March 1750, in Hanover, Germany, the younger of two girls in the Herschel household. Against the desires of her mother, Caroline actively participated in philosophical and scientific discussions with her father and brothers and pursued instruction in a musical career. Following her father's death in 1767, Caroline performed the household duties for her mother, Anna, and older brother, Jacob, until William brought her to Bath, England, in 1772 to encourage her singing career. She sang in oratorios in Bath, Bristol, and other English cities until 1782, when she began to devote herself full-time to assisting William with his astronomical observations. She served as recorder of his observations, executed the extensive calculations necessary for his work, prepared the star cluster and nebulae catalog for publication, and edited his papers prior to their submission for publication. William gave Caroline a small refracting telescope in 1782, and she began independent studies of the heavens. After she discovered three new nebulae in 1783,

photometry: the science that deals with measurement of the intensity of light.

1781 William Herschel observes the planet Uranus with a telescope.

1786 Caroline Herschel discovers the first of eight comets.

1787 William discovers the two moons of Uranus.

1789 William discovers two moons around Saturn.

1819 John Herschel pioneers the use of chemical analysis of the Sun.

1834 John begins studying the southern hemisphere sky.

1836 John records the amount of the Sun's radiation.

1864 John studies the structure of solar floccules.

William gave her a larger reflecting telescope, which she used when William was away from home and opportunities for her to conduct independent research occurred. Caroline discovered eight comets between 1786 and 1797, a record by a woman astronomer, which was not surpassed until 1987 (by

Sir William Hershel and his sister Caroline at the telescope.

Carolyn Shoemaker). Caroline was granted a stipend by King George III in 1787 for serving as William's assistant. Shortly after the discovery of her last comet in 1797, Caroline compiled a cross index of Flamsteed's Star Catalogue, making it much more useful for astronomical observations. This index was published by the Royal Society in 1798 as the *Catalog of Stars*. Following William's death in 1822, Caroline returned to Hanover, where she compiled a new catalog of nebulae arranged by zone. Her astronomical contributions were acknowledged with gold medals from the Royal Astronomical Society (1828) and the King of Prussia (1846), and she was awarded honorary membership in the Royal Astronomical Society (1835), since women were not permitted to be full members at the time. Caroline died in Hanover on 9 January 1848.

> **In 1835, Caroline Herschel was awarded honorary membership in the Royal Astronomical Society, since women were not permitted to be full members at the time.**

The Herschel legacy was continued by William's only son, John, who was born on 7 March 1792, in Slough, England. Sir John Herschel contributed to many areas of science and mathematics, including terrestrial magnetism, photography, differential calculus, finite differences, summation of series, calculus of operations, and optics. John devoted much of his life to studies of the Sun, pioneering the use of chemical analysis of the solar spectrum in 1819, recording the first satisfactory measurements of the amount of solar radiations in 1836, and studying the structure of solar floccules in 1864. During the 1820s John continued and revised his father's studies of **binary** star systems, nebulae, and star clusters in the northern hemisphere. From 1834 to 1838, he observed the southern hemisphere sky from the observatory at the Cape of Good Hope in South Africa, concentrating on observations of nebulae and star clusters and revising the nomenclature of the southern stars. John was a cofounder of the Analytical Society of Cambridge in 1813, the same year he was elected a fellow of the Royal Astronomical Society. He served as president of the Royal Society between 1827 and 1832. He received numerous medals and awards from a variety of scientific societies throughout his lifetime, including a gold medal and the Lalande prize from the Royal Society in 1825. He also served in several nonscientific positions, including lord rector at Marischall College in Aberdeen (1842) and master of the mint (1850–1855). John died on 11 May 1871, in Collingwood, Kent, England. ◆

binary: consisting of two parts.

Hertz, Heinrich Rudolf

1857–1894 ● PHYSICS

> *"I am here to support the assertion that light of every kind is itself an electrical phenomenon—the light of the sun, the light of the candle, the light of a glow worm."*
> — Heinrich Rudolf Hertz

German physicist Heinrich Hertz's experimental work provided the first proof of the existence of electromagnetic radiation. Hertz was born the son of a successful Hamburg lawyer and parliamentarian, and was raised as a devout Lutheran despite his father's Jewish origins. He excelled at school, exhibiting particular talent in language and natural sciences. By the time of his matriculation, Hertz was beset by uncertainty about a suitable career: his first intention was to study engineering, and in 1876 he enrolled in the Dresden Polytechnic. However, he soon realized that the regulated life of an engineer did not suit his temperament, and after consulting with his father decided to go into academic research.

After completing a year of mandatory military service in 1877, Hertz entered the University of Munich to study applied mathematics. The following year he moved to Berlin, which at the time was a major center of physics research. Although only in his second year of study, his individual research and dedication quickly drew the attention of Hermann von Helmholtz, the noted professor of physics in Berlin. Helmholtz was to fill the role of his mentor and, later, close friend.

Hertz began his doctoral dissertation into electromagnetic **induction** at the end of 1879, completing it with distinction within just three months. His first salaried position was as Helmholtz's assistant at the Berlin Physical Institute, where he remained for the next three years, publishing diverse papers and building a sound reputation, particularly in the field of electricity.

Transferring to Kiel as a *privatdozent* (lecturer) in 1888, Hertz was pleased to find his lectures popular, both for their content and for his manner of presentation. However, he was frustrated by the lack of a physics laboratory, and when Kiel offered him an associate professorship in 1885, he refused it, preferring to find a faculty that could offer him more than just theoretical experience.

That offer came from Karlsruhe, where he spent the following four years in research that was to make him famous. By the end of 1888 he had demonstrated the existence of finitely propagated electric waves of air and proven that electromagnetic radiation traveled at the speed of light. His work drew immediate acclaim worldwide. At the age of thirty-one Hertz found himself a much sought-after physicist. He could now select a chair that best suited his wish to extend his practical research, and accepted the physics professorship in Bonn.

Hertz began to amass an impressive array of awards and accolades. However, at about this time he began to suffer from a malignant facial bone condition. His first symptom was a mild toothache and by early 1889 he had had all his teeth pulled. He was forced to stop work for some time in 1892, due to the extreme pain he was enduring in his throat and nose. His doctors were baffled and unable to prevent further deterioration. Over the next few months, depressed as much by his forced retirement as by the disease, Hertz underwent several operations to no avail. He intermittently worked on a theoretical study of the principles of mechanics, which he managed to hand to the publishers in December, 1893, dedicating it to Helmholtz. On New Years Day 1894, Hertz died at thirty-six.

induction: the process by which an electrical conductor becomes electrified when near a charged body, or a magnetized body becomes magnetized when near a magnetic field.

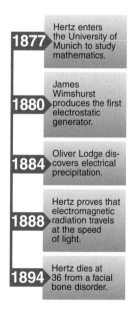

1877 Hertz enters the University of Munich to study mathematics.

1880 James Wimshurst produces the first electrostatic generator.

1884 Oliver Lodge discovers electrical precipitation.

1888 Hertz proves that electromagnetic radiation travels at the speed of light.

1894 Hertz dies at 36 from a facial bone disorder.

The unit of frequency was named "the hertz" to honor his work, though because of his Jewish background that name was dropped in Germany during Nazi rule, when his wife and two children were forced to emigrate to England in 1937 because of their Jewish origin. ◆

Hippocrates

C. 460–C. 370 BCE ● MEDICINE

> *"As to diseases make a habit of two things—to help, or at least, to do no harm."*
>
> — Hippocrates

pathological: caused or altered by disease.

The most famous physician of antiquity and founder of modern scientific medicine, Hippocrates became known as "the father of medicine." Very little is known with certainty about his life. He came from a family with a tradition of practicing medicine and was born in Cos, off the coast of Asia Minor. There, he founded a school of medicine at the famous temple of Asclepius, the god of healing and medicine. Traveling extensively, Hippocrates taught and practiced throughout Greece. He became so famous that he was consulted by kings—among them King Artaxerxes I of Persia—and his help was requested by the Athenians during a severe epidemic that struck the city-state in 430 BCE.

Hippocrates favored prognosis over diagnosis. A good physician, he believed, should learn through observation to foretell the course of a disease; after the initial manifestations of the malady appear, the physician should be able to predict its course. In most cases, he believed, there is a critical stage, the crisis, that indicates the forthcoming end—of the disease or of the patient. The almost mathematical calculation of the day of the crisis was a characteristic element of Hippocrates' theory. If, during the crisis, the natural heat of the body of the patient can overcome the **pathological** elements and reject them, recovery follows. Nature, that is the constitution of the patient, is always the main healing factor; the physician can only decrease or eradicate the obstacles opposing the natural defenses of the body. That is why Hippocrates did not make much use of drugs; instead, he prescribed fresh air, enemas, **emetics**, massages, bleeding, cupping, and hydrotherapy. He primarily prescribed a healthy way of life to prevent illness.

emetic: an agent that induces vomiting.

Of the extant collection of works related to medicine known as the Hippocratic Collection (*Corpus Hippocraticus*), very few can be definitively attributed to Hippocrates. The works cover all fields of medicine: surgery, dietetics, pharmacology, prognostics, therapeutics, and ethics. Presumably they are, in part, remains of the medical literature of the fifth and fourth centuries BCE, including that of the Hippocratic school. Among the more important of these writings are the book on epidemics, which includes case studies; the treatise on epilepsy, in which the ailment is explained by natural causes rather than by demonic possession; and the *Aphorisms*, which were used as textbooks until the nineteenth century. Another work, *Airs, Waters, and Places*, can be considered today as a treatise on human ecology, as it stresses the effects of food, occupation, and climate in causing disease.

Hippocrates gained eternal fame as the ideal physician, in part because he ennobled the medical profession by emphasizing medical ethics. In taking the Hippocratic oath (ascribed to him almost certainly incorrectly), physicians down through the ages have sworn to maintain the ethics associated with him and his school. ◆

Hubble, Edwin Powell

1889–1953 ● ASTRONOMY

Hubble was born in Marshfield, Missouri, November 20, 1889, the third of seven children. In 1898 his father transferred to the Chicago agency of his fire insurance firm and moved the family first to Evanston, and then to Wheaton, just outside Chicago. At Wheaton High School, Hubble was a star athlete as well as a scholar, and he continued his athletic accomplishments at the University of Chicago. Hubble was two years younger than most of his classmates, but he was 6' 3" tall and very well coordinated. He starred on the basketball team that won the Big Ten title his senior year, and he often placed in Big Ten dual track meets in both the shot put and the high jump. He was also elected vice president of his senior class. In 1910 Hubble went to Oxford University as a Rhodes Scholar, a high honor awarded to a single outstanding student-athlete-leader in each state.

After three years at Oxford studying law, traveling through Europe during vacations, and competing in athletics (high jump, broad jump, shot put, hammer throw, running events, and water polo), Hubble returned to the family home, now in Louisville, Kentucky. For a year he taught physics and Spanish at a high school across the river, in New Albany, Indiana, and coached the basketball team to an undefeated regular season and a trip to the state championship, where the team won its first two games before being eliminated. Hubble also passed the Kentucky bar exam, but he did not practice law.

In 1914 Hubble returned to the University of Chicago and the Yerkes Observatory as a graduate student in astronomy. He hoped to finish his doctoral dissertation on a photographic investigation of faint nebulae (wispy patches of light barely visible in the heavens with a good telescope) and take up a position at the Mount Wilson Observatory in southern California in the summer of 1917. In April, however, the United States declared war on Germany. Hubble rushed through his dissertation, took his final oral exam, and reported to the army for duty three days later. He served in France and made the rank of major before the war ended. In 1919 he finally joined the Mount Wilson Observatory.

In 1924 Hubble married the sister-in-law of a colleague from the Lick Observatory in northern California, but the Hubbles had no children. During World War II Hubble was chief of ballistics and director of the Supersonic Wind Tunnels Laboratory at the Army Proving Grounds in Aberdeen, Maryland, and was awarded the Medal for Merit for his wartime work. Except for this period, he worked all his life at Mount Wilson. Hubble's scientific achievements made him the foremost astronomer of the twentieth century and

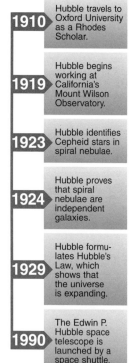

1910 Hubble travels to Oxford University as a Rhodes Scholar.

1919 Hubble begins working at California's Mount Wilson Observatory.

1923 Hubble identifies Cepheid stars in spiral nebulae.

1924 Hubble proves that spiral nebulae are independent galaxies.

1929 Hubble formulates Hubble's Law, which shows that the universe is expanding.

1990 The Edwin P. Hubble space telescope is launched by a space shuttle.

one of the most influential scientists of all time in changing our understanding of the universe. He was on the cover of *Time* magazine in 1948 and the Hubble Space Telescope is named after him. Perhaps the best indication of his fame, though, is the renaming of the Wheaton high school in 1991 after Hubble rather than the school's star football player, the legendary Red Grange—the "Galloping Ghost" at the University of Illinois, All-American halfback in 1923 and 1924, All-American quarterback in 1925, member of the college Football Hall of Fame, player for the Chicago Bears, and a charter member of the Professional Football Hall of Fame.

> Scientists, including Albert Einstein, had assumed the universe to be static; Hubble showed that it is expanding.

What Hubble did to make himself even more famous than the Galloping Ghost was, first, demonstrate conclusively after centuries of fruitless speculation by other astronomers that spiral nebulas (faint patches of light in the sky) are independent galaxies at great distances beyond our own galaxy. Using the new 100-inch. telescope at Mount Wilson, Hubble found Cepheid variable stars in spiral nebulas. These stars are a useful indicator of distances because their brightness correlates with the duration of time of their change from maximum to minimum and back to maximum brightness. Hubble used the relationship established for Cepheids in our galaxy between absolute luminosity (apparent brightness measured at a standard distance from the object) and period (the time it takes for the star to vary in brightness from maximum to faintest and back to maximum). He measured periods for Cepheids in spiral nebulas and then assumed they had the absolute luminosity corresponding to Cepheids of the same period in our galaxy. (Knowing the period, he could read off the expected absolute luminosity from a graph of the period-luminosity relation.) Finally, with an estimated absolute luminosity, he calculated how far away the Cepheids (and the nebulas they were embedded in) had to be for their absolute luminosity to be diminished to the apparent luminosity that he measured (luminosity is reduced in inverse proportion to the distance squared).

Proving in the mid-1920s that spiral nebulas are galaxies, a great accomplishment in itself, was only the starting point for Hubble. Step by step, he determined distances to ever more distant galaxies, first using Cepheid variables, and later calculating an average absolute luminosity for galaxies at known distances and then using this in conjunction with

The Hubble Space Telescope

In 1990, the crew of a space shuttle placed the Hubble Space Telescope into orbit about 300 miles above the Earth's surface. Because of its orbit above the atmosphere, the telescope can see much finer detail than ground-based telescopes and also observe wavelengths that do not reach the Earth. Some astronomers are using the Hubble Space Telescope to continue Edwin Hubble's search for Cepheid variable stars, which they hope can reveal the size of the universe and when the Big Bang occurred.

measured apparent luminosities of galaxies so distant that Cepheids were not detectable in them to estimate distances for these galaxies (again calculating distance from the difference between estimated absolute luminosity and measured apparent luminosity). A few velocities had been measured by other astronomers, including Vesto M. Slipher at the Lowell Observatory in Arizona, from the Doppler effect (a redshift in the spectrum of light from an object moving away from the observer). At the Mount Wilson Observatory, Hubble directed a program (largely carried out by his colleague Milton Humason) of measuring velocities for the galaxies whose distances he also was determining. By 1935 they had determined velocities and distances for more than 100 galaxies. Hubble's work throughout the 1930s demonstrated that more distant galaxies are moving away from us at greater velocities (his famous velocity-distance relation, which can, in turn, be used to estimate distances for even more distant galaxies from their measured velocities, or Doppler redshifts). Scientists, including Albert Einstein, had assumed the universe to be static; Hubble showed that it is expanding.

> By 1935, Hubble and his colleagues had determined velocities and distances for more than 100 galaxies.

World War II interrupted Hubble's work on cosmology, and his life ended in San Marino, California, on September 28, 1953, soon after completion of the 200-in. telescope on Palomar Mountain and too soon for conclusive answers from the research program he planned. Although subsequent investigations generally have confirmed Hubble's relativistic, expanding model of the universe, evaluation of his work should not be based solely on this fact. Instead, Hubble's cosmology should be appreciated more for the assumptions it overthrew, for the vistas it opened, and for its being one of the great accomplishments of human intellect. ◆

Humboldt, Alexander

1769–1859 ● GEOLOGY & BOTANY

German naturalist and explorer Alexander Humboldt was born in Berlin. In 1790 he accompanied George Foster, Captain Cook's companion on his second voyage, on a visit to England, beginning a series of journeys which were to shape his life and thinking.

In 1792 Humboldt was given the position of assessor of mines in Berlin, quickly made his way up to the highest post in his department, and was given important diplomatic assignments. At the same time he published, in 1793, a paper entitled *Florae Fribergensis Specimen*, based on his research of the plant life of the Freiburg mines, and in 1794 published another paper on the results of lengthy experiments on muscular irritability.

In 1796, following the death of his mother, Humboldt left his work to devote himself to travel. Accompanied by the French botanist Aimé Bonpland, he journeyed to Madrid and unexpectedly received the patronage of the Spanish minister d'Urquijo. As a result, he and Bonpland set out on an exploration of Spanish America, a voyage which was to form the foundation of Humboldt's greatest meteorological and geographical discoveries.

The two set sail from Corunna in 1799 and landed at Cumana in Venezuela. On the night of November 12–13, 1799, Humboldt observed a meteor shower, which led him to begin the study of the periodicity of meteors. In 1800 he charted the course of the Orinoco river; after traveling 1,725 miles in four months, he successfully discovered where the Orinoco and the Amazon divided. He and Bonpland continued their lengthy journey, traveling to the sources of the Amazon on their way to Lima. Humboldt noted the fertilizing properties of **guano** and published his findings on the subject, leading to the importation and use of guano as a fertilizer in Europe. After spending a year in Mexico, he and Bonpland returned to Europe in 1804.

Humboldt's findings on the expedition, published in thirty volumes, devised ways to show that climatic conditions in countries could be compared. He investigated the rate of

> *"Man cannot have an effect on nature, cannot adopt any of her forces, if he does not know the natural laws in terms of measurement and numerical relations."*
>
> — Alexander Humboldt, *Cosmos*

guano: a substance composed chiefly of the excrement of sea birds.

decrease in mean temperature with the increased elevation above sea level, and through his research into the origin of tropical storms, was able to deduce one of the main laws on atmospheric disturbances in higher altitudes. He also published an essay about the correlation between the distribution of organic life and physical conditions. He also discovered that the earth's magnetism decreases from the poles to the equator. Through his studies of the New World's volcanoes, he showed that they fell into a pattern of linear groups that probably corresponded with underground fissures. He also debunked many previously held theories on rocks thought to have **aqueous** origins when he proved their **igneous** properties.

aqueous: made with or by water.

igneous: resulting from volcanic activity.

In Europe Humboldt visited Italy with Joseph Gay-Lussac to investigate the law of magnetic declination, and stayed for two years in Berlin. He settled in Paris in 1808 and, supported by Paris' scientific circles, spent the next twenty-one years working on the information he had gathered on his voyages. His fame had spread through Europe and America and academies all over the world sought to have him as a member. But it was in Paris that Humboldt felt most at ease, and when he received a summons to join the court in Berlin, he made a point of traveling to Paris as often as possible. In 1827, he settled permanently in Berlin.

In Berlin Humboldt began to study "magnetic storms"—a term he invented for abnormal disturbances of the earth's magnetism. In 1829 he made a request to the Russian government to set up a line of magnetic and meteorological stations across northern Asia; he also obtained the cooperation of the British Empire for his project. By so doing, he established the basis of the first international scientific joint effort, believing that science should be above nationality.

Humboldt did not resume his journeys until he was sixty. In 1829, he crossed the Russian Empire in twenty-five weeks, covering 9,615 miles from Neva to Yenesei. As a result of this trip, Humboldt was able to correct the exaggerated estimate then held of the height of the central Asian plateau; he also discovered diamonds in the gold areas of the Ural.

Between 1845 and 1847, Humboldt published the first two volumes of his greatest work, *The Cosmos.* The third and fourth volumes appeared between 1850 and 1858 and the fifth was published in 1862, after his death. Humboldt died at ninety and was honored by a state funeral. He never married

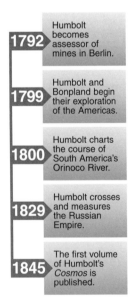

1792 Humbolt becomes assessor of mines in Berlin.

1799 Humbolt and Bonpland begin their exploration of the Americas.

1800 Humbolt charts the course of South America's Orinoco River.

1829 Humbolt crosses and measures the Russian Empire.

1845 The first volume of Humbolt's *Cosmos* is published.

and left his entire estate to his loyal servant Seifert. He was remembered not only for his scientific discoveries, but also for fighting for improved conditions for the miners of Galicia and Franconia. He was also an outspoken opponent of slavery.

Humboldt's brother, Karl Wilhelm von Humboldt (1767–1835), was an educator and scholar of languages. He pioneered in ethnolinguistics and more particularly in the study of the Basque language, and also worked on the languages of the East and the South Sea islands. From 1809 he was Prussia's first minister of public instruction and founded the university in Berlin, now known by his name. He was also a noted diplomat, serving as Prussian ambassador to Vienna from 1812. ◆

> *"By asserting the unity of the human race, we also oppose every distasteful assumption of higher and lower races of man."*
> — Alexander Humbolt, *Cosmos*

Huxley, Thomas Henry

1825–1895 ● NATURAL SCIENCES

> *"I asserted—and I repeat—that a man has no reason to be ashamed of having an ape for his grandfather."*
> — T. H. Huxley

English naturalist, writer, and lecturer Thomas Huxley was a proponent of Charles Darwin's theory of evolution. He was born at Ealing, London; at ten he went to Coventry, where he was introduced to medicine by his elder sister's husband. By age sixteen he had become an assistant to a medical doctor, despite a professed interest in becoming a mechanical engineer.

In 1842 Huxley moved to London where he entered Charing Cross Hospital's medical school. He received his M.B. three years later at London University and had his first medical paper published, "On a Hitherto Undescribed Structure in the Human Hair-Sheath." He later said of himself on becoming a natural scientist instead of an engineer: "I am not sure that I have not, all along, been a sort of mechanical engineer. . . . Physiology is the mechanical engineering of living machines." Later critics did, in fact, fault his mechanistic view of human evolution.

Huxley was assigned to Haslar Hospital in 1846 as lieutenant, R.N. Medical Service; that winter he sailed as assistant surgeon to survey Australasian waters. "On the Anatomy and Affinities of Medusae" was written during this time, based on his research at sea. Upon his return from this four-year voyage on H.M.S. *Rattlesnake* he discovered that it had been published by the Royal Society.

Huxley was frustrated at first in his attempts to have the rest of his work published and to find a suitable position, despite receiving the Royal Medal of the Royal Society in 1852. Two years later he was offered the post of paleontologist and lecturer on natural history at the Government School of Mines. He refused the former, not caring for paleontology (the study of fossils), and agreed to lecture on natural history only until he could find a position in physiology. "But I held the office for thirty-one years, and a large part of my work has been paleontological," he later wrote. He had another paper published, "On the Educational Value of the Natural History Sciences."

In 1856 Huxley went on an expedition to Switzerland to study the structure of glaciers. He continued to publish papers and in 1859 his review of *The Origin of Species* appeared in *The Times*. The 1860 meeting of the British Association for the Advancement of Science was a victory for Darwin's theories. Deeply committed to the advancement of the scientific method, a firm believer in rationality and "the development and organization of scientific education," Huxley was, in his own words, in an "endless series of battles over evolution." He considered religion to be "that ecclesiastical spirit. . . [which is] the deadly enemy of science." Huxley saw religion and sci-

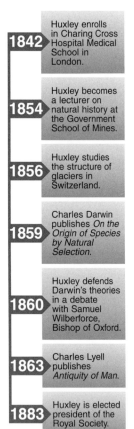

1842 Huxley enrolls in Charing Cross Hospital Medical School in London.

1854 Huxley becomes a lecturer on natural history at the Government School of Mines.

1856 Huxley studies the structure of glaciers in Switzerland.

1859 Charles Darwin publishes *On the Origin of Species by Natural Selection.*

1860 Huxley defends Darwin's theories in a debate with Samuel Wilberforce, Bishop of Oxford.

1863 Charles Lyell publishes *Antiquity of Man.*

1883 Huxley is elected president of the Royal Society.

ence as inimical and questioned any belief in God or in the spiritual world that could not be objectively proven, coining the term "agnostic" to describe this view. Huxley also introduced the term "biogenesis" to describe his view of the origins of life—that life only arises from another life—in juxtaposition to the description in the Book of Genesis (where life is created by God **ex nihilo**). Huxley spoke of having "helped that movement of opinion which has been called the New Reformation." Yet this "New Reformation," as its name implies, itself became a kind of secular, unprovable religion. One of the dogmas of Huxley's new creed was a belief in the dominance of the strong over the weak, the survival of the strongest.

During the next decade, Huxley's *Evidence as to Man's Place in Nature and Lectures on the Elements of Comparative Anatomy* were published, among other works. In 1871 he was appointed secretary of the Royal Society. A breakdown in his health soon followed, but a sizable gift from his friends enabled him to take a complete rest. In 1880 his book *The Crayfish* appeared. Huxley was elected president of the Royal Society in 1883 and appointed to the Privy Council in 1892. He was awarded the Darwin Medal of the Royal Society in 1894. Altogether he wrote one hundred essays, two hundred scientific papers, and twenty books.

Three of Huxley's grandsons made notable achievements, two of them in scientific endeavors. Sir Julian Sorell Huxley (1887–1975), a noted biologist, helped establish the United Nations Educational, Scientific and Cultural Organization (UNESCO), of which he was its first director general; Andrew Fielding Huxley (born 1917) shared the Nobel Prize for physiology in 1963; and Aldous Leonard Huxley (1894–1963) was a famous novelist who protested the excesses of scientific thought and deplored the tendency toward the mechanization of life in the modem age. ◆

> *"The great tragedy of Science—the slaying of a beautiful hypothesis by an ugly fact."*
> — T. H. Huxley

ex nihilo: latin for "from nothing."

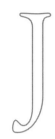

Jackson, Shirley Ann

1946–Present
Theoretical physics

Washington, D.C, was where Shirley Jackson was born on August 5, 1946. It was also where she was raised and educated. Jackson was one of only thirty or so women who entered the Massachusetts Institute of Technology in 1964. She was awarded a B.S. in physics in 1968 and a Ph.D. in 1973 for her work in elementary particle physics. Jackson's was the first female African-American doctorate from M.I.T. After earning her degree, she was a research associate (1973–1974, 1975–1976) at the Fermi National Accelerator Laboratory in Batavia, Ill., and a visiting scientist (1974–1975) at the European Center for Nuclear Research (CERN), where she worked on theories of strongly interacting elementary particles.

In 1975 Jackson moved to the Stanford Linear Accelerator Center and Aspen Center for Physics before leaving the following year to work for the Bell Laboratories of American Telephone and Telegraph in Murray Hill, New Jersey. During her early years at Bell Laboratories, Jackson's research was in the areas of theoretical physics, scattered- and low-energy physics, and solid-state quantum physics. She studied the electrical and optical properties of semiconductors.

Jackson was elected in 1975 as a member of the Massachusetts Institute of Technology Corporation, the institute's board of trustees. She was made a lifetime trustee in 1992. In 1985, New Jersey governor Thomas Kean appointed her to the state's Commission on Science and

"Making careers in science, especially in research, takes daring. All too often, I see people making choices below their capabilities because of fear— fear of taking risks, fear of failure."

— Shirley Ann Jackson

185

Technology. Specializing in optical physics research, she was named a distinguished member of the technical staff of Bell Laboratories in 1990. In 1991 she received an appointment as professor of physics at Rutgers University. Jackson's achievements in science have been recognized by other scientists through her election as a fellow of the American Physical Society and the American Academy of Arts and Sciences. ◆

Jenner, Edward

1749–1823 ● MEDICINE

"The deviation of man from the state in which he was originally placed by nature seems to have proved to him a prolific source of diseases."

— Edward Jenner

lymph: a pale fluid in the human body that bathes the body's tissues.

English physician Edward Jenner discovered the vaccine against smallpox, an often fatal disease that in former times was epidemic worldwide. Born to a family of landed gentry in Berkeley, Gloucestershire, Jenner was orphaned at age five and brought up by his three sisters. In 1757 he was sent to the local grammar school as a boarder, and while there was inoculated against smallpox through the primitive and risky method of variolation, an arduous process that consisted of inoculating the patient with a small amount of smallpox **lymph**, and which sometimes proved fatal. This traumatic experience gave Jenner insomnia as a child, and he was persistently plagued by imaginary noises. While at school, he also developed an interest in fossil collecting, a hobby he maintained for the rest of his life.

At age twelve, he was accepted as an apprentice surgeon to John Ludlow, with whom he remained for the next six years. He then enrolled as a student at Saint George's Hospital, London, where he lodged with John Hunter, the most eminent surgeon of his time. Hunter's wife, Anne Home, was a Scottish poet who hosted an artists' salon which Jenner, a fair poet and musician, frequented.

In 1771, when Captain James Cook returned from a voyage of scientific discovery aboard the ship *Endeavour*, Hunter recommended Jenner for the task of classifying the thousands of natural specimens, never before seen in Europe, which had been collected. Pleased with Jenner's work, the ship's chief botanist invited the young man on Cook's next trip, but Jenner turned down this and other offers of work abroad due to his deep attachment to Gloucestershire and his family.

Jenner returned to Berkeley, where he lived in his brother's house, and worked as a country doctor. In 1783, after the Montgolfier brothers launched the first balloon flight in history, Jenner organized the first flight of a hydrogen balloon in England, assisted by the earl of Berkeley.

In 1785, Jenner bought Chauntry Cottage and began work on a paper on the breeding habits of the cuckoo, the publication of which led to his acceptance as a member of the Royal Society in 1788.

As a country doctor, Jenner regularly inoculated against smallpox using the variolation method. However, finding some patients to be resistant to smallpox, he discovered that they had all previously had cowpox, corroborating the old wives' tale that cowpox provides immunization against smallpox. Jenner distinguished between two forms of cowpox, only one of which provides protection against smallpox and only when the lymph extracted from **vesicles** is administered when still fresh.

In 1796 Jenner inoculated James Phipps, the eight-year-old son of a landless laborer who had often worked for the Jenners, with cowpox lymph extracted from a vesicle from a milkmaid's arm. James was subsequently inoculated with smallpox, but the disease did not manifest itself. This led to Jenner's publication in 1798 of *An Inquiry into the Causes and Effects of the Variolae Vaccinae*, in which he coined the word "virus." Had Jenner decided to keep the nature of his findings to himself, he could have profited handsomely. Instead, he shared his findings and the practice of vaccination had spread, with cowpox lymph being transferred from arm to arm. Jenner stood by his findings in the face of sometimes fierce opposition.

Jenner discovered that cowpox lymph could be kept for up to three months if preserved in dried form, thus facilitating the worldwide distribution of the vaccine. The success of vaccinations in Moscow prompted the dowager empress Marie to send Jenner a diamond ring, while in the United States,

vesicle: a small, abnormal, fluid-filled pouch on the skin of an animal.

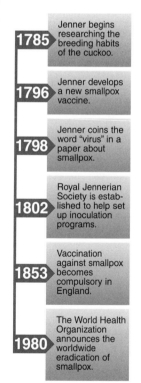

1785 Jenner begins researching the breeding habits of the cuckoo.

1796 Jenner develops a new smallpox vaccine.

1798 Jenner coins the word "virus" in a paper about smallpox.

1802 Royal Jennerian Society is established to help set up inoculation programs.

1853 Vaccination against smallpox becomes compulsory in England.

1980 The World Health Organization announces the worldwide eradication of smallpox.

President Thomas Jefferson wrote to Jenner: "Mankind can never forget that you have lived." After personally sending pamphlets about the vaccine to the Abenaqui tribe of Canadian Indians, Jenner received a reply with an address of thanks from ten chiefs, communicated by a string of **wampum**. Napoleon Bonaparte had a medal struck in Jenner's honor, made vaccination compulsory in the French army and, in response to Jenner's request in 1813 for the release of an English captain, is said to have replied: "*Ah, Jenner, je ne puis rien refuser à Jenner.*"

wampum: strings of polished shells.

Jenner, who vaccinated the poor free of charge, was awarded two separate grants from the British Parliament, amounting to £30,000, in recognition of his work, and the Royal Jennerian Society was established in 1802, leading to a widespread program of inoculation.

In 1817 Jenner was appointed to serve as mayor of Berkeley. From then until the end of his life, he resumed his inquiries into the migration of birds, and continued to collect fossils.

In 1980 the World Health Organization announced the worldwide eradication of smallpox as "an unprecedented event in human history," and with it the fulfillment of Jenner's dream. ◆

Controlling Smallpox

Smallpox, one of history's most deadly diseases, first appeared in Asia thousands of years ago. Smallpox is caused by a virus that spreads when an uninfected person comes into contact with an infected person and inhales the virus. The first symptoms are fever, headache, and muscle pain. Soon, the victim's skin erupts with red spots, which gradually turn into painful, pus-filled blisters. About a quarter of those infected die. Survivors are left with severely scarred skin and, in some cases, blindness.

The smallpox virus reached Europe in the 5th century and became one of the continent's leading causes of death. Beginning in the 16th century, Europeans carried the virus to the Americas, where it wiped out millions of indigenous people. Edward Jenner's vaccine, developed in 1796, was the first step toward controlling smallpox. Nevertheless, by the middle of the 20th century, smallpox still infected 10 to 15 million people every year. In 1967, the World Health Organization began a massive international vaccination program to eradicate the disease worldwide. The program was a remarkable success, and the last death from smallpox occurred in Britain in 1978. Today, the only remaining stocks of smallpox virus are kept frozen in high-security laboratories in Atlanta, Geogia, and Koltsova, Russia. These stocks will be destroyed on 30 June 1999, after research on the virus has been completed.

Jung, Carl Gustav

1876–1961 ● PSYCHIATRY & PSYCHOLOGY

> *"The separation of psychology from the premises of biology is purely artificial, because the human psyche lives in indissoluble union with the body"*
>
> — Carl Gustav Jung

Swiss psychiatrist and analytical psychologist Jung was a highly original thinker. His central theoretical concept was that of the collective unconscious, which has significantly enriched psychological thought and saved it from the barrenness of a purely individualistic psychology. Jung never restricted himself solely to the dry discipline of academic psychology, believing rather that in order to establish an understanding of the links between the individual personality and the symbolic field it inhabits, it was necessary to undertake wider ranging sociocultural studies. A talented linguist and a scholar of sufficient ability to read medieval Latin texts in the original, it was he who elucidated the important relations between religion and psychology.

As a child, Jung had remarkably striking and unusually intense dreams and fantasies, which he was in later years to posit came from the area of the mind he called the collective unconscious. The son of a pastor, he was expected to follow the family tradition and become a clergyman. However, his observation of his father's failing belief and his own inability to communicate his experience of God to the elder Jung led him to reject the expected course and opt to study medicine in Basel. He also read widely in the field of philosophy. Following a Ouija board session where a young girl adopted a

Jung discovered that the same symbols and themes recurred in widely different times and places in mythologies and religions, as well as art.

"The shoe that fits one person pinches another; there is no recipe for living that suits all cases."
— C. G. Jung

variety of roles suggested to her in the course of the seance, Jung determined to take up psychiatry that he might discover "the intruders of the mind."

After completing his studies at the universities of Basel and Zurich, he joined the Bergholzli Asylum in Zurich in 1902. There he made his name through his outstanding success in using association tests as an indicator of hidden emotional activity. For the constellation of activity within the unconscious mind he coined the term "complex," now a familiar usage in everyday speech. Many of his findings led him to champion the then hotly disputed theories of Sigmund Freud. For a period of some five years, from 1907, the two men collaborated closely, even engaging in mutual analysis.

Jung was widely expected to succeed Freud as the leader of the psychoanalytic movement headquartered in Vienna, and was elected president of the International Psychoanalytic Society in 1911. The two came, however, to disagree significantly on certain matters: Jung could not accept Freud's insistence on the sexual bases of neurosis, while Jung's views on symbolism conflicted sharply with Freud's more formalized approach. The formal break occurred in 1912; resigning from the Psychoanalytic Society, Jung founded a new school based in Zurich.

Disturbed by the break with Freud, Jung studied the reasons for it and was led to conclude that a constitutional difference in type inevitably led each to approach clinical and other problems from different angles. From these findings he evolved his differentiation of people into two attitude types: extroverted (outward looking) and introverted (inward looking). He went on to posit four basic mind functions—thinking, feeling, sensation, and intuition—one or more of which predominated in any given person. This outstandingly important—albeit controversial—theoretical development was delineated in his work *Psychological Types* (1923), which also manifested the breadth of his scholarship.

Jung believed that the free association technique used by Freudian analysts lead away from the complexes of which we need to become aware. He also believed that the types of neuroses that could be adequately dealt with in Freudian terms were characteristic of the earlier part of life. He stressed that a neurotic symptom cannot be explained solely through reference to the patient's past: it also represents an attempt to deal

1902 Jung joins the staff of the Bergholzli Asylum in Zurich.

1907 Jung begins his collaboration with Freud.

1912 Jung formally breaks with Freud by resigning from the International Psychoanalytic Society.

1917 Jung publishes *Psychology of the Unconscious.*

1923 Jung publishes *Psychological Types.*

1943 Jung joins the psychology department at Basel University.

with the present problems confronting the patient. He called the process by which patients could discover their own balanced synthesis of the competing demands of their drives and circumstances "individuation."

Due to his interest in the unconscious, unapprehended, background of conscious life, Jung stressed the importance of dreams. The appearance in the dreams of many of his patients of apparently ancient material, which he could not explain in terms of the personal history of the dreamer, led him to the study of **ethnology** and comparative religion with special emphasis upon religious symbolism. He conducted field research in Africa and the Americas and launched an extensive study of world religions. He was to discover that the same symbols and themes recurred in widely different times and places in mythologies and religions, as well as in art. He concluded that the mind, like the body, had a long ancestry and that just as the traces of our mammalian descent are plain on the physical level, so the mind too bears archetypal patterns, inherited tendencies of psychic functioning common to the species, through which the collective unconscious reveals itself.

> **ethnology:** the comparative and analytical study of cultures.

Jung believed that people have a strong need for religious beliefs and experiences since it is through these that they are able to encounter and accept the contents of the collective conscious, a process he deemed necessary to psychological health. In addition to his fascination with **alchemical** symbolism, Jung was especially interested in Chinese thought, meeting the noted **Sinologist** Richard Wilhelm and contributing commentaries to his translations of the *I Ching* and *The Secret of the Golden Flower*, two of the most noted Chinese religious-philosophical works.

> **alchemical:** relating to a medieval science that sought to change base metals into gold.

Jung held that the increase in scientific understanding had led to a dehumanization of the natural and social worlds and a corresponding lack of awareness of the powers of human nature; to this he ascribed the increased propensity to psychological disorder in modern society. He dated this process of disorientation as beginning with the original Christian break with paganism and accelerating after the Enlightenment.

> **Sinologist:** a person who studies Chinese history, language, and culture.

This approach helped make him a pioneer in the psychotherapy of the middle-aged and elderly, in whom he was able to reinstate a sense of the value of their lives in the context of the sequence of history.

Jung was in demand as a skilled lecturer, often visiting the United States and Great Britain; he was awarded numerous honorary degrees. A chair of medical psychology was created for him by Basel University in 1943. By the time of his death in his eighty-sixth year, institutes teaching Jungian methods were well established, most notably the famous C. G. Jung Institute in Zurich. ◆

Kelvin, Lord

1824–1907 • Chemistry & Physics

Lord Kelvin was born William Thomson on June 26, 1824, in Belfast to James and Margaret Thomson. James Thomson was a mathematics teacher who wrote an influential textbook promoting the analytical methods of the continental mathematicians instead of Newton's **fluxions**, which were still used in Britain at that time. In 1832, James Thomson moved to the University of Glasgow as professor of mathematics. Shortly before the move to Glasgow, Margaret Thomson died, and William, his three brothers, and two sisters were raised by Margaret's sister. The future Lord Kelvin's early education was at home by his father. At age ten he started taking classes at the University of Glasgow and enrolled at Cambridge University in 1841. His first paper (on Fourier series) was published in the *Cambridge Mathematical Journal* when he was fifteen years old. More than six hundred publications followed. He obtained a degree in natural philosophy (physics) in 1845 and the next year, at age twenty-two, was elected to the chair of physics at the University of Glasgow. He was the professor of physics at Glasgow for fifty-three years and after his retirement as professor continued his association with the University of Glasgow as chancellor until his death in 1907.

Professor Thomson did much to improve the quality of physics teaching. He established instructional laboratories for his students and involved students in his research. He was a strong proponent of the metric system and worked through the British Association to develop a set of electrical units. In collaboration with Peter Tait, he wrote a textbook of physics that was widely used. He was an enthusiastic lecturer who was popular with students. In discussing a topic, Thomson fre-

> *"When you can measure what you are speaking about, and express it in numbers, you know something about it; but when you cannot measure it, when you cannot express it in numbers, your knowledge is of a meager and unsatisfactory kind."*
>
> —Lord Kelvin

fluxions: results arising from a mathematical function.

quently had new insights, which he would explain on the spot, and sometimes became so involved with demonstrations and measurements that he forgot the multiplication table and had to ask his assistant to do simple arithmetic calculations.

Thomson did research and published in many areas including mathematics, electricity and magnetism, and hydrodynamics, but his most fundamental contributions were to **thermodynamics**. He worked closely with James Joule on the law of conservation of energy and the "dynamical theory of heat"—that is, the concept that heat is associated with molecular motion. He developed the thermodynamic temperature scale (for which he is now honored by the SI unit kelvin), and he showed that the efficiency of the Carnot cycle can be expressed in terms of temperatures and that the thermodynamic and perfect gas temperature scales are the same. Measurements of the temperature change when various gases expand led Joule and Thomson to what is now called the Joule-Thomson coefficient of a gas.

In the 1850s and 1860s, Thomson was very involved in designing and laying transatlantic telegraph cables. He developed and manufactured devices to detect and record the weak signals transmitted through submarine cables. His telegraphic signal recorders made him very wealthy.

However, not all of Lord Kelvin's ideas have withstood the test of time. Long after Maxwell's electromagnetic wave theory of the propagation of light and the results of the Michelson-Morley experiment were widely accepted, Kelvin continued in his attempt to explain the properties that the "luminiferous ether" must have if it were the material in which light waves are transmitted. For example, he struggled with the problem that the ether must be extremely rigid yet allow the Earth, Moon, and other objects to pass through it with ease.

In the mid-nineteenth century, evolutionary biologists and geologists found evidence that indicated that Earth must be billions of years old. Lord Kelvin estimated the age of Earth to be a few million years, with an upper limit of 200 million years. His calculations were based on (1) the rate at which Earth's speed of rotation is decreasing due to tidal action, (2) the rate at which the sun is losing energy, assumed to be due to gravitational collapse, and (3) the rate of heat flow from the interior to the surface of Earth. Kelvin never fully accept-

thermodynamics: the branch of physics that deals with the mechanical action of heat.

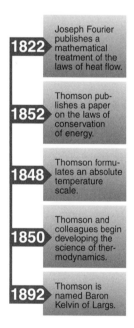

1822 Joseph Fourier publishes a mathematical treatment of the laws of heat flow.

1852 Thomson publishes a paper on the laws of conservation of energy.

1848 Thomson formulates an absolute temperature scale.

1850 Thomson and colleagues begin developing the science of thermodynamics.

1892 Thomson is named Baron Kelvin of Largs.

ed radioactivity and nuclear reactions as sources of heat within Earth and Sun.

In 1852 Thomson married Margaret Crum, who was an invalid for much of their marriage and died in 1870. Sir William (he was knighted in 1866) was remarried in 1874 to Francis Blandy. He had no children by either marriage. In 1892, he was made Baron Kelvin of Largs (Ayrshire, Scotland, near his home at Netherhall). Lord Kelvin was in generally good health most of his life, but "caught a chill" in November 1907 and died on December 18, 1907. He is buried at Westminster, near Isaac Newton. ◆

Kepler, Johannes

1571–1630 ● ASTRONOMY

K epler, who was born in Germany on December 27, 1571, had a childhood that was decidedly unhappy. He described his mother to be "of a bad disposition," while his father, a soldier of fortune, left home never to return. Kepler was fortunate to reside in Protestant Württemberg, which progressively provided university scholarships to talented but needy students. Kepler graduated from the University of Tübingen and accepted a position as teacher of mathematics and astronomy at the University of Graz, which, as was then common, also involved duties in astrology. Early successes in astrological prediction may have saved his position; his success in teaching was dubious, as no students registered for his course in his second year.

Kepler became an advocate of the Copernican solar system while at Tübingen and pondered the significance of its heliocentric distances. He was greatly impressed that there are exactly five regular or Pythagorean solids, objects whose faces are identical regular polygons. A cube and tetrahedron

> *"So long as the mother, Ignorance, lives, it is not safe for Science, the offspring, to divulge the hidden causes of things."*
> — Johannes Kepler

are familiar examples; the octahedron, dodecahedron, and icosahedron are less well-known. These solids can be inscribed in a sphere so that each corner just touches its surface, or circumscribed about a sphere that is then tangent to each face; the ratio of the radii of the circumscribed and inscribed spheres is fixed. The structure of the universe thus followed for Kepler: five solids—five spaces between planetary orbits, the relative sizes of which were determined by geometry. This notion, a brilliant inspiration which happens to be wrong, determined his future career.

His discovery was published in his first book, *The Mysterium Cosmographicum* (1596; *The Mystery of Cosmography*). Much of the book is medieval and mystical; a typical argument in favor of his model was that, since God must create a perfect world, it must be based on the five solids. It is a shock, then, when the second half of the book opens with: "Now we shall proceed to the astronomical determination of the orbits. . . . If these do not confirm the thesis, then all of our previous efforts have doubtless been in vain." In stating that truth is to be decided by the observed facts, Kepler leaped the gulf between mysticism and science.

His leap to science worked fairly well for some planets but not for others. Kepler questioned the quality of the data that had been compiled by Copernicus. Kepler also speculated, based on the periods and heliocentric distances of the planets, that there must be a force emanating from the Sun that drives the planets in their orbits and which decreases in ratio to distance "as does the force of light." Kepler's intuition forecasts the future work of Galileo and Newton.

Kepler needed better data to prove his theory, and he knew that they could only be obtained from Tycho Brahe, the last and greatest pretelescopic observational astronomer. Tycho, unable to accept the motion of the Earth in the Copernican model, had developed a compromise model in which the Sun circles the Earth but the other planets orbit the Sun. This model correctly explained the motions of planets seen from Earth without requiring the Earth to move. Tycho wished for a skilled mathematician to use his data to confirm his model, and he had his eye on Kepler ever since he read the *Mysterium*.

Tycho's major work had been done in his native Denmark, but in 1599 he accepted a position as Imperial Mathematicus

Kepler's intuition forecasts the work of Galileo and Newton.

1596 Kepler publishes *Mysterium Cosmography*.

1600 Kepler begins working with Tycho Brahe.

1601 Kepler becomes official court astronomer and astrologer to Emperor Rudolf II.

1604 Kepler publishes influential writings on optics.

1609 Kepler publishes *The New Astronomy*, outlining his first two laws of planetary motion.

1618 Kepler publishes the true orbits of all the planets in *Survey of Copernican Astronomy*.

1619 Kepler publishes *Harmonics of the World*, outlining his third law of planetary motion.

for Emperor Rudolph II and moved to Prague. Kepler's time in Graz was running out because of religious strife, so he set out for Prague, meeting Tycho early in 1600. Tycho assigned Kepler the task of determining Mars's orbit, a fortunate choice because Mars's large orbital eccentricity and proximity to Earth maximized the difficulty of fitting its motions with prevailing theory. Kepler and Tycho did not "hit it off" very well. Fortunately, Kepler was absent from Prague for several months on personal business, so he and Tycho were not exposed to each other enough to sabotage the relationship.

The idea that theories must confront accurate experimental data may be Kepler's greatest legacy to Western science.

Tycho died unexpectedly in October 1601, and Emperor Rudolph II appointed Kepler to be his successor as Imperial Mathematicus, possibly the most prestigious post for a scientist in Europe. Kepler managed to retain Tycho's data upon his death and proceeded to attack the problem of Mars's motions. His attempt to solve the problem using a traditional eccentric circular orbit fit Tycho's observations near oppositions but resulted in errors of up to eight minutes of arc when applied to all data. Previous astronomers would have been satisfied with the result; Kepler was not. In Kepler's words: "Now, because they could not have been ignored, these eight minutes alone will have led the way to the reformation of all of astronomy." The idea that theories must confront accurate experimental data may be Kepler's greatest legacy to Western science.

Kepler reexamined the problem, discarding many preconceived notions that had stood for centuries. He discovered that the Earth moves faster the closer it is to the Sun rather than uniformly, at constant speed. This led to Kepler's law of equal areas. Subsequently, Kepler concluded that the orbit must be an oval, although some time passed before he finally recognized that his formula was that of an **ellipse**. Four additional years passed before these results were published in *The New Astronomy* in 1609, due to squabbles with Tycho's son-in-law, who felt, with some justification, that Kepler had expediently misappropriated Tycho's data when he died.

ellipse: a closed plane curve where the sums of its distances from two fixed points is constant.

Kepler's work by no means ended with the publication of this book. In 1618 he published the true orbits of all the planets as well as of the satellites of Jupiter in *Survey of Copernican Astronomy*. *The Harmony of the World* (1619) introduced Kepler's third law relating periods and heliocentric distances. *The Rudolphine Tables* (1629) completed the task originally given to Tycho by Emperor Rudolph; namely, tabulating the positions of the planets. And, despite his scientific reputation being based on his contributions to astronomy, Kepler also published influential works on optics (1604), the theory of the telescope (1611), the geometrical structure of snowflakes (1611), and mathematics antecedent to the development of calculus (1615).

He died at Regensburg, Germany, on November 15, 1630. Although Kepler's grave was destroyed during the Thirty Years War, his epitaph remains:

I measured the skies, now the shadows I measure
Skybound was the mind, earthbound the body rests. ◆

Koch, Robert

1843–1910 ● BACTERIOLOGY

"*It is certainly a one-sided opinion—even though generally adopted at the moment—that all infectious agents which are still unknown must be bacteria. Why should not other microorganisms just as well be able to exist as parasites in the body of animals?*"
— Robert Koch

German physician Robert Koch is recognized as the principal founder of modern bacteriology for his discoveries of the tuberculosis and cholera bacteria. Koch was awarded the Nobel Prize for Medicine in 1905.

Koch was the son of a mining official in Clausthal, Germany. His parents were industrious and disciplined Lutherans who encouraged Koch in his natural inquisitiveness. The young Koch was particularly attracted to the natural sciences, collecting insects and plant specimens, and identifying and dissecting them meticulously.

In 1862 Koch was admitted to Göttingen University to study sciences, but after one year transferred to medicine. One of his first teachers, Henle, who had twenty years previously proposed theories on bacteriology, influenced profoundly the course of Koch's life. Koch was not a brilliant student, but his insatiable curiosity and unparalleled thoroughness—which characterized his career—were evidence of a different type of genius. He graduated in 1866 with the highest honors.

Koch's preferred career was to travel the world as a ship's doctor or to join the military, but his recent marriage mitigated against such choices. After several moves, he finally settled in Rakwitz to establish his own practice, and his earnest manner and efficiency won him a good reputation and a fair income. During the Franco-Prussian War (1870–1871) Koch volunteered for work in a field hospital, and on his return he received an appointment as the district physician for Wollstein. There, in what little spare time he had available, he established a small laboratory at the rear of his home, and began the bacteriological research that was to make him famous.

Koch first investigated **anthrax**, which at the time was ravaging his district's herds. He traced the cause of the disease to rodlike microorganisms and went on to study techniques of culturing them, developing an effective methodology to determine their life cycle and formation. His reputation in the field was established almost overnight, and his self-confidence grew. He became very much a man of the Second Reich: pugnacious, arrogant, quick to condemn, and unwilling to admit error or acknowledge the ability of others. He spent the next few years improving his methods for fixing, staining, and photographing bacterial cultures as well as investigating the cause and nature of surgical infections.

In 1880 Koch was appointed to the imperial health ministry office in Berlin, where he continued his work with the assistance of his own research team. The bacteriological methodology he developed and published at this time became the basic instructional text in this subject for many years. He demonstrated **in-vitro** pure culture techniques, using **aniline**

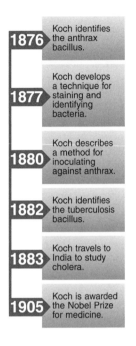

1876 Koch identifies the anthrax bacillus.

1877 Koch develops a technique for staining and identifying bacteria.

1880 Koch describes a method for inoculating against anthrax.

1882 Koch identifies the tuberculosis bacillus.

1883 Koch travels to India to study cholera.

1905 Koch is awarded the Nobel Prize for medicine.

anthrax: an infectious disease of animals characterized by ulcerating lesions in the lungs.

in-vitro: in an artificial environment outside the living body.

aniline: a synthetic organic dye.

agar: a gelatinous
extract of red algae.

dyes for staining and gelatin, and later **agar**, as the solidifying agent. Using these techniques he successfully isolated the small tuberculosis bacteria and proved its transmissibility. Paul Ehrlich, on seeing a spellbinding demonstration of this by Koch, improved the staining method overnight. He presented the results to Koch, and the two great researchers became close professional and personal friends. At the same time Koch began a decade-long rivalry with Louis Pasteur, which was exacerbated by nationalistic pride and professional jealousies.

In 1883 Koch traveled to India, where a cholera epidemic was raging. He identified the source of the epidemic as water infected with a particular comma-shaped bacillus. However, he was unable to induce the disease in experimental animals with this bacillus, so was uncertain as to whether it was indeed the direct cause of cholera. Nevertheless he returned triumphantly in 1884 to Berlin where he became the chief adviser on state hygiene and was appointed director of the Berlin Hygiene Institute the following year.

At the end of a routine lecture in 1890, Koch announced that he had "hit upon a substance which had the power of preventing the growth of tubercle bacilli." People flocked to his institute for inoculation. He was lauded by governments, and even Pasteur praised his efforts, but his vaccine proved ineffective. Koch had ignored his years of meticulous attention to detail and for the first time in his career prematurely made a claim founded on insufficient data, a fault he often found in others.

Koch was shaken by the debacle, but was redeemed by his tireless drive to help Hamburg through a cholera epidemic in 1892. He instituted treatment of the city's water supply after showing a direct correlation between the dispersion of victims and infected water. In 1905 he was awarded the Nobel Prize in medicine for his discovery of the tuberculosis bacillus. ◆

Latimer, Lewis Howard

1848–1928 ● INVENTOR

Lewis Latimer was born in Chelsea, Massachusetts, September 4, 1848, the son of runaway slaves from Virginia. In his youth Latimer worked at a variety of odd jobs, including selling copies of William Lloyd Garrison's *Liberator*, sweeping up in his father's barbershop, hanging paper, and waiting tables. In 1863 he joined the Union Navy and worked as a cabin boy aboard the U.S.S. *Massasoit*. He served on the James River in Virginia until the end of the war in 1865.

After the war Latimer returned to Boston where, in 1871, he was hired by patent lawyers Crosby and Gould. Although hired as an office boy, he became an expert mechanical drafter. He also tried his hand at inventing, and on February 10, 1874, he patented a pivot bottom for a water closet for railroad cars. The inventor of the telephone, Alexander Graham Bell, retained Crosby and Gould to handle his patent application, and Latimer helped sketch the drawings for Bell's 1876 patent.

In 1880 Latimer was hired by inventor Hiram Maxim's United States Electric Lighting Company in Bridgeport, Connecticut. Maxim was a competitor of Thomas A. Edison, who had patented the incandescent light bulb in 1879. In 1881 Latimer and his colleague Joseph V. Nichols shared a patent for an electric lamp. Latimer's most important invention, patented in 1882, was a carbon filament that increased the brightness and longevity of the light bulb. Because of its decreased costs, the resulting product made electric lighting more accessible. Latimer also invented a locking rack for hats, coats, and umbrellas in 1896.

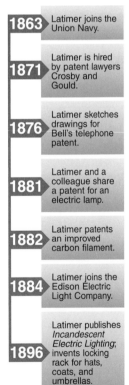

1863 Latimer joins the Union Navy.

1871 Latimer is hired by patent lawyers Crosby and Gould.

1876 Latimer sketches drawings for Bell's telephone patent.

1881 Latimer and a colleague share a patent for an electric lamp.

1882 Latimer patents an improved carbon filament.

1884 Latimer joins the Edison Electric Light Company.

1896 Latimer publishes *Incandescent Electric Lighting*; invents locking rack for hats, coats, and umbrellas.

Latimer's most important invention was a carbon filament that increased the brightness and longevity of the light bulb.

From 1880 to 1882, Latimer oversaw the establishment of factories for U.S. Electric's production of the filaments and the installation of electric-light systems in New York City and Philadelphia and later in London. After his return from Britain, he worked for firms in the New York area until he joined the Edison Electric Light Company in 1884. (Edison Electric soon bought out other companies to form General Electric.) There he served as engineer, chief draftsman, and an expert witness for Edison in patent infringement lawsuits. Latimer was author of *Incandescent Electric Lighting* (1896), one of the first textbooks on electric lighting. When General Electric and Westinghouse decided that year to pool patents, they created the Board of Patent Control to monitor patent disputes and appointed Latimer to the board. He used his drafting techniques and knowledge of patent law in this capacity until 1911, when the board was disbanded. He then did patent law consulting with the New York firm of Hammer & Schwarz.

Latimer moved to Flushing, New York, in the late nineteenth century and was active in New York City politics and civil rights issues. In 1902 he circulated a petition to New York City Mayor Seth Low, expressing concern about the lack of African-American representation on the school board. He also taught English and mechanical drawing to immigrants at the Henry Street Settlement in 1906. In 1918 Latimer became a charter member of the Edison Pioneers, an honorary group of scientists who had worked for Thomas Edison's laboratories. Latimer's booklet, *Poems of Love and Life*, was privately published by his friends on his seventy-fifth birthday in 1925. Latimer died in Flushing on December 11, 1928. On May 10, 1968, a public school in Brooklyn was named in his honor. ◆

Lavoisier, Antoine Laurent

1743–1794 ● CHEMISTRY

Considered by many to be the father of modern chemistry, Antoine Laurent Lavoisier was born on August 26, 1743, in Paris. Following his elementary education, he attended the Collège Mazarin and then studied law. He received his license in 1764 but was drawn toward a career in the sciences. His initial venture into science began in 1763, when he was invited by his geology teacher to assist in preparing the first mineralogical atlas of France.

Lavoisier's efforts in geology earned his election to the Academy of Science in 1768, an honor rarely extended to someone his age. In an effort to obtain a higher salary to support his research, he joined the despised taxation committee. While not winning favor among Academy colleagues, the move did allow him to continue his experiments. It also provided Lavoisier with an introduction to Marie Ann Paulze, a committee member's daughter, whom he married in 1771.

When the French government took over the production of gunpowder, Lavoisier headed the committee overseeing the operation. This provided him with a house at the Arsenal, and in it he used his own money to set up a fully equipped laboratory. It soon became a meeting place for prominent scientists, including Joseph Priestley, Benjamin Franklin, and James Watt. To encourage the development of younger scientists, he provided financial assistance and positions as laboratory assistants. Among these promising young researchers was Pierre Samuel du Pont de Nemours, who went to America in 1800 to build the first gunpowder factory.

In addition to his governmental duties, Lavoisier studied numerous topics in chemistry. In experiments begun in 1772, he defined combustion as the "combination of a burnable substance with oxygen." Having provided definitive evidence against the **phlogiston** theory of combustion, he continued to investigate "elastic aeriform fluids," or gases. His experiments extended to acids and bases, and with the help of his wife he organized his results, writing *Elements of Chemistry*, published

> *"If, by the term elements, we mean to express the simple and indivisible molecules that compose bodies, it is probable that we know nothing about them; but if, on the contrary, we express by the term elements or principles of bodies the idea of the last point reached by analysis, all substances that we have not yet been able to decompose by any means are elements to us."*
>
> — Antoine Lavoisier

phlogiston: regarding fire as a material substance.

in 1789. In the preface, Lavoisier outlined his methodical approach to scientific experimentation. He emphasized the importance of basing scientific ideas upon observable facts and stressed the necessity of carefully planned experiments and accurately collected data. The third section of his text described the instruments and operations of chemistry, accompanied by detailed illustrations. He pioneered gas handling and calorimetric methods, and he worked toward developing a chemical nomenclature. His preliminary efforts on a standard system of weights and measures were later to become the metric system.

Despite philanthropic works and his position as the director of the Academy of Sciences, Lavoisier's role in taxation led to his imprisonment during the Reign of Terror. Following a trial before the Revolutionary Tribunal, he was sentenced to death for "contributing to a conspiracy against the people of France." He rejected suicide as an alternative because it would "acquit the madmen who are sending us to death." He was executed by guillotine at the Place de la Révolution on May 8, 1794, and his body was thrown into a nameless grave in the cemetery of Parc Monceau. ◆

1763 Lavoisier helps prepare the first mineralogical atlas of France.

1772 Lavoisier begins experiments on combustion.

1775 Lavoisier becomes head of gunpowder production in France.

1789 Lavoisier publishes *Elements of Chemistry*.

1794 Lavoisier is executed by guillotine.

Lawrence, Ernest Orlando

1901–1958 ● NUCLEAR PHYSICS

Ernest Lawrence, the son of Norwegian-American educators Carl Gustavus and Gunda Jacobson Lawrence, was born in Canton, South Dakota, on August 8, 1901. After attending public schools in Canton and Pierre, South Dakota, Lawrence entered St. Olaf's College in Northfield, Minnesota. A year later he transferred to the University of South Dakota, from which he received a bachelor's degree in 1922. Lawrence earned a master's degree from the University of Minnesota (1923) and a doctorate from Yale (1925), both

under the direction of W. F. G. Swann. Remaining at Yale as a research fellow and then an assistant professor, Lawrence quickly gained a reputation for his ability to create ingenious experimental devices. His research at that time was on spark discharges and the ionization of atoms. In 1928 the University of California at Berkeley offered him an associate professorship and as many graduate students as he could handle. Lawrence accepted, saying that at Berkeley he would have an importance he could not attain at Yale for years. Within two years, he became the youngest full professor at Berkeley. Lawrence married Mary Kimberly Blumer, a daughter of the dean of Yale's medical school, in 1932; they had six children.

M. Stanley Livingston and Ernest O. Lawrence with a cyclotron, 1934.

Lawrence's research on nuclear reactions and particle accelerators began at Berkeley. He conceived the idea for accelerating particles to great speeds while scanning an article that Norwegian engineer Rolf Wideröe had published on the linear acceleration of positive ions. Unable to read

German, Lawrence studied the diagrams, recognizing that he could reduce the size of the apparatus by applying a magnetic field to make the charged particles move in a spiral path. With his first graduate students, Niels E. Edlefsen and M. Stanley Livingston, Lawrence in 1929 produced a test model of a circular particle accelerator, later called a cyclotron, in which a magnetic field constrained charged particles to move in a circular path while an electrical charge jolted them on each trip around the circle, accelerating them to higher velocities. Previous researchers had achieved 125,000 volts of electricity with which to bombard atomic nulcei. Lawrence's goal was one million volts, and in February 1932 he and Livingston succeeded. Their cyclotron, less than a foot in diameter, accelerated protons to about five percent of light's speed and, upon bombarding lithium nuclei, disintegrated them. The cyclotron quickly became a powerful investigative instrument that renewed interest in nuclear research and led to the discovery of a large number of new isotopes.

In 1936 Lawrence became the director of the Berkeley Radiation Laboratory, where during World War II, he and close friend J. Robert Oppenheimer helped devise an electromagnetic method for separating uranium–235, the fissionable uranium isotope used in the Hiroshima atomic bomb. After the war, Lawrence and Edward Teller supported the U.S. fusion, or hydrogen, bomb program and played key roles in establishing a second laboratory for research on nuclear weapons at Livermore, California. However, Lawrence later spoke against the proliferation of nuclear weapons. While participating in a nuclear test ban conference at Geneva, Switzerland, in 1958, Lawrence became ill and died after an operation for ulcerative **colitis**.

Among the numerous awards Lawrence received were the National Academy of Sciences' Comstock Prize (1937), the Royal Society's Hughes Medal (1937), and the Nobel Prize for physics (1939). His name is commemorated in the Lawrence Berkeley Laboratory, the Lawrence Livermore Laboratory in California, and the Annual Lawrence Awards, which the U.S. Atomic Energy Commission (now the Department of Energy) gives to honor young scientists. In addition, element number 103, discovered at Berkeley, is named lawrencium in his honor. ◆

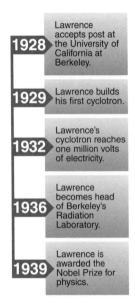

1928 Lawrence accepts post at the University of California at Berkeley.

1929 Lawrence builds his first cyclotron.

1932 Lawrence's cyclotron reaches one million volts of electricity.

1936 Lawrence becomes head of Berkeley's Radiation Laboratory.

1939 Lawrence is awarded the Nobel Prize for physics.

colitis: inflammation of the colon.

Leakey, Louis Seymour Bazett

1903–1972 ● PALEONTOLOGY

> **"I was told, as a young student, not to waste my time searching for Early Man in Africa, since 'everyone knew he had started in Asia.'"**
> — Louis Leakey, preface to *White African*

L eakey was born in Kabete, Kenya, on August 7, 1903. He was the son of Canon Leakey of the Church Missionary Society in Kenya and was brought up with the native Kikuyu. After attending Weymouth College he went to St. John's College, Cambridge, from which he graduated in archaeology and anthropology and took his Ph.D. in African prehistory. He then became a research fellow of the college and, in 1966, an honorary fellow. His interests in prehistory and ethnology were stimulated by M. C. Burkitt and A. C. Haddon. He was a member of the British Museum East African Expedition to **Tanganyika** in 1924 and from 1926 led his own East African archaeological research expeditions. Leakey's important discoveries about the prehistory of East Africa and his discovery of early hominids were published in *The Stone Age Cultures of Kenya* (1931), *The Stone Age Races of Kenya* (1935), and *Stone-Age Africa* (1936).

His archaeological and paleontological work did not detract from his interest in Kenya and its politics, an interest which his close association with the Kikuyu made him particularly well equipped to pursue, as can be seen from his autobiographical *White African* (1937). The results of his

Tanganyika: a former country in east Africa; now part of Tanzania.

research for the Rhodes Trustees into the customs of the Kikuyu tribe (1937-1939) are still in print. At the outbreak of World War II he was in charge of special branch 6 of the Criminal Investigation Department in Nairobi; he continued as a handwriting expert to the department until 1951.

At the end of the war he returned to his archaeological and paleontological researches, as curator of the Coryndon Memorial Museum, Nairobi (1945–1961), and later as honorary director of the National Centre of Prehistory and Paleontology in Nairobi, and on behalf of various research foundations. He founded the Pan-African Congress on Prehistory, of which he was general secretary (1947–1951) and president (1955–1959). On periods of leave during the war Leakey and his second wife, the former Mary Douglas Nicol, discovered the Acheulean site of Olorgesailie in the **Rift Valley**. He continued his researches after the war. His work on the **Miocene** deposits of western Kenya produced among other discoveries the almost complete skull of *Proconsul africansus*, the earliest ape yet found.

Financed largely by the National Geographic Society of Washington, Leakey and his family, beginning in 1959, undertook large-scale work at Olduvai. There, in their first season, Mary Leakey found the skull of *Australopithecus (Zinjanthropus) boisie*; and in 1960 their son Jonathan discovered the first remains of *Homo habilis*, a **hominid** dated by the potassium-argon method at 1.7 million years. Also in 1960 Leakey discovered the skull of one of the makers of the **Acheulean** culture at Olduvai, which he named *Homo erectus*. These remarkable researches have been published and are still being published in a series of books entitled *Olduvai Gorge*. After his death his work was continued by his wife and his son Richard, who just before his father's death in London, October 1, 1972, was able to show him the remains of a human being found on the shores of Lake Rudolf below a tufa dated at 2.6 million years.

Charles Darwin speculated that Africa might be the continent where man had emerged; and Leakey's fieldwork seems to have shown this guess to be a sound one. After his death the Kenya authorities established a museum and research institute which they propose to call The Louis Leakey Memorial Institute for African Prehistory.

Rift Valley: a depression in southwest Asia and East Africa extending from the valley of the Jordan River to central Mozambique.

Miocene: a period beginning about 24 million years ago.

hominid: a family of primate mammals who stood erect and walked on two feet.

Acheulean: relating to an early Stone Age culture that used rough, chipped stone tools.

A man of very wide interests and a great lover of both domestic and wild animals, Leakey was a trustee of the National Parks of Kenya and of the Kenya Wild Life Society and president of the East Africa Kennel Club. An enthusiastic and inspiring teacher, he was keen to demonstrate flint knapping, a technique he had learnt from Llewellyn Jewitt's account of the methods used by the nineteenth-century flint forger Edward Simpson, and from watching the knappers at Brandon in Suffolk. He travelled extensively, lecturing to large European and American audiences, and worked tirelessly to disseminate knowledge of this discoveries. His enthusiasm, it was claimed, often carried him to extremes. Although intolerant of opposing views that he considered ill-informed, he realized that, in his field, it was necessary to be a competent archaeologist, human paleontology, zoologist, anatomist, and geologist—and that hardly anyone could be expert in all of them. Many of his discoveries were controversial but his persistence and faith were amply justified. No one has hitherto contributed more to the direct discovery of early man and his ancient culture. ◆

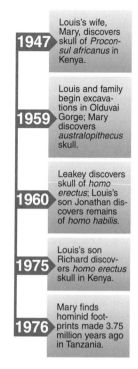

1947 Louis's wife, Mary, discovers skull of *Proconsul africanus* in Kenya.

1959 Louis and family begin excavations in Olduvai Gorge; Mary discovers *australopithecus* skull.

1960 Leakey discovers skull of *homo erectus*; Louis's son Jonathan discovers remains of *homo habilis*.

1975 Louis's son Richard discovers *homo erectus* skull in Kenya.

1976 Mary finds hominid footprints made 3.75 million years ago in Tanzania.

Leeuwenhoek, Antonie van

1632–1723 ● BIOLOGY

Dutch biologist Leeuwenhoek was born in Delft, Holland, son of a basket maker, Philips Thoniszoon, who died when his son was six years old. The surname by which he became famous was taken from a house named "Lion's Corner," which his father owned.

Leeuwenhoek was educated at Warmond grammar school and in 1648 commenced an apprenticeship to an Amsterdam cloth merchant. He returned to his native town and opened a draper's shop in 1652. In 1660 he obtained a **sinecure** position as an usher at Delft town hall, a post he retained for the

> *"A man is always to be busy with his thoughts if anything is to be accomplished."*
>
> — Antonie van Leeuwenhoek

sinecure: a position that requires little work, but provides an income.

rest of his life. In 1677 he was made chief warden and in 1679 winegauger. His business was prosperous and the additional income from municipal office meant he could afford to give time to scientific experiment.

Leeuwenhoek was familiar with the glasses used to inspect the quality of cloth. He experimented with grinding glass and mounting the lens on a specimen holder that could be revolved in three planes: the result was an effective microscope. He was not the first person to make such a device but the lenses he ground were of greater mathematical accuracy and power than any previously known. Although these lenses were tiny and of short focus, they provided almost two hundred times magnification. In the course of his life he ground 419 lenses, attaining as much as five hundred times magnification. With this powerful microscope an exciting new world of biological observation opened up. Within a few years of commencing his experiments in 1671, Leeuwenhoek discovered that microorganisms are living creatures and was the first to reveal the single-celled organisms now called protozoa. Leeuwenhoek investigated the life cycle of the flea and found "this minute and despised creature. . . endowed with as great perfection in its kind as any large animal." He even found tiny parasites living on fleas and this find brought him the distinction of inspiring the poet Jonathan Swift to write:

> *So naturalists observe, a flea*
> *Has smaller fleas that on him prey;*
> *And these have smaller still to bite 'em;*
> *And so proceed ad infinitum.*

Taking samples from such varied sources as ditch water, tooth scrapings, and sperm, Leeuwenhoek made significant contributions to man's knowledge of bacteria. He developed a method for measuring such minute creatures, using for a scale such tiny objects as a hair from his beard and a grain of sand.

Leeuwenhoek's research extended understanding of the fertilization process in animals and plants. It had been believed for many years that certain tiny creatures like fleas or weevils in grain were generated spontaneously or somehow developed out of the decay of natural matter. He demonstrat-

1660 Leeuwenhoek becomes usher at Delft town hall.

1665 Robert Hooke publishes a paper called *Micrographia* on the microscope.

1671 Leeuwenhoek discovers that microorganisms are living creatures.

1680 Leeuwenhoek is elected a member of the Royal Society.

1684 Leeuwenhoek publishes his studies.

ed conclusively that they were really little creatures with reproductive processes comparable to those in larger animals. In the same way he refuted the widespread belief that eels developed from dew: his studies showed that they had an ordinary process of generation.

A Dutch correspondent of the Royal Society of London initiated a correspondence between Leeuwenhoek and the society in 1673. At first members were skeptical concerning his work but he sent to London twenty-six microscopes so they could make their own investigations to confirm his conclusions. Contact with the Royal Society was important in disseminating this new knowledge since he did not publish his findings until 1684 and he wrote mostly in Dutch, a language not widely read outside Holland. In 1680 he was elected a fellow of the Royal Society and in 1697 he was similarly honored by the Paris Academy of Sciences.

His discoveries brought Leeuwenhoek international fame and he was visited by many of the great figures of Europe, including King James II of England and Czar Peter the Great of Russia. In Delft his achievements were not properly understood and he was annoyed to find many townsmen considered him a magician. The municipality, however, did show appreciation to their most eminent citizen, awarding a pension. He was able to continue his work into a ripe old age. ◆

> Leeuwenhoek investigated the life cycle of the flea and even found tiny parasites living on fleas.

Libby, Willard
1908–1980 ● CHEMISTRY & INVENTOR

Willard F. Libby was a nuclear chemist, best remembered as the originator and developer of the C^{14} (radiocarbon) dating method, for which he received the Nobel Prize in chemistry in 1960.

Libby was born on 17 December 1908 in Grand Valley, Colorado, and grew up in a farming community in northern California. He entered the University of California,

Berkeley, in 1927 intending, as he often said, to learn enough science to be a modern farmer. He was diverted from this goal by the chemistry faculty, however. As a result he went straight from undergraduate studies to graduate work, receiving his Ph.D. degree in chemistry in 1933, during the Great Depression. He gladly accepted an instructorship in the department. In the following years he did research in several areas of physical and nuclear chemistry, gaining a reputation for originality and daring. In 1941, still an assistant professor, he received a Guggenheim fellowship at Princeton University. While he was there the United States entered World War II. Libby was one of the first two people invited by Professor Harold Urey to join his project at Columbia University to separate the light fissionable isotope U^{235} by a **diffusion** method, as part of what became the Manhattan Project, the U.S. program to build an atomic bomb. Libby accepted and became the head of the chemistry division of that very large enterprise.

diffusion: scattering.

The separation of an uncommon isotope of a heavy element in the kilogram quantities needed for nuclear weapons was an unprecedented undertaking. A number of methods were developed at least to a pilot plant stage. It was clear that in principle diffusion of a uranium-containing gas was the most straightforward approach to large-scale production. For several reasons the fluoride UF^6 was the gas to use. There were two major obstacles: (1) the problem of large-scale production of the fine grained, thin membranes or diffusion barriers and their assembly to perform the multi-stage separation, and (2) the extreme corrosiveness of the gas. The key invention was made by Libby and Anthony Turkevich, who were issued a secret patent for the design and manufacturing method. Libby led the research needed to enable production of the barriers, which was completed while the huge separation plant was under construction at Oak Ridge, Tennessee. The barriers were delivered in time to permit the plant to begin functioning on schedule. The first bomb was exploded over Japan in August 1945.

After the war Libby, along with Urey, Enrico Fermi, Edward Teller, Leo Szilard, and other famous physicists and chemists, accepted professorial positions in newly established science institutes at the University of Chicago, where Fermi and others had earlier achieved the first self-sustained

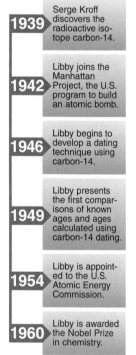

1939 Serge Kroff discovers the radioactive isotope carbon-14.

1942 Libby joins the Manhattan Project, the U.S. program to build an atomic bomb.

1946 Libby begins to develop a dating technique using carbon-14.

1949 Libby presents the first comparisons of known ages and ages calculated using carbon-14 dating.

1954 Libby is appointed to the U.S. Atomic Energy Commission.

1960 Libby is awarded the Nobel Prize in chemistry.

release of nuclear energy in 1942. The Institute for Nuclear Studies there, now the Fermi Institute, housed an extraordinary concentration of scientific talent. Confidence was high. Discipline boundaries were to a great extent ignored, providing fertile soil for original projects. It was in this environment that Libby's C^{14} dating project began to take shape.

The method was based on a few critical assumptions, which had to be verified at the start. The first was that the radioactive isotope of carbon, C^{14}, is made naturally in the earth's atmosphere by cosmic rays (already suggested by Serge Korff a few years earlier), and that it quickly oxidizes to carbon dioxide, CO_2. Next, that this material, combined with the much more abundant nonradioactive CO_2, quickly mixes uniformly throughout the earth's atmosphere and through carbonate dissolved in the ocean as well. Next, that it quickly enters the "carbon cycle" in which living plants incorporate it, and animals take it in from their food, and that the death and decay of organisms liberates it for the next cycle. Finally, it must be assumed that materials formerly living and preserved, like wood or textiles, no longer are exchanging material with the atmosphere or biosphere, and

Five winners of the 1960 Nobel Prizes stand together at the ceremony in Stockholm. They include (from left) Willard F. Libby; Peter Brian Medawar of Britain and Frank MacFarlane Burnet of Australia, co-winners of the award for Medicine; Donald A. Glaser of the United States, winner of the Physics award; and St John Perse of France, winner of the Literature award.

that, when life stops, C^{14} begins to decay (to nonradioactive N^{14}) at a rate set by its half life. With these assumptions and appropriate measurements, an age (or time of death) can be calculated. When Libby began his studies in 1946, none of these assumptions had been tested. Even the half life of C^{14} was extremely uncertain. Moreover, at that time there was no way with existing equipment to measure the C^{14} content or decay rate at the levels that occur in nature without expensive, difficult isotopic enrichment. In the next few years he and his junior collaborators provided proof, at the working level of precision, of all the assumptions listed, measured the half-life still in use in the field today, and built counting equipment capable of measuring the effect. This research was one of the last examples of a major scientific development designed and led to a successful outcome by a single individual.

The first direct comparison of ages calculated from C^{14} with known (historical) ages appeared in 1949. Since the measured half-life is about 5,700 years, the method is especially suited to studies of human history and prehistory. When the first "date list" of unknowns was published in 1951, the statistical error of the measurements (one standard deviation) was about 200 years for samples younger than a few thousand years. The range of applicability was about 20,000 years. Since then both measuring methods and fundamental understanding have improved, accompanied by a great increase in the number of laboratories set up for the purpose. There is a scientific journal, *Radiocarbon*, devoted entirely to this subject. It would be difficult to overstate the achievements made by C^{14} analyses in archeology, earth sciences, and many other disciplines, such as the study of solar changes.

In the next few years Libby and his students discovered and studied the natural distribution of the radioactive isotope of hydrogen, H^3 or tritium, which has a half-life of 12.3 years and is also produced by cosmic rays in the atmosphere. It was fortunate that this work preceded by a few years the large-scale testing of nuclear weapons in the atmosphere. The tritium content of the megaton "hydrogen bombs" tested and distributed first through the northern hemisphere and then around the whole earth, swamped the natural tritium level, which could not be freely studied again for decades afterward.

> It would be difficult to overstate the achievements made by carbon 14 analysis in archeology, earth sciences, and many other disciplines.

Radiocarbon Dating

Before 1949, geologists and anthropologists had no accurate method for measuring the age of very old wood, bones, cloth, and other artifacts. They estimated an artifact's age by studying the location where it was found, other artifacts found near it, tree rings and silt layers in nearby riverbeds, and related historical documents. Such dating methods are useful, but often inaccurate. In 1949, Willard Libby developed an accurate method for measuring the age of ancient artifacts. All animals and plants contain carbon-14, which they absorb during their lifetimes by breathing and eating. When an organism dies, its carbon-14 begins to decay at a constant rate of approximately 50% every 5,700 years. Libby worked out a formula for measuring this rate of carbon-14 decay. Using Libby's technique, scientists can determine the date an organism died to within 1% accuracy. Scientists have learned much about prehistoric people, animals, and plants using carbon-14 dating. Libby's formula has greatly changed the way we understand the history of the Earth and the development of living organisms.

Even the C^{14} content of the atmosphere doubled in the interval before the United States and the Soviet Union stopped major atmospheric testing.

In this same period Libby began a small research program to observe the atmospheric and surface distribution of nuclear fission products, especially long-lived Sr^{90} and Cs^{137}, resulting from atmospheric tests and other releases. When fallout became a major issue after the U.S. H-bomb tests in the Marshall Islands in the Pacific in 1954, this project provided much of the limited scientific understanding then available of the processes involved, and of the potential hazards.

In that year Libby accepted an appointment as one of the five U.S. Atomic Energy Commissioners, and moved to Washington, DC. An early achievement was the release of information possessed by the Atomic Energy Commission (AEC) on the fallout resulting from H-bomb tests. Up to his arrival this information had been classified secret.

In his role as commissioner, and afterward, Libby was a tireless advocate of the peaceful uses of nuclear science and technology. These included the relatively noncontroversial use of radioactive isotopes in medical and industrial research as well as the worldwide generation of nuclear power as a substitute for the use of fossil fuels, and projects for large-scale public works, such as the digging of canals and artificial harbors using nuclear explosives. This point of view involved him in many debates, especially in later years.

After the expiration of his term as commissioner, Libby returned to academic life as professor of chemistry at U.C.L.A. There he took an active role in developing new interdisciplinary programs, first as director of the University of California's multicampus Institute of Geophysics and Planetary Physics, and later, among other things, in the creation of U.C.L.A.'s unique Environmental Doctor degree program. He continued to serve on numerous boards and committees concerned with science policy, nuclear matters, and the environment.

Throughout his academic career Libby had a strong interest in teaching, and particularly in the training of research students. He was not an especially gifted classroom lecturer. At the same time his skill in selecting students capable of first-class research achievement, and in developing their motivation and talents, was remarkable.

As a scientist and as a policymaker, Willard Libby was an important figure. Especially in later years, his originality and fearlessness in crossing disciplinary boundaries sometimes led him into error. Still, his contributions to science were most impressive, both through his own work and through the students he trained. Some of his policy views are now widely seen as incorrect. Others, especially his commitment to openness in government, and his enthusiasm for science as an adventure perennially appealing to the young in spirit, are fortunately still with us. Libby died on 8 September 1980 in Los Angeles, California. ◆

> Libby's enthusiasm for science as an adventure perennially appealing to the young in spirit is fortunately still with us.

Linné, Carl von (Carolus Linnaeus)

1707–1778 ● BOTANY

> *"Minerals grow; plants grow and live; animals grow and live and feel."*
> — Carl von Linné, *Systema Naturae*

S weden was the home of the naturalist Carl von Linné, of whom it was said, "God created, Linnaeus set in order." His father, Nils, was a country parson in Stenbrohult, southern Sweden, who laid out a beautiful flower garden around the parsonage and instilled in his son his passion for botany.

Linné was a mediocre student at school; plants were all he really cared to learn about. Botany might be a hobby, but Nils Linné doubted it could provide his son a livelihood; poor progress at academic studies ruled out holy orders. In 1726 he considered apprenticing him to a tailor or shoemaker, but Dr. Johan Rothman, one of Linné's teachers, persuaded him that Carl could be usefully employed in medicine.

In 1727 Linné began medical studies at Lund University, but the instruction available there was of poor quality. However, it proved to be a good place for botanical studies. He had at his disposal an extensive library and collection of specimens, and he explored the surrounding countryside, augmenting his knowledge of plant life. He gained his medical degree and meanwhile also attracted the sponsorship of fellow botany enthusiasts Professor Rudbeck and Olaf Celcius. With the latter, he undertook field trips investigating the flora of the region.

flora: plant or bacterial life.

By 1730 Linné had developed his theory of plant classification based on sexuality. That year he was appointed lecturer on botany at Uppsala University and gave demonstrations in the botanical gardens. In 1732, on behalf of the university, he made a historic forty-six hundred mile four-month tour through Lapland, recording its **flora** and the customs of the natives. He discovered one hundred new species of plants, and described the small plant *Linnaea borealis* as "lowly, insignificant, flowering for only a short while, named after Linné who resembles it." It was he who showed that any species of plant—or, indeed, of any other living being—could be described in two words, denoting it and its relationship.

genus: a biological group of structurally related species.

The first word, a Latin noun, gives the **genus**, the second, a Latin adjective, the organism. His best known definition is *Homo sapiens*.

Linné left for Holland to take a doctorate at the University of Harderwijk in 1735, when he also published his *Systema Naturae*, a pioneering classification of the animal, plant, and mineral kingdoms. Originally it consisted of just seven folio leaves, but by the tenth edition had expanded to twenty-five hundred pages. It marked Linné's emergence as the leading European botanist and he drew many patrons willing to finance his books. In 1737 he published a book on his travels in Lapland and *Genera Plantarum*, an important reference work describing all 935 plant species then recognized.

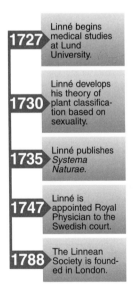

1727 Linné begins medical studies at Lund University.

1730 Linné develops his theory of plant classification based on sexuality.

1735 Linné publishes *Systema Naturae*.

1747 Linné is appointed Royal Physician to the Swedish court.

1788 The Linnean Society is founded in London.

In 1738 Linné returned to Sweden and started practicing as a physician in Stockholm, where he was appointed physician to the Admiralty. In 1742 he returned to Uppsala university, this time as holder of the chair of botany and medicine. The rest of his life he devoted to development of the university's botanical garden and to teaching enthusiastic students who flocked to Uppsala from many different countries. His students sent him plants from their own regions and he proceeded to cultivate these in the garden at Uppsala. The Swedish parliament also commissioned him to travel around the country surveying natural resources.

In his later years Linné developed his views on a natural order in which every component filled a set role. He was amazed at the smooth working of all the interlocking components in this world, writing of "seeing the infinite, all-knowing and all-powerful God from behind." In all creation he sensed "an eternal wisdom and power, an inscrutable perfection."

Linné took pride in his fame and was intolerant of other botanists challenging his work. He said of himself that God had bestowed on him the greatest insight into the knowledge of nature, more than any one had hitherto enjoyed. As a teacher he was a gifted communicator, a charismatic figure inspiring devotion. He sent pupils on study trips to America, China, Japan, and other distant lands. These expeditions made significant contributions to botanical knowledge but were so dangerous that an estimated one-third of the students sent out never returned.

Linné' field studies around Uppsala were outstandingly popular. Two to three hundred students at a time, clad in light linen garments and equipped with collecting tools, would set off with him into the surrounding countryside, all marching in formation to the accompaniment of French horns and drums.

Linné was a welcome visitor to the Swedish court and in 1747 was appointed Royal Physician. In 1761 he was ennobled. An attack of apoplexy forced him into retirement in 1774. His only son (also called Carl) succeeded him in the professorship. Sir James Smith bought his botanical collection for 900 guineas and removed it to Burlington House, London, where in 1788 the Linnaean Society was founded. ◆

> *"A professor can never better distinguish himself in his work than by encouraging a clever pupil, for the true discoverers are among them, as comets amongst the stars."*
> — Carl von Linné

Lister, Joseph Baron

1827–1912 ● MEDICINE

British surgeon Joseph Baron Lister developed the use of antiseptics in medical practice. Born to Quaker parents in Upton, Essex, Lister inherited a fascination for natural history from his father, a successful businessman who had won membership to the Royal Society for his discoveries in the field of optics. From an early age Lister expressed a desire to enter surgery, but as the universities of Oxford and

Cambridge were barred to him on religious grounds, he entered the nonsectarian University College, London, in those days popularly known as the "Godless College in Gower Street."

Lister boarded in London with other Quaker students, but soon fell victim to a nervous breakdown induced by his austere lifestyle combined with the rigor of studies and an attack of smallpox. He resumed his education later that year and received his medical degree in 1852, along with a fellowship in the Royal College of Surgeons.

In 1853 Lister began work under James Symes, professor of clinical surgery at the University of Edinburgh, and the two became good friends. Lister became resident house surgeon in 1854, marrying Symes's eldest daughter, Agnes, in 1856. Marriage to a non-Quaker compelled Lister to resign from the Society of Friends, much to the consternation of his family, who nevertheless maintained their close ties with him.

Upon returning from a lengthy tour of Europe, Lister took up the post of assistant surgeon at Glasgow's Royal Infirmary, and worked as an extramural lecturer at the medical school. He accepted a professorship at the University of Glasgow in 1860 and was elected to the Royal Society. His lectures were held in a dim, dusty operating theater where students sat in semicircles around the kitchen table at which he operated and behind which hung a blackboard.

After taking charge of the surgical wards at the Royal Infirmary in 1861 Lister contributed to the rapid progress being made in surgery—following the advent of anesthesia—through his invention of several instruments. He was remarkably deft in surgery and his innovations included radical **mastectomy** for breast cancer and the pinning together of fractures. In those days hospitals were filthy and infection was rife; 40 percent of patients died from **septicemia** following limb amputation. Lister, who insisted upon scrupulous cleanliness in order to prevent infection, was mocked by colleagues for being overly fastidious.

As only external wounds were subject to infection, Lister postulated that the festering of wounds was a form of decomposition produced by something in the hospital air. On reading of Louis Pasteur's discovery that airborne microorganisms on contact with an appropriate medium cause fermentation or decomposition and multiply, he deduced that these airborne

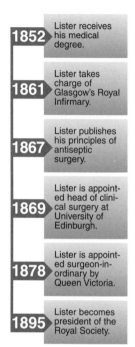

1852 Lister receives his medical degree.

1861 Lister takes charge of Glasgow's Royal Infirmary.

1867 Lister publishes his principles of antiseptic surgery.

1869 Lister is appointed head of clinical surgery at University of Edinburgh.

1878 Lister is appointed surgeon-in-ordinary by Queen Victoria.

1895 Lister becomes president of the Royal Society.

mastectomy: surgery to remove the breast.

septicemia: blood poisoning.

microbes might cause the infection of wounds and began to search for a chemical destroyer. Carbolic acid, which destroyed **entozoa** when spread on polluted fields could, he thought, act as an effective antiseptic on wounds.

Between 1865 and 1867 Lister successfully used carbolic acid to prevent infection in cases of compound fractures and created an antiseptic putty for use on abscesses. He constantly modified and improved upon his techniques, which were based on methodical and thorough testing, and began to use carbolic acid in surgery. Many fellow surgeons, however, were skeptical of Lister's findings, published in *The Lancet* in 1867.

In 1869 Lister was appointed professor of clinical surgery at the University of Edinburgh, and devoted himself to the perfection and promulgation of the antiseptic system. He left Edinburgh in 1877 to take up the professorship of the newly created chair of clinical surgery at Kings College, London, where he encountered a hostile reception. His ideas were, however, received enthusiastically abroad, and the following year Lister was appointed surgeon-in-ordinary by Queen Victoria. He carefully followed developments in aseptic surgery in Germany in the 1880s, appreciating its importance in view of the fact that antiseptics can damage the body's natural healing processes but stood by his conviction that antiseptics still had an important role to play in medical treatment.

Lister retired in 1892 and was made president of the Royal Society in 1895. In his final years he suffered from rheumatism and lived with his sister-in-law in a small town on the coast of Kent. in accordance with his own wish he was buried alongside his wife in West Hampstead cemetery. A funeral service was held at Westminster Abbey where a marble medallion now hangs in his honor.

Lister's antiseptic system transformed the ancient craft of surgery into an enlightened profession. His work resulted in a huge reduction in deaths following surgery, and made possible abdominal, chest, and later brain operations, which had formerly been inconceivable. Lister received many honors and in 1897 was raised to the peerage. ◆

> *"Since the antiseptic treatment has been brought into full operation, and wounds and abscesses no longer poison the atmosphere with putrid exhalations, my wards, though in other respects under precisely the same circumstances as before, have completely changed their character.*
>
> — Joseph Lister

entozoa: parasites, especially worms, that live inside animals.

Lumière, Auguste

1862–1954 ● INVENTOR

Lumière, Louis

1864–1948 ● INVENTOR

Louise Lumière was the first person to recognize the cinema as a profitable form of public entertainment.

rench photographic and cinema entrepreneurs, the Lumière brothers are credited with the invention of cinematography. Born in France, near Lyons, the sons of a prosperous manufacturer of photographic plates, Lumière and his older brother Auguste (1862–1954) studied at the Martinier School of Industry and Commerce. Both brothers joined their father in the family business and quickly showed signs of the ingenuity and business acumen that was to become their trademark. Before he was twenty, Lumière had perfected his father's production techniques to the point where their factory was a leader in this new field. Within fifteen years the Lumière brothers had become important industrialists; they kept up to date with the latest developments in photography and soon became interested in the development of motion pictures, a field very much in its technological infancy a that time.

In 1894 the Lumière brothers came into contact with Thomas Edison's Kinetoscope, a primitive contraption by which a short sequence of moving images could be viewed by one customer at a time. They were immediately inspired with the idea of projecting moving images onto a screen in front of an audience and within a year they had developed an elegant machine that combined camera, processor, and projector. Its original contribution was a system of claws that moved the film. Patented under the name *Cinématographe*, from which the word *cinema* is derived, this machine was used to shoot one-minute films that were first shown privately throughout 1895. Confident of their technique, the brothers premiered their films to the paying public on December 28, in a basement of the Grand Café in Paris. The ten films totalled twenty minutes, and there were twenty screenings a day. Each film was limited to a physical length of fifty feet, which was the capacity of the spool box holding the negative.

Not only did the Lumière brothers' *Cinématographe* produce high quality images, it had the added advantage of being portable, so that for the first time the cameraman was able to leave the studio and record the outside world at work and play. The Lumières' films were short, lively documentaries that presented a warm, secure image of bourgeois life at the turn of the century. Initially, the Lumières made use of family and friends in their films. Their first production, *Workers Leaving the Factory*, shows their own employees leaving the family photographic factory. Another early work, *Baby's Tea*, is a charming sequence that features Louis Lumière, his wife, and their baby daughter. From the beginning, Louis also showed a lively comic talent and produced many popular comic sketches.

The Early Film Industry

Although many inventors and scientists contributed to the development of motion pictures, Louis and Auguste Lumière are usually credited with inventing the movie industry in 1895 when they presented a program of brief motion pictures to a paying audience in the basement of a Paris cafe. By 1896, motion pictures were commercial successes in many parts of the world. The earliest films were 15- to 60-second glimpses of real life scenes or staged theatrical performances. In the United States, these short films were usually shown in vaudeville theaters as one act on a bill of live performances. By 1903, a growing number of small theaters called nickelodeons began to show movies exclusively. Patrons paid a nickel to see a program of five or six 10-minute films, usually including an adventure, a comedy, a drama, and a documentary. Longer feature films first appeared in the United States in 1912, when *Queen Elizabeth,* starring Sarah Bernhardt, was imported from France. Bernhardt, along with Mary Pickford and Charlie Chaplin, was one of the first movie stars.

The Lumières started to send cameramen all over the world to cover international events and satisfy audiences' curiosity about foreign lands and cultures. People queued up for hours to be astounded by the Lumières' lifelike moving images. One of their most famous films, *The Arrival of the Train*, caused an uproar when it was first shown as many people thought that the approaching train on the screen was actually going to hit them. Despite the fact that none of the Lumières' works lasted more than a few minutes, they were skillfully organized in terms of time and space, testifying to Louis Lumière's experience as a stills photographer.

The Lumière brothers set out to market their films internationally and jealously guarded the secret of the *Cinématographe*, employing their own cameramen and projectionists. However, imitators proliferated and the brothers soon found themselves in competition with English and American filmmakers. Despite considerable financial success, they never had the resources of their rivals and as a result grew discouraged. Louis Lumière gradually wound down his production of films and by 1903 had returned to photography and developing the production of color plates. During World War I the company diversified its production, working on ways of heating aircraft, and in 1920 Louis Lumière abandoned direction of the factory to concentrate on technical inventions. In 1934 he returned to the cinema with three-dimensional films, which were premiered in Paris in 1936. Meanwhile Auguste Lumière had directed his energies to medical research and published many respected articles.

Louis Lumière was the first person to recognize the cinema as a profitable form of public entertainment, and the artistic excellence and sound marketing of his films ensured that the cinema would be more than just a passing technological novelty. The irony is that Louis Lumière himself never believed that the cinema had a long-term future or that it could ever do more than represent everyday life; it was left for others to exploit the narrative and aesthetic properties of the medium. The Lumière factory in Lyons is now a museum and archives, and the gates featured in his first film are still in place. ◆

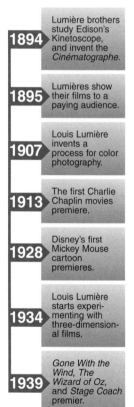

1894 Lumière brothers study Edison's Kinetoscope, and invent the *Cinématographe*.

1895 Lumières show their films to a paying audience.

1907 Louis Lumière invents a process for color photography.

1913 The first Charlie Chaplin movies premiere.

1928 Disney's first Mickey Mouse cartoon premieres.

1934 Louis Lumière starts experimenting with three-dimensional films.

1939 *Gone With the Wind*, *The Wizard of Oz*, and *Stage Coach* premier.

Lyell, Charles

1797–1875 ● GEOLOGY

"It may undoubtedly be said that strata have been always forming somewhere, and therefore at every moment of past time Nature has added a page to her archives."

— Charles Lyell

harles Lyell was born at Kirriemuir, Angus, Scotland, on 14 November 1797, the eldest child of Charles Lyell and Frances (Smith) Lyell. In 1798 his father moved to Hampshire in southern England, where Lyell grew up. After attending school at Midhurst in Sussex, Lyell entered Exeter College, Oxford, where he received the usual classical education and graduated with a Bachelor of Arts degree in 1819. At Oxford, William Buckland's lectures on mineralogy and geology aroused Lyell's interest in geology. In 1817 he visited the island of Staffa to study its **columnar basalt** and in 1818, while traveling with his family through Switzerland, Lyell observed the effects of glaciers in the Alps.

In 1819 Lyell was elected to the Geological Society of London and entered Lincoln's Inn to study law. In 1822 he was admitted to the bar, but defective eyesight (he was shortsighted) made reading for the law difficult. He turned to geology and in 1823 spent two months in Paris, where he met leading naturalists, including the director of the Museum of Natural History, Georges Cuvier, and the famous traveler and geologist, Alexander von Humboldt. The geologist Constant Prevost showed him that the alternation of freshwater and marine formations in the Paris basin did not require the geological catastrophes postulated by Cuvier. In 1824 Lyell found

columnar basalt: column-shaped formations of basalt, a dark grey or black rock.

that modern limestones formed in Scottish lakes were exactly like ancient fresh water limestones of the Paris basin, suggesting a close analogy between ancient and modern conditions.

In 1828 a geological tour through France and Italy convinced Lyell that the elevation and disturbance of **sedimentary** rocks had occurred gradually as a result of earthquakes and volcanic activity occurring on the same scale as in the present. He found analogies among rocks formed at widely different geological periods and decided that in the past, geological processes were identical to those of the present. In his *Principles of Geology*, published in three volumes from 1830 to 1833, Lyell argued that the geological past was uniform with the present. During his travels, Lyell recognized that the **Tertiary** formations of France and Italy were of various ages and might be classified by the proportion of living species among their fossil shells. Lyell noted that throughout the Tertiary period species of shells gradually became extinct to be replaced by new species, their extinction brought about by geological change. According to the proportion of living species among their fossil shells, a **seminal** observation in the development of historical geology, Lyell classified Tertiary formations into four epochs: Eocene, Miocene, and the older and newer Pliocene.

On 12 July 1832 Lyell married Mary Elizabeth Horner, daughter of Leonard Horner, geologist and educator. The Lyells then took a house in London, where they resided except when on their frequent and often extended travels. Fluent in French and German, Mary Lyell assisted Lyell in his scientific work and usually accompanied him on his travels. Through the 1830s Lyell was occupied continually with revision of the *Principles of Geology*, which was published in a fifth edition in 1837 and exerted a profound influence, especially on young geologists, including Charles Darwin. Lyell showed how the detailed study of rocks, and especially of fossils, could be used to reveal the history of the earth. In 1838 he published the *Elements of Geology*, an introductory work describing the classes of rocks and the succession of geological formations then known.

In July 1841 the Lyells sailed for the United States, where that autumn Lyell delivered the Lowell lectures at Boston. The Lyells remained in America until August 1842, traveling

sedimentary: formed from material deposited by water, wind, or glaciers.

Tertiary: a geological period beginning about 65 million and ending about 5 million years ago.

seminal: something original that contributes to later development.

widely to examine the geology of New York State and Pennsylvania, the Atlantic coastal plain as far south as Georgia, and Nova Scotia. In 1845 Lyell published his *Travels in America* and the same year returned to America to deliver the Lowell lectures and to travel widely through the South and along the Mississippi River, travels described in 1849 in his *Second Visit to the United States*. In 1852 he made a third visit to the States to deliver the Lowell lectures, and in 1853 returned a fourth time as a representative of Great Britain at the New York Industrial Exhibition.

During 1853–1854 the Lyells visited Madeira and the Canary Islands to examine the evidence for Leopold von Buch's theory of craters of elevation, which postulated the sudden catastrophic elevation of volcanic mountains. Finding that Madeira and the Canary Islands had been formed by ordinary volcanic eruptions, in 1857 Lyell revisited Sicily to learn whether Elie de Beaumont was correct that, when lavas were found steeply inclined, they must have been poured out originally on a horizontal surface and uplifted later, an assumption necessary to the theory of craters of elevation. On Mount Etna and Vesuvius, Lyell found that lavas could harden into thick sheets of compact rock on steep slopes and that the mountains had been built up gradually by a long succession of ordinary volcanic eruptions. Lyell's 1858 paper, "On the Structure of Lavas Which Have Consolidated on Steep Slopes. . . ," effectively destroyed the theory of craters of elevation and with it the scientific basis for catastrophism.

In 1859, when Lyell was preparing the sixth edition of the *Elements of Geology*, the discovery of flint implements at Brixham in Devonshire and in the Somme Valley in France, coupled with the recent discovery of a fossil human skeleton at Neanderthal in Germany, suggested that humans had lived in Europe much earlier than was thought previously. As Lyell compared the evidence for early humans to that for successive glacial periods, he found the subject too large to include within the *Elements*, so in 1863 he published a separate work titled *Antiquity of Man*. In *Antiquity of Man* Lyell argued that immense periods of time had been necessary for the differentiation of the various human races and human languages. If the various human races were descended from common ancestors, related species of animals might likewise share a common ancestry. Lyell laid out a broad array of evidence to indi-

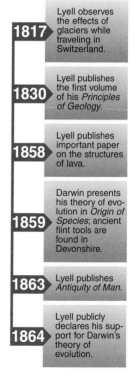

1817 Lyell observes the effects of glaciers while traveling in Switzerland.

1830 Lyell publishes the first volume of his *Principles of Geology*.

1858 Lyell publishes important paper on the structures of lava.

1859 Darwin presents his theory of evolution in *Origin of Species*; ancient flint tools are found in Devonshire.

1863 Lyell publishes *Antiquity of Man*.

1864 Lyell publicly declares his support for Darwin's theory of evolution.

". . . the human mind is not only enabled to number worlds beyond the unassisted ken of mortal eye, but to trace the events of indefinite ages before the creation of our race . . ."
— Charles Lyell,
Principles of Geology

tectonics: a branch of geology concerned with the structure of the earth's crust.

cate that species had changed over time, that such change may have occurred as a result of natural selection, and that humankind had evolved from lower animals. Lyell did not draw conclusions from such evidence, thereby inducing his readers to decide its meaning for themselves.

Antiquity of Man enjoyed a large sale, the first edition of four thousand copies disappearing almost immediately and the book moving rapidly through second and third editions. In the second edition, at Charles Darwin's urging, Lyell expressed his opinion that scientists would ultimately agree that change of species had been brought about by variation and natural selection. In 1864, Lyell publicly declared his faith in Darwin's theory and he thoroughly revised the tenth edition of the *Principles of Geology* (1867–1868) to conform to it.

On 25 April 1873 Lady Lyell died of typhoid ever. Her death was a severe blow to Lyell and, after some months of illness, he died on 22 February 1875. Lyell exerted a profound influence on geologists both during his lifetime and later, especially by his insistence that geological phenomena are explicable by natural causes. His objection to catastrophism was that, once a catastrophe was postulated, geological inquiry ceased. Lyell's uniformitarian geology could not be fitted within the brief age of the earth postulated by Lord Kelvin and widely accepted in the late nineteenth century, but in the twentieth century the much greater age of Earth determined by radioactive methods and the low and extremely steady rates of geological change suggested by the theories of continental drift and plate **tectonics** have vindicated Lyell's confidence in the uniformity of Earth history. ◆

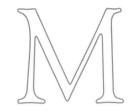

Marconi, Guglielmo

1874–1937 ● INVENTOR

Inventor of wireless telegraphy and winner of the Nobel prize, Guglielmo Marconi was born in Bologna, Italy, where the differences between his Irish mother and Italian father made his childhood insecure and unstable. His strict, disapproving father condemned Marconi's boyhood fascination with dismembering electrical devices and constructing new gadgets from the pieces as a nonsensical waste of time better spent in study. He felt that Marconi would never amount to anything, especially after he failed the naval academy's entrance exams. However, his doting mother got him into a technical institute, where his scientific interests found an outlet and he became an avid student of practical physics and electricity, although he still failed to get into the University of Bologna.

By then, an extensive telephone and telegraph system had been developed, information on electricity was readily available, and Heinrich Hertz had just discovered that electrical energy could be radiated through space. Marconi read about

Marconi studied Hertz's experiments with electromagnetic waves, and created a system of wireless telegraphy based on them.

Hertz's experiments with electromagnetic waves and, becoming obsessed with the idea of creating a system of wireless telegraphy based on them, began experimenting with home-made equipment.

Marconi's ability to tinker with equipment, modifying it until it achieved good results, was always one of his greatest assets. After two years of experimentation, he developed a model, which he first offered to the Italian government; when it rejected it, he went to England where he patented his device and demonstrated it to the British post office, which was extremely impressed and sponsored a further series of tests that brought Marconi international fame.

Marconi's flair for staging dramatic, attention-getting, and successful demonstrations contributed to the phenomenal speed with which his inventions were developed and adopted. The scientific community continually criticized his dramatics as an unseemly, unscholarly, and unethical means of grabbing credit for the scientific discoveries of others. However, Marconi himself never claimed to have discovered the principles upon which his inventions were based; he was just the first to make use of them for practical applications.

Italy became interested in Marconi's invention and criticized him for having taken it to England, and for avoiding his obligatory Italian military service. He turned the criticism to acclaim by accepting the nominal position of a naval cadet attached to Italy's London embassy—which allowed him to continue his work uninterrupted—and giving an extensive demonstration of his invention for the Italian navy. From then on, Italy was his most consistent supporter. Marconi's good relations with the British post office never recovered from his decision to form a company (1897) for commercial exploitation of his patents—the British expected favored treatment because they had helped him get started.

Marconi hoped to use his invention to solve the problem of communicating with ships at sea. He successfully demonstrated it to the British, Italian, and French navies, but his demonstration to the American navy failed because rival companies' broadcasts interfered with his transmissions (Marconi soon worked out how to fine-tune his transmitters and receivers to exclude such interference). The intense rivalry between wireless companies involved Marconi's company in many legal battles over patent rights, kept it short of

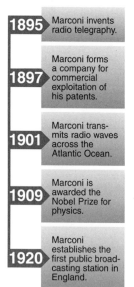

1895 Marconi invents radio telegraphy.

1897 Marconi forms a company for commercial exploitation of his patents.

1901 Marconi transmits radio waves across the Atlantic Ocean.

1909 Marconi is awarded the Nobel Prize for physics.

1920 Marconi establishes the first public broadcasting station in England.

money, and necessitated constant innovation on Marconi's part, to keep ahead of the competition.

Marconi attempted to establish his company's clear superiority over its competitors by achieving commercially viable transatlantic wireless communication. Using powerful generators and tall antennae to transmit and receive the hundreds-of-meter long electromagnetic waves then thought necessary, transatlantic transmission was achieved in 1901 (thanks to the existence of a previously unidentified reflective **ionosphere** encircling the earth). However, this achievement resulted in a temporary loss of customers when, despite Marconi's own objections, the Marconi Company announced that transatlantic commercial wireless communication was available before it had been sufficiently perfected.

ionosphere: a part of the atmosphere that helps transmit radio waves.

Marconi continued to improve and demonstrate his wireless, receiving a Nobel Prize in physics in 1909 for his work. The following year he lost his right ear in a car accident. Marriage to the young Irishwoman, Beatrice O'Brien, had little effect on his preoccupation with his work and his traveling, or on his enjoyment of high living and other women. He was a very proud and private person, and the association of his name with the Marconi scandal (the 1912 revelation of financial speculation in Marconi stock by British government figures) outraged him, especially since he was not even involved in it.

His patriotism led Marconi to spend World War I serving Italy by inspecting and improving mobile wireless stations, procuring military equipment, checking the uses of wireless in airplanes, experimenting with short-wave communication, and participating in a goodwill mission to the United States. Marconi was also an Italian emissary to the Paris Peace Conference, where he signed the peace treaties with Austria and Bulgaria.

Marconi's flair for staging dramatic demonstrations contributed to the phenomenal speed with which his inventions were developed and adopted.

Marconi continued his work on short-wave communication after the war. He persuaded the British government to try short-wave stations for the imperial wireless scheme linking the British Empire. The contract he received contained stiff penalties for failure, which were never enforced since short-wave communication was a success, and Marconi's great ambition of creating a worldwide wireless network was realized.

Beatrice and Marconi were divorced in 1923 after living increasingly separate lives for years. His role in his company decreased as it became less involved with research and innovation. Italy bestowed on him many honors, including a life membership in the Senate. After his marriage to Cristina Bezzi-Scali of the Roman nobility in 1927, his interests were increasingly Italian.

Marconi refused to stop working or even slow down, despite a series of heart attacks. He continued his research in microwaves (waves under a meter long) that led, after his death, to the development of radar and television. He also did extensive public relations work abroad for Fascist Italy (having become a member of the Fascist party in 1923). He suffered a fatal heart attack in 1937, and wireless stations worldwide observed two minutes of silence. ◆

McClintock, Barbara

1902–1992 ● GENETICS

"When you know you're right, you don't care what others think. You know sooner or later it will come out in the wash."
— Barbara McClintock

Barbara McClintock was born June 16, 1902. She was the third child of Dr. Henry Thomas McClintock and his wife Sara (Handy). Mrs. McClintock gave birth to another child two years later; four youngsters close in age proved too much for the mother and Barbara was turned over to relatives for a brief spell. But it wasn't long before the mother's tolerance—and the family's income—improved. The brood, along with Barbara, relocated to Flatbush, Brooklyn. There, an adolescent Barbara McClintock attended Erasmus High School.

Always a tomboy with an avid love for sports, McClintock surprised more than a few friends and relatives when, in 1919, she announced she wanted to attend Cornell University in nearby Ithaca to study agriculture. In her junior year she took a course in genetics. It was the beginning of a career that led her through not only many professional challenges, but past many social obstacles in a world where males predominated.

McClintock was fascinated with genetics, but because she was a woman, she was refused entry into Cornell's plant breeding department, where most of the genetics courses were taught. Instead she entered the botany department, where she became the assistant to a staff member who quickly spotted her talents.

McClintock received her B.A. in 1923 and her M.A. two years later. Remaining at Cornell, she earned a Ph.D. in **cytology** in 1927. It was during her graduate years that scientists were beginning to perceive a connection between heredity and genetics. Simultaneously, Cornell was pioneering the development of corn. McClintock made her first contribution to the latter science when she identified all 10 chromosomes in maize corn.

cytology: a branch of biology dealing with the structure, function, and life history of cells.

She remained at Cornell as botany instructor and researcher until 1931. These years reaped new and amazing findings from her microscope. Observing and recording changes in plants, and noting cell divisions, she named the function of each chromosome. These startling observations appeared in nine papers published between 1929–1931 by the National Academy of Sciences. These papers are considered the cornerstone of the search to clarify the role of chromosomes.

Despite such success, which brought major grant funding to Cornell, McClintock could not obtain a full-time faculty position, chiefly because of her gender.

Over the next decade, McClintock taught at the California Institute of Technology (1931) and the University of Missouri (1936). She was brought to the latter by Lewis Staller, who admired her work and sought her assistance on a project involving **mutagenic** effects of X-rays on corn.

mutagenic: relating to mutation—a relatively permanent change in hereditary that is usually caused by a physical change in chromosome relations.

At Missouri, she turned her sights toward chromosomes that were affected by radiation and, from them, created methods to generate new mutations. Her hypotheses underscored the existence of a structure on the tip of the chromosome that kept the chromosome stable; she called this structure the telomere. She also concentrated on a pattern of chromosomal behavior, which she aptly named the break-fusion-bridge (BFB) cycle, in which the cycle is initiated by a breakage, followed by fusion to other plant members, thereby creating a new bridge which is ripped apart again by **meiosis** or **meitosis**, beginning the same cycle over again.

Her successes at the University of Missouri created a rivalry with a resident geneticist. McClintock resigned from the post in 1940. After a summer at the botany department at Columbia University with Marcus Rhoades, she accepted a series of temporary, then full-time, positions at Cold Spring Harbor Laboratory, New York, run by the Carnegie Foundation. Here she was to spend the rest of her career and began the work that would eventually result in a Nobel Prize.

Her initial work at Cold Spring produced results. She observed unusual characteristics in maize corn seedlings—odd streaks and assorted discolorations, as well as evidence of mutations within the plants. She had, by this time, become so familiar with maize that she could immediately recognize an abnormality. The pattern, she determined, was not caused by X-rays, as others thought, but seemed to be caused by something internal. Upon closer observation, she observed that because of the seemingly consistent mutations something was regulating the rate of the mutations in the pigment genes, and that in certain areas the mutation either increased or decreased. Further, she discovered that many color patches likewise appeared in opposite pairs of seeds. She came to the conclusion that somewhere in a single cell there existed a gene that actually did regulate these actions and had itself changed, had in fact "jumped" from one part of the chromosome to another.

She called this jumping effect "transposition." She described it as the relocation of genes from one position to another within the same chromosome, thus contributing to the development of large organisms. Until that time scientists were certain that genes were stable, static, and never moved.

meiosis: a type of nuclear cell division in which one cell produces four cells.

meitosis: a type of nuclear cell division in which one cell produces two cells.

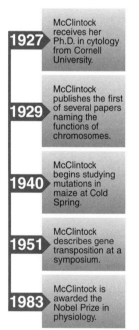

1927 McClintock receives her Ph.D. in cytology from Cornell University.

1929 McClintock publishes the first of several papers naming the functions of chromosomes.

1940 McClintock begins studying mutations in maize at Cold Spring.

1951 McClintock describes gene transposition at a symposium.

1983 McClintock is awarded the Nobel Prize in physiology.

When she presented her discovery at a 1951 symposium, her peers were amazed and shocked. Not surprisingly, some were greatly upset. Some skeptics jeered—she had, after all, undermined the established foundation of chromosome research; one group called her findings with maize inconsequential. But, through time, as transposition was discovered in other genetic systems, the world began to realize that McClintock's theories were true and had indeed altered the course of genetics.

Even though it took the world more than 30 years to formally recognize her achievement with presentation of the 1983 Nobel Prize in physiology or medicine, and even though she had to overcome gender prejudice, she remained determined. She was elected to the National Academy of Science (1944) and the Genetics Society (1945); won the Wolfe Prize in Medicine (1981); and received the first Prize Fellow laureate from the MacArthur Foundation (1981). In her later years, she engaged in writing children's stories. ◆

McCoy, Elijah J.

1843–1929 ● INVENTOR

Elijah McCoy was born on May 2, 1843, in Colchester, Canada West (now Ontario), the third of twelve children, to former slaves who had fled Kentucky. After attending grammar school, McCoy moved to Scotland, where as an engineer's apprentice he acquired technical training that was hard for blacks to obtain in North America. Moving to Ypsilanti, Michigan, after the Civil War, the only railroad work he could find was as a locomotive fireman, despite his background in engineering. His duties led him to consider the limitations in existing lubrication technology. Railroad engines were lubricated only periodically, so they tended to overheat and cause the entire train to stop. Relubrication was awkward and wasted oil, labor, and time.

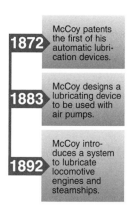

1872 McCoy patents the first of his automatic lubrication devices.

1883 McCoy designs a lubricating device to be used with air pumps.

1892 McCoy introduces a system to lubricate locomotive engines and steamships.

hydrostatic: dealing with fluids at rest and the pressures they exert.

After two years of experimenting, McCoy developed a "lubricating cup" for steam engines that would, in his words, "provid[e] for the continuous flow of oil on the gears . . . and thereby do away with the necessity of shutting down the machine." His next three patents, issued in 1872, 1873, and 1874, were for improvements on the lubricator. In order to finance a machine shop to advance his research, McCoy assigned his patents to various companies and individuals. While this enabled him to work continuously on his own inventions and assured him due credit, it meant that almost all of the profits made from his machines went to others. McCoy was only a minor stockholder in the Elijah McCoy Manufacturing Company of Detroit.

In 1883 McCoy designed a lubricating device to be used with air pump brakes. Previously, oil had been depleted in the brakes whenever the steam was cut off. McCoy placed an additional lubricator on top of the brake cylinder, assuring a continuous flow of oil into the system. The patent for this device, known as the **hydrostatic** oil lubricator, was assigned to the Hodges Company of Detroit. In 1892 McCoy introduced a system that soon lubricated most locomotive engines in the West and those on steamships of the Great Lakes. He also experimented with solid lubricants, such as graphite, which, when applied to machine gears, enabled them to glide smoothly over one another.

By the time of his death on October 10, 1929, in Eloise, Michigan, McCoy held over fifty-eight patents, including a folding iron table and an automatic sprinkler and was known as the "father of lubrication." Many believe that his reputation for quality and authenticity was the source for the phrase "the real McCoy," but conclusive evidence for its origins is lacking. ◆

Meitner, Lise

1878–1968 ● N<small>UCLEAR PHYSICS</small>

Meitner's work spanned the development of twenti-eth-century atomic physics from radioactivity to nuclear fission. Albert Einstein called her "our Marie Curie." It is true that Meitner, like Curie, was a brilliant experimental physicist of exceptional prominence.

She was born in Vienna, Austria, on November 7, 1878, to intellectual, politically liberal parents, the third of eight children of Philipp (a lawyer) and Hedwig Meitner. Although the family background was Jewish, Judaism played no role in the children's upbringing, and all were baptized as adults, Lise as a Protestant in 1908.

At the time, schooling for Austrian girls ended at age fourteen, but in 1897 Austria opened its universities to women. Lise attended university from 1901 to 1906, the second woman to receive a physics doctorate in Vienna (the first was Olga Steindler in 1903). There she learned physics from Ludwig Boltzmann, a brilliant teacher who gave her the "vision of physics as a battle for ultimate truth." Her doctoral research was experimental; she was introduced to radioactivity by Stefan Meyer in 1906.

There were no jobs for women physicists, however, and in 1907 Meitner went to Berlin to study under another great

> Meitner's vision of physics as a battle for ultimate truth culminated in her discovery of nuclear fission in 1938.

beta decay: radiation resulting from the loss of certain particles from the nucleus of an atom.

spectra: sequences of waves arranged according to their wavelengths.

1897 Austrian universities begin admitting women.

1907 Meitner moves to Berlin and begins working with Otto Hahn.

1918 Meitner and Hahn discover protactinium.

1938 Meitner's research team discovers fission of uranium nuclei; Meitner flees Nazi Germany.

1943 Meitner refuses on principle to help the United States build an atomic bomb.

1944 Otto Hahn is awarded the Nobel Prize for chemistry.

theoretical physicist, Max Planck, who became her mentor and friend. For research she found a partner in Otto Hahn, a radiochemist just her age. Berlin became her professional home, and she stayed thirty-one years.

With Hahn she found new radioactive species, studied **beta decay** and beta **spectra**, and in 1918 discovered protactinium, element 91.

Between 1920 and 1934 Meitner, independent of Hahn, pioneered in nuclear physics. From studies of beta-gamma spectra, she clarified the radioactive decay process by proving that gamma radiation follows the emission of alpha (or beta) particles; her studies of the absorption of gamma radiation verified the formula of Oskar Klein and Yoshio Nishina and indirectly the relativistic electron theory of Paul Dirac. Meitner was among the first to determine the mass of neutrons and to observe the formation of electron-positron pairs.

In 1934 Meitner began studying the products formed when uranium is bombarded with neutrons; the investigation, led by Meitner and including Hahn and chemist Fritz Strassmann, culminated in the discovery of nuclear fission in December 1938. Five months earlier, however, Nazi racial policies forced her to flee Germany, and although she conducted an intense scientific correspondence with Hahn from exile in Stockholm, she was not credited with her share of the discovery. In early 1939 she and her physicist nephew Otto Robert Frisch published the first theoretical explanation for the process and named it fission. Hahn was awarded the 1944 Nobel chemistry prize alone, an injustice that clouded Meitner's reputation in later years.

Meitner had a talent for friendship and a deep love for music and the outdoors. She served in the Austrian army as an X-ray nurse in World War I and retained her Austrian citizenship all her life. In 1943 she was asked to join the atomic bomb project at Los Alamos but refused on principle; years later she said that her "unconditional love for physics" had been damaged by the knowledge that her work had led to nuclear weapons.

Dr. Meitner died at Cambridge, England, October 27, 1968.◆

Mendel, Gregor Johann

1822–1884 ● BOTANY & GENETICS

"The theory is confirmed that pea hybrids form egg and pollen cells, which, in their constitution, represent in equal numbers all constant forms which result for the combination of the characters united in fertilization."

— Gregor Mendel

Austrian monk Mendel was the first discoverer of laws of heredity. Born in Heinzendorf, Austria, he early showed an interest in the natural sciences. He attended the Philosophical Institute at Olmutz for two years and entered the Augustinian monastery at Brno in 1843; he was ordained there in 1847. Throughout this period he taught himself science.

In 1851 Mendel's abbot sent him to the University of Vienna, where he studied physics, chemistry, mathematics, zoology, and botany. In 1854 he returned to Brno, where he taught natural sciences at the technical high school. In 1868 he was elected abbot of his monastery and ceased teaching.

As early as 1856, Mendel had begun to work in the small monastery garden, conducting experiments that were to lead to his discovery of the basic principles of heredity and to the founding of the science of genetics. Mendel found support among the other teachers at the high school, several of whom were active in the sciences and had helped found the Natural Science Society in Brno in 1862. Mendel participated in the

Mendel established the foundations for understanding heredity and evolution.

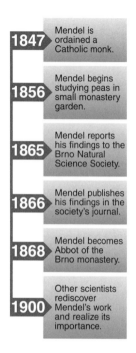

1847 Mendel is ordained a Catholic monk.

1856 Mendel begins studying peas in small monastery garden.

1865 Mendel reports his findings to the Brno Natural Science Society.

1866 Mendel publishes his findings in the society's journal.

1868 Mendel becomes Abbot of the Brno monastery.

1900 Other scientists rediscover Mendel's work and realize its importance.

axil: the angle between a branch and a leaf.

society's meetings and often borrowed books from its library, as well as that of the monastery, concentrating especially on agriculture, horticulture, and botany—subjects with which he was already familiar, since his father owned an orchard and farm.

Mendel also bought his own books and was aware of Charles Darwin's publications of the 1860s and 1870s. He had already started his experiments before Darwin published his first book and before heredity was widely regarded as the basis of evolutionary change. Reporting his findings, which he called "plant hybridization," to the Natural Science Society in 1865, he stated that his experiments went further than any others in the subject "to make it possible to determine the number of different forms under which the offspring of hybrids appear, or to change these forms with certainty according to their separate generations, or definitely to ascertain their statistical relations." Hence Mendel for the first time defined the imperatives for studying heredity through experimentation and provided the data that fulfilled these imperatives; these established the foundations for understanding heredity and evolution as well as biological processes.

Mendel carried out his experiments on garden peas, which he crossed to gather data on single alternative characteristics: tallness, dwarfness, presence or absence of color in the blossoms and leaf **axils**, alternative differences in seed color and seed shape, position of flowers on the stem, and the pod's shape. He found that each cross exhibited a "dominant character" for one of the alternative types in the hybrids (e.g., tallness over dwarfness). Yet when these crosses reproduced by self-fertilization, the second showed both grandparental types in the same constant proportion: approximately three-quarters exhibited the dominant type, and one quarter the recessive type. Mendel also proved that when the second-generation hybrids were individually tested, about one quarter of them resembled one of the pure parent varieties in the single character being observed, one quarter the other pure variety, and half resembled in appearance and behavior the first generation hybrid.

The essential part of his hypothesis was that paired elementary units, now known as genes, caused the occurrence of visible alternative characters in the plants in the constant varieties and in their descendants. These units he symbolized by letters; he assumed that they occurred in alternative forms *AA* and *aa* in the constant parent variety and *Aa* in the hybrid. Where the "dominant" feature—such as tallness—appeared, he labeled it *Aa*, resembling *AA*. The other, "recessive," feature—in this example, dwarfness—was to be found in *aa* individuals.

Mendel showed how his findings were based on a simple statistical law whereby the reproductive cells of one hybrid transmitted half the unit, A, and the other transmitted the other half, *a*. The separation of alternatives in the reproductive cells (or the principle of segregation) came to be known as Mendel's first law and could be used in predicting the occurrence of features in living organisms. Mendel went further and showed how a range of combinations of features could be obtained by crossing several pairs of alternative characters. He observed this when he crossed peas with seven pairs of differentiating characters and found that they recombined randomly, governed by the law of independent assortment. More is now known of this phenomenon: this law or principle applies only to units, or genes, which are transmitted in different linkage groups, now called "chromosomes," where genes are organized.

The publications of Mendel's results in 1866 had little effect at the time. He continued his experiments on other plants and maintained a lifelong interest in botany, bee culture, and meteorology, but could not devote much time to them due to his increasing administrative duties as abbot. It was not until 1900, well after his death, that he was rediscovered when other scientists obtained results similar to his. ◆

It was not until 1900, well after Mendel's death, that scientists rediscovered his work.

Mendeleyev, Dmitri Ivanovich

1834–1907 ● CHEMISTRY

"There will come a time when the world will be filled with one science, one truth, one industry, one brotherhood, one friendship with nature."
— Dmitri Ivanovich Medeleyev

Russian chemist Mendeleyev was famed for his work on periodic law. He was the first to determine that "the properties of the elements are in periodic dependence upon their atomic weights." This statement, found in his best known textbook, *The Principles of Chemistry* (two volumes: 1868–1870), was the first to assert that the atomic weights of elements reflect the connections between the elements themselves and their properties. Mendeleyev went on to state that this law of nature could be used to determine new classifications and facts about the elements.

Mendeleyev was the fourteenth child in a family from Tobolsk, Siberia. His father was blind, and his mother, who directed a glass factory, looked after the family. In 1848 she traveled thousands of miles to Moscow in order to enroll Mendeleyev in the university. However, at that time no Siberians were allowed to enter that institution, so they set out again, this time for Saint Petersburg. In 1850 Mendeleyev was admitted to a training college for teachers; his mother died soon after, but his love and devotion to her memory remained with him all his life.

Receiving his degree in chemistry, in 1856 Mendeleyev became a *privatdozent* (official but unpaid lecturer). In 1859 he spent two years in Heidelberg working out his own theories and ideas. Upon his return to Saint Petersburg he became a professor at the university, where he remained until 1890, when he resigned after a dispute with the administration over his liberal views. From 1893 he directed the bureau of weights and measures.

In Saint Petersburg, Mendeleyev investigated the periodic law, the composition of solutions, and the nature and origin of petroleum. His first periodic table (developed in 1869), which contested accepted atomic weights, became an extensive paper presented in German in 1871. His new finds led him to believe that three previously unknown elements existed. He assigned these elements and their compounds specific structures, terming them boron, eka-aluminum, and eka-silicon. Chemists took an interest in his findings when they were confirmed within fifteen years: the discovery of gallium, scandium, and germanium earned him considerable respect throughout the scientific community.

Mendeleyev also undertook extensive research on the nature of solutions and the thermal expansion of liquids. His work in this area, conducted in the early 1860s, predated the findings of Thomas Andrews on the critical temperature of gases. Independently, they both defined the absolute boiling point of a substance as "the temperature at which cohesion and heat of vaporization become equal to zero and the liquid changes to vapor, irrespective of the pressure and volume."

The Royal Society honored Mendeleyev with the Davy medal in 1882, and the Copley medal in 1905. ◆

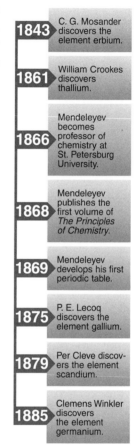

1843 C. G. Mosander discovers the element erbium.

1861 William Crookes discovers thallium.

1866 Mendeleyev becomes professor of chemistry at St. Petersburg University.

1868 Mendeleyev publishes the first volume of *The Principles of Chemistry*.

1869 Mendeleyev develops his first periodic table.

1875 P. E. Lecoq discovers the element gallium.

1879 Per Cleve discovers the element scandium.

1885 Clemens Winkler discovers the element germanium.

Morton, William Thomas Green

1819–1868 ● MEDICINE

> *"... still and motionless, as if already in the embrace of death."*
> —William T. G. Morton, describing the effect of ether

ether: a light, flammable liquid used primarily as a solvent and anesthetic.

An American dental surgeon, Dr. Morton was a pioneer of anesthesia through the use of **ether**. He was the son of Massachusetts farmer whose family was among the earliest settlers in New England. He went to Boston to work as a salesman, but the commercial life did not satisfy him for long and in 1840 he enrolled at the College of Dental Surgery in Baltimore, finding a profession more appropriate to his talents and interests.

Morton opened a practice in Farmington, Connecticut, and later in Boston. He did not succeed financially and felt that he lacked sufficient medical training, and so enrolled in Harvard Medical School in 1844. This was also the year of his marriage, and his new responsibilities led to financial difficulties: leaving Harvard without completing his degree, he returned to working as a dentist.

A Harvard professor, Charles T. Jackson, had demonstrated to his chemistry class that the inhalation of sulfuric ether caused loss of consciousness. Jackson gave Morton the idea of using this as a local anesthetic for dental fillings. Previously Morton had investigated narcotics, intoxicants, and even mesmerism in order to remove the pain from dental surgery, but none of these had worked satisfactorily.

Morton carried out his tests of the power of ether on his own body. Initially, he mixed it with opium and was encouraged by the numbness produced by prolonged inhalation. Further experiments followed at the family farm, where he etherized a hen and then cut off its comb without the bird showing any signs of discomfort. Encouraged, he returned to Boston and gave himself a heavy dose of sulfuric ether, even though the effects of this inhalation were then unknown. He lost consciousness for eight minutes without ill-effect.

When a patient named Frost arrived at the surgery with a painful toothache, Morton told him he had something much more effective than mesmerism to remove the pain of the extraction. He administered ether from a handkerchief and

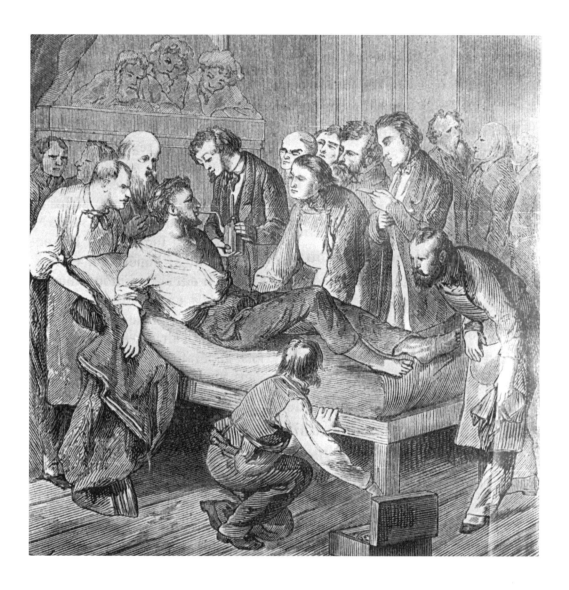

the patient was soon unconscious. The tooth was removed without reaction, Frost remaining, as Morton later described it, "still and motionless as if already in the embrace of death." For a moment he feared he had killed his patient but Frost revived when he threw a glass of water over him. Frost could not believe the tooth had been extracted, for he had felt nothing.

Morton chose to publicize his discovery through a demonstration in the Massachusetts General Hospital. The operating theater was crowded with doctors eager to see the new process. As the doubting medical men looked on,

William Morton's first experiments with anesthesia.

Morton administered the ether and the patient lapsed into unconsciousness. A tumor was removed without any sign of pain and all sensed a historic step forward in medical practice had just been witnessed.

Morton did not want to have to share the rewards for the discovery with Professor Jackson, and refused to accept an award from the French Academy of Medicine since Jackson was named as joint discoverer. He refused to disclose the ingredients of the ether and named it "letheon," suggesting a new, previously unknown substance. He allowed certain charity hospitals to use this free of charge.

The last twenty years of Morton's life were spent on his farm at Wellesley. He was awarded medals from Russia and Sweden, but at home there was a long legal struggle both for recognition as discoverer of the anesthetic and for appropriate financial reward. Although he maintained his temper and did not seek to retaliate against his opponents, it was a bitter fight and reduced him to abject poverty. His death was ascribed to an apoplectic attack that occurred while driving in New York's Central Park reading an article by Professor Jackson attempting to impede efforts by Morton's supporters to raise a testimonial subscription for him. ◆

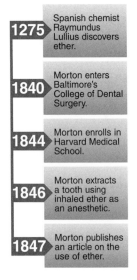

1275 Spanish chemist Raymundus Lullius discovers ether.

1840 Morton enters Baltimore's College of Dental Surgery.

1844 Morton enrolls in Harvard Medical School.

1846 Morton extracts a tooth using inhaled ether as an anesthetic.

1847 Morton publishes an article on the use of ether.

Newton, Isaac

1642–1727 ● Astronomy & Physics

Newton was born on Christmas Day, 1642, at Woolsthorpe, England. He was the offspring of a yeoman family of southwestern Lincolnshire, none of whom before him could read; their steadily increasing prosperity indicates that his forebears were not short of ability, however. Newton's father, also named Isaac, died in October 1642, two months before his only child was born.

When his mother remarried, Newton was left in the care of his maternal grandparents at Woolsthorpe. His mother's family, the Ayscoughs, had a tradition of education. Consequently, following primary instruction in local day schools, Newton began attending grammar school in Grantham in 1655, after his mother, now with three more children, Newton's half-brother and half-sisters, had been widowed a second time. In June 1661, Newton enrolled in Trinity College, Cambridge, the college of his mother's brother.

From the notebooks that he kept, we know a good deal about Newton's undergraduate education and how, around 1664, he discovered the new natural philosophy of René Descartes, Pierre Gassendi, and others. The influence of a friend and patron from Lincolnshire, highly placed in Trinity, led the college to elect him to a scholarship in April 1664 and a fellowship in 1668 upon the completion of his M.A. degree. The influence of Isaac Barrow added the Lucasian Professorship of Mathematics in 1669. Trinity remained Newton's home for the following twenty-seven years; all of his achievements in science stem from the years in Cambridge.

The period 1665–1666 has been called Newton's *annus mirabilis*, his wonderful year. It was, first of all, the period of

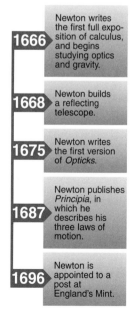

1666 Newton writes the first full exposition of calculus, and begins studying optics and gravity.

1668 Newton builds a reflecting telescope.

1675 Newton writes the first version of *Opticks*.

1687 Newton publishes *Principia*, in which he describes his three laws of motion.

1696 Newton is appointed to a post at England's Mint.

his greatest achievement in mathematics, leading up to an essay composed in October 1666 that set down the first full exposition of what he called the fluxional method, what is now called calculus. Calculus became and remains the basic tool of modern physics.

During the *annus mirabilis*, as he pursued the new natural philosophy, Newton also began the work that would transform physics. He took up the science of mechanics and explored the law of impact and the dynamics of circular motion. Substituting the relations of Johannes Kepler's third law into his formula for the **radial** force in circular motion, Newton concluded that the radial force in the solar system varies inversely as the square of the planets' distances from the Sun. He also compared the force acting on the Moon with the force of gravity at Earth's surface and found a very rough approximation to the inverse square relation. No one any longer accepts the myth that with this calculation Newton effectively discovered the law of universal gravitation in 1666. The radial force in orbital motion, as he then conceived of it, was **centrifugal** rather than **centripetal**. In comparison with what would follow twenty years later, Newton's early work in mechanics was relatively crude. Nevertheless, it marked an important step in his development.

His early work in optics was more conclusive. Around 1665 Newton became interested in the phenomena of colors. He began to entertain the then novel ideas that light, as it comes from the Sun, is not simple and pure but heterogeneous and that phenomena of colors arise from the separation of the mixture into its components. He had seen the colored fringes around bodies observed through a prism. If rays differ both in their degree of refrangibility (refraction) and in the sensation of color they provoke, his idea would explain this appearance.

He first tested the notion by a simple experiment with a prism and then proceeded to a more elaborate one. Making a small hole in the shutter to his window, he admitted a narrow beam of light into the otherwise darkened room and refracted the beam through a prism onto a wall about twenty-two feet away. He saw, as he expected to see, an elongated spectrum about five times as long as it was broad. Newton went on to devise a variety of further experiments with prisms, of which two were especially important. When he intercepted the diverging spectrum with a board and isolated the rays of one

radial: developing uniformly around a central axis.

centrifugal: a force that tends to impel a thing outward from a center of rotation.

centripetal: a force that is directed inward toward the center of rotation.

color, which passed through a hole in the board to be refracted through a second prism, he observed no further dispersion, but different parts of the spectrum did refract different amounts in exact proportion with the refractions at the first prism. In the second experiment he played the diverging spectrum onto a lens, which brought the rays back to a focus. When a screen was placed at the focus, the spot appeared white, the sensation caused by the mixture of rays that comes from the Sun. When the screen was moved beyond the focus, the spectrum reappeared in reverse order.

By 1669 Newton had worked out the full implications of his theory for presentation in his first series of Lucasian lectures. To avoid the problems of **chromatic** aberration present in refracting telescopes, he constructed the first reflecting one about this time. He published a brief statement of the theory in the *Philosophical Transactions* of the Royal Society in 1672, and some thirty years later he rewrote the material of the lectures as Book I of his *Opticks* (1703).

chromatic: relating to color.

He had also to explain the colors of solid bodies if his theory were to be complete. Newton was convinced that differential reflections can also separate the heterogeneous mixture of sunlight into its components. In the phenomena of thin transparent films he found a means to investigate this notion. Pressing a lens of known curvature against a flat sheet of glass and playing a beam of sunlight onto the apparatus, he observed a pattern of colored rings, which continue to be called Newton's rings, reflected from the film of air between the lens and the sheet. From the measured diameters of the rings, the geometry of circles allowed him to calculate the thickness of the film that corresponded to individual rings and individual colors, the first successful venture of mathematical physics into quantities this small. In 1703 this investigation became Book II of the *Opticks*.

Newton's work in optics was not as determinative for the future as his work in mechanics and cosmology would be. His **corpuscular** conception of light had to be replaced by the wave theory in the early nineteenth century before optics could move on, and the details of his explanation of the colors of solid bodies have not survived. Nevertheless, he effected an immense step forward. He established the heterogeneity of light—extended in the nineteenth century to the heterogeneity of electromagnetic radiation—apparently for all

corpuscular: dealing with minute particles.

alchemy: a medieval science that aimed to change base metals into gold.

time, and his measurements of Newton's rings first demonstrated the periodicity of an optical phenomenon, though he did not consider that periodicity was a property of light itself.

About 1670, Newton's interest shifted away from the topics we associate with his name to alchemy and theology, which dominated his life for roughly fifteen years. He pursued **alchemy** with great intensity, though his work did not affect the development of chemistry; his study of theology, which he kept very secret, led him to doubt the divinity of Christ and the doctrine of the Trinity. In August 1684, a visit from Edmond Halley with a question about orbital dynamics brought Newton back to physics. The steadily expanding enquiry that Halley's question opened led to his 1687 masterpiece, *The Mathematical Principles of Natural Philosophy* (or *Principia*, from the key word in its Latin title).

In the *Principia*, Newton returned to the science of mechanics. The work opened with a system of dynamics, the three laws of motion still taught as the foundation of modern physics. In Book I he then proceeded to apply the laws to problems of orbital motion, developing for the first time a successful orbital dynamics. He enunciated the concept of centripetal force, reversing the centrifugal force that he and other scientists had associated with bodies in circular motion, and he showed that orbital motion reduces to two essential elements, an inertial motion that is constantly deflected by a centripetal force sufficiently strong to hold a body in a closed circuit. Whenever a body in inertial motion is diverted from its rectilinear path by any centripetal force, Johannes Kepler's law of areas is obeyed. Orbital motion in an ellipse with a centripetal force directed to one focus requires the force to vary inversely as the square of the distance, and a system of satellites orbiting a center that attracts them with an inverse square force must obey Kepler's third law, which relates periods to orbital radii.

After Book II, which examined motions in and of material media, Book III applied the conclusions of Book I to the observed phenomena of the heavens. Newton demonstrated that planets orbiting the Sun and satellites orbiting Jupiter and Saturn, all three systems in accordance with Kepler's third law, require the presence of inverse square attractions toward the central bodies. There must likewise be some attraction toward Earth that holds the Moon in an orbit about it.

He compared the centripetal acceleration of the Moon, calculated from its observed orbit, with the acceleration of gravity on Earth's surface, measured by experiments with pendulums. This was the comparison he had made in 1666, but now he had an accurate measurement of Earth's size, and the correlation agreed with a high degree of accuracy. He concluded then that the inverse square force present in the cosmos is identical to the force that causes bodies to fall to the earth, and in Proposition 7 of Book III Newton pronounced the law of universal gravitation.

The rest of Book III applied the concept of universal gravitation with quantitative precision to a series of known phenomena that had not been used in its derivation—the perturbations of the Moon's orbit, the tides, a conical motion of Earth's axis that gives rise to an appearance called the precession of the equinoxes, and finally comets, which he showed to be planet-like bodies orbiting the Sun. He succeeded in defining the orbit of the great comet of 1681-1682, treating it as a **parabola** in the first edition and as a greatly elongated **ellipse** in subsequent ones. Newton's *Principia* was received at once as an epochal achievement in England. His newly won prominence led Newton to abandon Cambridge in 1696 for London, where he was first Warden and then Master of the Mint and, after 1703, President of the Royal Society, positions that he filled until his death. On the continent, the work met opposition from the entrenched **Cartesian** natural philosophy. Nevertheless, there too Newtonian science was triumphant well before the middle of the eighteenth century. It shaped and dominated the development of the physical sciences until the beginning of the twentieth century, and even then such developments as relativity and quantum mechanics were possible only because Newtonian science had prepared the way for them.

Sir Isaac died in London on March 20, 1727. ◆

parabola: a type of curved plane.

ellipse: an type of oval.

Cartesian: relating to French scientist and philosopher René Descartes.

Nobel, Alfred Bernhard

1833–1896 ● INVENTOR

"My factories may make an end to war sooner than your congresses. The day when two army corps can annihilate each other in one second, all civilized nations, it is to be hoped, will recoil from war and discharge their troops."
— Alfred Nobel

philanthropist: a person who actively promotes the welfare of other human beings.

Stockholm, Sweden was the birthplace of Alfred Nobel, the inventor of dynamite and **philanthropist**. However, he spent many of his younger years in Saint Petersburg, Russia, a year in Paris, and four years in the United States. From 1859 he lived in Sweden and spent his final years in San Remo, Italy. Nobel was a frail and sickly child who required constant care by his attentive mother. As an adult Nobel wrote the following poem in memory of early childhood: "My cradle looked like a deathbed and for years /A mother watched with ever anxious care / Though little chance to save the flickering light."

He was devoted to his mother his entire life, foregoing marriage. Because of this, unfounded rumors abounded that he was a homosexual. The Nobel Foundation abetted the rumors by keeping his love letters secret for fifty years following his death. It then transpired that Nobel had hired prostitutes and had one eighteen-year love affair in the autumn of his life. Nobel's father, Immanuel, was a chemist who began experimenting with explosives in 1837. His experiments led to the development of land mines for the Russian army and an interest in the subject by his three eldest sons. At Immanuel's insistence Alfred conducted research with **nitroglycerin**, which had been developed by an Italian, Aslanio Sobero, in 1847. Sobero mixed nitric acid with sulphuric acid and glycerine to yield an oily liquid that was very powerful but very unstable.

Alfred Nobel initially succeeded in taming the violent explosive in underwater experiments. Later his older brother Oscar discovered a granular powder that could soak up the liquid nitroglycerin, thereby making the material less volatile. Nobel devised a method of securely sealing the explosive material in a cylinder that could accommodate a primary charge and fuse in order to be safely detonated on land. After patenting "Dynamite" in 1862, he built mass production factories to meet the great demand by mining and excavation companies and by the military around the world. Nobel would personally demonstrate that dynamite was safe to use by throwing sticks, dropping sticks onto rocks, and by burning them. Then he would attach the primary charge and detonate the dynamite from a safe distance.

His development of dynamite was not without personal cost. His younger brother was killed, along with three other people, when nitroglycerine in the Stockholm laboratory unexpectedly blew up. Nobel concluded that the nitro, which was not mixed with granular power, exploded when the temperature inside the laboratory building exceeded thirty degrees centigrade. While saddened by the death of his brother, he bore no moral guilt as he believed that the power of explosives would ultimately serve humanity.

One morning in 1888 Alfred was shocked as he read his own obituary in a French newspaper. In fact, his brother had died but the reporter erroneously thought that the deceased was the inventor of dynamite. The negative article centered on the "Dynamite King" becoming extremely wealthy over bodies of soldiers whose deaths were caused by his weapons of destruction. Nobel was obsessed with the idea that the public would only remember him in terms of war when in fact he had developed dynamite to serve mankind. As a result, he decided to leave his fortune to a foundation that would distribute its earnings in equal prizes to individuals in five fields for their preceding years' work. Alfred Nobel bequeathed the then-princely sum of $9,200,000 to establish his foundation, but he

nitroglycerin: an explosive poisonous liquid, now primarily used to make dynamite.

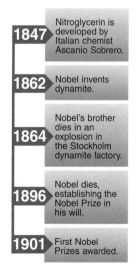

1847 Nitroglycerin is developed by Italian chemist Ascanio Sobrero.

1862 Nobel invents dynamite.

1864 Nobel's brother dies in an explosion in the Stockholm dynamite factory.

1896 Nobel dies, establishing the Nobel Prize in his will.

1901 First Nobel Prizes awarded.

was also generous during his lifetime. "As a rule," he wrote, "I'd rather take care of the stomachs of the living than the glory of the departed in the form of monuments." From his letters we learn about a case in which the pastor of the Swedish Church in Paris turned to him with a request for aid on behalf of a needy Swede. Nobel wrote, "I always feel happy to be able to help honest and industrious people in difficulties against which they struggle in vain. Mr. B. felt he could get along with 600 francs, but since I know very well that inadequate help and no help at all are not very far apart, I increased the amount on my own accord to 1,000 francs." ◆

Oppenheimer, J. Robert

1904–1967 ● NUCLEAR PHYSICS

"In some sort of crude sense which no vulgarity, no humor, no overstatement can quite extinguish, the physicists have known sin; and this is a knowledge which they cannot lose."
— J. Robert Oppenheimer

Oppenheimer grew up in splendid surroundings. He was born in New York, New York, April 22, 1904. From his boyhood home, an apartment high above New York City's Riverside Drive, he could gaze out over the Hudson River and watch the sun setting in the west. Hanging on the walls of his home were magnificent paintings by Van Gogh, Cezanne, and Gauguin. During the hot Manhattan summer months, Oppenheimer, his younger brother (Frank), and his parents (Julius and Ella) could escape to their shoreline home on Long Island, where two sailboats awaited.

Oppenheimer's interest in science came early. He collected minerals and, at age twelve, presented his first paper to the New York Mineralogy Club. He attended a private school, the Ethical Culture School, and was a superior student. In

spectroscopy: the study of spectra (the distribution of wavelengths of increasing magnitude), especially electromagnetic spectra.

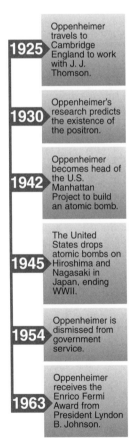

1925 Oppenheimer travels to Cambridge England to work with J. J. Thomson.

1930 Oppenheimer's research predicts the existence of the positron.

1942 Oppenheimer becomes head of the U.S. Manhattan Project to build an atomic bomb.

1945 The United States drops atomic bombs on Hiroshima and Nagasaki in Japan, ending WWII.

1954 Oppenheimer is dismissed from government service.

1963 Oppenheimer receives the Enrico Fermi Award from President Lyndon B. Johnson.

September 1922, upon completion of high school, Oppenheimer entered Harvard University, where he began a major in chemistry. Quickly, however, he was drawn to physics and, based on his extensive reading, was granted advanced standing in the physics department, where he was invited to work in Percy Bridgman's laboratory.

The laboratory was not fitting for the talents of Oppenheimer, but that was all he knew. In the 1920s American physics was recognized for its experimental prowess; theoretical physics was largely the domain of European physicists. Thus, when he approached his graduation, Oppenheimer acted on what he knew and applied for a position at Cambridge University with the eminent experimental physicist Ernest Rutherford, who, in 1911, discovered the atomic nucleus. When Rutherford rejected Oppenheimer's application, he wrote to another renowned experimentalist, J. J. Thomson, who had discovered the electron in 1897. Thomson accepted Oppenheimer, and in the summer of 1925 he traveled to Cambridge, England, to begin work in Thomson's laboratory.

Fortunately, for Oppenheimer and for physics, Cambridge was an active center and Oppenheimer quickly met other Cambridge physicists such as Paul Dirac and Ralph Fowler, as well as visiting physicists Niels Bohr and Paul Ehrenfest. All these men were theoretical physicists. At Fowler's suggestion, Oppenheimer began to learn Dirac's new quantum mechanics and apply the theory to a problem in **spectroscopy**. Oppenheimer was soon absorbed in his theoretical work and he was demonstrating a level of brilliance that had been masked by the laboratory. Max Born, a theoretical physicist from the University of Göttingen, was another visitor to Cambridge and he was so impressed by Oppenheimer that he invited Oppenheimer to come to Göttingen to do his doctoral dissertation research. Four months after his arrival at Göttingen, Oppenheimer submitted a paper that was his dissertation, and three months after that, he received his doctor of philosophy degree.

Oppenheimer returned to the United States in the summer of 1929, where he accepted a dual appointment at the University of California, Berkeley, and the California Institute of Technology. During the period from 1929 to 1942, Oppenheimer and his students worked at the cutting edge of physics. Owing to his command of theoretical physics, his wide-ranging **erudition**, and his personal charm, bright students flocked to Berkeley and Pasadena to work with Oppenheimer. A school of theoretical physics formed around him which, by the mid-to-late 1930s, had helped to launch American physics into the forefront of world physics.

Before he left Europe, however, Oppenheimer had written two very important papers. First, a short paper that Born, aghast at its brevity, expanded. This paper became known as the Born-Oppenheimer approximation and is the contemporary basis for the quantum mechanical study of molecules. In a second paper, Oppenheimer showed that electrons could be extracted from the surface of a metal by a weak electric field. The mechanism for this is quantum mechanical tunneling that, fifty-four years later, became the basis for the scanning tunneling microscope.

In 1930 Oppenheimer conducted research that fell just short of predicting the existence of the positron—the antiparticle of the electron. Two years later, the positron was discovered. Later in the 1930s Oppenheimer and his students applied the general theory of relativity to examine stellar collapse. In this work they showed that stars can collapse into both neutron stars and black holes.

Oppenheimer's physics is very impressive; however, it is for his work during World War II that he is more widely known. In 1942 Oppenheimer became the director of the Manhattan Project's laboratory in Los Alamos, New Mexico—the site where the atomic bomb was developed. Many of the world's greatest physicists worked under intense pressure from 1943 to mid-1945. With few exceptions, the participants in the project acknowledged Oppenheimer as a superb leader. His brilliance put him in command of every technical issue; his attention extended to the everyday problems of family members.

The first atomic explosion occurred in the predawn darkness on July 16, 1945, over the sand of Alomogordo desert. Each witness to this event, in his own way, was moved by the awesome sight. To Oppenheimer's mind came the words from the Hindu scripture in the *Bhagavadgita*: "I am become death, the shatterer of worlds."

After the end of World War II, Oppenheimer became a public figure. He advised presidents and was the chairman of

"We knew the world would not be the same. A few people laughed, a few people cried. Most people were silent."

— J. Robert Oppenheimer

erudition: extensive knowledge acquired chiefly from books.

high-level government committees. He had an international stage and, for a few years, he was universally admired—until 1954.

During the postdepression days of the 1930s, Oppenheimer had been sympathetic with the idealist ideas of socialist and even communist groups. During the time of the Manhattan Project, there were a few highly placed individuals who were suspicious of Oppenheimer. Their suspicions continued to fester after the war, and when the Science Advisory Committee, which Oppenheimer chaired, recommended against a crash program to develop the hydrogen bomb, these suspicions were activated. In 1954 a three-man board was formed to conduct a hearing to determine whether Oppenheimer's security clearance should be revoked. The hearing was brutal. Oppenheimer's character was called into question, and he was demeaned. In this hostile environment, he was unable to defend himself effectively. By a vote of 2 to 1, the board recommended revocation of Oppenheimer's clearance. With this decision, his public service came to an end.

In 1947 Oppenheimer had been named the director of the Institute for Advanced Study in Princeton, New Jersey. After the results of the 1954 hearing were announced, Oppenheimer's colleagues at the Institute, including Albert

The Manhattan Project

In 1938, just before World War II began, German physicists discovered nuclear fission. The following year, Albert Einstein warned President Roosevelt that Germany was close to creating an atomic bomb. The United States soon set up its own bomb program. Known as the Manhattan Project, it involved teams of scientists working at several locations. The first milestone occurred in 1942 in Chicago when a team lead by Enrico Fermi produced the first controlled chain reaction. Soon, scientists at Los Alamos in New Mexico began building a bomb under the direction of J. Robert Oppenheimer. The first test bomb was exploded in the New Mexico dessert on July 16, 1945. On August 6, a United States B-29 aircraft dropped an atomic bomb on the Japanese city of Hiroshima, leveling most of the buildings and killing tens of thousands of people. Three days later, a second bomb was dropped on Nagasaki. Japan surrendered on August 15, ending World War II. Since then, most nations have signed international treaties providing for the nonproliferation and reduction of nuclear weapons.

Einstein, proclaimed their confidence in Oppenheimer. The board of directors of the Institute reappointed Oppenheimer as director. In 1963 he received the Atomic Energy Commission's Enrico Fermi Award from President Lyndon B. Johnson. This award, in a small way, acknowledged the wrong that had been done to Oppenheimer in 1954.

In the spring of 1966 Oppenheimer announced his early retirement from the Institute effective June 30 of that year. Oppenheimer died at Princeton on February 18, 1967, less than eight months after his retirement. ◆

Pascal, Blaise

1623–1662 ● MATHEMATICS

> *"What is man in nature? Nothing in relation to the infinite, everything in relation to nothing, a mean between nothing and everything."*
> — Blaise Pascal

French mathematician, philosopher, scientist, and writer Blaise Pascal was born at Clermont-Ferrand but after the death of his mother in 1626, the family moved to Paris. His father, a tax administrator, was an eminent mathematician and under his instruction Pascal displayed mathematical genius from an early age. In 1640 he completed an analytic study of the work of Girard Desargues on synthetic projective geometry, and wrote an essay on conic sections based on his analysis. During the years 1642–1644 Pascal worked on the construction of a calculating device, originally designed as an aid for his father's tax computations. The mechanism was acclaimed in mathematic circles and Pascal's work was noted by René Descartes, the illustrious philosopher and mathematician.

There followed an intense period of scientific work. He corresponded with the leading scientist Marin Mersenne and began to test the theories of Galileo and Evangelista Torricelli (the Italian physicist who invented the barometer) by means

hydrodynamics: a branch of physics that deals with the motion of fluids and the forces acting on solid bodies immersed in them.

hydrostatics: a branch a physics that deals with fluids at rest and the pressure they exert.

of experiments using mercury barometers to measure air pressure. His experiments led to further studies in **hydrodynamics** and **hydrostatics** and during the course of this work Pascal developed an improved version of Torricelli's barometer and also invented the syringe. His major success at this time was the invention of the hydraulic press, which was based upon a formula that came to be known as Pascal's law. This theory states that in a fluid at rest in a closed container, a pressure change in one part is transmitted undiminished through the liquid to the walls of the container in all directions, regardless of the area to which the pressure is applied. A modern application of the principle is its utilization in hydraulic brakes. Pascal also published a number of essays and treatises during this period (1646–1654) dealing with the problem of the vacuum, the equilibrium of liquid solutions, the weight and density of air, and the arithmetic triangle, in which he formulated the foundations for the modern theory of probabilities.

As a young man Pascal embraced the theological teachings of Jansenism, a religious movement centered at the abbey of Port Royal. Contrary to classical Jesuit principles, Jansenist doctrine accepted predestination and rejected free will: it held that divine grace alone was capable of restoring man to true freedom. Under Pascal's influence, his entire family turned to Jansenism in 1646 as an expression of spiritual and religious life. Pascal himself experienced a mystical revelation in 1654 which he interpreted in terms of "conversion." He kept his account of it sewn in his coat for the rest of his life: "From about half past ten at night to about half after midnight, Fire. God of Abraham, God of Isaac, God of Jacob, not of the philosophers and the wise. Security, security. Feeling, joy, peace. Righteous Father, the world has not known you but I have known you. Joy, joy, joy, tears of joy."

In 1655 Pascal joined the Port-Royal solitaries, those who without taking vows undertook a religious life outside the convent under the direction of its leaders.

Pascal's writings during the subsequent year, in particular *Lettres écrites par Louis de Montalte à un provincial*, better known as *Les Provinciales* ("Provincial Letters"), and *Pensées* ("Thoughts"), established him as a master of French prose. The *Provinciales* were written in defense of Antoine Arnauld, a Jansenist who had been expelled by the faculty of theology in Paris for his controversial religious works opposing Jesuit

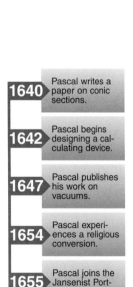

1640 Pascal writes a paper on conic sections.

1642 Pascal begins designing a calculating device.

1647 Pascal publishes his work on vacuums.

1654 Pascal experiences a religious conversion.

1655 Pascal joins the Jansenist Port-Royal solitaires.

interpretation of Roman Catholic orthodoxy and adherence to dogma. Pascal vigorously attacked the lax moral teachings and ethical code of the Jesuits and advocated a more spiritual approach emphasizing the soul's union with the body of Christ. The *Provinciales*, written in brilliant rhetorical style, replaced the **vituperative** monotony of conventional French writers with a brevity and sarcasm that proved immensely popular among French literary critics. Pascal's other major work of this period was his *Apologie de la religion chrétienne* ("Defense of Christianity"), which he began as a composition of Christian **apologetics** based on his meditations on the proofs of Christianity and intended to vanquish skepticism. He insisted upon a sharp separation of theology from philosophy, maintaining that much of the spirit of Christianity conflicted with the requirements of human physiology and reason and concluded that there is a continuous "guerre intestine de l'homme entre la raison et les passions" (internal war in human beings between reason and passion). The work, comprising a collection of fragmented notes, remained unfinished at his death; it was edited by his executors and published under the title *Pensées*.

> **vituperative:** characterized by criticism and verbal abuse.

> **apologetics:** a branch of theology devoted to defense of divine origin and the authority of Christianity.

Following a severe illness in 1659, Pascal spent his final years devoted to spiritual concern and care of the poor. He remained periodically active in the controversy over the formulary, the church document that called for universal condemnation of Jansenism, but withdrew from the dispute as a result of a disagreement with the school of Port-Royal.

Pascal's achievements in the realms of mathematics and science constitute important developments in these areas; however, as a religious philosopher Pascal firmly believed that the scientific approach could never yield certainty in its own right: he maintained that experience of God was to be attained through the heart and rejected the "truths of fact" and reason in an almost **existentialist** fashion (doctrines that influenced later philosophers such Jean-Jacques Rousseau). ◆

> **existentialism:** a 20th century philosophical movement centering on analysis of individual existence in an unfathomable universe.

Pasteur, Louis

1822–1895 ● CHEMISTRY
& MICROBIOLOGY

*"When meditating over a disease, I never
think of finding a remedy for it, but,
instead, a means of preventing it."*

— Louis Pasteur

ouis Pasteur's life is not just a story about dates and places. It is about a human being who, like many students, was just average in secondary schools and college at Arbois and Besançon, and was "mediocre" on the chemistry entrance exams to the École Normale in Paris, where all university professors trained. The traits that set Pasteur apart as a great chemist and brought him top honors in mathematics, physics, and chemistry while at the École were his fiery enthusiasm and hard work. His teachers were the great chemists Jean Batiste Dumas, Antoin-Jerome Balard, and M. Laurent. They recognized that his intense power of concentration, his methodical selection of significant experimental details, and his intuitive explanations of experimental results were the secrets of his genius. Under their influence, he made his first major discovery—the relation of **dissymmetry** and the direction of rotation of **plane-polarized** light in crystals—and solved many practical problems in agriculture, industry, and medicine. Through persuasive arguments on the validity of his experimental results, he convinced others that he was not a "mere chemist and a medical dabbler." His story of success includes support given by his family and friends when, because of fragile health, he needed energy to pursue his studies uninterrupted.

dissymmetry: absence of symmetry; lack of balanced proportion.

plane-polarized: the breaking of light into planes.

Pasteur continued studying crystal structures after receiving the his doctorate (1847) and while teaching at Dijon and Strasbourg. Sir John Herschel's findings on quartz crystals, which showed the direction of rotation of plane-polarized light to be dependent on the direction of arrangement of the crystal facets, together with Biot's work on **tartrate** crystals gathered from wine barrels, showing that both crystals and solutions of these crystals rotate plane-polarized light in the same direction—right, or **dextrorotatory**—led Pasteur to the discovery that tiny facets on tartrate crystals were dissymmetrical in the same direction—to the right. He found that **racemic** tartrates, which have no effect on polarized light, contained equal quantities of crystals with right-handed facets, as in common tartrate, and left-handed facets. In experiments analogous to Biot's, he found that solutions of each type crystal retained its optical rotatory pattern. Also, a mixture made from equal amounts of solutions of each type of crystal had no effect on plane-polarized light—it was racemic. His intuitive prediction, that dissymmetry arose from the atomic and molecular level, laid the groundwork for stereochemisty, the study of spatial arrangements of molecules.

While teaching at Lille (1855) and at the École (1857), Pasteur solved some problems facing French agriculture and industries. First, he determined that the manufacture of beer and wine by fermentation depended upon specific microorganisms that grow in the absence of oxygen (anaerobic organisms), and that the sterilization of wine and beer, and protection from other microscopic organisms, prevented abnormal fermentations. This process, called pasteurization, is used today to prevent spoilage in beverages, medicines, and foods. Pasteur's persuasive arguments convinced those who believed in spontaneous generation that fermentation was a microbial process.

By pursuing the same arguments, Pasteur was able to identify the microbial origins of two diseases, pebrine and flachery, which threatened to ruin France's silkworm industry. Careful inspection of eggs, worms, chrysalides, and moths of silkworms that carried the brown-black spots characteristic of pebrine led Pasteur to an egg-selection process that produced uninfected adults and saved the silkworm industry.

tartrate: a salt or ester of tartaric acid (a strong acid of plant origin).

dextrorotatory: rotating the plane of polarization of light to the right.

racemic: relating to a compound that rotates the plane of polarization of light to the right and to the left in equal amounts.

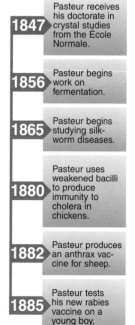

1847 Pasteur receives his doctorate in crystal studies from the École Normale.

1856 Pasteur begins work on fermentation.

1865 Pasteur begins studying silkworm diseases.

1880 Pasteur uses weakened bacilli to produce immunity to cholera in chickens.

1882 Pasteur produces an anthrax vaccine for sheep.

1885 Pasteur tests his new rabies vaccine on a young boy.

The Pasteur Institute

Louis Pasteur founded the Pasteur Institute in Paris in 1887 as a clinic for treating rabies. Today, the Pasteur Institute is one of the world's leading biomedical research organizations. It employs almost three thousand people, including more than a thousand scientists, who have the common goal of fighting disease and improving the health of people everywhere. Along with its research facilities, the Pasteur Institute includes a teaching hospital, a graduate study center, and a network of associated foreign institutes devoted to medical problems in third world countries. The institute also includes an Epidemiological Reference Center that helps to monitor epidemics and control outbreaks of infectious diseases throughout the world. Over the years, Pasteur Institute scientists have been responsible for breakthrough discoveries that have helped doctors to control such diseases as diphtheria, tetanus, polio, influenza, yellow fever, and plague. Recent research has focused on the prevention and treatment of such infectious diseases as AIDS, malaria, and tuberculosis, as well as the development of new treatments for cancer.

anthrax: an infectious disease of warm-blooded animals, characterized by lesions in the lungs.

In 1877, using his knowledge of Koch's discovery of the cholera bacillus, Pasteur isolated the bacteria that caused **anthrax** and in two years determined the pathway of transmission of the disease. By 1880 he developed immunity to cholera in chickens by inoculating them with **attenuated** cultures of the bacteria. Later, he used similar techniques to develop an attenuated form of anthrax that caused a mild attack but rendered the inoculated animal immune to virulent cultures. Pasteur saw the analogy of his vaccination process to Jenner's use of cowpox to protect against smallpox.

attenuated: weakened.

medulla oblongata: a part of the brain of vertebrate animals.

Pasteur's discovery of a rabies vaccine brought him greatest recognition. Injections of a suspension of **medulla oblongata** from a rabid dog into a healthy animal produced the symptoms of rabies. Even though he was unable to isolate the microbial cause, he produced a vaccine by using the same procedures developed for anthrax and cholera vaccines. On July 6, 1885, Pasteur used the vaccine on a nine-year-old boy, who had been badly bitten by a rabid dog. The experiment worked and his technique became a treatment for rabies. The Pasteur Institute in Paris, founded for the further investigation and prevention of rabies, is a tribute to the genius of Pasteur. ◆

Pauli, Wolfgang

1900–1958 ● PHYSICS

"It was absolutely marvelous working for Pauli. You could ask him anything. There was no worry that he would think a particular question stupid, since he thought all questions were stupid."
— Physicist Victor Weisskopf

Wolfgang Pauli, the son of a professor of physical chemistry, was born in Vienna on April 25, 1900. While still in his teenage years, Pauli was considered a mathematical prodigy. At nineteen years of age he published a paper on the general theory of relativity that attracted even Einstein's interest. Pauli studied under Arnold Sommerfeld at the University of Munich, obtaining his doctorate in 1921. His post doctorate work was with Niels Bohr in Copenhagen and with Max Born in Göttingen. In 1923 he joined the faculty of the University of Hamburg. During his time there he announced his exclusion principle. His teachers Bohr and Sommerfeld had determined the energy levels of electrons within atoms, which were expressed as Quantum Numbers. Three quantum numbers had been established. Pauli allowed for a fourth quantum number, supposing that in any energy level only two electrons are permitted: one electron spinning clockwise and the second one spinning counterclockwise. It was now possible to arrange the electrons of elements in shells and subshells. Many years later (1945),

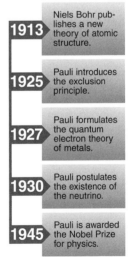

1913 Niels Bohr publishes a new theory of atomic structure.

1925 Pauli introduces the exclusion principle.

1927 Pauli formulates the quantum electron theory of metals.

1930 Pauli postulates the existence of the neutrino.

1945 Pauli is awarded the Nobel Prize for physics.

Pauli was awarded the Nobel Prize in physics for this all-important discovery.

After five years at the University of Hamburg, Pauli was appointed a professor at the Federal Institute in Zurich. During his time in Zurich, Pauli proposed the existence of the neutrino. The neutrino, a chargeless and massless particle, was Pauli's explanation for the loss of energy encountered when **beta particles** are emitted. The energy loss was previously unaccounted for and almost led to the destruction of the law of conservation of energy. Although Pauli died at a relatively young age, he did live to see his hypothesis proved. Practically undetectable, the neutrino was considered a gimmick to preserve energy bookkeeping until 1956, when it was finally detected and its existence proven through elaborate nuclear-power station experiments.

During World War II Pauli, feeling that remaining in Switzerland was too risky, moved to the United States and joined the Institute for Advanced Study at Princeton. Despite having lived in Switzerland for many years, he remained an Austrian citizen. Although during World War II an emphasis was laid on nuclear physics, Pauli was not interested in such studies, in spite of the fact that he had discovered nuclear spin. Pauli brought attention back to studies of fundamental physics. Shortly after the war he returned to Zurich. The Swiss did not consent to give him citizenship until after he received the Nobel Prize in 1946.

Pauli is often remembered as an unpleasant character. His highly publicized roughness was merely an expression of his dislike of half-truths. He wanted people to understand concepts thoroughly and correctly. Instead of for his roughness, he should be remembered for his effort to provide clarity and purity in science and human relations. Pauli died on December 14, 1958, in Zurich. ◆

beta particle: a high speed electron.

Pauling, Linus Carl

1901–1994 ● CHEMISTRY

"Science is the search for truth—it is not a game in which one tries to beat his opponents, to do harm to others."
— Linus Carl Pauling, *No More War*

L inus Pauling—a two-time Nobel Prize winner, peace activist, and passionate Vitamin C advocate—was one of the most prominent scientists of the twentieth century. Pauling was born in Portland, Oregon, on February 28, 1901, and died August 19, 1994, at age 93. He was awarded the Nobel Prize in chemistry in 1954 for his work on the molecular structure of proteins, and the Nobel Prize in peace in 1962 for his efforts to halt nuclear testing.

Linus Pauling's first chemistry laboratory was created from an old abandoned iron smelter near Oswego, Oregon. At the age of fifteen, Pauling found an old testing laboratory in the smelter and loaded up an old suitcase with everything that he could carry.

Linus Pauling received his bachelor's degree in chemical engineering at Oregon State University in 1922 and went on to receive his Ph.D. from the California Institute of Technology in 1925. Linus Pauling received a Guggenheim fellowship to study quantum theory in Europe and applied quantum mechanics to chemistry, developing a new theory of the chemical bond. In 1939 he published *The Nature of the Chemical Bond*, an influential scientific book. Other books written by Pauling that have influenced science include

1939 Pauling publishes *The Nature of the Chemical Bond*.

1954 Pauling wins the Nobel Prize for chemistry.

1958 Pauling warns the United Nations about radioactive fallout.

1962 Pauling wins the Nobel Peace Prize.

1971 Pauling publishes *Vitamin C and the Common Cold*.

1973 Pauling establishes the Linus Pauling Institute of Science and Medicine.

General Chemistry, Vitamin C and the Common Cold, and *Vitamin C, the Common Cold, and the Flu.*

Pauling, a professor emeritus of chemistry at Stanford University, won the Nobel Prize for chemistry in 1954 for his outstanding contributions toward understanding chemical bonding. The work started in the mid-1930s when Pauling became interested in biological molecules. Pauling performed magnetic studies on oxygen-carrying **hemoglobin** molecules with C.D. Coryell. Pauling and A. E. Mirsky developed a structural theory of **denatured** and coagulated protein molecules. During World War II, Pauling's research projects were interrupted when he had to work on explosives. During this time he also developed an oxygen detector. In the early 1950s, Pauling proposed the alpha **helix** as the basic structure of proteins and barely missed discovering the double helix structure of DNA.

Pauling became concerned about the dangers of radioactive fallout from nuclear weapons testing after World War II. In 1958 Pauling presented a petition to the United Nations signed by more than eleven thousand scientists warning about the problems of radioactive fallout. Pauling was awarded the 1962 Nobel Peace Prize on October 10, 1963, the effective date for the U.S.-Soviet test ban treaty.

In 1973, Linus Pauling founded the Linus Pauling Institute of Science and Medicine, an institute in Palo Alto, California, where research is conducted in three areas: **cardiovascular** disease; nutrition, biochemistry, and cancer; and genetics. Pauling has become well known for his research and advocacy of the health benefits of Vitamin C, which he believed warded off everything from the common cold to cancer. Pauling himself took many times more the FDA's recommended dosage of Vitamin C to fight his own cancer. Pauling's death from prostate cancer does not contradict his argument on the benefits of Vitamin C. He was active well into his nineties and lived longer than the typical American male. Linus Pauling believed his inevitable death was postponed by the high doses of Vitamin C he took. ◆

hemoglobin: an iron-containing pigment in red blood cells.

denatured: to modify the molecular structure by heat, acid, or radiation.

helix: spiral in form.

cardiovascular: involving the heart and blood vessels.

Pavlov, Ivan Petrovich

1849–1936 ● PHYSIOLOGY

"The naturalist must consider only one thing: what is the relation of this or that external reaction of the animal to the phenomena of the external world?"
— Ivan Petrovich Pavlov

Pavlov, a Russian physiologist and pioneer in the field of conditioned reflexes, was the winner of the 1904 Nobel Prize in physiology. Born in Ryazan, Russia, the son of a poor priest, Ivan Pavlov loved to work with his father in gardens and orchards and his interest in botany lasted all his life. Each spring he planted flowers in his home and then transplanted seedlings to formal gardens at his Estonia **dacha**. During the famine years of the Russian Revolution, he grew food in space allotted to the staff of the Institute of Experimental Medicine in Saint Petersburg. His godfather, the head of an abbey, influenced him spiritually, instilled in him a pride for work, and expanded his mind by giving him reading assignments.

dacha: a Russian country cottage.

Upon completion of schooling at the ecclesiastical seminary in Ryazan, Pavlov attended the University of Saint Petersburg. His graduation was delayed a full year because of his involvement in his first experiment on the nerves of the **pancreatic gland**. Scientific research and experimentation was to become his life work. Graduate work was at the Military-Medical Academy, where he became a professor in 1890, holding the chair of pharmacology and, from 1895, the chair of physiology. He made innovative changes in teaching methods by introducing demonstrations within lectures. As a

pancreatic gland: a gland in animals that secretes digestive enzymes and hormones.

rule, he would lecture sedately from a chair behind a table until he began to conduct a demonstration, at which time he would become very animated. His teaching talents, however, did not extend to creating good illustrations on the blackboard. His crude drawings were a constant source of amusement to the students.

During his years of teaching he continually conducted and supervised experiments. Visiting his laboratory assistants to inspect their progress, he usually carried a mug of tea, which he sipped while nibbling cubes of sugar taken from his pocket.

In 1904 Pavlov won the Nobel Prize in physiology and medicine for his research on digestion and the nervous system, which disclosed how nerves control the flow of digestive juices of the stomach and pancreas. Upon being informed of the prize he was in a state of shock, partly because his book *Lectures on the Works of the Digestive Glands* had not been well received. Following presentation of the prize by the king of Sweden, sales of the book improved. He deposited the prize money, approximately thirty-six thousand U.S. gold dollars, with the Saint Petersburg branch of Nobel's Russian firm. Following the Russian revolution of 1917, he lost all his money because the Bolsheviks liquidated all stocks and bonds of value.

Pavlov was a man of integrity, principle, and personal courage. In 1922 Vladimir Lenin refused his request to relocate his laboratory outside the country but, as a consolation, offered him the same food rations as an honored Communist. Pavlov refused on the grounds that his colleagues were excluded. In 1924 he voluntarily and publicly resigned from the Military-Medical Academy because the authorities did not permit children of clergy to receive higher education. As the son of a clergyman, he felt that it was an injustice arbitrarily to deprive a portion of the population of university education. In addition, he wrote to Joseph Stalin in 1927 stating, "You are depriving and annihilating the intelligentsia to such an extent that I am ashamed to be called a Russian." Upon returning to Russia from a visit to the United States in 1929, he publicly denounced Communism.

Although Pavlov won the 1904 Nobel Prize, he is best known for his later development work in the field of conditioned reflexology, and his famous experiment with salivating

---

Pavlov wrote to Stalin in 1927 stating, "You are depriving and annihilating the intelligentsia to such an extent that I am ashamed to be called a Russian."

1890 Pavlov becomes a Professor at the Military-Medical Academy.

1904 Pavlov wins the Nobel Prize in physiology.

1922 Stalin refuses Pavlov's request to move his laboratory abroad.

1924 Pavlov resigns his post at the Military-Medical Academy.

1929 Pavlov publicly denounces communism.

dogs. That experiment involved bringing food, accompanied by a ringing bell, to hungry dogs. The normal physiological reaction of the dogs was to salivate upon smelling the food. In time Pavlov was able to get the dogs to salivate only upon hearing the bell, an artificial stimulus, even when the food was withheld. Pavlov believed that conditioned reflexes controlled all acquired habits. He continued to work in his laboratories until his death at age eighty-seven. ◆

Plank, Max Karl Ernst Ludwig

1858–1947 ● THEORETICAL PHYSICS

"We have no right to assume that any physical laws exist, or if they have existed up to now, that they will continue to exist in a similar manner in the future." — Max Planck, *The Universe in the Light of Modern Physics*

Planck was born on April 23, 1858, at Kiel, Germany. His father was a distinguished professor of civil law at the University of Kiel. Max was the youngest of six children. In 1867 the family moved to Munich, where the children benefitted from their father's high position in Bavarian society, learning the cultural graces as well as their academic subjects. A program of music, mountain climbing, and religious training instilled in the Planck children a devotion to God, family, and country as well as respect for discipline and hard work.

Planck attended secondary school at the Maximilian Gymnasium in Munich from 1867 until his graduation in 1874. Although a shy student, he excelled in mathematics, astronomy, languages, and physics. He would later fondly recall his favorite teacher, Hermann Müller, as a master in the art of making his pupils visualize and understand the meaning of the laws governing the physical world. Planck then attended the University of Munich (1874–1877), where he decided to study physics and devoted himself to finding the most fundamental physical laws and constants.

In 1877 he left Munich for a year of study at the University of Berlin where he came under the tutelage of Hermann von Helmholtz and Gustav Kirchhoff, two pioneers in the field of **thermodynamics**. Although not impressed with their teaching styles, Planck readily took their subject as his own. Inspired by the writings of Rudolf Clausius, Planck worked on sharpening the distinction between the first and second laws of thermodynamics. His doctoral dissertation asserted that all "natural processes" were irreversible and that the sum of the entropies of all bodies in such processes would always increase. He was awarded his Ph.D. from the University of Munich in July 1879.

In 1885 Planck was offered the position of associate professor of theoretical physics at the University of Kiel. Soon thereafter, he married his fiancée, Marie Merck. The couple would eventually have four children: a son, Karl, twin daughters, Margrete and Emma, and a younger son, Erwin. Planck called this period "one of the happiest of my life."

In addition to his teaching duties, Planck published several important papers on the thermodynamics of physical and chemical reactions. He continued to focus his research on the concept of **entropy** "since its maximum value indicates a state of **equilibrium** [and] all the laws of physical and chemical equilibrium follow from a knowledge of [it]." By 1889 he had earned a strong enough reputation to be offered the position of associate professor of theoretical physics at the University of Berlin, a position that was vacant owing to the death of Kirchhoff. Planck became an active member of the Berlin (later German) Physical Society, was promoted to full

thermodynamics: the branch of physics that deals with the mechanical action of heat.

entropy: a measure of the disorder of a system.

equilibrium: a state of balance between opposing forces.

professor in 1892, and was elected to the Prussian Academy of Sciences in 1894.

This slow, steady ascent up the professional ladder suited Planck's conservative temperament, but in 1894 a series of events accelerated his progression. Heinrich Hertz, the young physicist who had experimentally proven the existence of electromagnetic waves, died prematurely in the winter of 1894. Several months later the deaths of August Kundt, the Director of the Berlin Physics Institute, and Helmholtz, the leading authority in German physics, propelled Planck into a position of leadership at the age of thirty-six. Characteristically, though deeply saddened by the loss of three of his closest friends and colleagues, Planck accepted as his duty the many new demands thrust upon him.

In the mid-1890's many of the Berlin physicists, including Planck, were investigating the light spectrum emitted by a perfect radiator of light, which was termed a blackbody since it was also a perfect absorber of light. The problem was of interest because at thermal equilibrium the emitted radiation was known to depend only on the temperature of the emitting object, not its composition. Planck theorized that minute, charged **resonators** comprising the walls of the blackbody could absorb and emit light by oscillating at the same frequency as the light waves. This resonance would result in the body proceeding to an equilibrium temperature.

On October 19, 1900, Planck announced that he had found a formula for the radiant energy emission for the blackbody spectrum that exactly matched the experimental data. He immediately devoted himself "to the task of investing [his radiation formula] with a true physical meaning. . . [which] led me to study the interrelation between entropy and probability." He theorized that the total energy was divided into small, quantized units and then determined the probability W of how these energy quanta could be distributed among the resonators. Applying Boltzmann's equation, $S = k \ln W$ (k is Boltzmann's constant) to calculate the entropy S led Planck to the correct radiation formula. The energy of each quantum was found by multiplying the frequency v of the oscillating resonator by a new constant h, which Planck called "the quantum of action" but which is now universally referred to as Planck's constant. He reported these findings to the Berlin Physical Society on December 14, 1900.

resonators: something that enhances or intensifies an atomic, nuclear, or particle reaction.

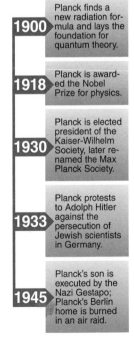

1900 Planck finds a new radiation formula and lays the foundation for quantum theory.

1918 Planck is awarded the Nobel Prize for physics.

1930 Planck is elected president of the Kaiser-Wilhelm Society, later renamed the Max Planck Society.

1933 Planck protests to Adolph Hitler against the persecution of Jewish scientists in Germany.

1945 Planck's son is executed by the Nazi Gestapo; Planck's Berlin home is burned in an air raid.

"An important scientific innovation rarely makes its way by gradually winning over and converting its opponents; it rarely happens that Saul becomes Paul. What does happen is that its opponents gradually die out and that the growing generation is familiarized with the idea from the beginning."

— Max Planck,
The Philosophy of Physics

Others, including Albert Einstein and Niels Bohr, would later use energy quanta to prove the atomic nature of matter, but to Planck, the radiation constants themselves were of fundamental significance. He calculated numerical values for both k and h from the experimental data on blackbody radiation. The value of k allowed him to calculate Avogadro's number and the value of the elementary electric charge. In addition, by using the constants h and k along with the gravitation constant G and the speed of light c, he devised a system of units for the fundamental quantities of mass, length, time, and temperature that were independent of arbitrary standards and so would "retain their significance for all times."

In the years that followed, Planck was an early supporter of Einstein's theory of relativity. Later, as Planck's supervisory role at the university increased, his direct participation in theoretical research lessened. He maintained a full schedule of teaching throughout his career, wrote textbooks on most of the major fields of physics, and played an instrumental role in revising the university science curriculum. As a firm believer in a balanced life, Planck also retained his passion for piano playing and hiking, often in the company of family and friends. He corresponded with the other leading scientific figures throughout Europe and lectured widely on topics ranging from the role of science in society to the relationship between science and religion. As a man of faith, Planck argued that the two were not mutually exclusive and that seeking an understanding of both were required for a complete world view.

Just as Planck began to acquire widespread professional acclaim, his personal life was marred by tragedy. In 1909 his wife died. In 1916 his elder son was killed in action during World War I. The twin girls both died while giving birth to daughters, Margrete in 1917 and Emma in 1919. Although he eventually remarried, Planck wrote mournfully that "no man is born with a legal claim to happiness, success, and prosperity in life" and that one had no alternative but to "fight bravely in the battle of life, and to bow in silent surrender to the will of a higher power which rules over him."

After the war, most German scientists were ostracized by international organizations, but Planck's reputation for hon-

esty and integrity remained intact. He was awarded the 1918
Nobel Prize in physics for "his contribution to the development of physics by his discovery of the element of action." He
was the leading German authority on scientific matters and
was instrumental in the reacceptance of German scientists by
the international scientific community after the war. He was
elected as a member to most of the leading scientific organizations in the world. Planck retired from the University of
Berlin in 1927 after a career spanning more than forty years.
He remained active in the Kaiser-Wilhelm Society, which was
created to support German scientific research, and to establish and fund new scientific institutes. In 1930 Planck was
elected as its President (it would later be renamed the Max
Planck Society). He guided and protected the Society
through the rise of the Nazi regime, and on one occasion
protested personally to Adolf Hitler about the Nazis' anti-
Semitic policies.

Even retirement could not shield Planck from more
tragedy. His son Erwin, the remaining child from his first
marriage, was implicated in the 1944 assassination attempt
on Hitler and was brutally executed by the Gestapo in 1945.
Planck's home in a Berlin suburb was leveled in an allied air
raid. Although he survived the raid, all of his personal
belongings, including his library, were destroyed. At the end
of the war an American officer brought Planck and his second wife to the city of Göttingen. Although in failing
health, he continued to travel and lecture for two more
years in the hope of encouraging "people struggling for truth
and knowledge, especially young people." Having enjoyed
the best of life with humility and accepted the worst with
dignity, Max Planck died on October 4, 1947, at the age of
eighty-nine. ◆

Planck's son Erwin was implicated in the 1944 assassination attempt on Hitler and was brutally executed by the Gestapo.

Powell, John Wesley

1834–1902 ● Geology, Anthropology, & Ethnology

Powell led the first expedition down the Colorado River and through the Grand Canyon.

A geologist, ethnologist, and anthropologist, John Wesley Powell explored the Grand Canyon and the Colorado River, became director of the United States Geological Survey, and developed a useful classification system of American Indian languages. He was born in Mount Morris, New York.

Before Powell turned to science and exploration, he served in the Union Army during the Civil War and attained the rank of major. He fought with great gallantry and, at the Battle of Shiloh, lost his right arm. After the war, he became a professor of geology at Illinois Wesleyan University in 1865 and at Illinois Normal College in 1867. Powell did not remain within the confines of the classroom for long. In 1867 and 1868, he led field trips into the Rocky Mountains, where the Ute Indians called him Karpurats—"one-arm man." In July and August 1869, having secured support from the Smithsonian Institution and an appropriation from Congress, he led eleven others in the first expedition down the Colorado River and through the Grand Canyon. The expedition faced both natural and human hazards; three of the party were killed by hostile Paiute Indians.

The expedition brought funding from the Department of the Interior for a "U.S. Geographical and Geological Survey of the Rocky Mountain Region" from 1871 to 1879. In 1871 and 1874, Powell personally led expeditions, which not only added vastly to the information on public lands in the Rocky Mountains, but provided photographer John K. Hillers with the opportunity to document the Grand Canyon in a spectacular series of images. Laying the groundwork for a vast part of the national park system, Powell's reports and Hillers's photographs sparked interest in preserving the Grand Canyon as a national scenic area. Remarkably, while undertaking geological studies, Powell also conducted ethnological work among the Native Americans of the region. He published *An Introduction to The Study of Indian Languages* in 1877, a pioneering effort in the linguistic and ethnological classification of Indian languages and dialects, which organized them into fiffy-six well-defined linguistic families. Powell also led expeditions into Utah and Arizona and charted large tracts in the region.

In 1879, the so-called Powell Survey, the Hayden Survey (conducted by Ferdinand Vandeveer Hayden), and the King Survey (led by Clarence King) were merged into the U.S Geological Survey under the aegis of the Department of the Interior. King served as the survey's first director and was succeeded by Powell in 1881. Also in 1879, Powell became the first director of the Smithsonian Institution's Bureau of Ethnology (renamed the Bureau of American Ethnology in 1894). As director of the Geological Survey, Powell was dynamic and energetic but also generally heedless of politics. He built the U.S. Geological Survey into a well-organized, well-funded, and powerful federal agency, which produced a large volume of scientific information through the publication series Powell instituted: the Bulletin series (from 1883), the Monograph series (from 1890), and the folio atlas series (begun in 1894). As early as his *Report on the Lands of Arid Regions* in 1878, Powell had advocated government-funded irrigation and reclamation projects, and in 1888, as a result of his work at the Geological Survey, Congress began authorizing funds. However, his unbending advocacy of these government-regulated irrigation projects, coupled with his insistence on stringent forest preservation measures, caused great

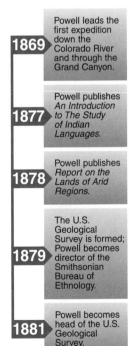

1869 Powell leads the first expedition down the Colorado River and through the Grand Canyon.

1877 Powell publishes *An Introduction to The Study of Indian Languages.*

1878 Powell publishes *Report on the Lands of Arid Regions.*

1879 The U.S. Geological Survey is formed; Powell becomes director of the Smithsonian Bureau of Ethnology.

1881 Powell becomes head of the U.S. Geological Survey.

Powell built the U.S. Geological Survey into a well-organized, well-funded, and powerful federal agency.

consternation among Western landowners and capitalists, who pressured Congress into forcing Powell to resign from the survey in 1894.

Powell continued as director of the Bureau of Ethnology until his death. He directed expeditions to study the Zunis of New Mexico and the Pueblo Indians of the Southwest. He brought into the Bureau of Ethnology the leading anthropologists of the day, including Adolph Alphonse Bandeiler, Frank Hilton Cushing, James Owen Dorsey, Jesse Walker Fewkes, William Henry Holmes, Washington Matthews, James Mooney, Matilda Coxe Stevenson, and William Orrie Tuggle.

Powell's reports on his early geological studies were published in 1875 as *Explorations of the Colorado River of the West and Its Tributaries*, which was revised and enlarged in 1885 as *Canyons of the Colorado*. Not only were these works invaluable for what they revealed about the Southwest, they also developed much of the terminology and many of the concepts used by geologists to this day. ◆

Ptolemy, Claudius

C. 100–170 ● GEOGRAPHY, MATHEMATICS, & ASTRONOMY

"Everything that is hard to attain is easily assailed by the generality of men."

— Claudius Ptolemy

Greece was the homeland of this mathematician, astronomer, and geographer, though Ptolemy was actually born in Egypt. Little is known about Ptolemy's early life except that he was born in Alexandria, then one of the world's great centers of learning, of Greek and Egyptian parents. Demonstrating an encyclopedic breadth and depth of erudition he gathered all the theories that were prominent in his time and tested them against the knowledge of the physical world that had been accumulated. Although his knowledge was necessarily limited by ancient theories, Ptolemy's use of mathematics and derivation of precise observation makes him a precursor of later scientific method. Indeed, his synthesis was so powerful that it lasted for thirteen centuries, dominating

European thinking and acting as the cornerstone of scientific knowledge until the Copernican Revolution.

Ptolemy inherited a wealth of Greek philosophical, astronomical, and geographical works: from the philosophy of Plato he adopted the assumption that the Earth was that most perfect of geometric forms, a sphere; following Aristotle, he further saw the Earth as the center of the universe, surrounded by fixed celestial spheres, including one that held the multiplicity of stars (another trend in Greek thought, that placed the Sun at the center of the universe, was thereby ignored); from Hipparchus, the preeminent astronomer of antiquity, Ptolemy inherited a star map with the locations of 850 stars, the first such compilation of its kind, which increased the number of charted stars to 1,022. He also adopted Hipparchus's tradition of dividing a circle or sphere into 360 degrees, and invented the map grid charting longitude and latitude, which is still utilized to the present day. With his sphere projected on a flat surface divided by latitude and longitude Ptolemy charted the locations of eight thousand places in the known world, including the entire Roman Empire, which spanned the known continents of his times—Africa, Asia, and Europe. His maps situated the northern lands at the top of the page with east at the right, a convention still observed in cartography.

Ptolemy erred in his estimate of the size of the Earth: attributing fifty miles to one degree of latitude, he underestimated the circumference of the planet by some thirty percent. Moreover, on Ptolemy's maps the majority of the Earth's surface is covered by land (which in fact only accounts for about one-quarter of the planet's surface area), incorrectly making the distance from Europe to its neighboring continent seem smaller than it really is. Ptolemy studied spherical geometry, inventing a sundial that was of great significance in an age before the advent of the mechanical clock. He also worked in harmonics, measuring the lengths of chords, and propounded theories in optics for phenomena that had previously escaped scientific explanation. In addition, he developed a calendar that indicated meteorological factors as well as charting the locations of stars at sunrise and sunset.

Ptolemy's major work in astronomy is the thirteen-volume *Almagest*. Ptolemy put the Earth at the center of the universe, followed by the Moon, Mercury, Venus, the Sun, Mars,

> Ptolemy put the Earth at the center of the universe followed by the Moon, Mercury, Venus, the Sun, Mars, Jupiter, and Saturn.

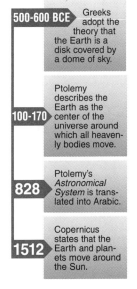

500-600 BCE Greeks adopt the theory that the Earth is a disk covered by a dome of sky.

100-170 Ptolemy describes the Earth as the center of the universe around which all heavenly bodies move.

828 Ptolemy's *Astronomical System* is translated into Arabic.

1512 Copernicus states that the Earth and planets move around the Sun.

Jupiter, and Saturn. He correctly placed the planets closer to Earth than the stars, which he believed were held in fixed positions by a crystalline sphere. Like Aristotle, he held that the outermost sphere was set into motion by the Prime Mover. The planets were conceived of as revolving around the earth on a circular course known as a deferrent. The system was complicated by the need to account for the occasional dimming of a planet's light that could be observed. A more significant problem was the observation of retrograde motions, when planets seemed to move backward in their course. Ptolemy explained this phenomenon by proposing that while the planet revolved in its larger circles around the Earth, they also turned in an epicycle, a smaller cycle that gave the planet a second revolving course.

geocentric: having the earth as center.

The *Almagest* also offered proofs for a **geocentric** universe, based on the observable fact that an object when dropped falls toward the Earth and not toward some other center. It also argued that the Earth was stationary for otherwise an object dropped from a height would land at a distant location. These beliefs, consistent with the teaching of the church, remained unchallenged until the fifteenth century when accumulated observation made the Ptolemaic system less tenable than a **heliocentric** model. ◆

heliocentric: have the sun as center.

Pythagoras

C. 580–C. 500 BCE ● Physics, Mathematics, & Astronomy

"Reason is immortal, all else mortal."

— Pythagoras

Ancient Greece was the birthplace of western philosophy and science. If, as Alfred North Whitehead claimed, European philosophy is simply "a series of footnotes to Plato," Pythagoras, a Greek, can rightfully be considered the father of philosophy—a term he coined—and of mathematics, physics, and astronomy. Although his teachings were handed down secretly to a select body of disciples, contemporary scholars have been able to reconstruct much of what he said and present plausible interpretations of the numerous **cryptic maxims** attributed to him. The events of Pythagoras's life have been obscured by countless legends promulgated by fervent devotees attempting to deify their master. Some considered him the incarnation of the **Hyperborean** Apollo; others claim that Apollo was his father. Actually, Pythagoras was probably the son of Mnesarchus, a merchant or jeweler from the island of Samos, then a major Mediterranean commercial center. To explain his preoccupation with numbers, some biographers claim that he trained to be a bookkeeper. More likely, he studied under the three foremost contemporary thinkers: Pherekydis of Syros and Thales and Anaximander of Miletus, to each of whom central elements of his doctrines can be traced. He seems to have rejected the Hellenic ideal of physical perfection, possibly because of a large golden birthmark on his thigh, which he later pointed to as evidence of his divine origins. The reasons for Pythagoras's sudden departure for Egypt remain obscure. In one account, he fled the dictator Polycrates, but that same source claims that he brought with him a letter of introduction signed by Polycrates. Another possibility is that, having mastered astrology under Anaximander, he wanted to continue his studies under Thales, but the latter, being too old, encouraged him to study abroad. Whatever the reason, his twenty years there proved vital in formulating his philosophy. He was initiated into several **esoteric** sects and adopted many of their beliefs. Most notable was the belief in reincarnation—he later claimed to remember his previous lives—and in a living universe governed by mathematical principles.

Egypt was conquered by Cambyses in 525 BCE and Pythagoras was exiled to Babylon. For ten years, he mastered Chaldean mysticism, including the use of opium to attain enlightenment and the complicated procedures of ritual purification, before returning to Samos to establish his ideas.

Back home, however, Pythagoras, who now sported long hair, an unshaven beard, and trousers, was regarded as an eccentric figure, more barbarian than Greek. Since no one would attend his school, he bribed a young boy to study mathematics with him. The boy then shared his knowledge with his peers who became increasingly fascinated by Pythagoras. Suddenly, Pythagoras refused to teach unless he was paid. Not only the boy, but many other young aristocrats flocked to him

cryptic maxims: secret or mysterious sayings.

Hyperborean: relating to a group of people believed by the ancient Greeks to live beyond the north wind in a region of perpetual sunshine.

esoteric: limited to a small, specially-initiated group of people.

until, unwilling to fulfill disagreeable social obligations, Pythagoras fled to Croton.

There, Pythagoras quickly reestablished his brotherhood of disciples, called mathematikoi. Its beliefs were a well guarded secret, but probably included the belief that the entire universe was a living organism governed by mathematical principles. Man's soul was immortal, but subject to reincarnation, possibly as an animal or even a plant. Ritual purity was essential; his followers were strict vegetarians who also abstained from eating beans because of the similarity between their shape and that of the human embryo. The brotherhood was governed by a strict moral code that emphasized communal property and, above all, secrecy. Pythagoras encouraged the reputation that he was divine by refusing to eat or perform other physical needs in public. He was surrounded by legends—on one occasion, a heavenly voice called out his name. He once stopped a dog from being beaten because he recognized in its whining the voice of a dead friend, while on another occasion, he made a fisherman agree to release his catch if he told him exactly how many fish were in the net.

Pythagoras once stopped a dog from being beaten because he recognized in its whining the voice of a dead friend.

The Pythagoreans governed Croton for about fifteen years, until a native rebellion forced Pythagoras to flee to Metapontum amidst rumors that he committed suicide. Conflicting accounts exist as to how Pythagoras died; one disciple later claimed that he rose bodily to heaven. His school, however, continued to function for four hundred years, influencing many prominent Greek philosophers, among them Plato. Today, it is difficult to determine what was originally taught by Pythagoras and what was discovered by his pupils— they generally attributed all their knowledge to him. In mathematics, he is attributed with the Pythagorean Theorem (the square of the hypotenuse of a right angle triangle is equal to the sum of the square of both sides). In physics, he taught the mathematical relationship between the length of a string and its tone when plucked. In astronomy, he was the first to propose that the earth was spherical and that the evening star and the morning star were the same planet, which he identified as Aphrodite (later known as Venus). ◆

Richter, Charles

1900–1985 ● SEISMOLOGY

Charles F. Richter was born in Hamilton, Ohio, on 26 April 1900. He earned a bachelor's degree in physics at Stanford in 1920, enrolled at the California Institute of Technology (CalTech) for graduate study, and received his Ph.D. in theoretical physics in 1928. Richter began working at the **Seismological** Laboratory of the Carnegie Institution of Washington a year before receiving his Ph.D. degree. The Seismological Laboratory was then located in Pasadena, California, and jointly operated by the Carnegie Institution and CalTech. Richter worked first as an employee of the Carnegie Institution and later as a member of CalTech when the laboratory was transferred to CalTech in 1936. He continued to work at CalTech as professor of seismology until his retirement in 1970. He taught seismology in Japan as a Fulbright scholar during 1959–1960. He served as president of the Seismological Society of America from 1959 to 1960 and was the second recipient of its medal in 1977. Richter married Lillian Brand in 1928. The Richters had no children.

In the 1930s, the Seismological Laboratory was preparing to issue regular reports of earthquakes occurring in southern California. While tabulating 200 to 300 earthquakes a year, Richter wanted to devise some means of grading them on a quantitative basis (the systems then in use were extremely qualitative). He measured the amplitudes of seismic waves recorded with the Wood—Anderson seismographs that just had been deployed in southern California. Using this data set, Richter introduced a local magnitude scale, M_L, to represent the physical size of earthquakes in southern California. M_L is determined by the logarithm of the amplitude A measured at a distance Δ from the earthquake's epicenter (the point on the

seismological: relating to the study of earthquakes.

> While tabulating 200 to 300 earthquakes a year, Richter wanted to devise some means of grading them on a quantitative basis.

earth's surface directly above the focus of an earthquake): $M_L = \log A + f(\Delta)$. Here $f(\Delta)$, called the amplitude attenuation function, is a function of Δ, but does not depend on A. Thus, at a given distance, M_L increases by one unit as the amplitude of seismic waves increases 10 times. $f(\Delta)$ is adjusted such that $M_L = 3$, if $A = 1$ mm at $\Delta = 100$ km. This scale, though developed **empirically** with data from only a few stations, turned out to be extremely useful not only for earthquake reporting purposes but also for various scientific and engineering studies. For this reason, Richter's paper on the local magnitude published in 1935 is generally regarded as a milestone in seismology. Later analyses using many more earthquakes and seismic stations confirmed that the function $f(\Delta)$ Richter determined is very accurate.

Although M_L was originally introduced to measure earthquakes only in southern California, the concept—the Richter scale—was later extended to earthquakes all over the world by Beno Gutenberg (then director of the Seismological Laboratory of CalTech), Richter, and subsequently by many other seismologists. With the introduction of the magnitude scale, seismologists could begin to study earthquakes quantitatively, and earthquake seismology, which had been a somewhat descriptive science, became a modern quantitative science.

Another major contribution by Richter was his 1958 book *Elementary Seismology*. This book is in a way an encyclopedia of seismology; it touches on practically every aspect of earthquakes with a strong emphasis on field observations. It includes not only the conventional subjects like descriptions of important earthquakes, seismic waves, magnitude, intensity, seismographs, and distribution of earthquakes, but also sections on the effects of earthquakes on ground and surface water, insurance, seismic zoning, and earthquake-resistant construction. It is remarkable that even today not only students but also professional seismologists often refer to this thirty-five-year-old text. Although Richter did not have many students from his own laboratory, through this book he probably has more students than any other seismologist. Richter's descriptions of earthquakes is always very detailed and accurate. Very often when the original account was written in a foreign language he had someone translate it before writing his own account.

empirically: through observation and verifiable data.

1927 Richter begins working at the Seismological Laboratory of the Carnegie Institution.

1928 Richter earns his Ph.D. in theoretical physics.

1935 Richter establishes the Richter Scale of earthquake magnitude.

1949 Richter publishes *Seismicity of the Earthquake*.

1958 Richter publishes *Elementary Seismology*.

Another important contribution is the book *Seismicity of the Earthquake*, which Gutenberg and Richter published in 1949. This is not merely a catalog of earthquakes but a monumental work on **tectonics** of Earth as viewed from a seismological point of view.

Richter also coauthored with Gutenberg a series of monographs, *On Seismic Waves* (1934, 1935, 1936, and 1939). Interpretation of seismograms is one of the most important tasks in seismology. Many of the important features of Earth's interior and of earthquakes are determined by the interpretation of very subtle features in **seismograms**. The descriptions of seismic waves and their theoretical interpretations described in *On Seismic Waves* helped many seismologists to extract useful information from seismograms, which eventually led to many important discoveries.

Although Richter's works are generally on the observational aspects of seismology and appear descriptive, he was also interested in basic theories in seismology, as is evidenced by his paper on mathematical questions in seismology.

For many years until his retirement, Richter was in charge of the measuring room of the Seismological Laboratory. He examined literally thousands of seismograms to study every detail of earthquakes. In this capacity, Richter played an important role in educating the public about earthquakes. Whenever a major earthquake occurred, not only in southern California but also in other seismic regions in the world, reporters from the news media called Richter at his home or at the laboratory for his comments. Richter responded to these requests day and night. Talking to the press about earthquakes was apparently one of Richter's joys and pleasures. Richter was a man with remarkable memory and his account of an earthquake that just occurred in relation to the historical background of the area intrigued not only the general public but also professional seismologists.

Richter was known to be a man of good humor, but whenever he saw something that ran counter to his scientific or professional beliefs, he expressed his opinion in candid words, which can be seen in some of his writings.

Richter died on 30 September 1985 in Altadena, but the tradition he established of making detailed analysis of earthquakes in southern California and reporting the results to the public is maintained at the Seismological Laboratory. ◆

tectonics: geology dealing with the structure, folds, and faults of the earth's crust.

seismogram: the record of an earth tremor.

Whenever major earthquakes occurred, reporters called Richter at his home or at the laboratory for his comments.

Röntgen, Wilhelm Conrad

1845–1923 ● PHYSICS

> *"I shall use the expression 'rays' and to distinguish them from others of this name, I shall call them 'x-rays.' "*
> — Wilhelm Conrad Röntgen

The newly discovered rays cast curious shadows of hidden things: brass weights in a wooden box, a steel compass needle in a metal case, the bones of a living hand inside the outline of its flesh.

Röntgen was born at Lennep, Germany, March 27, 1845, the only child of Friedrich Conrad Röntgen, a merchant and cloth manufacturer of Lennep in Germany, and Charlotte Constanze Frowein from Apeldoorn in Holland, to which the family moved in 1848. When Röntgen would not tattle on a classmate, he was expelled from school before graduation. Now ineligible for the Dutch and German universities, he wound up in Switzerland in 1865 to study mechanical engineering at the Federal Polytechnic in Zurich.

Zurich was splendid. Röntgen skipped lectures to enjoy the mountains and lake, fell in love with Bertha Ludwig, daughter of a German political refugee, earned his diploma in 1868, and was recruited for research by August Kundt, the professor of physics. In 1869 he qualified for a Ph.D. at the university; then, as Kundt's assistant, he moved to Würzburg and Strassburg, marrying Bertha in 1872. In 1874 he acquired the faculty status that freed him for an independent career and brought him back to Würzburg as a professor of physics in 1888.

He was fifty in 1895 when he first glimpsed the X-rays. They were strange, something like light, but of an oddly penetrating kind that would not bend for prisms or focus for lenses. They cast curious shadows of hidden things: brass weights in a wooden box, a steel compass needle in a metal case, the bones of a living hand inside the outline of its flesh. They were impossible to explain, but he could still describe them by recording their behavior, and he stretched his imagination for experiments to reveal every quirk of it.

That description filled seventeen numbered sections in the report that he mailed out as a preprint to announce his discovery on January 1, 1896. With each, he enclosed a set of his shadow photographs, hoping that the pictures might confirm the text and the text might validate the pictures.

Both were effective. Anyone who read the paper could produce X-rays; skeletal hands appeared by the dozens, and Röntgen became a reluctant celebrity. He declined the aristocratic title of *von Röntgen,* moved grudgingly when he was called to Munich in 1899, and did not lecture at Stockholm when he received the first Nobel Prize for physics in 1901.

Bertha's health was failing, and Munich was less congenial than Würzburg. They missed their old friends but rejoined them in summer at Pontresina in the Swiss Alps (where Röntgen still enjoyed climbing, as he also enjoyed hunting at their country place in Weilheim). He kept working through the hard days of World War I and the bitter defeat that followed and tried to manage Bertha's bouts of pain with morphine injections. She died on October 1, 1919, and he followed three years later, on on February 10, 1923, active to the end.

Was Röntgen a great scientist? In his own way he was. In three brief months he created a new science and gave it to the world. Although the talents by which he established it also kept him from going farther, he opened a new territory for other scientists to prospect and explore for years to come. ◆

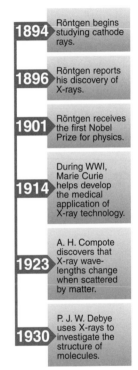

1894 Röntgen begins studying cathode rays.

1896 Röntgen reports his discovery of X-rays.

1901 Röntgen receives the first Nobel Prize for physics.

1914 During WWI, Marie Curie helps develop the medical application of X-ray technology.

1923 A. H. Compote discovers that X-ray wavelengths change when scattered by matter.

1930 P. J. W. Debye uses X-rays to investigate the structure of molecules.

Rutherford, Ernest

1871–1937 ● PHYSICS & CHEMISTRY

> *"When we have found how the nucleus of atoms are built up we shall have found the greatest secret of all, except life. We shall have found the basis of everything—of the earth we walk on, of the air we breathe, of the sunshine, of our physical body itself, of everything in the world, however small—except life."*
>
> — Ernest Rutherford, *Passing Show 24*

E rnest Rutherford was born on August 30, 1871, near Nelson on New Zealand's South Island. He was the fourth of the twelve children of James and Martha Rutherford, who had migrated to New Zealand from the British Isles. He obtained a scholarship to attend Nelson College (a secondary school) and then went on to Canterbury College, Christchurch, where he received a B.A. in 1892, with "first class honours" in mathematics and physics, and an M.A. in 1893. Rutherford stayed at Canterbury College for a fifth year to do research on the detection of radio waves. He became engaged to Mary Newton, his landlady's daughter; they were married when Rutherford returned to New Zealand for the summer of 1900. Their only child, Eileen, was born in 1901.

In 1895 Rutherford went to work under J. J. Thomson at the Cavendish Laboratory of Cambridge University, supported by an 1881 Exhibition Scholarship. At first he continued his research on the magnetic detection of radio waves, but he soon switched, at Thomson's direction, to the ionization of gases by X-rays. Shortly after the discovery of radioactivity, Rutherford investigated the ionization of gases by the radiation from radioactive sources. He soon discovered two types of radiation, which he named alpha and beta, and eventually proved that alpha particles are doubly charged helium. Rutherford became professor of physics at McGill University in Montreal in 1898. He continued to study alpha particles, working with Frederick Soddy, a chemist. This work led Rutherford to the conclusion, in 1902, that radioactivity is the result of the disintegration or transmutation of elements. For this discovery he was awarded the 1908 Nobel Prize in chemistry.

In 1907 Rutherford moved back to England to the University of Manchester. He continued to study the alpha particle (which he considered his alpha particles). Based on measurements of the scattering of alpha particles by thin foils, mostly done by Hans Geiger and Ernest Marsden under his direction, Rutherford demonstrated in 1911 that atoms consist of a tiny, very dense, positively charged nucleus surrounded by electrons. Niels Bohr worked with Rutherford for a year before returning to Copenhagen to develop his model of the electronic structure of atoms.

Rutherford was knighted in 1914. He had become world-famous as the large and boisterous but friendly and extremely effective leader of one of the most important physics research groups. During World War I he studied underwater acoustics for submarine detection. This work laid the foundation for the later development of **sonar**. Continued work with alpha particles led, in 1919, to the discovery of the first artificial transmutation—the bombardment of nitrogen by alpha particles resulted in oxygen and hydrogen. In 1919 he succeeded J. J. Thomson as director of the Cavendish Laboratory. Much of his time in the 1920s and 1930s was spent in seeking government support of basic research and in being a leader of the international scientific community. Rutherford speculated on the existence of the neutron, which James Chadwick discovered at the Cavendish Laboratory in 1932. It was under Rutherford's leadership that Cockcroft and Walton first observed a transmutation induced by artificially accelerated protons.

In 1931 Rutherford was made a baron, Lord Rutherford of Nelson. He was quite healthy most of his life but did have a small **umbilical hernia**. A strangulation of the hernia led to his death at Cambridge on October 19, 1937. ◆

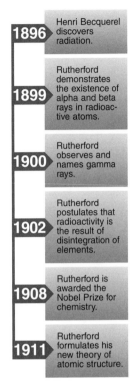

1896 Henri Becquerel discovers radiation.

1899 Rutherford demonstrates the existence of alpha and beta rays in radioactive atoms.

1900 Rutherford observes and names gamma rays.

1902 Rutherford postulates that radioactivity is the result of disintegration of elements.

1908 Rutherford is awarded the Nobel Prize for chemistry.

1911 Rutherford formulates his new theory of atomic structure.

sonar: a method for locating underwater objects using sound waves.

umbilical hernia: a protrusion of an organ through the naval area of the abdomen.

Sakharov, Andrei Dmitrievich

1921–1989 ● NUCLEAR PHYSICS

> *"Intellectual freedom is the only guarantee of a scientific-democratic approach to politics, economic development, and culture."*
> — Andrei Sakharov, *Progress, Coexistence, and Intellectual Freedom*

Sakharov was born in Moscow, Russia, May 21, 1921, into a family of intellectuals; his father was a well-known physics teacher and the author of textbooks and popular articles. Sakharov graduated with honors from Moscow University in 1942, perhaps the best physics major they had ever had. He spent the years of World War II in a munitions factory, where his creativity was already evident. After the war, he did his graduate work at the Physics Institute of the Academy of Sciences (FIAN). Immediately after that, Sakharov joined the Installation, which was the Soviet atomic bomb laboratory. He worked closely with four great theoretical physicists: Yakov Zeldovich, Nikolai Bogolubov, Igor Tamm, and Isaak Pomeranchuk. Sakharov is often credited with being the "father" of the Soviet hydrogen bomb.

Besides his military work (which involved a deep knowledge of nuclear and **plasma** physics), Sakharov made major contributions to basic science in three areas. In plasma physics he was the first in the Soviet Union to suggest the use

plasma: a collection of charged particles containing about equal numbers of positive ions and electrons.

of lasers to initiate a controlled thermonuclear burn. He also proposed the tokamak (a device using a large current induced directly in the plasma) which is, even to this day, a major line of fusion energy research. In particle physics he put forward the first rational explanation of the baryon asymmetry of the universe; that is, why there are more particles than antiparticles; in short, why we exist. His explanation is based on the elementary violation of CP invariance: under simultaneous charge conjugation (C) and parity inversion (P) the universe is not invariant. In cosmology Sakharov proposed an alternative gravitational theory to that of Albert Einstein. In sum, his work was recognized early, and at age thirty-two he was elected to the Soviet Academy of Sciences, an honor that has no precedent in Soviet science.

Sakharov devoted himself to the societal aspects of science. He was one of the first to realize the health consequences of atmospheric nuclear explosions, and he was instrumental in convincing Nikita Krushchev to sign an agreement with John Kennedy that ended such tests. He was also very concerned about the uses of nuclear weapons. His 1968 publication on "Coexistence" galvanized the world's attention onto this subject, while causing him, within the Soviet system, much personal distress.

It is on human rights that Sakharov is best known. In fact, his work in the defense of human rights resulted in his being awarded the Nobel Peace Prize in 1975. He was active in the defense of many dissidents, including Sergei Kovalev and Yuri Orlov. For this activity, he was tried and sentenced, in January 1980, to house arrest in the (closed city) of Gorky. He was released by Mikhail Gorbachev in December 1986. In his last years, Sakharov was elected to the Congress of People's Deputies. Many feel he would have played a significant role in the transition from the Soviet Union to Russia, if it had not been for his early death in Moscow on December 14, 1989. ◆

1945 Sakharov joins the Lebedev Physics Institute in Moscow to work on cosmic rays.

1950 Sakhorov proposes the tokamak.

1954 USSR explodes its first hydrogen bomb, which Sakharov helped design.

1975 Sakharov is awarded the Nobel Prize for peace.

1980 Sakharov is tried as a dissident and sentenced to house arrest in Gorky.

1986 Mikhail Gorbachev releases Sakharov from house arrest.

Salk, Jonas

1914–1995 ● MEDICINE

"The people—could you patent the sun?"
—Jonas Salk, when asked who owned the
patent for his vaccine.

Before Salk developed an effective vaccination against poliomyetis, commonly referred to as polio, contraction of the disease often meant enduring a lifetime of paralysis to its victims. In 1955 Salk gave the world the first effective means of preventing the disease.

Salk was born in New York City on Oct. 28, 1914, to immigrants from Russia. His mother lacked any formal education while his father completed some elementary grades. Salk was the oldest of three boys and the first in his family to go to college. Although both his parents had very little education, both wanted more for their children, and encouraged them in whatever field they chose, although Salk once said his mother wasn't happy with his first career choice—becoming a lawyer.

Although he entered the City College of New York as a prelaw major, Salk later switched to premed. While receiving training as a medical doctor, Salk never strayed from his main goal of becoming a research scientist. When Salk graduated in 1939 from New York University's Medical School, he continued research on influenza that he had started as a medical student.

Salk did research for the government, which was interested in keeping its soldiers and those who returned home from spreading the flu virus. Successful in developing a vaccine that stopped the spread of the flu, Salk then turned his attention to fighting polio, which he undertook while serving as a research professor at the University of Pittsburgh School of Medicine.

Salk was approached by the research director of the National Foundation for Infantile Paralysis, who wanted to know if he would be interested in a program seeking to classify various polio viruses. Provided with funding and equipment, Salk accepted the challenge.

Salk knew that if he used a "killed virus" instead of a weakened virus, it would eliminate the risk of infection, which would make the vaccine much safer. Despite a large number of skeptics who said it couldn't be done, Salk continued his research.

In 1952, Salk found that his early vaccine produced an antibody response in humans. It was the first solid evidence that his research was headed in the proper direction. After Salk discovered the vaccine, the next step was to test it on people. Field trials on human beings began in July 1954; by April 1955, the announcement was made that a vaccine had been successfully tested. Salk went from anonymous research

The War Against Polio

Until the mid-1950s, polio was the most feared disease in America. Polio is caused by a virus that enters the body through the nose or mouth. The virus may eventually attack nerve cells in the spinal cord or the brain, causing paralysis and, in severe case, death. In the United States, polio outbreaks often occurred in cities in the summer, and it was common for swimming pools and other recreational facilities to be closed down after cases were reported in an area. In the 1930s, President Franklin D. Roosevelt, who had been infected with polio in 1921, declared war on the disease. Fundraising and public awareness campaigns were held, and large grants were made to medical institutions to find a cure or a vaccine. Jonas Salk began experimenting on killed-virus vaccines in 1950. Four years later, he had a polio vaccine ready. Trials showed Salk's vaccine to be effective, and extensive mass immunization programs were quickly implemented. In 1960, Dr. Albert Sabin developed an oral form of the polio vaccine. Although there is still no cure for polio, Salk and Sabin's vaccines have virtually eradicated the disease in industrialized countries. The World Health Organization hopes to eliminate polio worldwide by the year 2000.

scientist to international hero overnight, in part because he refused to patent his vaccine, which would have made him millions.

However, some problems arose. After the field trials ended and the vaccine was licensed, reports filtered back in that instances of polio had occurred due to the vaccine. Further investigation revealed that a manufacturer had not followed the proper procedures with the vaccine. The federal government ordered that the vaccine be filtered, a move Salk rejected, saying it made his vaccine less efficient.

When Albert Sabin developed a "live virus" oral vaccine, there was controversy over which was safer. Other "live virus" vaccines had a history of causing the very disease the vaccine was attempting to fight, especially in people with weakened immune systems. The U.S. government decided to issue Sabin's oral vaccine, which some believe has caused new cases of polio.

In 1963, Salk founded the Salk Institute for Biological Studies, which he hoped would not only perform scientific work but would also address issues outside of science that affect everyone, what Salk called the "human dimension." It is located in La Jolla, California.

Salk wrote three books. The first, *Man Unfolding*, came out in 1972. It was followed by *The Survival of the Wisest*, written with his son Jonathan in 1973, and *Anatomy of Reality*, which was published in 1983.

Late in his life, Salk began to research the AIDS epidemic, hoping to find a cure for the virus. However, he was never able to complete this research, dying on June 23, 1995, at the age of eighty.

Of his life, Salk once said, "There have to be people who are ahead of their time. And that is my fate." ◆

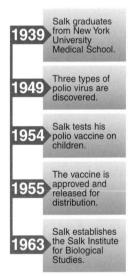

1939 Salk graduates from New York University Medical School.

1949 Three types of polio virus are discovered.

1954 Salk tests his polio vaccine on children.

1955 The vaccine is approved and released for distribution.

1963 Salk establishes the Salk Institute for Biological Studies.

Schliemann, Heinrich

1822–1890 ● ARCHEOLOGY

"I have gazed on the face of Agamemnon."
— Heinrich Schliemann

Homeric: relating to the Greek poet Homer, who lived during the 8th to 9th century BCE and is credited with writing the *The Illiad* and *The Odyssey*.

This German archeologist proved that the Heroic Age of Greece was not myth but reality. Schliemann was born at Neu Buckow in Mecklenburg-Schwerin to a poor pastor. Obsessed by the **Homeric** stories, he wanted to become a linguist and came to know eight languages apart from German, including ancient and modern Greek.

After being sent out to Saint Petersburg by a commercial house in 1846, he set up his own company and traded in indigo. He made a fortune during the Crimean War, partly as a military contractor. In 1868 he moved to Greece, where he spent his time visiting Homeric sites. He then published a book, *Ithaka, der Peloponnes und Troja* (1869), in which he put forward two theories which he was later to test: that Hissarlik (about four miles from the mouth of the Dardanelles) rather than Bunarbashi was the site of Troy, and that the Atreid graves that Pausanias saw at Mycenae were within the citadel wall.

In 1870 he started working on Calvert's excavations at the former site and, believing that Troy was on the lowest level, cut downwards, disregarding the upper strata, where the remains of the Troy of Homer that he was seeking in fact lay. In 1873, the day before he was due to cease his digging for the season, he made the sensational discovery of 8,700 pieces, which he called "Priam's Treasure." He had unearthed large fortifications and other remains of a very ancient city that had been burned. Although Schliemann announced that it was Troy, this city is now known to have belonged to the middle pre-Mycenaean period, a thousand years before Homer's Archaeans. At the time, he was widely supported in his claim; only later was it realized that he had in fact destroyed much of the remains of the real Troy.

In 1874 Schliemann was prohibited by the Ottoman government from continuing his work, as they were dissatisfied with their share of the treasure. Only two years later did he receive permission to resume his excavations. In the meantime he had published *Troja und Seine Ruinen* (*Troy and Its Remains*, 1875) and gone to Mycenae. In 1877 he began investigating the dome-tombs and the area near the Lion Gate, and opened up a large pit just inside the citadel of Mycenae. Here he discovered the now-famous double ring of slabs and stone reliefs. In the rock shaft, six royal graves were discovered, containing the most valuable treasure trove known, including gold, silver, bronze, fine stone and ivory objects, proving the existence of a great pre-Hellenic civilization. The find was deposited in Athens, and Schliemann published *Mykenä* (*Mycenae*, 1878), becoming famous for his discoveries. He had by then settled in Athens and married a Greek woman, building two magnificent houses that became notable centers for Athenian society.

Further excavations in Ithaca in 1878 were unsuccessful, and so he again took up his work at Hissarlik. Based on this, he published his *Ilios* (1881) and, in 1883, *Troja*. In 1880 he found the beautiful ceiling in the remains of the ruined dome-tomb of Orchomenus and in 1885, aided by Wilhelm Dorpfeld, cleared away earth on the rock of Tiryns, traditional birthplace of Hercules, to reveal a complete ground plan of a Mycenaean palace. This proved to be his last major discovery. He was unsuccessful in his searches for the Caesareum at Alexandria, the palace of Minos at Knossos in Crete, and the Aphrodite temple at Cythera (1888). He died while planning further digs at Hissarlik. His autobiography was published in 1892. ◆

In Mycenae, Schliemann discovered six royal graves that contained gold, silver, bronze, fine stone, and ivory.

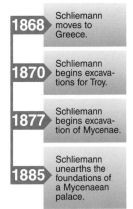

1868 Schliemann moves to Greece.

1870 Schliemann begins excavations for Troy.

1877 Schliemann begins excavation of Mycenae.

1885 Schliemann unearths the foundations of a Mycenaean palace.

Schrödinger, Erwin

1887–1961 ● PHYSICS

> *"Thus the task is not so much to see what no one has yet seen; but to think what nobody has yet thought, about that which everybody sees."*
>
> — Erwin Schrödinger, quoted in *Problems of Life*, by L. Bertlanffy

The Austrian physicist Erwin Schrödinger was born in Vienna on August 12, 1887, the only child of Georgine and Rudolf Schrödinger. As was common practice for upper-middle-class children, Erwin was tutored at home as a child in preparation for the entrance examination to a gymnasium. He passed the examination easily and entered the Akademisches Gymnasium in 1898 at age eleven.

In the fall of 1906 Schrödinger entered the University of Vienna, where he quickly gained a reputation as an outstanding student and performed brilliantly in physics and mathematics. He was greatly influenced by Professor Fritz Hasenohrl's courses on theoretical physics and became focused mainly on theory while at the university. Schrödinger stated that no one except his father had a more profound influence on his life than Hasenohrl. In 1910 he received a doctor of philosophy degree, roughly equivalent to a master's degree in American universities.

After a one-year stint as a volunteer in the Austria Hungary Army reserves, he returned to the University of Vienna, where he was appointed to an assistantship in experimental physics under Franz Exner and Fritz Kohlrausch. He missed an opportunity to take an assistantship with Fritz Hasenohrl in theoretical physics because of his military service, but he was happy to have had the practical laboratory experience, which influenced what he would eventually accept as possible in the realm of theoretical physics.

Schrödinger presented his first theoretical paper in 1912 at the Vienna Academy as part of his *habilitation*, a process similar to obtaining a Ph.D. in American universities. In 1914 he completed his *habilitation* at the University of Vienna and was paid to teach courses there. Schrödinger then spent 1914 to 1918 in military service during World War I. He was able to continue some scientific work while in uniform. After the war, he resumed his research at the Institute of Physics at the University of Vienna. He continued there until 1920, when he married Annemarie Bertel and took a position teaching physics at the University of Jena in Germany. He went from the University of Jena to other teaching and research positions at the universities of Stuttgart (Germany), Breslau (Poland), Zurich (Switzerland), and Berlin (Germany). At Berlin he was Max Planck's successor. Out of disgust for the Nazis, he left Berlin in 1933 and took a fellowship at Oxford University in England. He then taught at the University of Graz in Austria before becoming director of theoretical physics at the Institute for Advanced Studies in Dublin from 1940 until his retirement in 1955. He returned to the University of Vienna as a professor emeritus in 1958.

Schrödinger's important research included work on atomic **spectra** and statistical **thermodynamics**. However, he is best known for the development of wave mechanics, a mathematical description of the wave behavior of electrons as they orbit atomic nuclei. His theory of wave mechanics published in 1926 was considered the mathematical equivalent of the theory of matrix mechanics proposed by Werner Heisenberg in 1925. These contributions of Schrödinger and Heisenberg are considered to be the foundation of quantum mechanics. Schrödinger received a Nobel Prize in 1933 for his contribution to the development of quantum mechanics.

Schrödinger died in Vienna on January 4, 1961, and is buried in Alpbach, Tirol. ◆

1910 Schrödinger receives his Ph.D. in physics.

1926 Schrödinger publishes his theory of wave mechanics.

1933 Schrödinger wins the Nobel Prize in physics; leaves Berlin out of disgust for the Nazis.

1944 Schrödinger publishes *What is Life?*

1940 Schrödinger becomes director of physics at the Institute for Advanced Studies in Dublin, Ireland.

spectra: the distribution of wavelengths of increasing magnitude.

thermodynamics: the branch of physics that deals with the mechanical action of heat.

Thomson, Joseph John

1856–1940 ● PHYSICS

Joseph John Thomson was born at Cheetham Hill near Manchester, England, December 18, 1856. He is best remembered for his experimental discovery of the electron in 1897, for which he won the Nobel Prize in physics in 1906, but his influence was much wider. His lifelong interest was the relationship between the **ether** and matter, and his theoretical virtuosity was much admired by contemporaries. He was the first to suggest electromagnetic mass; his work on the structure of light, from 1907 onwards, paved the way for the acceptance of the quantum theory of radiation in Britain; and he laid the foundations for theories of ionic chemical bonding. Thomson was a leading spokesman for science to the government and guided the increasing professionalism of science in Britain. Finally, Thomson was a renowned research supervisor, and eight of his students won Nobel Prizes.

Thomson's father, Joseph James Thomson, was a Manchester bookseller. His mother was Emma Swindells. Thomson's younger brother, Frederick Vernon Thomson,

ether: a medium that in the wave theory of light permeates all space and transmits waves.

303

went into business with a firm of calico merchants. Thomson's parents sympathized with his scientific interests, encouraged his lifelong interest in botany, and intended for him to become an engineer. At fourteen, Thomson entered Owens College, Manchester, to begin his training. His father died two years later, leaving the family poorly off and compelling Thomson to rely on scholarships, concentrating on subjects he excelled in—mathematics and physics, taught by Thomas Barker and Balfour Stewart, respectively.

In 1876 Thomson went to Cambridge to study mathematics. He received a thorough grounding in analytical dynamics (the use of Lagrange's equations and Hamilton's principle of least action) from his coach, Edward Routh. The emphasis on physical analogies and a mechanical world view is evident throughout the rest of his work. In 1880 he graduated as Second Wrangler (second place).

electrodynamics: a branch of physics that deals with the interactions of electric currents with magnets, with other currents, or with themselves.

Thomson's early work was dominated by his commitment to analytical dynamics and Maxwell's **electrodynamics**, which he first encountered at Owens College and later learned from William Niven at Cambridge. In 1881 he showed, for the first time, that the mass of a charged particle increases as it moves. He thought the increase was due to the particle dragging some of the ether with it. In 1882 he won the Adams Prize with "A Treatise on Vortex Motion," investigating the stability of interlocked vortex rings and developing the then popular ether-vortex model of the atom to account for the periodic table.

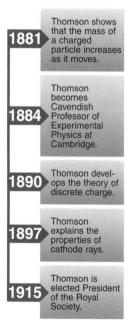

1881 Thomson shows that the mass of a charged particle increases as it moves.

1884 Thomson becomes Cavendish Professor of Experimental Physics at Cambridge.

1890 Thomson develops the theory of discrete charge.

1897 Thomson explains the properties of cathode rays.

1915 Thomson is elected President of the Royal Society.

Through this work, Thomson allied himself with the goals of the elite of Cambridge mathematical physicists, and he also identified himself with Cambridge values and social mores. In 1890 he married Rose Paget, daughter of a professor of medicine. He sent his son, George, and daughter, Joan, to private schools. He appeared religiously devout. He also joined the Athenaeum and Saville clubs. His conventionality and scientific accomplishments paid off, and in 1884 Thomson was elected Cavendish Professor of Experimental Physics at Cambridge, one of the top university positions in Britain, at the early age of twenty-eight.

Overnight, Thomson became a leader of science. He wrote review articles and held an increasing number of positions in scientific administration, as editor of journals, on education committees, and on the Board for Invention and

Research during World War I. He was elected president of the Royal Society in 1915 and after the war became science's leading spokesman in Britain to the new Department for Scientific and Industrial Research. The esteem he gained was confirmed by a knighthood in 1908, the Order of Merit in 1912, and his election in 1918 as Master of Trinity College, a Crown appointment.

Under Thomson's leadership, the Cavendish Laboratory became a place of lively debate, at the forefront of modern experimental physics, but also one of great financial stringency. He instituted a **colloquium**, and the laboratory developed a social life of teas and an annual dinner.

colloquium: an academic meeting where specialists deliver addresses then answer questions.

As Cavendish Professor, Thomson had free choice of scientific direction, coinciding with a change in attitude away from analytical dynamics and toward a more experimental approach. He chose the academically unpopular subject of discharge of electricity through gases, and continued to experiment with it for the rest of his life. Around 1890 Thomson developed a concept of a discrete charge, modeled by the terminus of a **vortex** tube in the ether, which guided his subsequent experimental work. The discovery of X-rays in 1895 was the turning point of Thomson's work on discharge. X-rays ionized the gas in a controllable manner and clearly distinguished the effects of ionization and secondary radiation. By the end of 1896 Thomson and Ernest Rutherford had convincing evidence for Thomson's theory of discharge by ionization of gas molecules.

vortex: something that resembles a whirlpool.

The discovery of X-rays revived interest in the nature of cathode rays. With new confidence in his apparatus and theories, derived from his success with X-ray ionization, Thomson in 1897 showed that all of the properties of **cathode rays** could be explained by assuming that they were subatomic charged particles, which were a universal constituent of matter. He called these "corpuscles" but they soon became known as electrons.

cathode rays: the stream of high-speed electrons emitted from the electrode of a vacuum tube.

Over the next few years Thomson unified his ionization and corpuscle theories into a general theory of gaseous discharge that is still largely accepted today.

Thomson next investigated the role of corpuscles in matter. His "plum pudding" model of the atom, in which thousands of corpuscles orbited in a sphere of positive electrification, worked until 1906 when he calculated that the number of corpuscles in the atom was comparable with the atomic weight, raising problems with the origin of the atom's mass and of its stability. He began experimenting with the positive ions in a discharge tube to account for the mass of the atom. This work eventually led to the discovery of the first nonradioactive isotopes, those of neon, in 1913, and the invention by Thomson's collaborator Francis Aston of the mass **spectrograph** in 1919.

spectrograph: an instrument for dispersing radiation and mapping its pattern.

In 1919 Thomson resigned the Cavendish Professorship, a year after his appointment as Master of Trinity College, Cambridge. He now had a major social and administrative role. When he died twenty-one years later, on August 30, 1940, his ashes were buried in Westminster Abbey. ◆

Vesalius, Andreas

1514–1564 ● MEDICINE & ANATOMY

This Belgian physician who revolutionized the study of modern medicine and anatomy was born in Brussels to a family of physicians. Vesalius entered the University of Louvain at the age of fourteen, studying Latin, some Greek, and medieval writings on science; he also performed dissections on small animals.

His study of medicine began in earnest in 1533 at the University of Paris. One of his teachers, Johann Guinther, had translated Galen's work on anatomy. Galenic anatomy derived from the dissection of animals, since Roman law had forbidden human autopsies, and extrapolated to what was presumed to be the human condition. Galen's theories were a marked advance on Hippocratic medicine, which had been more philosophical and less grounded in practical demonstration, but it still lacked real examples of human anatomy. Galen's work, imperfect as it was, had been forgotten during the Middle Ages, while lesser scientific attitudes prevailed; only with the beginning of the Renaissance was it brought to light. During the rare dissections that were performed, the professor would read out from a text while a demonstrator, usually a barber or executioner, dissected the corpse, exhibiting its various parts. Even this limited exposure to real human anatomy was infrequent; Vesalius attended less than a handful of such demonstrations during his three years at the university.

Curious and frustrated, Vesalius stole from the **charnel houses** of Paris the bodies of those who had been executed or had been victims of the plague and buried in the Cemetery of Innocents. Using these dismembered parts, he performed his own dissections in order to see for himself the structures of the

> *"I myself cannot wonder enough at my own stupidity and too great trust in the writings of Galen and other anatomists."*
>
> — Andreas Vesalius

charnel house: a building in which dead bodies or bones are deposited.

human body. In 1536, due to war conditions, he had to return to Louvain for a year. On the road into town he found a hung cadaver, which he stole; it was his first articulated skeleton. During that year he obtained permission from the **burgomeister** to obtain whatever body he sought. In 1537 he received his medical doctorate "with highest distinction." The next day he was appointed Professor of Surgery; the day after that he began teaching anatomy.

burgomeister: mayor.

Vesalius, who performed his own dissections in front of his well-attended classes, also used sketches to illustrate the workings of the body. In 1538 he published *Tabulae Sex*, a series of six charts, of which three (drawn by him) mapped out the **vascular** system and three (drawn by Jan Stefan van Kalkar, a student of Titian) illustrated the skeletal form. A year later he published his *Venesection Letter*, which presented actual observations of the body and greatly influenced William Harvey in his studies of the circulatory system.

vascular: relating to the blood vessels.

Meanwhile, Vesalius had already begun the great multi-volume work that was to take him several years to complete: *De humani corporis fabrica libri septem* (*The Seven Books on the Structure of the Human Body*). This was significantly more accurate than any other medical work of its time, and more extensive than most published since. It is particularly famed for its cross referencing and its anatomical illustrations. *Fabrica* faced severe criticism for its modern approach, which exposed the weaknesses in Galen's works.

In 1543, the same year that *Fabrica* was published, Vesalius—still only twenty-eight—also produced *Epitome*, which was largely pictorial with little text, cheaper, and therefore more accessible to students. This popular work was dedicated to Philip (later Philip II of Spain), son of the Holy Roman emperor Charles V. Vesalius presented his works to the emperor personally, received a court appointment, and gave up his academic career. During that winter his father died and he came into his inheritance, which included the family home in Brussels. As court physician during the war of 1544 he had the opportunity to perform autopsies on some of the victims of gunpowder. With the war's end, he returned home to settle on his estate.

During his years with the emperor, Vesalius gained experience in surgery and a reputation for giving accurate prognoses. In 1555 he published his augmented second edition of

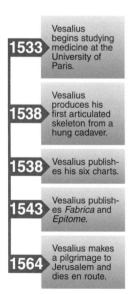

1533 Vesalius begins studying medicine at the University of Paris.

1538 Vesalius produces his first articulated skeleton from a hung cadaver.

1538 Vesalius publishes his six charts.

1543 Vesalius publishes *Fabrica* and *Epitome*.

1564 Vesalius makes a pilgrimage to Jerusalem and dies en route.

the *Fabrica*, with a corrected text based on his more recent findings. The following year Charles gave up his throne to Philip, granted Vesalius a lifetime pension, made him a count, and had him appointed to Philip's court. In 1559 Vesalius and his family moved to Madrid.

In Spain, Vesalius was not chief court physician but merely physician in ordinary. He found the atmosphere there contrary to his more rational and modern tendencies, and he was often involved in controversies with the other attending physicians, whom he considered little more than faith healers. In 1564 he was given permission to leave Spain and make a pilgrimage to Jerusalem. While traveling, he died; on the Greek island of Zante stands a grave with the inscription "The tomb of Andreas Vesalius of Brussels, who died October 15 of the year 1564 at the age of fifty years, on his return from Jerusalem." ◆

Vesalius stole bodies of people who had been executed or had been victims of the plague, and dissected them.

Wassermann, August von

1866–1925 ● MEDICINE & BACTERIOLOGY

German bacteriologist August von Wassermann discovered a blood serum test for **syphilis**. Born in Bamberg, Germany, he took his medical degree at the University of Strasbourg in 1888 and was then appointed assistant to Robert Koch at the Koch Institute of Infectious Diseases in Berlin (1890–1906). In 1891, in collaboration with another scientist, Wassermann reported on the toxins of diptheria and became famous after publishing a paper on immunity and toxin fixation in 1892. His reputation was enhanced in 1898 by a further paper on tetanus toxin in which he showed its affinity to nervous tissue. This work led to the development of biological methods of differentiating animal **albumins**. The precipitin reaction he produced became important medicolegally. He also developed innoculations against cholera and typhoid.

He received the titular rank of professor in 1898 and was appointed professor at the University of Berlin in 1903. In 1906 Wassermann announced his development of a **serodiagnostic** test for syphilis (the Wassermann test) following Jules Bordet and Octave Gengou's discovery of complement fixation. Blood or spinal fluid producing a positive reaction indicates the existence of antibodies formed as a result of infection with syphilis. Wassermann also proved that **tabes dorsalis** and progressive paralysis were late results of syphilis. This achievement revolutionized the diagnosis, control, and treatment of syphilis.

In 1907 he became director of therapeutic and serum research at the University of Berlin. From 1913 he directed

syphilis: a sexually transmitted disease.

albumins: any of numerous water-soluble plant and animal proteins.

serodiagnostic: diagnosis of a disease with the use of serum (animal or plant fluid).

tabes dorsalis: a disorder of the nervous system.

1892 Wassermann publishes a paper on immunity and toxin fixation.

1898 Wassermann publishes a paper on tetanus toxin.

1906 Wassermann announces his development of a test for syphilis.

1904 Wassermann publishes *Immune Sera, Haemolysins, Cytotoxins and Precipitins.*

the department of experimental therapy at the Kaiser Wilhelm Institute of Experimental Therapy, at Dahlem, Germany. He was responsible for discovering diagnostic tests for tuberculosis.

Wassermann's main genius as a brilliant scientific worker was to adapt and develop the research of others into practical use. He wrote over sixty scientific papers on serology and immunology and published a book, *Immune Sera, Haemolysins, Cytotoxins and Precipitins*, in 1904 (translated into English). Together with the German bacteriologist Wilhelm Kolle, he published the six-volume *Handbook of Pathological Micro-organisms* (1903–1909). ◆

Watt, James

1736–1819 ● INVENTOR

Watt was born at Greenock and at the age of nineteen traveled to London to be apprenticed as an instrument maker but was forced to return home, unable to stand up to the hard work and poverty. In 1756, using knowledge he had acquired in London, he tried to set up as an instrument maker in Glasgow, but the city guilds refused to recognize him as a craftsman as he had not completed his apprenticeship. The University of Glasgow helped him, however, and in 1757 he was given the title of mathematical instrument maker to the university.

Watt became a close friend of Joseph Black, who had discovered latent heat, and his student John Robinson, who later became professor of natural philosophy at Edinburgh. By then Watt was already considering how to improve the best available steam engine, the Newcomen engine, which was mainly used for pumping water, notably in draining mines. In 1764 he was able to make some progress in his experiments when he was given a Newcomen engine to repair. Observing its huge consumption of steam, Watt began studying the properties of the latter, particularly the relationship between density and pressure in determining the temperature of steam. From his experiments he concluded that two factors were important for the economical use of steam in a condensing machine: the temperature of the condensed steam had to be as low as possible (1,000°F. or less) to insure a good vacuum and the cylinder had to be as hot as the steam that entered it.

In 1765 Watt successfully solved the problem by condensing the steam in a separate vessel, thereby keeping the temperature of the condensation low and that of the cylinder high. A vacuum was maintained by adding an air pump for the removal of condensed steam. In 1769 Watt took out a patent for his invention. As a repayment to John Roebuck, the founder of Carron ironworks, for his financial backing, Watt gave him two-thirds of the profits. An engine was built near Linlithgow, allowing Watt to make further improvements.

In 1768 Matthew Boulton of Soho engineering works in Birmingham took over Roebuck's share of the invention's proceeds, and in 1775 successfully applied to parliament to continue the patent for another twenty-five years. Watt moved to Birmingham, where steam engines were manufactured by the firm Boulton and Watt. He took out a second steam engine patent in 1781 that showed five methods of converting the reciprocating motion to the piston into a rotating motion, enabling the engine to be adapted for driving ordinary machinery. In 1782 Watt took out a third patent for his invention of the double-action engine, in which both ends of the cylinder came into contact with the boiler and condenser instead of just one. A fourth patent in

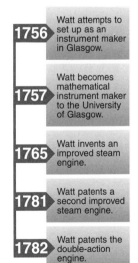

1756 Watt attempts to set up as an instrument maker in Glasgow.

1757 Watt becomes mathematical instrument maker to the University of Glasgow.

1765 Watt invents an improved steam engine.

1781 Watt patents a second improved steam engine.

1782 Watt patents the double-action engine.

1784 covered the way he arranged the links so that the top of the piston rod was connected to the beam, giving it the ability to pull or push.

A later invention was the centrifugal governor, which ensured the control of the speed of the rotary engines and was an early application of feedback, an important aspect of automation. Watt also invented the indicator diagram which showed the relation between the steam's pressure to its volume as the strokes proceeded.

Watt's invention helped revive the mining industry, which had suffered greatly due to the difficulties of draining mines. By 1873 his engine had replaced all but one of the Newcomen pumping engines. Watt's first invention speeded up the work and increased the power of the steam engine, but it was essentially a steam pump; his later invention adapted the steam engine to drive all kinds of machinery.

In 1800, when the act extending the patent of 1769 expired, Watt handed over his share in the business to his sons, and spent the rest of his years at Heathfield Hall near Birmingham, where he continued his research in mechanics and inventing. ◆

> Watt's inventions not only increased the speed and power of steam engines, but adapted steam engines to drive many kinds of machinery.

Westinghouse, George

1846–1914 ● INVENTOR

George Westinghouse was one of the most productive and prolific inventors during the time when America was emerging from its rural roots and entering the Industrial Revolution. Westinghouse's work with railroad air brakes and alternating current helped the United States become powerful in the latter half of the nineteenth century.

Westinghouse was born on October 6, 1846, in Central Bridge, New York, the son of a manufacturer of farm equipment. He was one of 10 children, the eighth born to George and Emeline Westinghouse. He married Marguerite Erskine

Walker in 1867 and she gave him one son, the third generation to carry the name George Westinghouse.

Showing determination even in his youth, Westinghouse attempted to join the Union Army during the American Civil War, but was sent home with his parents after it was discovered he was underage. When he reached an age acceptable to the recruiter, Westinghouse was allowed to enlist as a Union soldier. Receiving an honorable discharge, Westinghouse then joined the Navy, where he was also discharged honorably after serving as an engineer.

After his military service, Westinghouse enrolled at Union College in Schenectady, New York, but a few months later he decided to enter his father's business. By the time Westinghouse began to dabble in railroad engineering, the rail system had already proven itself to be the most important technological advance in the mid-eighteenth century. As the United States sought to expand the railroads westward and open up the vast riches and natural resources the area held, Westinghouse realized that the braking system used by the railroads was dangerous and in great need of improvement.

The brake for each car had to be worked separately, and the conductor had no means of stopping the entire train if needed. Westinghouse observed this problem first hand when he was riding on a passenger train that had to stop abruptly to avoid an accident further down the track.

On April 13, 1869, almost one month before the historic May 10, meeting of the Union Pacific and Central Pacific railroads at Promontory Point, Utah, Westinghouse was granted the first air-brake patent. Six months later, he formed the Westinghouse Air Brake Company in Pennsylvania.

While the air-brake made travel by rails safe, Westinghouse continued to improve and revise his invention. His intuitiveness paid off when he standardized the air-brake, which allowed even older models of locomotives to be retrofitted and therefore made safe.

Along with other inventions such as the refrigerated car and Pullman sleeping car, the air-brake brought railroad travel and commerce into the twentieth century.

While it was the air-brake that brought the Westinghouse name to prominence, it was his work with alternating currents and electricity that has kept it there to this day.

> *"George Westinghouse was, in my opinion, the only man on this globe who could take my alternating current system under the circumstances then existing, and win the battle against prejudice and money power."*
>
> Nikola Tesla

Some researchers believe it was Westinghouse's work on railroad signal devices, which needed electricity to work, that prompted his foray into the world of electrical currents. Working with three electrical engineers, William Stanley, O. B. Shallenberger and Albert Schmid, Westinghouse set out to improve a French-designed single-phase alternating current system that traveled at a high voltage, but was modified to a lower voltage by the use of a "core-type" transformer.

Westinghouse founded the Westinghouse Electric Company on January 8, 1886. However, Westinghouse was forced to compete with Thomas Edison, whose system of direct current was believed at the time to be safer. A dozen or so state legislatures prohibited the installation of alternating current systems. The low point for the alternating current system came when it was approved for use in executing criminals convicted in capital cases in New York state.

Westinghouse's system eventually gained acceptance from communities throughout the east, and eventually the rest of the world. Buffalo, New York, became the first community in America to be powered entirely by alternating current. Westinghouse even provided power for the Chicago World's Fair.

While the alternating current system proved safe and effective for lighting, Westinghouse wasn't satisfied because motors could not be operated on alternating current. Westinghouse turned to Nikola Tesla, an immigrant from Budapest who had already patented a motor that used alternating current. Purchasing Tesla's patent, Westinghouse then put the young man to work on improving his system.

Westinghouse had developed a reputation as a fair and benevolent employer who sought to improve worker's conditions while other factory owners and industrialists were labeled "robber barons." Tesla was so impressed with Westinghouse that he once said "George Westinghouse was, in my opinion, the only man on this globe who could take my alternating current system under the circumstances then existing, and win the battle against prejudice and money power." While Westinghouse's paternalism toward his workers was based in part on pragmatism—he hoped to keep the unions from his factories—his companies also developed sanitary washrooms and other amenities that most factory workers only dreamed of.

At its peak, Westinghouse's fifteen factories around the world employed 50,000 workers; it was the largest business of

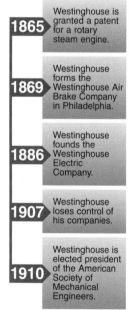

1865 Westinghouse is granted a patent for a rotary steam engine.

1869 Westinghouse forms the Westinghouse Air Brake Company in Philadelphia.

1886 Westinghouse founds the Westinghouse Electric Company.

1907 Westinghouse loses control of his companies.

1910 Westinghouse is elected president of the American Society of Mechanical Engineers.

its time. The net worth of his many different business concerns was estimated at $120 million.

In 1907 a financial panic swept the nation. Westinghouse was forced to give up control of his companies. By 1911 he broke all ties to the companies he had built. Westinghouse continued to enjoy great popularity with the public and the engineering profession, which elected him president of the American Society of Mechanical Engineers in 1910. By 1913 a heart ailment forced Westinghouse into a wheelchair, and on March 12, 1914, he died. His memory has been enshrined in a George Westinghouse Museum in Wilmerding, Pennsylvania, and with a memorial in Pittsburgh. ◆

Whitney, Eli

1765–1825 ● INVENTOR

"One of my primary objects is to form the tools so the tools themselves shall fashion the work and give to each part its proportion—which, when once accomplished, will give expedition, uniformity and exactness to the whole."

— Eli Whitney

Eli Whitney is credited with two inventions that helped change the face of American agriculture and industry. The cotton gin, which he developed in 1793, made it economically possible to raise short-fiber cotton for sale to textile mills. Before Whitney's invention it had taken so much labor to clean seeds out of short-fiber cotton that the

Eli Whitney's Cotton Gin

A cotton gin is a machine used to gin (pull the seeds) from cotton. For centuries, workers ginned cotton slowly by hand. Then, inventors in India developed a simple ginning machine. Such machines were known in America by the mid-1700s, but they did not work well on the type of cotton that grew best in the colonies. American farmers felt that cotton could never be grown profitably because it took too much time to clean. In 1793, Eli Whitney designed a machine that contained a revolving cylinder covered with rows of spiked teeth. As a worker turned a crank, the teeth drew the cotton through narrow slots that trapped the seeds. A second roller with brushes freed the fibers from the teeth. Whitney's new gin could clean cotton faster than 50 people working by hand. Whitney's gin worked so well that American farmers greatly expanded cotton production. Today, the United States is one of the world's leading producers of cotton. The word "cotton gin" now refers to sophisticated mechanical systems that dry, clean, de-seed, and bale huge amounts of cotton each day.

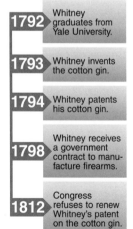

1792 — Whitney graduates from Yale University.

1793 — Whitney invents the cotton gin.

1794 — Whitney patents his cotton gin.

1798 — Whitney receives a government contract to manufacture firearms.

1812 — Congress refuses to renew Whitney's patent on the cotton gin.

crop was hardly worth the trouble of raising and cleaning it. After the cotton gin was developed, southern farmers and plantation owners turned to cotton growing on lands that could only support the short-fiber types of cotton.

Whitney had another major industrial development to his credit. After he received a contract to manufacture muskets for the U.S. government, he developed a system of making the weapons with interchangeable parts. The use of parts made so much alike that any one could be used as a replacement or assembly item in a whole line of muskets paved the way for mass production in other American industries.

Whitney was born at Westboro, Massachusetts, on December 8, 1765. He was a lifelong tinkerer and mechanical genius. He had a very good education, even though he turned into a serious student much later than most other people did. He was eighteen years old, and already an experienced mechanic, before he decided to pursue a formal education. He graduated from Yale in 1792 and spent several months after his graduation working in Georgia. There, he lived with the family of the Revolutionary War hero, General Nathanael Greene, while studying law. Whitney developed his cotton gin at the Greene plantation. The invention, so important and valuable in American agriculture, did not bring him much in the way of monetary rewards. Many planters built gins without paying him a royalty, and he was involved in a long series of law cases, trying to protect his patents. However, Whitney did make a great deal of money from his military contracts, which enabled him to return to Connecticut, establish a factory, and organize a system of assembling muskets that used precision tools and relatively less skilled labor.

He died January 8, 1825, at New Haven, Connecticut. ◆

Woods, Granville T.

1856–1910 ● INVENTOR

Born in Columbus, Ohio, on April 23, 1856, Granville Woods began work at age ten as an apprentice in a machine shop that repaired railroad equipment. From 1882 to 1884, he worked as an engineer for the Danniville Southern railroad. He then decided to become an inventor and opened a shop with his brother in Cincinnati. From 1884 to 1907, Woods received thirty-five U.S. patents for inventions that contributed to the development of the transportation and communication industries. He received his first patent in early 1884 for a steam-boiler furnace that required less fuel than the existing models. That same year, he was awarded a second patent for a telephone transmitter. This invention, which he sold to American Bell Telephone Company in Boston, produced voice signals clearer than those of other telephonic devices at the time. His third patent, granted in April 1885, made it possible for telephone messages to be transmitted over the same wires used for carrying telegraphic messages. In November 1887, Woods patented an Induction Telegraph System, which improved communication between moving trains. It also allowed station houses to ascertain the exact location of trains on the rails, thereby greatly reducing accidental train collisions, which were

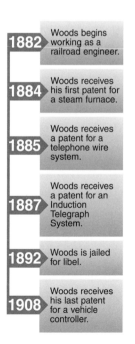

1882 Woods begins working as a railroad engineer.

1884 Woods receives his first patent for a steam furnace.

1885 Woods receives a patent for a telephone wire system.

1887 Woods receives a patent for an Induction Telegraph System.

1892 Woods is jailed for libel.

1908 Woods receives his last patent for a vehicle controller.

frequent in the early days of the railroads. Other inventions in the late 1880s also improved the safety of railway travel. They included an electromagnetic brake, an automatic cutoff for electric circuits, and a regulator for electric motors.

In 1890, Woods moved to New York City. There he patented more electrical devices. Despite his prolific work, Woods was never able to market his inventions successfully. Instead, Woods had to sell his inventions at little profit to the well-financed white owned corporations, such as General Electric and American Bell Telephone. The last years of Woods's life were difficult. He lived in virtual poverty and turmoil in New York City as he faced costly legal and court fees battling businessmen for control of his inventions. In 1892, he was briefly jailed for libel after accusing the American Engineering Company of infringing on his patents. Three years before his death, Woods was still receiving patents. His last recorded invention was a vehicle controlling device in 1907. Woods died in New York City on January 18, 1910. ◆

Wren, Sir Christopher

1632–1723 ● ASTRONOMY & MATHEMATICS

Although renowned as the architect who rebuilt Saint Paul's Cathedral after the Great Fire of London (1666), Wren began his career as a scientist. Turning to architecture late in life, he nontheless achieved a prodigious output and popularized the Renaissance Palladian style.

Wren's family was prosperous and powerful; his father, the Dean of Windsor, was a devoted Tory and a staunch supporter of the Church of England. In 1641 Wren entered the Westminster School, which had a reputation for science, mathematics, and Latin, and performed brilliantly. In about 1646 he went to Oxford, graduating in 1653 with an M.A. He became an admired colleague among a brilliant circle who would be the leading scientists and scholars in England after the Restoration. He was a scientist, mathematician, and inventor and made significant scientific discoveries, especially in astronomy.

In 1657, upon his appointment as Gresham Professor of Astronomy in London, he pronounced in his inauguration speech that "Mathematical demonstrations being built upon the impregnable foundations of Geometry and Arithmetik are the only Truths that can sink into the mind of Man, void of all uncertainty." He was one of the founders of the Royal Society, and became Savillian Professor of Astronomy at Oxford in 1661, holding this position until 1673.

Wren ventured into architecture at a time when building was in a state of stagnation. The Italian Renaissance style had been introduced by Inigo Jones but was not widely accepted and the Civil War had discouraged building. Wren received his first architectural commission in 1662 to design the Sheldonian Theater at Oxford, which he modeled on the open air theaters of Roman antiquity. In 1665 he traveled to France to study art and architecture.

Wren returned from France inspired, loaded with books, engravings, and other materials on European architecture. These sources influenced his future work and his theories on beauty and taste, which he formulated in his essays on the development of architecture: "Architecture aims at eternity; and therefore the only Thing uncapable of Modes and Fashions in its Principals. . . Beauty, Firmness and Convenience are the Principles; the two first depend upon geometrical Reasons of opticks and staticks; the third only makes the Variety. There are natural Causes of Beauty. Beauty is a Harmony of Objects, begetting Pleasure by the Eye."

In London Wren became involved in planning the repair of Saint Paul's Cathedral but in 1666, days after his suggestions for an ambitious reconstruction were accepted, the Great Fire of London broke out. After most of London was destroyed in the fire Wren was appointed "Principal Architect" for the reconstruction of the city. His main project was the rebuilding of Saint Paul's and some fifty other city churches.

He was able to experiment with the designs for these churches, creating loose classical forms and devising ingenious solutions to the problems of cramped space and limited time. Most of the churches were based on plans of Roman basilicas. Saint Paul's Cathedral was conceived as a bold land-

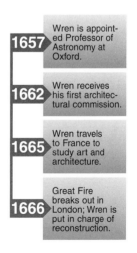

1657 Wren is appointed Professor of Astronomy at Oxford.

1662 Wren receives his first architectural commission.

1665 Wren travels to France to study art and architecture.

1666 Great Fire breaks out in London; Wren is put in charge of reconstruction.

> ***"If you would see this man's monument, look around."***
> — Inscription in St. Paul's Cathedral

mark for the newly built London. The dome, influenced by the work of Donato Bramante and Michelangelo, dominates the skyline. A work group of master craftsmen was chosen and their exceptional workmanship established a precedent for masterly design in England.

Wren was also commissioned to design royal buildings such as the Kensington and Hampton Court palaces, and public buildings including the Royal Marine Hospital at Greeenwich, Chelsea Hospital, and the western towers and northern transept of Westminster Abbey. The royal palaces were built on a grand scale, influenced by glorious French Renaissance palaces such as Versailles. Wren was the first English architect to incorporate Baroque details into his buildings. The Doric order that encompasses the Chelsea Hospital foreshadows the Baroque style of the reign of Queen Anne and a number of his churches designed in the late 1600s embody a true Baroque vocabulary.

During his long and rich career Wren applied his genius so successfully to his work that he became a pivotal influence on the development of English architecture and a symbol of the flourishing of scholarship and the arts in seventeenth-century England. He was buried in Saint Paul's Cathedral. ◆

Wright, Wilbur

1867–1912 ● INVENTOR

Wright, Orville

1871–1948 ● INVENTOR

American aviation pioneers, Wilbur and Orville Wright are credited with the invention of the airplane. Their father was Milton Wright, bishop of the Church of the United Brethren in Christ. After finishing high school, the brothers set up the newspaper *West Side*

Orville (left) and
Wilbur Wright.

News, which was printed on a homemade press. In 1893 they opened a bicycle repairing and manufacturing business.

Wilbur and Orville had already shown an interest in aerodynamics as boys, when they had access to a toy helicopter powered by rubber bands, and later closely followed the exploits of the German pioneer aviation engineer Otto Lilienthal. His death in 1896 prompted them to undertake experiments in gliding based on his findings. They now read Lilienthal's *The Problems of Flying and Practical Experiments in Soaring* and Octave Chanute's *Progress in Flying Machines*. Wilbur corresponded with Chanute and over the years the brothers kept him updated on their experiments.

Orville sought to improve flying machines through increased control. He also believed that sidewise balance could be attained by presenting the left and right wings at different angles to the wind; this was achieved by Wilbur twisting or warping the wings. When their initial experiments in increased control succeeded, they decided to build a man-carrying glider.

In 1900, after discovering from the U.S. Weather Bureau that Kitty Hawk, North Carolina, was the breeziest place in the country and that its sand hills made it suitable for gliding, they took their first man-carrying glider there. It spanned eighteen feet from tip to tip and was unique in having a horizontal front rudder or elevator which was approximately four

1893 The Wright brothers open a bicycle repair shop.

1900 The Wright brothers take their first man-carrying glider to Kitty Hawk.

1902 The Wright brothers fly an improved glider at Kitty Hawk.

1903 The Wright brothers accomplish the first successful flight in a motorized, manned airplane.

1908 The Wright brothers receive a contract from the U.S. government to build military aircraft.

feet in front of the lower main plane; the rear edge could be raised or lowered for fore-and-aft balance.

The brothers planned to fly the glider as a pilot-guided kite as a means of practicing, but they found that they could only do this when wind speed was over twenty-five miles an hour. Although the glider did not lift as it should have done according to Lilienthal's air pressure tables, Wilbur and Orville were encouraged by the success of their method of control. They then took their machine to Kill Devil Hill near Kitty Hawk and made a number of dives down the hillside. They were, however, dissatisfied with the glider's lifting ability and decided to return the following year with a larger machine with wings of deeper curvature.

Because of their problems with Lilienthal's tables and other air pressure figures that were used as standard references, the brothers began questioning the validity of the existing data and started to conduct their own experiments. The design of their glider of 1902 reflected their own calculations; it had a wingspan of thirty-two feet and sported a tail with fixed twin vertical vanes: this was used for balancing, essential to add to the presentation of the wings at different angles to the wind. Using their new machine, the brothers made glides of over 600 feet and were able to glide at narrower angles of descent.

The following year the Wright brothers built a flying machine with a motor and on December 17, 1903, they took

Faster and Faster Airplanes

In 1903, Orville and Wilbur Wright accomplished the first successful flight in a piloted, engine-powered airplane. The Wrights' first plane flew about 31 miles per hour. During the next several decades, rapid advances were made in airplane design and technology. Larger and larger planes could fly ever higher, faster, and farther. By the end of World War I, most planes could fly faster than 130 miles per hour. In 1939, engineers in Germany developed the first jet plane. By 1944, German jets were flying over Europe at close to 500 miles per hour. During World War II, German engineers also developed rocket-powered planes that could fly even faster. In 1947, U.S. Air Force officer Chuck Yeager made the first supersonic flight when he piloted a rocket plane at the speed of sound (about 760 miles per hour at sea level). By the end of the century, supersonic flights were common.

it to Kitty Hawk, where Orville made a flight of 120 feet, with Wilbur later flying 852 feet in 59 seconds. Between 1904 and 1905 they carried out further refinements, which resulted in Wilbur flying as far as twenty-four miles. In 1908 they established their own company and received a contract with the U.S. War Department for the first army plane, development of which was completed the following year. Neither brother married; Wilbur died in 1912 of typhoid fever, while Orville survived him for another thirty-six years during which he made more important contributions to aviation. ◆

Sources

The biographies in *Macmillan Profiles: Scientists and Inventors* were extracted from the following sources:

Dictionary of Scientific Biography, Macmillan Reference USA, 1981.
Encyclopedia of African-American Culture and History, Macmillan Reference USA, 1996.
Encyclopedia of The American West, Macmillan Reference USA, 1996.
Macmillan Encyclopedia of Chemistry, Macmillan Reference USA, 1997.
Macmillan Encyclopedia of Computers, Macmillan Reference USA, 1992.
Macmillan Encyclopedia of Earth Sciences, Macmillan Reference USA, 1996.
Macmillan Encyclopedia of Physics, Macmillan Reference USA, 1996.
Record of America: A Reference History of the United States, Charles Scribner's Sons, 1974.
Scribner Encyclopedia of American Life, Charles Scribner's Sons, 1998.
They Made History: A Biographical Dictionary, Simon & Shuster, 1993.

The following authors contributed articles to the publications listed above:

Arnold, James: Willard Libby
Axelrod, Alan: John Wesley Powell
Barbeau, Art: Dian Fossey
Barlow, Nadine G.: Herschel Family
Bedini, Silvio A.: Benjamin Banneker
Bergstrom, Anna R.: Wolfgang Pauli
Bishop, Muriel B.: Louis Pasteur
Bradford, Marlene: Ernest Orlando Lawrence
Bruno, Mark S.: Max Karl Ernst Ludwig Planck
Cassidy, David C.: Werner Karl Heisenberg
Choppin, Gregory R.: Marie Curie
Daniel, Glyn: Louis Seymour Bazett Leakey
Dasch, Patricia: Rachel Carson
Davenport, Derek: Sir Humphry Davy
Falconer, Isobel: Joseph John Thomson
Fox, Robert: Nicholas-Léonard-Sadi Carnot
Gee, Mary: Erwin Schrödinger
Geringer, Joseph: Francis Harry Compton Crick, Stephen William Hawking, Barbara McClintock, James Dewy Watson
Hayden, Robert C.: Shirley Ann Jackson, Granville T. Woods
Herschbach, Dudley: Benjamin Franklin
Hetherington, Norriss S.: Edwin Powell Hubble
Hofmann, James R.: André-Marie Ampère
Holley, Kathleen: Antoine-Laurent Lavoisier
James, Philip B.: Johannes Kepler
Kanamuri, Hiroo: Charles Richter
Kauffman, George B.: Robert Boyle
Kragh, Helge: Paul Adrien Maurice Dirac

McCullough, Thomas F., CSC: Francis Bacon
McMurry, Linda O.: George Washington Carver
Miller, Allison X.: Lewis Howard Latimer, Elijah McCoy
Norman, Jack C.: Lord Kelvin, Ernest Rutherford
Pais, Abraham: Niels Henrik David Bohr
Parker, Kevin: Lewis Howard Latimer
Rattenberry, Richard C.: John Moses Browning
Reynolds, Clark G.: R(ichard) Buckminster Fuller (Jr.)
Rigden, John S.: J. Robert Oppenheimer
Romer, Alfred: Wilhelm Conrad Röntgen
Russell, Thaddeus: Matthew Alexander Henson
Schoch, Robert M.: Jean Louis Rodolphe Agassiz
Schweber, S.S.: Richard Phillips Feynman
Sessler, Andrew M.: Andrei Dmitrievich Sakharov
Shea, William R.: Galileo Galilei
Sime, Ruth Lewin: Lise Meitner
Spencer, Donald D.: Charles Babbage
Stachel, John: Albert Einstein
Stranges, Anthony N.: Ernest Orlando Lawrence
Talkmitt, Marcia J.: Linus Carl Pauling
Turner, R. Steven: Hermann L. F. von Helmholtz
Wattenberg, Albert: Enrico Fermi
Westfall, Richard S.: Isaac Newton
Wick, Rob: Jacques Yves Cousteau, Rudolf Diesel, Jane Goodall, Charles Goodyear, Jonas Salk, George Westinghouse
Williams, L. Pearce: Michael Faraday
Wilson, Leonard: Charles Lyell
Yochelson, Ellis Y.: Charles Darwin

Photographs and images used in this volume were obtained from the following sources:

Stock Montage, Inc.:

Louis Agassiz (page 1)
Aristotle (page 8)
Charles Babbage (page 13)
Francis Bacon (page 16)
Benjamin Banneker (page 18)
Alexander Graham Bell (page 21)
Niels Bohr (page 24)
Tycho Brahe (page 31)
Rachel Carson (page 38)
George Washington Carver (page 43)
Nicolaus Copernicus (page 47)
Marie Curie (page 56)
Louis-Jacques Daguerre (page 59)
Charles Darwin (page 62)
Leonardo da Vinci (page 66)
Sir Humphry Davy (page 70)
René Descartes (page 72)
Rudolf Diesel (page 76)
Thomas Alva Edison (page 83)
Albert Einstein (page 87)
Michael Faraday (page 97)
Enrico Fermi (page 107)
Sir Alexander Fleming (page 115)
Henry Ford (page 117)
Benjamin Franklin (page 122)
Sigmund Freud (page 126)
Galileo Galilei (page 137)
Carl Friedrich Gauss (page 143)
Charles Goodyear (page 147)

Johannes Gutenberg (page 150)
William Harvey (page 153)
Hermann von Helmholtz (page 162)
Matthew Henson (page 166)
William and Caroline Herschel (page 170)
Heinrich Rudolph Hertz (page 172)
Thomas Henry Huxley (page 181)
Carl Gustav Jung (page 189)
Robert Koch (page 198)
Ernest O. Lawrence (page 205)
Carl von Linné (page 217)
Auguste and Louis Lumière (page 222)
Guglielmo Marconi (page 229)
Gregor Johann Mendel (page 239)
Dmitri Ivanovich Mendeleyev (page 242)
Alfred Nobel (page 252)
Blaise Pascal (page 261)
Louis Pasteur (page 264)
Linus Pauling (page 269)
Ivan Pavlov (page 271)
Wilhelm Conrad Röntgen (page 288)
Ernest Rutherford (page 290)
Jonas Salk (page 295)
Heinrich Schliemann (page 298)
Sir Joseph John Thomson (page 303)
James Watt (page 312)
Eli Whitney (page 317)
Orville Wright (page 323)
Wilbur Wright (page 323)

Yann Arthus-Bertrand/Corbis: Dian Fossey (page 119)

Jonathan Blair/Corbis: Louis Leakey (page 207)

Corbis-Bettmann: Werner Karl Heisenberg (page 158), Charles Lyell (page 225), William T.G. Morton (page 245), J. Robert Oppenheimer (page 255)

Leonard de Selva/Corbis: André-Marie Ampère (page 4)

Shelley Gazin/Corbis: Richard Feynman (page 111)

Library of Congress/Corbis: Lise Meitner (page 237)

The National Archives/Corbis: John Wesley Powell (page 278)

Peter Turnley/© Corbis: Andrei Sakharov (page 293)

UPI/Corbis-Bettmann: Jacques Yves Cousteau (page 49), Crick & Watson (page 53), Paul Dirac (page 79), R. Buckminster Fuller (page 133), Willard F. Libby (page 213), Barbara McClintock (page 232), Wolfgang Pauli (page 267), Max Planck (page 273), Erwin Schrödinger (page 300)

© Kennan Ward Phtotgraphy/Corbis: Jane Goodall (page 144)

Michael S. Yamashita/Corbis: Stephen Hawking (page 155)

Suggested Reading

Agassiz, Louis

Lurie, Edward. *Louis Agassiz: A Life in Science*. Johns Hopkins University Press, 1988.

Ampère, André-Marie

Hofmann, J. *Andre-Marie Ampere, Enlightenment and Electrodynamics*, Cambridge University Press, 1995.

Archimedes

Dijksterhuis, E. J. *Archimedes*. Princeton University Press, 1987.

Aristotle

Byrne, Patrick H. *Analysis and Science in Aristotle* (SUNY series in ancient Greek philosophy). State University of New York, 1997.

Ross, David. *Aristotle*, Routledge, 1995.

Babbage, Charles

Bernstein, J. *The Analytical Engine*. William Morrow, 1981.

Hyman, A. *Charles Babbage: Pioneer of the Computer*. Princeton University Press, 1982.

Bacon, Francis

Peltonen, Markku (editor). *The Cambridge Companion to Bacon* (Cambridge Companion to Philosophy). Cambridge University Press, 1996.

Rossi, Paolo. *Francis Bacon: From Magic to Science*, Routledge and Kegan Paul, 1968.

Banneker, Benjamin

Conley, Kevin; Huggins, Nathan Irvin; Washington B. (editors). *Benjamin Banneker: Scientist and Mathematician* (Black Americans of Achievement). Chelsea House, 1989.

Jackson, Garnet N. *Benjamin Banneker, Scientist*. Modern Curriculum Press, 1992.

Bell, Alexander Graham

Bruce, Robert V.; Grosvenor, Edwin; Wesson, Morgan; *Alexander Graham Bell: The Life and Times of the Man Who Invented the Telephone*. Harry N. Abrams, 1997.

MacKay, James A. *Alexander Graham Bell: A Life*. John Wiley & Sons, 1998.

Bohr, Niels

Franch, A.P.; and P.J. Kennedy, (editors). *Niels Bohr: a Centenary Volume.* Harvard University Press, 1985.

Pais, Abraham. *Niels Bohr's Times: In Physics, Philosophy, and Polity.* Oxford University Press, 1993.

Boyle, Robert

Sargent, Rose-Mary. *The Diffident Naturalist: Robert Boyle and the Philosophy of Experiment (Science and Its Conceptual Foundations).* University of Chicago Press, 1995.

Tiner, John H. *Robert Boyle: Trailblazer of Science.* Fromm Intl., 1989.

Brahe, Tycho

Thoren, Victor E. *The Lord of Uraniborg: A Biography of Tycho Brahe.* Cambridge University Press, 1991.

Browning, John M.

Hogg, Ian V. *The Story of the Gun.* St Martins Press, 1996.

Zwoll, Wayne Van. *America's Great Gunmakers.* Stoeger Publishing Company, 1993.

Carnot, Nicolas-Leonard-Sadi

Cardwell, D.S.L. *From Watt to Clausius: The Rise of Thermodynamics in the Early Industrial Age.* Heinemann, 1971.

Carson, Rachel

Lear, Linda J. *Rachel Carson: Witness for Nature.* Henry Holt & Company, 1997.

Ring, Elizabeth. *Rachel Carson.* Millbrook Press Trade, 1994.

Carver, George Washington

McLoone, Margo. *George Washington Carver.* Capstone, 1997.

Nicholson, Lois P.; Epes, William. *George Washington Carver* (Junior World Biographies). Chelsea House Pub., 1994.

Copernicus, Nicolaus

Rosen, Edward. *Copernicus and his Successors.* Hambledon Press, 1995.

Rosen, Edward. *Copernicus and the Scientific Revolution.* Krieger Publishing Company, 1984.

Cousteau, Jacques

Markham, Lois. *Jacques-Yves Cousteau: Exploring the Wonders of the Deep.* Raintree/Steck Vaughn, 1997.

Reef, Catherine; Raymond, Larry (illustrator). *Jacques Cousteau: Champion of the Sea.* Twenty First Century Books, 1992.

Crick and Watson

Newton, D. *James Watson and Francis Crick: Discovery of the Double Helix and Beyond*. Fact on File, 1992.

Sherrow, Victoria. *James Watson & Francis Crick: Decoding the Secrets of DNA (Partners)*. Blackbirch Marketing, 1995.

Curie, Marie

Fisher, Leonard Everett. *Marie Curie*. Atheneum, 1994.

Giroud, F; David L. (translator). *Marie Curie: A Life*. Homes & Meier, 1986.

Quinn, Susan. *Marie Curie: A Life* (Radcliffe Biographical Series). Addison-Wesley Publishing Co., 1996.

Daguerre, Louis-Jacques

Barger, M. Susan; White, William B. *The Daguerreotype: Nineteenth Century Technology and Modern Science*. Smithsonian Institution Press, 1991.

Bisbee, A. *The History and Practice of Daguerreotyping*. Ayer Co. Publishing, 1973.

Darwin, Charles

Anderson, Margaret J. *Charles Darwin: Naturalist* (Great Minds of Science). Enslow Publishers Inc., 1994.

Bowlby, John. *Charles Darwin: A New Life*. W. W. Norton & Company, 1992.

Twist, Clint. *Charles Darwin: On the Trail of Evolution* (Beyond the Horizons). Raintree/Steck Vaughan, 1994.

da Vinci, Leonardo

O'Malley, Charles; Saunders, L.B. De C.M.; *Leonardo da Vinci on the Human Body: The Anatomical, Physiological and Embryological Drawings of Leonardo da Vinci*. Outlet, 1997.

Frere, Jean Claude; Clarke, Jean-Marie; *Leonardo: Painter, Inventor, Visionary, Mathematician, Philosopher, Engineer*. Terrail, 1995.

Davy, Humphry

Hartley, H. *Humphry Davy*. Oxford University Press, 1972.

Knight, David. *Humphry Davy, Science and Power*. Cambridge University Press. 1996.

Descartes, René

Cottingham, John, ed. *The Cambridge Companion to Descartes* (Cambridge Companions to Philosophy). Cambridge University Press, 1992.

Gaukroger, Stephen. *Descartes: An Intellectual Biography*. Oxford University Press, 1997.

Diesel, Rudolf

Cummins, C. Lyle Jr. *Diesel's Engine: From Conception to 1918*. Carnot Press, 1993.

Dirac, Paul

Kragh, H. *Dirac: A Scientific Biography*. Cambridge University Press, 1990.

Pais, Abraham (editor); Jacob, Maurice; Olive, David. *Paul Dirac: The Man and His Work*. Cambridge University Press, 1998.

Edison, Thomas Alva

Baldwin, Neil. *Edison: Inventing the Century*. Hyperion, 1996.

Josephson, Matthew. *Edison: A Biography*. John Wiley & Sons, 1992.

Einstein, Albert

Folsing, Albrecht. *Albert Einstein: A Biography*. Viking Press, 1997.

Goldberg, Jacob. *Albert Einstein* (Impact Books - Biographical Series). Franklin Watts, 1996.

Pais, A. *"Subtle is the Lord . . .": The Science and Life of Albert Einstein*. Oxford University Press. 1982.

Euclid

Artmann, Benno. *Euclid - The Creation of Mathematics*. Springer-Verlog TELOS, 1998.

Frankland, F.W. *Story of Euclid*. Gordon Press Publications, 1986.

Faraday, Michael

Gooding, David, and Frank James, (editors). *Faraday Rediscovered: Essays on the Life and Work of Michael Faraday 1791-1867*. Stockton Press, 1985.

Ludwig, Charles. *Michael Faraday: Father of Electronics*. Herald Press, 1988.

Williams, L. P. *Michael Faraday, A Biography*. Chapman & Hill, 1965.

Fermi, Enrico

Fermi, L. *Atoms in the Family*. University of Chicago Press, 1954.

Segre, Emilio. *Enrico Fermi Physicist*. University of Chicago Press, 1995.

Feynman, Richard

Gleick, James. *Genius: The Life and Science of Richard Feynman*. Random House, 1992.

Mehra, Jagdish. The *Beat of a Different Drum: The Life and Science of Richard Feynman*. Oxford University Press, 1996.

Fleming, Alexander

Gottfried, Ted. *Alexander Fleming: Discoverer of Penicillin* (Book Report Biographies). Franklin Watts, 1997.

Hughes, W. Howard. *Alexander Fleming and Penicillin*. Crane Russak & Co., 1977.

Macfarlane, Gwyn. *Alexander Fleming: the Man and the Myth*. Oxford University Press, 1985.

Ford, Henry

Bryan, Ford R. *Beyond the Model T: The Other Ventures of Henry Ford*. Wayne State University Press, 1997.

Lewis, David L. *The Public Image of Henry Ford: An American Folk Hero and His Company*. Wayne State University Press, 1987.

Fossey, Dian

Freedman, Suzanne. *Dian Fossey: Befriending the Gorillas*. Raintree/Steck Vaughn, 1997.

Matthews, Tom. *A Light Shining Through the Mist: Dian Fossey and the Mountain Gorillas*. National Geographic Society, 1998.

Roberts, Jack. *The Importance of Dian Fossey*. Lucent Books, 1995.

Franklin, Benjamin

Cohen, I. Bernard. *Science and the Founding Fathers: Science in the Political Thought of Jefferson, Franklin, Adams, and Madison*. W. W. Norton & Company, 1995.

Durham, Jennifer L. *Benjamin Franklin: A Biographical Companion*. ABC-Clio, 1997.

Franklin, Benjamin. *Autobiography of Benjamin Franklin*. Yale University Press, 1964.

Freud, Sigmund

Appignanesi, Richard; Zarats, Oscar; Engelhardt, Tom. *Freud for Beginners*. Pantheon Books, 1990.

Neu, Jerome (editor). *The Cambridge Companion to Freud*. Cambridge University Press, 1992.

Sulloway, Frank J. *Freud: Biologist of the Mind*. Basic Books, 1979.

Fuller, Buckminster

Baldwin, J. *Bucky works: Buckminster Fuller's Ideas for Today*. John Wiley & Sons, 1996.

Pawley, Martin. *Buckminster Fuller*. Parkwest Publications, 1991.

Galen

Brock, Arthur J. (editor). *Greek Medicine, Being Extracts Illustrative of Medical Writing from Hippocrates to Galen* (Library of Greek Thought). AMS Press, 1976.

Singer, Charles J. *Greek Biology and Greek Medicine*. AMS Press, 1985.

Galilei, Galileo

Bagioli, M. *Galileo Courtier*. University of Chicago Press, 1993.

Drake, S. *Galileo: Pioneer Scientist*. University of Toronto Press, 1990.

Fantoli, A. *Galileo: For Copernicanism and for the Church*. Vatican Observatory Publications, 1994.

Gauss, Carl Friedrich

Bohler, Walter Kauffman. *Gauss: A Biographical Study*. Springer-Verlag, 1981.

Goodall, Jane

Pratt, Paul. *Jane Goodall.* Lucent Books, 1996.

Ferber, Elizabeth. *Jane Goodall: A Life With Animals.* Marshall Cavendish Corp., 1997.

Gutenberg, Johann

Fisher, Leonard Everett. *Gutenberg.* Simon and Schuster, 1993.

Kapr, Albert; Martin, Douglas (translator). *Johann Gutenberg: The Man and His Invention.* Scolar Press, 1996.

Harvey, William

Keynes, Geoffrey. *The Life of William Harvey.* Oxford University Press, 1978.

Yount, Lisa. *William Harvey: Discoverer of How Blood Circulates.* Enslow Publishers Inc., 1994.

Hawking, Stephen

Ferguson, K. *Stephen Hawking: Quest for a Theory of the Universe.* Franklin Watts, 1994.

McDaniel, M. *Stephen Hawking, Revolutionary Physicist.* Chelsea House, 1994.

Heisenberg, Werner Karl

Cassidy, David C. *Uncertainty: The Life and Science of Werner Heisenberg.* W. H. Freeman & Co., 1993.

Powers, Thomas. *Heisenberg's War: The Secret History of the German Bomb.* Alfred A. Knopf, 1993.

Helmholtz, Herman L.F. von

Cahan, D. *Hermann von Helmholtz and the Foundations of Nineteenth Century Science.* University of California Press, 1993.

Henson, Matthew

Ferris, Jeri. *Arctic Explorer: The Story of Matthew Henson.* Carolhoda Books, 1989.

Gilman, Michael. *Matthew Henson* (Black American Series). Holoway House Publishing Co., 1990.

Henson, Matthew A. *A Black Explorer at the North Pole.* University of Nebraska Press, 1989.

Herschel Family

Lubbock, C.A. *The Herschel Chronicles: The Life-Story of William Herschel and His Sister Caroline Herschel.* Cambridge University Press, 1993.

Hertz, Heinrich

Aitken, Jugh J.G. *Syntony and Spark: The Origins of Radio,* Princeton University Press, 1985.

Buchwald, J. Z., *The Creation of Scientific Effects: Heinrich Hertz and Electric Waves,* University of Chicago Press, 1994.

Susskind, C. *Heinrich Hertz: A Short Life.* San Francisco Press, 1995.

Hippocrates

Temkin, Owsei. *Hippocrates in a World of Pagans and Christians.* Johns Hopkins University Press, 1991.

Hubble, Edwin

Christianson, Gale E. *Edwin Hubble: Mariner of the Nebulae.* University of Chicago Press, 1996.

Fox, Mary Virginia. *Edwin Hubble: American Astronomer* (Book Report Biographies). Franklin Watts, 1997.

Hetherington, N. *Hubble's Cosmology: A Guided Study of Selected Texts.* Pachart, 1995.

Humboldt, Alexander

Bottling, D. *Humboldt and the Cosmos.* Harper Row, 1973.

Gaines, Ann; Collins, Michael. *Alexander Von Humboldt, Colossus of Exploration.* Chelsea House Publications, 1990.

Huxley, Thomas

Davis, Ainsworth. *Thomas H. Huxley.* AMS Press, 1991.

Desmond, Adrian. *Huxley: From Devil's Disciple to Evolution's High Priest.* Addison-Wesley Publishing Co., 1997.

Jackson, Shirley A.

Hayden, Robert C. "Dr. Shirley A. Jackson: From Bumblebees to Elementary Particles." *Seven African American Scientists.* 1992

Hayden, Robert C. "Nuclear Physicist at Fermi Lab," *Ebony* (November 1974): 113-122.

Jenner, Edward

Behbehani, Abbas M. *Smallpox Story: In Words and Pictures.* University of Kansas Medical Center, 1988.

Jenner, Edward. *Vaccination Against Smallpox* (Great Minds Series). Prometheus Books, 1996.

Jung, Carl Gustav

Dawson, Terence; Young-Eisendrath, Polly (editors). *The Cambridge Companion to Jung.* Cambridge University Press, 1997.

McLynn, Frank. *Carl Gustav Jung.* St. Martins Press, 1997.

Kelvin, Lord

Burchfield, J. D. *Lord Kelvin and the Age of the Earth.* Science History Publications, 1975.

Burchfield, Joe D. *Lord Kelvin and the Age of Faith.* University of Chicago Press, 1990.

Smith, Crosbie; Wise, M. Norton. *Energy and Empire: A Biographical Study of Lord Kelvin.* Cambridge University Press, 1989.

Kepler, Johannes

Casper, M. *Kepler*. Dover, 1990.

Tiner, John H. *Johannes Kepler: Giant of Faith and Science*. Mott Media, 1977.

Koch, Robert

Brock, Thomas. *Robert Koch: A Life in Medicine and Bacteriology*. American Society for Microbiology, 1998.

Latimer, Lewis

Ayer, Eleanor H. *Lewis Latimer: Creating Bright Ideas*. Raintree/Steck Vaughn, 1996.

Norman, Winifred Latimer; Patterson, Lily. *Lewis Latimer* (Black Americans of Achievement). Chelsea House Publishing, 1993.

Lavoisier, Antoine

Donovan, Arthur. *Antoine Lavoisier: Science, Administration, and Revolution*. Cambridge University Press, 1996.

Yount, Lisa. *Antoine Lavoisier: Founder of Modern Chemistry*. Enslow Publishers, Inc., 1997.

Lawrence, Ernest Orlando

Childs, H. *An American Genius: The Life of Ernest Orlando Lawrence*. Dutton, 1968.

Heilbron, J.L.; Seidel, Robert W.; Wheaton, Bruce R. *Lawrence and His Laboratory: Nuclear Science at Berkeley*. University of California Regents, 1981.

Leakey, Louis

Cole, Sonia. *Leakey's Luck: the Life of Louise Leakey, 1903-1972*. Harcourt Brace Jovanivich, 1975.

Leakey, Richard, *The Origin of Humankind*. Basic Books, 1994.

Morell, Virginia. *Ancestral Passions: The Leakey Family and the Quest for Humankind's Beginnings*. Touchstone Books, 1996.

Leeuwenhoek, Antonie van

Dobell, Clifford, ed. *Anthony Van Leeuwenhoek and his "Little Animals."* Dover Publications, 1960.

Yount, Lisa. *Anton Van Leeuwenhoek: First to See Microscopic Life*. Enslow Publishers, Inc., 1996.

Libby, Willard

Bowman, Sheridan. *Radiocarbon Dating (Interpreting the Past)*. University of California Press, 1990.

Jespersen, James; Fitz-Randolph, Jane; Hiscock, Bruce (illustrator). *Mummies, Dinosaurs, Moon Rocks: How We Know How Old Things Are*. Atheneum, 1996.

Linné, Carl von

Anderson, Margaret Jean. *Carl Linnaeus: Father of Classification*. Enslow Publishers, Inc., 1997.

Weistock, John. *Contemporary Perspectives on Linnaeus*. University Press of America, 1986.

Lister, Joseph

Fisher, Richard B. *Joseph Lister 1827-1912*. MacDonald and Jane's, 1977.

Lumière Brothers

Lumiere, Auguste; Lumiere, Louis; Rittaud-Hutinet, Jacques (translator). *Letters*. Faber & Faber, 1997.

Lyell, Charles

Wilson, L.G. (editors). *Sir Charles Lyell's Scientific Journals of the Species Question*. New Haven, 1970.

Marconi, Guglielmo

Aitken, Hugh. *Syntony and Spark: The Origin of Radio*. Princeton University Press, 1985.

Parker, Steve. *Guglielmo Marconi and Radio*. Chelsea House Publishing, 1995.

McClintock, Barbara

Keller, E.F. *A Feeling for the Organism: The Life and Work of Barbara McClintock*. Freeman, 1983.

Kittredge, Mary; Horner, Matina S. *Barbara McClintock* (American Women of Achievement). Chelsea House Publishing, 1991.

Heiligman, Deborah; Hamlin, Janet. *Barbara McClintock: Alone in Her Field*. W. H. Freeman & Co., 1994.

McCoy, Elijah

Jackson, Garnet; Thomas, Gary (illustrator). *Elijah McCoy: Inventor* (Beginning Biographies). Modern Curriculum Press, 1992.

Portia, James. *The Real McCoy: African American Invention and Innovation, 1619-1930*. Washington D.C. 1989.

Meitner, Lise

Sime, Ruth Lewin. *Lise Meitner: A Life in Physics*. University of California Press, 1997

Rife, Patricia; Meitner, Lise. *Lise Meitner and the Dawn of the Nuclear Age*. Birkhauser, 1998.

Mendel, Johann Gregor

Bowler, Peter J. *Mendelian Revolution: The Emergence of Hereditarian Concepts in Modern Science and Society*. Johns Hopkins University Press, 1989.

Orel, Viezslav. *Gregor Mendel: The First Geneticist*. Oxford University Press, 1996.

Morton, William T. G.

Fradin, Dennis Brindell. *We Have Conquered Pain: The Discovery of Anesthesia*. Margaret McElderry, 1996.

Rupreht, Joseph. *Anaesthesia: Essays on Its History*. Springer Verlag, 1985.

Newton, Isaac

Hitzeroth, Deborah; Leon, Sharon. *The Importance of Sir Isaac Newton.* Lucent Books, 1994.

Rankin, William. *Introducing Newton.* Totem Books, 1994.

White, Michael. *Isaac Newton: The Last Sorcerer.* Addison-Wesley Publishing Co., 1998.

Nobel, Alfred

Fant, Kenne. *Alfred Nobel: A Biography.* Arcade Publishing, 1998.

Lars-Ake; Varcoe, George. *The Remarkable Story of Alfred Nobel and the Nobel Prize.* Coronet Books, 1994.

Oppenheimer, J. Robert

Davis, Nuel Pharr. *Lawrence and Oppenheimer.* Da Capo Press, 1986.

Holloway, Rachel L. *In the Matter of J. Robert Oppenheimer: Politics, Rhetoric, and Self-Defense.* Praeger Publishing, 1993.

Rummel, Jack. *Robert Oppenheimer: Dark Prince* (Makers of Modern Science). Facts on File, 1992.

Pascal, Blaise

McPherson, Joyce. *A Piece of the Mountain: The Story of Blaise Pascal.* Greenleaf Press, 1995.

Nelson, Robert J. *Pascal: Adversary and Advocate.* Harvard University Press, 1982.

Pasteur, Louis

Geison, Gerald L. *The Private Science of Louis Pasteur.* Princeton University Press, 1995.

Reynolds, Moira David. *How Pasteur Changed History: The Story of Louis Pasteur and the Pasteur Institute.* McGuinn & McGuire, 1994.

Pauli, Wolfgang

Laurikainen, Kalervo Vihtori. *The Message of the Atoms: Essays on Wolfgang Pauli and the Unspeakable.* Springer Verlag, 1997.

Pauling, Linus

Newton, David E. *Linus Pauling: Scientist and Advocate.* Facts on File, 1994.

Serafini, Anthony. *Linus Pauling: A Man and his Science.* Paragon House, 1989.

Sherrow, Victoria. *Linus Pauling: Investigating the Magic Within.* Raintree/Steck Vaughn, 1997.

Planck, Max

Hielbron, J.L. *The Dilemmas of an Upright Man: Max Planck as Spokesman for German Science.* University of California Press, 1987.

Powell, John Wesley

Bruns, Roger A. *John Wesley Powell: Explorer of Grand Canyon*. Enslow Publishers, Inc., 1997.

Murphy, Dan. *John Wesley Powell: Voyage of Discovery*. K.C. Publications, 1991.

Ptolomy, Claudius

Stevenson, E.L., (editor). *Claudius Ptolemy: The Geography*. Dover Publications, 1991.

Taub, Liba Chaia. *Ptolomy's Universe: The Natural Philosophical and Ethical Foundations of Ptolomy's Astronomy*. Open Court Publishing Co., 1993.

Pythagoras

Guthrie, Kenneth Sylvan; Godwin, Joscelyn; Fideler, David R. *The Pythagorean Sourcebook and Library: An Anthology of Ancient Writings Which Relate to Pythagoras and Pythagorean Philosophy*. Phanes Press, 1991.

Schure, Edouard. *Pythagoras and the Delphic Mysteries*. Kessinger Publishing Co., 1997.

Richter, Charles

Levy, Matthys; Salvadori, Mario. *Why the Earth Quakes: The Story of Earthquakes and Volcanoes*. W.W. Norton & Company, 1995.

Röntgen, Wilhelm Conrad

Gherman, Beverly; Marchesi, Stephen. *The Mysterious Rays of Dr. Röntgen*. Atheneum, 1994.

Glassner, Otto. *Wilhelm Conrad Roentgen and the Early History of the Roentgen Rays*. Jeremy Norman Co., 1992.

Nitske, W. R. *The Life of Wilhelm Conrad Röntgen*. Univeristy of Arizona Press, 1971.

Rutherford, Ernest

Andrade, E. N. da C. *Rutherford and the Nature of the Atom*. Doubleday, 1964.

Wilson, D. *Rutherford: Simple Genius*. MIT Press, 1983.

Sakharov, Andrei

Babyonyshev, A. *On Sakharov*. Knopf, 1982.

Drell, Sidney D.; Kapitza, Sergei P. (editors). *Sakharov Remembered: A Tribute by Friends and Colleagues*, American Institute of Physics, 1991.

Sakharov, Andrei. *Memoirs*. Knopf, 1990.

Salk, Jonas

Curson, Marjorie. *Jonas Salk* (Pioneers in Change). Silver Burdett Press, 1990.

Radetsky, Peter. *The Invisible Invaders: Viruses and the Scientists Who Pursue Them*. Little, Brown, and Co., 1994.

Schliemann, Heinrich

Duchene, Herve; Leggatt, Jeremy. *Golden Treasures of Tory: The Dream of Heinrich Schliemann*. Harry N. Abrams, 1996.

Moorehead, Caroline. *Lost and Found: The 9,000 Treasures of Troy: Heinrich Schliemann and the Gold That Got Away*. Penguin USA, 1997.

Schrödinger, Erwin

Moore, Walter J. *Erwin Schrodinger: Una Vida*. Cambridge University Press, 1996.

Thomson, Joseph John

Thomson, G.P. *J. J. Thomson and the Cavendish Laboratory in His Day*. Doubleday, 1964.

Wheaton, B. *The Tiger and the Shark*. Cambridge University Press, 1983.

Vesalius, Andreas

Vesalius, Andreas. *The Illustrations from the Works of Andreas Vesalius of Brussels; With Annotations and Translations, a Discussion of the Plates and Their Background*. Dover Publications, 1973.

Westinghouse, George

Prout, Henry G. *Life of George Westinghouse*. Ayer Company Publishing, 1921.

Ravage, Barbara. *George Westinghouse: A Genius for Invention*. Raintree/Steck Vaughn, 1996

Whitney, Eli

Green, Constance Mclaughlin. *Eli Whitney and the Birth of American Technology*. Scott Foresman & Company, 1979.

Latham, Jean Lee. *Eli Whitney* (Discovery Biographies). Chelsea House Publishing, 1991.

Woods, Granville

Baker, Henry E. "The Negro in the Field in Invention." *Journal of Negro History* (January 1917): 21-36.

Hayden, Robert C. "The Inventive Genius of Granville Woods." *Journal of the National Teachers Association* (Summer 1990): 44.

Wren, Christopher

Bennett, James A. *The Mathematical Science of Christopher Wren*. Cambridge University Press, 1983.

Hutchinson, Harold Frederick. *Sir Christopher Wren: A Biography*. Stein & Day Publishing, 1976.

Wright Brothers

Crouch, Tom D. *The Bishop's Boys: A Life of Wilbur and Orville Wright*. W.W. Norton & Company, 1990.

Paul, Joseph, *The Wright Brothers (Inventors)*. Abdo & Daughters, 1996.

Taylor, Richard L. *The First Flight: The Story of the Wright Brothers*. Franklin Watts, Inc., 1990.

CHEMISTRY

1997 ◆ Paul D. Boyer and John E. Walker for work on the enzymatic mechanism underlying the synthesis of adenosine triphosphate, and Jens C. Skou for the discovery of the ion-transporting enzyme, Na+, K+-ATPase.

1996 ◆ Robert F. Curl, Jr., Sir Harold W. Kroto, and Richard E. Smalley for the discovery of fullerenes.

1995 ◆ Paul Crutzen, Mario Molina, and F. Sherwood Rowland for work concerning the formation and decomposition of ozone.

1994 ◆ George A. Olah for his contribution to carbocation chemistry.

1993 ◆ Kary B. Mullis for the invention of the polymerase chain reaction method, and Michael Smith for contributions to the establishment of oligonucleiotide-based, site-directed mutagenesis.

1992 ◆ Rudolph A. Marcus for work on electron transfer reactions in chemical systems.

1991 ◆ Richard R. Ernst for contributions to high resolution nuclear magnetic resonance spectroscopy.

1990 ◆ Elias James Corey for the development of organic synthesis.

1989 ◆ Sidney Altman and Thomas R. Cech for the discovery of catalytic properties of RNA.

1988 ◆ Johann Deisenhofer, Robert Huber, and Hartmut Michel for the determination of the three-dimensional structure of a photosynthetic reaction center.

1987 ◆ Donald J. Cram, Jean-Marie Lehn, and Charles J. Pedersen for the development and use of molecules with structure-specific interactions of high selectivity.

1986 ◆ Dudley R. Herschbach, Yuan T. Lee, and John C. Polanyi for contributions concerning the dynamics of chemical elementary processes.

1985 ◆ Herbert A. Hauptman and Jerome Karle for outstanding achievement in the development of direct methods for the determination of crystal structures.

1984 ◆ Robert Bruce Merrifield for chemical synthesis on a solid matrix.

1983 ◆ Henry Taube for work on electron transfer reactions, especially in metal complexes.

1982 ◆ Sir Aaron Klug for work on crystallographic electron microscopy and nuclei acid-protein complexes.

1981 ◆ Kenichi Fukui and Roald Hoffmann for theories concerning the course of chemical reactions.

1980 ◆ Paul Berg for studies of the biochemistry of nucleic acids, and Walter Gilbert and Frederick Sanger for work on the determination of base sequences in nucleic acids.

1979 ◆ Herbert C. Brown and Georg Wittig for development of the use of boron- and phosphorus-containing compounds, respectively, into reagents in organic synthesis.

1978 ◆ Peter D. Mitchell for work on biological energy transfer through the formulation of chemiosmotic theory.

1977 ◆ Ilya Prigogine for contributions to non-equilibrium thermodynamics.

1976 ◆ William N. Lipscomb for work on the structure of boranes illuminating problems of chemical bonding.

1975 ◆ Sir John Warcup Cornforth for work on the stereochemistry of enzyme-catalyzed reactions, and Vladimir Prelog for research into the stereochemistry of organic molecules and reactions.

1974 ◆ Paul J. Flory for achievements in the physical chemistry of the macromolecules.

1973 ◆ Ernst Otto Fischer and Sir Geoffrey Wilkinson for work on the chemistry of the organometallic, or sandwich compounds.

1972 ◆ Christian B. Anfinsen for work on ribonuclease, and Stanford Moore and William H. Stein for contributions to the understanding of the connection between chemical structure and catalytic activity of the ribonuclease molecule.

1971 ◆ Gerhard Herzberg for contributions to the knowledge of electronic stucture and geometry of molecules, particularly free radicals.

1970 ◆ Luis F. Leloir for the discovery of sugar nucleotides and their role in the biosynthesis of carbohydrates.

1969 ◆ Sir Derek H. R. Barton and Odd Hassel for contributions to the concept of conformation and its application in chemistry.

1968 ◆ Lars Onsager for the discovery of the reciprocal relations that are fundamental to the thermodynamics of irreversible processes.

1967 ◆ Manfred Eigen, Ronald George Wreyford Norrish, and Lord George Porter for studies of extremely fast chemical reactions.

1966 ◆ Robert S. Mulliken for work concerning chemical bonds and the electronic structure of molecules by the molecular orbital method.

1965 ◆ Robert Burns Woodward for achievements in the art of organic synthesis.

1964 ◆ Dorothy Crowfoot Hodgkin for determinations by X-ray techniques of the structures of biochemical substances.

1963 ◆ Karl Ziegler and Giulio Natta for discoveries in the field of the chemistry and technology of high polymers.

1962 ◆ Max Ferdinand Perutz and Sir John Cowdery Kendrew for studies of the structures of globular proteins.

1961 ◆ Melvin Calvin for research on the carbon dioxide assimilation in plants.

1960 ◆ Willard Frank Libby for developing a method to use carbon-14 for age determination in archaeology, geology, geophysics, and other branches of science.

1959 ◆ Jaroslav Heyrovsky for the discovery and development of polarographic methods of analysis.

1958 ◆ Frederick Sanger for work on the structure of proteins, especially insulin.

1957 ◆ Lord Alexander R. Todd for work on nucleotides and nucleotide co-enzymes.

1956 ◆ Sir Cyril Norman Hinshelwood and Nikolay Nikolaevich Semenov for research into the mechanism of chemical reactions.

1955 ◆ Vincent Du Vigneaud for work on sulphur compounds, especially for the first synthesis of a polypeptide hormone.

1954 ◆ Linus Carl Pauling for research into the nature of the chemical bond and its application to the structure of complex substances.

1953 ◆ Hermann Staudinger for discoveries in macromolecular chemistry.

1952 ◆ Archer John Porter Martin and Richard Laurence Millington Synge for the invention of partition chromatography.

1951 ◆ Edwin Mattison McMillan and Glenn Theodore Seaborg for discoveries in the chemistry of the transuranium elements.

1950 ◆ Otto Paul Hermann Diels and Kurt Alder for the discovery and development of diene synthesis.

1949 ◆ William Francis Giauque for contributions to chemical thermodynamics, particularly concerning the behaviour of substances at extremely low temperatures.

1948 ◆ Arne Wilhelm Kaurin Tiselius for research on electrophoresis and adsorption analysis.

1947 ◆ Sir Robert Robinson for investigations on plant products of biological importance, especially alkaloids.

1946 ◆ James Batcheller Sumner for the discovery that enzymes can be crystallized, and John Howard Northrop and Wendell Meredith Stanley for the preparation of enzymes and virus proteins in a pure form.

1945 ◆ Artturi Ilmari Virtanen for research and inventions in agricultural and nutrition chemistry.

1944 ◆ Otto Hahn for the discovery of fission of heavy nuclei.

1943 ◆ George De Hevesy for work on the use of isotopes as tracers in the study of chemical processes.

1942 ◆ The prize money was allocated to the Main Fund (1/3) and the
-1940 Special Fund (2/3) of the Chemistry Prize section.

1939 ◆ Adolf Friedrich Johann Butenandt for work on sex hormones, and
Leopold Ruzicka for work on polymethylenes and higher terpenes.

1938 ◆ Richard Kuhn for work on carotenoids and vitamins.

1937 ◆ Sir Walter Norman Haworth for investigations on carbohydrates
and vitamin C, and Paul Karrer for investigations on carotenoids,
flavins, and vitamins A and B2.

1936 ◆ Petrus Josephus Wilhelmus Debye for contributions to our knowledge of molecular structure through investigations on dipole
moments and on the diffraction of X-rays and electrons in gases.

1935 ◆ Frédéric Joliot and Irène Joliot-Curie for the synthesis of new
radioactive elements.

1934 ◆ Harold Clayton Urey for the discovery of heavy hydrogen.

1933 ◆ The prize money was allocated to the Main Fund (1/3) and to the
Special Fund (2/3) of the Chemistry Prize section.

1932 ◆ Irving Langmuir for discoveries and investigations in surface
chemistry.

1931 ◆ Carl Bosch and Friedrich Bergius for contributions to the invention and development of chemical high pressure methods.

1930 ◆ Hans Fischer for research into the constitution of haemin and
chlorophyll.

1929 ◆ Sir Arthur Harden and Hans Karl August Simon Von Euler-
Chelpin for investigations on the fermentation of sugar and fer-
mentative enzymes.

1928 ◆ Adolf Otto Reinhold Windaus for research into the constitution
of the sterols and their connection with vitamins.

1927 ◆ Heinrich Otto Wieland for investigations of the constitution of
the bile acids and related substances.

1926 ◆ Theodor Svedberg for work on disperse systems.

1925 ◆ Richard Adolf Zsigmondy for the demonstration of the heterogenous nature of colloid solutions.

1924 ◆ The prize money for 1924 was allocated to the Special Fund of the Chemistry Prize section.

1923 ◆ Fritz Pregl for the invention of the method of micro-analysis of organic substances.

1922 ◆ Francis William Aston for the discovery, by means of his mass spectrograph, of isotopes, in a large number of non-radioactive elements, and for the enunciation of the whole-number rule.

1921 ◆ Frederick Soddy for contributions to the chemistry of radioactive substances, and investigations into the origin and nature of isotopes.

1920 ◆ Walther Hermann Nernst for work in thermochemistry.

1919 ◆ The prize money for 1919 was allocated to the Special Fund of the Chemistry Prize section.

1918 ◆ Fritz Haber for the synthesis of ammonia from its elements.

1917 ◆ The prize money for 1917-1916 was allocated to the Special Fund
-1916 of the Chemistry Prize section.

1915 ◆ Richard Martin Willstätter for research on plant pigments, especially chlorophyll.

1914 ◆ Theodore William Richards for accurate determinations of the atomic weight of a large number of chemical elements.

1913 ◆ Alfred Werner for work on the linkage of atoms in molecules.

1912 ◆ Victor Grignard for the discovery of the Grignard reagent, and Paul Sabatier for his method of hydrogenating organic compounds in the presence of finely disintegrated metals.

1911 ◆ Marie Curie for the discovery of the elements radium and polonium.

1910 ◆ Otto Wallach for work on alicyclic compounds.

1909 ◆ Wilhelm Ostwald for work on catalysis and for investigations into the principles governing chemical equilibria and rates of reaction.

1908 ◆ Lord Ernest Rutherford for investigations into the disintegration of the elements and the chemistry of radioactive substances.

1907 ◆ Eduard Buchner for biochemical research and the discovery of cellfree fermentation.

1906 ◆ Henri Moissan for the investigation and isolation of the element fluorine, and for the electric furnace named after him.

1905 ◆ Johann Friedrich Wilhelm Adolf Von Baeyer for work on organic dyes and hydroaromatic compounds.

1904 ◆ Sir William Ramsey for the discovery of the inert gaseous elements in air and the determination of their place in the periodic system.

1903 ◆ Svante August Arrhenius for the electrolytic theory of dissociation.

1902 ◆ Hermann Emil Fischer for work on sugar and purine syntheses.

1901 ◆ Jacobus Henricus van't Hoff for the discovery of the laws of chemical dynamics and osmotic pressure in solutions.

PHYSIOLOGY & MEDICINE

1997 ◆ Stanley B. Prusiner for the discovery of Prions.

1996 ◆ Peter C. Doherty and Rolf M. Zinkernagel for discoveries concerning cell mediated immune defence.

1995 ◆ Edward B. Lewis, Christiane Nüsslein-Volhard, and Eric F. Wieschaus for discoveries concerning genetic control of early embryonic development.

1994 ◆ Alfred G. Gilman and Martin Rodbell for the discovery of G-proteins and their role in signal transduction in cells.

1993 ◆ Richard J. Roberts and Phillip A. Sharp for the discovery of split genes.

1992 ◆ Edmond H. Fischer and Edwin G. Krebs for discoveries concerning reversible protein phosphorylation as a biological regulatory mechanism.

1991 ◆ Erwin Neher and Bert Sakmann for discoveries concerning the function of single ion channels in cells.

1990 ◆ Joseph E. Murray and E. Donnall Thomas for discoveries concerning organ and cell transplantation in the treatment of human disease.

1989 ◆ J. Michael Bishop and Harold E. Varmus for the discovery of the cellular origin of retroviral oncogenes.

1988 ◆ Sir James W. Black, Gertrude B. Elion, and George H. Hitchings for the discovery of important principles for drug treatment.

1987 ◆ Susumu Tonegawa for the discovery of the genetic principle for generation of antibody diversity.

1986 ◆ Stanley Cohen and Rita Levi-Montalcini for discoveries concerning growth factors.

1985 ◆ Michael S. Brown and Joseph L. Goldstein for discoveries concerning the regulation of cholesterol metabolism.

1984 ◆ Niels K. Jerne, Georges J.F. Köhler, and César Milstein theories concerning the specificity in development and control of the immune system and the discovery of the principle for production of monoclonal antibodies.

1983 ◆ Barbara McClintock for the discovery of mobile genetic elements.

1982 ◆ S. K. Bergström, Bengt I. Samuelsson, and Sir John R. Vane for discoveries concerning prostaglandins and related biologically active substances.

1981 ◆ Roger W. Sperry for discoveries concerning the functional specialization of the cerebral hemispheres, and David H. Hubel and Torsten N. Wiesel for discoveries concerning information processing in the visual system.

1980 ◆ Baruj Benacerraf, Jean Dausset, and George D. Snell for discoveries concerning genetically determined structures on the cell surface that regulate immunological reactions.

1979 ◆ Alan M. Cormack and Sir Godfrey N. Hounsfield for development of computer assisted tomography.

1978 ◆ Werner Arber, Daniel Nathans, and Hamilton O. Smith for the discovery of restriction enzymes and their application to problems of molecular genetics.

1977 ◆ Roger Guillemin and Andrew V. Schally for discoveries concerning the peptide hormone production of the brain, and Rosalyn Yalow for the development of radioimmunoassays of peptide hormones.

1976 ◆ Baruch S. Blumberg and D. Carleton Gajdusek for discoveries concerning new mechanisms for the origin and dissemination of infectious diseases.

1975 ◆ David Baltimore, Renato Dulbecco, and Howard Martin Temin for discoveries concerning the interaction between tumour viruses and the genetic material of the cell.

1974 ◆ Albert Claude, Christian De Duve, and George E. Palade for discoveries concerning the structural and functional organization of the cell.

1973 ◆ Karl Von Frisch, Konrad Lorenz, and Nikolaas Tinbergen for discoveries concerning organization and elicitation of individual and social behaviour patterns.

1972 ◆ Gerald M. Edelman and Rodney R. Porter for discoveries concerning the chemical structure of antibodies.

1971 ◆ Earl W. Jr. Sutherland for discoveries concerning the action of hormones.

1970 ◆ Sir Bernard Katz, Ulf Von Euler, and Julius Axelrod for discoveries concerning the humoral transmittors in the nerve terminals and the mechanism for their storage, release, and inactivation.

1969 ◆ Max Delbrück, Alfred D. Hershey, and Salvador E. Luria for discoveries concerning the replication mechanism and the gentic structure of viruses.

1968 ◆ Robert W. Holley, Har Gobind Khorana, and Marshall W. Nirenberg for the interpretation of the genetic code and its function in protein synthesis.

1967 ◆ Ragnar Granit, Haldan Keffer Hartline, and George Wald for discoveries concerning the primary physiological and chemical visual processes in the eye.

1966 ◆ Peyton Rous for the discovery of tumorinducing viruses, and Charles Brenton Huggins for discoveries concerning hormonal treatment of prostatic cancer.

1965 ◆ François Jacob, André Lwoff, and Jacoues Monod for discoveries concerning genetic control of enzyme and virus synthesis.

1964 ◆ Konrad Bloch and Feodor Lynen for discoveries concerning the mechanism and regulation of cholesterol and fatty acid metabolism.

1963 ◆ Sir John Carew Eccles, Sir Alan Lloyd Hodgkin, and Sir Andrew Fielding Huxley for discoveries concerning the ionic mechanisms involved in excitation and inhibition in the peripheral and central portions of the nerve cell membrane.

1962 ◆ Francis Harry Compton Crick, James Dewey Watson, and Maurice Hugh Frederick Wilkins for discoveries concerning the molecular structure of nuclear acids and its significance for information transfer in living material.

1961 ◆ Georg Von Békésy for discoveries of the physical mechanism of stimulation within the cochlea.

1960 ◆ Sir Frank Macfarlane Burnet and Sir Peter Brian Medawar for the discovery of acquired immunological tolerance.

1959 ◆ Severo Ochoa and Arthur Kornberg for the discovery of the mechanisms in the biological synthesis of ribonucleic acid and deoxiribonucleic acid.

1958 ◆ George Wells Beadle and Edward Lawrie Tatum for the discovery that genes act by regulating definite chemical events, and Joshua Lederberg for discoveries concerning genetic recombination and the organization of genetic material in bacteria.

1957 ◆ Daniel Bovet for discoveries relating to synthetic compounds that inhibit the action of certain body substances, especially the vascular system and the skeletal muscles.

1956 ◆ André Frédéric Cournand, Werner Forssmann, and D. W. Richard for discoveries concerning heart atherization and pathological changes in the circulatory system.

1955 ◆ Axel Hugo Theodor Theorell for discoveries concerning the nature and mode of action of oxidation enzymes.

1954 ◆ John Franklin Enders, Thomas Huckle Weller, and Frederick Chapman Robbins for the discovery of the ability of poliomyelitis viruses to grow in cultures of various types of tissue.

1953 ◆ Sir Hans Adolf Krebs for the discovery of the citric acid cycle, and Fritz Albert Lipmann for the discovery of co-enzyme A and its importance for intermediary metabolism.

1952 ◆ Selman Abraham Waksman for the discovery of streptomycin, the first antibiotic effective against tuberculosis.

1951 ◆ Max Theiler for discoveries concerning yellow fever.

1950 ◆ Edward Calvin Kendall, Tadeus Reichstein, and Philip Showalter Hench for discoveries concerning the hormones of the adrenal cortex.

1949 ◆ Walter Rudolf Hess for the discovery of the functional organization of the interbrain as a coordinator of the activities of the internal organs, and Antonio Caetano De Abreu Freire Egas Moniz for the discovery of the therapeutic value of leucotomy in certain psychoses.

1948 ◆ Paul Hermann Müller for the discovery of the high efficiency of DDT as a contact poison against several arthropods.

1947 ◆ Carl Ferdinand Cori and Gerty Theresa Cori Née Radnitz for the discovery of the course of the catalytic conversion of glycogen, and Bernardo Alberto Houssay for the discovery of the part played by the hormone of the anterior pituitary lobe in the metabolism of sugar.

1946 ◆ Hermann Joseph Muller for the discovery of the production of mutations through X-ray irradiation.

1945 ◆ Sir Alexander Fleming, Sir Ernst Boris Chain, and Lord Howard Walter Florey for the discovery of penicillin.

1944 ◆ Joseph Erlanger and Herbert Spencer Gasser for discoveries relating to the highly differentiated functions of single nerve fibres.

1943 ◆ Henrik Carl Peter Dam for the discovery of vitamin K, and Edward Adelbert Doisy for the discovery of the chemical nature of vitamin K.

1942 ◆ The prize money was allocated to the Main Fund (1/3) and to the
-1940 Special Fund (2/3) of the Physiology and Medicine Prize section.

1939 ◆ Gerhard Domagk for the discovery of the antibacterial effects of prontosil.

1938 ◆ Corneille Jean François Heymans for the discovery of the role played by the sinus and aortic mechanisms in the regulation of respiration.

1937 ◆ Albert Szent-Györgyi Von Nagyrapolt for discoveries in connection with the biological combustion processes.

1936 ◆ Sir Henry Hallett Dale and Otto Loewi for discoveries relating to chemical transmission of nerve impulses.

1935 ◆ Hans Spemann for the discovery of the organizer effect in embryonic development.

1934 ◆ George Hoyt Whipple, George Richards Minot, and William Parry Murphy for discoveries concerning liver therapy in cases of anaemia.

1933 ◆ Thomas Hunt Morgan for discoveries concerning the role played by the chromosome in heredity.

1932 ◆ Sir Charles Scott Sherrington and Lord Edgar Douglas Adrian for discoveries regarding the functions of neurons.

1931 ◆ Otto Heinrich Warburg for the discovery of the nature and mode of action of the respiratory enzyme.

1930 ◆ Karl Landsteiner for the discovery of human blood groups.

1929 ◆ Christiaan Eijkman for the discovery of the antineuritic vitamin, and Sir Frederick Gowland Hopkins for the discovery of the growth-stimulating vitamins.

1928 ◆ Charles Jules Henri Nicolle for work on typhus.

1927 ◆ Julius Wagner-Jauregg for the discovery of the therapeutic value of malaria inoculation in the treatment of dementia paralytica.

1926 ◆ Johannes Andreas Grib Fibiger for the discovery of the spiroptera carcinoma.

1925 ◆ The prize money for 1925 was allocated to the Special Fund of the Physiology or Medicine Prize section.

1924 ◆ Willem Einthoven for the discovery of the mechanism of the electrocardiogram.

1923 ◆ Sir Frederick Grant Banting and John James Richard Macleod for the discovery of insulin.

1922 ◆ Sir Archibald Vivian Hill for the discovery relating to the production of heat in the muscle, and Otto Fritz Meyerhof for the discovery of the fixed relationship between the consumption of oxygen and the metabolism of lactid acid in the muscle.

1921 ◆ The prize money for 1921 was allocated to the Special Fund of the Physiology and Medicine Prize section.

1920 ◆ Schack August Steenberger Krogh for the discovery of the capillary motor regulating mechanism.

1919 ◆ Jules Bordet for discoveries relating to immunity.

1918 ◆ The prize money for 1918-1915 was allocated to the Special Fund **-1915** of the Physiology and Medicine Prize section.

1914 ◆ Robert Bárány for work on the physiology and pathology of the vestibular apparatus.

1913 ◆ Charles Robert Richet for work on anaphylaxis.

1912 ◆ Alexis Carrel for work on vascular suture and the transplantation of blood-vessels and organs.

1911 ◆ Allvar Gullstrand for work on the dioptrics of the eye.

1910 ◆ Albrecht Kossel for his work on proteins, including the nucleic substances.

1909 ◆ Emil Theodor Kocher for work on the thyroid gland.

1908 ◆ Ilya Ilyich Mechnikov and Paul Ehrlich for work on immunity.

1907 ◆ Charles Louis Alphonse Laveran for work on the role played by protozoa in causing diseases.

1906 ◆ Camillo Golgi and Santiago Ramon Y Cajal for work on the structure of the nervous system.

1905 ◆ Robert Koch for investigations and discoveries in relation to tuberculosis.

1904 ◆ Ivan Petrovich Pavlov for his work on the physiology of digestion.

1903 ◆ Niels Ryberg Finsen for contributions to the treatment of diseases, especially lupus vulgaris.

1902 ◆ Sir Ronald Ross for work on malaria.

1901 ◆ Emil Adolf Von Behring for work on serum therapy, especially its application against diphtheria.

PHYSICS

1997 ◆ Steven Chu, Claude Cohen-Tannoudji, and William D. Phillips for development of methods to cool and trap atoms with laser light.

1996 ◆ David M. Lee, Douglas D. Osheroff, and Robert C. Richardson for the discovery of superfluidity in helium-3.

1995 ◆ Martin L. Perl for the discovery of the tau lepton, and Frederick Reines for the detection of the neutrino.

1994 ◆ Bertram N. Brockhouse for the development of neutron spectroscopy, and Clifford G. Shull for the development of the neutron diffraction technique.

1993 ◆ Russell A. Hulse and Joseph H. Taylor Jr. for the discovery of a new type of pulsar.

1992 ◆ Georges Charpak for the invention and development of particle detectors.

1991 ◆ Pierre-Gilles de Gennes for discovering that methods developed for studying order phenomena in simple systems can be generalized to more complex forms of matter.

1990 ◆ Jerome I. Friedman, Henry W. Kendall, and Richard E. Taylor for investgations concerning deep inelastic scattering of electrons on protons and bound neutrons.

1989 ◆ Norman F. Ramsey for the invention of the separated oscillatory fields method and its use in the hydrogen maser and other atomic clocks, and Hans G. Dehmelt and Wolfgang Paul for the development of the ion trap technique.

1988 ◆ Leon M. Lederman, Melvin Schwartz, and Jack Steinberger for the neutri no beam method and the demonstration of the doublet structure of the leptons through the discovery of the muon neutrino.

1987 ◆ J. Georg Bednorz and K. Alexander Müller for the discovery of superconductivity in ceramic materials.

1986 ◆ Ernst Ruska for work in electron optics and for the design of the first electron microscope, and Gerd Binnig and Heinrich Rohrer for the design of the scanning tunneling microscope.

1985 ◆ Klaus Von Klitzing for the discovery of the quantized Hall effect.

1984 ◆ Carlo Rubbia and Simon Van Der Meer for contributions leading to the discovery of the field particles W and Z, communicators of weak interaction.

1983 ◆ Subramanyan Chandrasekhar for studies of the physical processes of importance to the structure and evolution of the stars, and William A. Fowler for studies of the nuclear reactions of importance in the formation of the chemical elements in the universe.

1982 ◆ Kenneth G. Wilson for the theory for critical phenomena in connection with phase transitions.

1981 ◆ Nicolaas Bloembergen and Arthur L. Schawlow for contributions to the development of laser spectroscopy, and Kai M. Siegbahn for contributions to the development of high-resolution electron spectroscopy.

1980 ◆ James W. Cronin and Val L. Fitch for the discovery of violations of fundamental symmetry principles in the decay of neutral K-mesons.

1979 ◆ Sheldon L. Glashow, Abdus Salam, and Steven Weinberg for contributions to the theory of the unified weak and electromagnetic interaction between elementary particles.

1978 ◆ Pyotr Leonidovich Kapitsa for inventions and discoveries in the area of low-temperature physics, and Arno A. Penzias and Robert W. Wilson for the discovery of cosmic microwave background radiation.

1977 ◆ Philip W. Anderson, Sir Nevill F. Mott, and John H. Van Vleck for investigations of the electronic structure of magnetic and disordered systems.

1976 ◆ Burton Richter and Samuel C. C. Ting for the discovery of a heavy elementary particle of a new kind.

1975 ◆ Aage Bohr, Ben Mottelson, and James Rainwater for the discovery of a connection between collective motion and particle motion in atomic nuclei and the development of the theory of the structure of the atomic nucleus.

1974 ◆ Sir Martin Ryle and Antony Hewish for research in radio astrophysics: Ryle for his observations and inventions, in particular of the aperture synthesis technique; and Hewish for his role in the discovery of pulsars.

1973 ◆ Leo Esaki and Ivar Giaever for experimental discoveries regarding tunneling phenomena in semiconductors and superconductors, respectively, and Brian D. Josephson for predictions of the properties of a supercurrent through a tunnel barrier.

1972 ◆ John Bardeen, Leon N. Cooper, and J. Robert Schrieffer for the theory of superconductivity, usually called the BCS-theory.

1971 ◆ Dennis Gabor for the invention and development of the holographic method.

1970 ◆ Hannes Alfvén for discoveries in magneto-hydrodynamics with applications in different parts of plasma physics, and Louis Néel for discoveries concerning antiferromagnetism and ferrimagnetism.

1969 ◆ Murray Gell-Mann for discoveries concerning the classification of elementary particles and their interactions.

1968 ◆ Luis W. Alvarez for contributions to elementary particle physics, in particular the discovery of a large number of resonance states, made possible through his development of the hydrogen bubble chamber and data analysis.

1967 ◆ Hans Albrecht Bethe for contributions to the theory of nuclear reactions, especially the discoveries concerning the energy production in stars.

1966 ◆ Alfred Kastler for the discovery of optical methods for studying hertzian resonances in atoms.

1965 ◆ Sin-Itiro Tomonaga, Julian Schwinger, and Richard P. Feynman for work in quantum electrodynamics.

1964 ◆ Charles H. Townes, Nicolay Gennadiyevich Basov, and Aleksandr Mikhailovich Prokhorov for work in quantum electronics, which has led to the construction of oscillators and amplifiers based on the maser-laser principle.

1963 ◆ Eugene P. Wigner for contributions to the theory of atomic nuclei and the elementary particles, and Maria Goeppert-Mayer and J. H. D. Jensen for discoveries concerning nuclear shell structure.

1962 ◆ Lev Davidovich Landau for theories concerning condensed matter, especially liquid helium.

1961 ◆ Robert Hofstadter for studies of electron scattering in atomic nuclei and for discoveries concerning the stucture of the nucleons, and Rudolf Ludwig Mössbauer for research concerning the resonance absorption of gamma radiation and the discovery of the effect named after him.

1960 ◆ Donald A. Glaser for the invention of the bubble chamber.

1959 ◆ Emilio Gino Segrè and Owen Chamberlain for the discovery of the antiproton.

1958 ◆ Pavel Alekseyevich Cherenkov, I. Mikhailovich Frank, and Igor Yevgenyevich Tamm for the discovery and the interpretation of the Cherenkov effect.

1957 ◆ Chen Ning Yang and Tsung-Dao Lee for investigations of parity laws, which have led to discoveries regarding elementary particles.

1956 ◆ William Shockley, John Bardeen, and Walter Houser Brattain for research on semiconductors and the discovery of the transistor effect.

1955 ◆ Willis Eugene Lamb for discoveries concerning the fine structure of the hydrogen spectrum, and Polykarp Kusch for determination of the magnetic moment of the electron.

1954 ◆ Max Born for research in quantum mechanics, especially for statistical interpretation of the wavefunction, and Walther Bothe for the coincidence method.

1953 ◆ Frits Zernike for demonstrating the phase contrast method and for inventing the phase contrast microscope.

1952 ◆ Felix Bloch and Edward Mills Purcell for the development of new methods for nuclear magnetic precision measurements.

1951 ◆ Sir John Douglas Cockcroft and Ernest Thomas Sinton Walton for work on the transmutation of atomic nuclei by artificially accelerated atomic particles.

1950 ◆ Cecil Frank Powell for the development of the photographic method of studying nuclear processes and discoveries regarding mesons made with this method.

1949 ◆ Hideki Yukawa for the prediction of the existence of mesons.

1948 ◆ Lord Patrick M. S. Blackett for the development of the Wilson cloud chamber method.

1947 ◆ Sir Edward Victor Appleton for investigations of the physics of the upper atmosphere, especially for the discovery of the so-called Appleton layer

1946 ◆ Percy Williams Bridgman for the invention of an apparatus to produce extremely high pressures, and for discoveries made in high pressure physics.

1945 ◆ Wolfgang Pauli for the discovery of the Exclusion Principle.

1944 ◆ Isidor Isaac Rabi for the resonance method for recording the magnetic properties of atomic nuclei.

1943 ◆ Otto Stern for contribution to the development of the molecular ray method and the discovery of the magnetic moment of the proton.

1942 ◆ The prize money was allocated to the Main Fund (1/3) and to the
-1940   Special Fund (2/3) of the Physics Prize section.

1939 ◆ Ernest Orlando Lawrence for the invention and development of the cyclotron.

1938 ◆ Enrico Fermi for demonstrating the existence of new radioactive elements produced by neutron irradiation, and for the related discovery of nuclear reactions brought about by slow neutrons.

1937 ◆ Clinton Joseph Davisson And Sir George Paget Thomson for the discovery of the diffraction of electrons by crystals.

1936 ◆ Victor Franz Hess for the discovery of cosmic radiation, and Carl David Anderson for the discovery of the positron.

1935 ◆ Sir James Chadwick for the discovery of the neutron.

1934 ◆ The prize money was allocated to the Main Fund (1/3) and to the Special Fund (2/3) of the Physics Prize section.

1933 ◆ Erwin Schrödinger and Paul Adrien Maurice Dirac for the development of new productive forms of atomic theory.

1932 ◆ Werner Heisenberg for the creation of quantum mechanics.

1931 ◆ The prize money was allocated to the Main Fund (1/3) and to the Special Fund (2/3) of the Physics Prize section.

1930 ◆ Sir Chandrasekhara Venkata Raman for work on the scattering of light and for the discovery of the effect named after him.

1929 ◆ Prince Louis-Victor De Broglie for his discovery of the wave nature of electrons.

1928 ◆ Sir Owen Willans Richardson for work on the thermionic phenomenon and for the discovery of the law named after him.

1927 ◆ Arthur Holly Compton for his discovery of the effect named after him, and Charles Thomson Rees Wilson for making the paths of electrically charged particles visible by condensation of vapour.

1926 ◆ Jean Baptiste Perrin for work on the discontinuous structure of matter, and especially for the discovery of sedimentation equilibrium.

1925 ◆ James Franck and Gustav Hertz for the discovery of the laws governing the impact of an electron upon an atom.

1924 ◆ Karl Manne Georg Siegbahn for discoveries and research in X-ray spectroscopy.

1923 ◆ Robert Andrews Millikan for work on the elementary charge of electricity and on the photoelectric effect.

1922 ◆ Niels Bohr for investigating the structure of atoms and of radiation emanating from them.

1921 ◆ Albert Einstein for services to theoretical physics and the discovery of the law of the photoelectric effect.

1920 ◆ Charles Edouard Guillaume for the discovery of anomalies in nickel steel alloys.

1919 ◆ Johannes Stark for the discovery of the Doppler effect in canal rays and the splitting of spectral lines in electric fields.

1918 ◆ Max Karl Ernst Ludwig Planck for the discovery of energy quanta.

1917 ◆ Charles Glover Barkla for the discovery of characteristic Röntgen radiation of the elements.

1916 ◆ The prize money for 1916 was allocated to the Special Fund of the Physics Prize section.

1915 ◆ Sir William Henry Bragg and Sir William Lawrence Bragg for analysis of crystal structure by means of X-rays.

1914 ◆ Max Von Laue for the discovery of the diffraction of X-rays by crystals.

1913 ◆ Heike Kamerlingh-Onnes for investigations on the properties of matter at low temperatures.

1912 ◆ Nils Gustaf Dalén for the invention of automatic regulators to be used with gas accumulators for illuminating lighthouses and buoys.

1911 ◆ Wilhelm Wien for discoveries regarding the laws governing the radiation of heat.

1910 ◆ Johannes Diderik van der Waals for work on the equation of state for gases and liquids.

1909 ◆ Guglielmo Marconi and Carl Ferdinand Braun for their contributions to the development of wireless telegraphy.

1908 ◆ Gabriel Lippmann for the method of reproducing colors photographically based on the phenomenon of interference.

1907 ◆ Albert Abraham Michelson for the development of optical precision instruments and for the spectroscopic and metrological investigations carried out with their aid.

1906 ◆ Sir Joseph John Thomson for investigations on the conduction of electricity by gases.

1905 ◆ Philipp Eduard Anton Lenard for work on cathode rays.

1904 ◆ Lord John William Strutt Rayleigh for investigations of the densities of gases and for the discovery of argon.

1903 ◆ Antoine Henri Becquerel for the discovery of spontaneous radioactivity, and Pierre Curie and Marie Curie for research on the radiation phenomena discovered by Becquerel.

1902 ◆ Hendrik Antoon Lorentz and Pieter Zeeman for research into the influence of magnetism upon radiation phenomena.

1901 ◆ Wilhelm Conrad Röntgen for the discovery of the rays named after him.

abscess A localized collection of pus surrounded by inflamed tissue.

absolute magnitude The brightness a star would have if it were placed at a distance of ten parsecs from the earth.

acid Any of various water soluble compounds that in a solution are capable of reacting with a base to form a salt.

acoustics The science or study that deals with the production, control, transmission, reception, and effects of sound.

aeronautics The science or study that deals with the operation of aircraft.

agar A gelatinous extract of red algae, used in culture media or as a stabilizing and gelling agent in foods.

agriculture The science, art, or practice of cultivating soil, producing crops, and raising livestock.

AIDS (Acquired Immune Deficiency Syndrome) A disease of the human immune system that is caused by infection with the HIV virus.

alchemy A medieval chemical science aimed at achieving the transmutation of base metals into gold.

algae A plant organism usually found growing in water.

alpha helix A protein structure characterized by a single, spiral chain of animo acids stabilized by hydrogen bonds.

alpha particle A positively charged nuclear particle identical with the nucleus of a helium atom, consisting of two protons and two neutrons, ejected at high speeds in certain radioactive transformations.

alternating current (AC) An electrical current that reverses its direction at regularly occurring intervals.

amino acid Any of a class of organic compounds, especially those that form proteins.

amphibian A class of cold-blooded vertebrates intermediate in many characteristics between fishes and reptiles (i.e., frogs, toads, salamanders).

analytical (coordinate) geometry Study of geometric properties by means of algebraic operations on symbols defined in terms of a coordinate system.

anatomy A branch of morphology that deals with the structure of organisms.

ancestors Those from whom a person is descended, usually used to refer to those more remote than a grandparent.

anesthesia A loss of sensation with or without loss of consciousness.

anion a negatively charged ion; the ion in the electrolyzed solution that migrates to the anode.

anode The electrode of an electrochemical cell at which oxidation occurs; the positive terminal of an electrolytic cell to the negative terminal of a galvanic cell.

antenna Slender, moveable, sensory organ on the head of insects, myriapods, and crustaceans; a metallic device for radiating or receiving radio waves.

anthrax An infectious disease of warm-blooded animals, such as cattle or sheep, caused by a spore-forming bacterium, characterized by external ulcerating nodules or by lesions in the lungs.

antibiotic A substance produced by or derived from a microorganism, able in a dilute solution to kill or inhibit another microorganism.

apparent magnitude The brightness of a star as viewed from earth.

binary star systems A system of two stars that revolve around each other by means of their mutual gravitation.

biochemistry The science or discipline of chemistry that deals with the chemical compounds and processes occurring in organisms.

biogenesis The development of life from pre-existing life.

biology The science or study that deals with living organisms and their vital processes.

bioluminescence The emission of light from and produced by living organisms.

biosphere The part of the world in which life exists.

biota The flora and fauna of a region.

bitumen An asphalt used in ancient times as a cement and mortar.

black hole A hypothetical celestial object with a gravitational field so strong that not even light can escape from it, believed to be created by the collapse of a very massive star.

blackbody An ideal body or surface that completely absorbs all radiant energy falling upon it with no reflection, and that radiates at all frequencies with a spectral energy distribution dependent on its absolute temperature.

boron A metalloid element found in nature only in combination, used primarily in metallurgy and in composite structural materials.

boson An elementary particle, such as a meson, that has zero spin.

botany The branch of biology dealing with plant life.

Boyle's Law A law in physics that states that the volume of a gas at constant temperature varies inversely with the pressure exerted on it.

C¹⁴ (radiocarbon) dating A method of determining the age of old material, such as a fossil or relic, by measuring the content of carbon 14, a heavy, radioactive isotope of carbon of mass number 14.

cadaver A dead body intended for dissection.

calcination The act or process of heating materials to a high temperature but without fusing in order to drive off volatile matter or to effect changes.

calcium A metallic element of the alkaline-earth group, occurring in nature only in combination.

calculus A mathematical method of computation or calculation in a special notation, comprised of differential and integral calculus; a system or arrangement of intricate or interrelated parts.

calorie A unit for the measure of heat or energy.

camera obscura An early method of photography, consisting of a darkened enclosure having an opening, usually provided with a lens, through which light from external objects enters to form an image of the objects on the opposite surface.

cancer A malignant tumor of potentially unlimited growth that expands locally by invasion and systematically by metastasis.

capacitor From **capacitance**: the property of an electric nonconductor that permits the storage of energy.

Carbolic acid Also known as **phenol**, a caustic, white crystalline compound.

carbon dioxide (CO²) A heavy, odorless gas produced primarily by human and animal respiration and the decay or combustion of animal or vegetable matter.

carbon monoxide (CO) A colorless, odorless, very toxic gas, produced as a result of the incomplete combustion of carbon.

cardiology The science or study of the heart and its actions and diseases.

cardiovascular disease Disease or illness of or relating to the heart and its blood vessels.

Carnot cycle Developed by Nicolas Carnot, an early precursor of the second law of thermodynamics.

cartography The science or art of making maps.

catheter A tubular medical device for insertion into canals, vessels, passageways, or body cavities, usually to permit the injection or withdrawal of fluids or to keep a passage open.

cathode The electrode of an electrochemical cell at which induction occurs.

cation A positively charged ion; the ion in an electrolyzed solution that migrates to the cathode.

causality The relationship between a cause and its effect, or between regularly coordinated events and phenomena.

celestial equator A great circle on the celestial sphere in the same plane as the earth's equator.

celestial sphere An imaginary sphere of infinite extent with the earth at its center.

cell A small microscopic mass of protoplasm bound externally by a membrane including one or more nuclei and various other organelles with their products.

centrifugal force The force that tends to propel a thing or parts of a thing outward from its center of rotation.

centripedal force The force that is necessary to keep an object moving in a circular path, that is directed inward toward the center of rotation.

Cepheid variable stars A class of pulsating stars whose very regular light variations are related directly to their intrinsic luminosities, and whose apparent luminosities are used to estimate astronomical distances.

chlorine A halogen element that is isolated as a heavy, greenish yellow gas of pungent odor, used especially as a bleach, oxidizing element, and disinfectant in water purification.

cholera Any of several diseases of humans and domesticated animals usually characterized by severe gastrointestinal symptoms.

cinematography The art or science of motion picture photography.

circulatory system The system of blood, blood vessels, lymphatics, and heart concerned with the circulation of the blood and lymph.

collective unconscious The hypothesized pool of memories, experiences, and feelings shared by all human beings.

colloid The suspension of tiny particles of one substance, called the dispersed phase, in another phase, called the dispersion medium.

combustion A rapid chemical process that produces heat an usually light.

comet A celestial object consisting of a solid body in a highly eccentric orbit, which when it approaches the point of its orbit closest to the sun often develops a characteristic "tail" that points away from the sun.

comparative Characterized by systematic comparison especially of likeness and dissimilarities.

Compton effect The increase in the wavelength of high-energy electromagnetic radiation when it collides with electrons.

condensation A chemical reaction involving union between molecules, often with the elimination of a simple molecule to form a new, complex compound of often greater molecular weight; the conversion of a substance, such as water, from vapor to a denser liquid or solid state, usually caused by a reduction in the temperature of the vapor.

conductor A material or object that permits an electric current to flow easily.

continental drift A hypothetical slow movement of the continental plates on a deep-seated viscous zone within the earth.

corpuscle A living cell, one not aggregated into a continuous body, or any of various circumscribed multicellular bodies.

cosmic rays Streams of atomic nuclei of extremely penetrating nature that enter the earth's atmosphere from outer space at speeds approaching the speed of light.

cosmology The branch of astronomy that deals with the origin, structure, and space-time relationships of the universe.

cowpox A mild eruptive disease of cows that when communicated to humans protects against smallpox.

Cretaceous The last period of the Mesozoic era characterized by the dominance of reptiles.

cross-fertilization Fertilization in which the gametes are produced by separate individuals.

crystal A body that is formed by the solidification of a chemical element, a compound, or a mixture, and has regularly repeating internal arrangement of its atoms and often external plane faces.

cupping An operation of drawing blood to the surface of the body by use of a glass vessel evacuated by heat.

cyclotron An accelerator in which charged particles are propelled by an alternating electric field in a constant magnetic field.

daguerreotype An early photograph produced on a silver plate, named for its inventor, Louis-Jacques-Mande Daguerre.

decomposition The separation into constituent parts or elements, or into simpler compounds.

deoxyribonucleic acid (DNA) Any of various nucleic acids that are usually the molecular basis of heredity and are constructed of a double helix held together by hydrogen bonds.

diamagnetic Having a magnetic permeability less than that of a vacuum.

dietetics The science or art of applying the principles of nutrition to the diet.

difference engine Considered the first automatic counting machine. Designed by Charles Babbage in 1922, it was constructed for the purpose of preparing mathematic tables.

differential calculus A branch of mathematics concerned primarily with the study of the rate of change of functions with respect to their variables.

diffusion The process whereby the particles of liquids, gases, or solids intermingle as a result of movement brought on by thermal agitation, and in dissolved substances change from a higher composition to a lower.

digestion The process in the living body of making food absorbable by dissolving it and breaking it down into simpler chemical compounds.

diphtheria A contagious disease characterized by the formation of a false membrane, especially in the throat, that produces a toxin causing inflammation in the heart and nervous system.

dissymmetry The absence or lack of symmetry.

distillation The process of purifying a liquid by successive evaporation and condensation.

dodecahedron A geometric figure with 12 sides or plane faces.

Doppler effect A change in the frequence in which waves of sound or light are perceived by an observer, when the source and the observer are in motion with respect to each other, so that the frequency increases or decreases according to the speed at which the distance between the two is increasing or decreasing.

double helix A spiral consisting of two strands in the surface of a cylinder that coil around its axis; characteristic of the DNA molecule.

double star Two stars in much the same line of sight, but distinct from each other.

dymaxion A play on the words *maximum*, *dynamic*, and *ion*, coined by R. Buckminster Fuller to describe a variety of his innovative designs.

Earth Day An event, now yearly, first observed internationally on April 22, 1970, to bring attention to ecological issues and the necessity for the conservation of the earth's natural resources.

eclipse The total or partial obscuring of one celestial body by another.

ecology The branch of science concerned with the interrelationship of organisms and their environment.

electricity A fundamental force of nature consisting of positive and negative kinds, produced naturally, as in lightning and friction, and man-generated.

electrochemistry The branch of science that deals with the relation of electricity to chemical changes, and with the relationship between chemical and electrical energy.

electrodes Conductors used to establish contact with the nonmetallic part of a circuit, or an element in a semiconductor device, such as a transistor, that emits or collects electrons and controls their movement.

electrodynamics The branch of physics that deals with the effects arising from the interaction of electric currents with magnets.

electrolysis Chemical change, especially decomposition, produced in an electrolyte by an electric current, or the destruction of living tissue by an electrical current.

electrolyte A chemical compound that ionizes when dissolved to produced an electrically conductive medium.

electromagnetic field A magnetic field created about a current-carrying conductor.

electromagnetic induction The creation of an electric current in a conductor moving across a magnetic field.

electromagnetic radiation Energy waves produced by the oscillation or acceleration of an electric charge.

electromagnetic spectrum The entire range of radiation, from cosmic rays to radio waves.

electromagnetic waves Energy waves produced by an electric charge, possessing both electric and magnetic components.

electromagnetism Magnetism produced by an electric charge in motion.

electron An elementary particle orbiting the nucleus of an atom, possessed of a negative charge.

electrostatics A branch of physics that deals with the phenomena due to attraction and repulsion of electric charges.

elementary particle A subatomic particle, particularly those regarded as irreducible.

elements The fundamental substances that consists of atoms of only one kind, that singly, or in combination, constitute all matter.

embryology The branch of biology that deals with embryos and their development.

emetics Medicinal agents used to induce vomiting.

Enceladus A moon of the planet Saturn.

enema The injection of liquid into the rectum for cleaning or other therapeutic purposes.

energy The capacity of acting or being active.

Eocene The second oldest epoch of the Tertiary Period, marked by the rise of mammals.

ephemeris The calculation, expressed in a tabular statement, of the position in the night sky as seen from earth of a celestial body for regular intervals.

epidemic A contagious disease that spreads rapidly, infecting a significant percentage of subjects.

epilepsy Any of various neurological disorders marked by loss of consciousness or convulsive seizures.

epoch A particular period of history, especially one that is noteworthy, or a unit of geologic time that is a division of a period.

equator The imaginary circle around a planet's surface, equidistant from the poles and perpendicular to the axis of rotation, that divides the Northern from the Southern hemisphere.

equilibrium A condition of balance between opposed forces, influences, or actions.

equinox Either of the two times during the year when the sun crosses the celestial equator, making the length of day and night approximately equal.

eruption A violent outbreak from restraints or limits, as in a volcanic eruption or a rash or blemish on the skin.

ethics A system or discipline dealing with good and bad, and with moral duty and obligation.

ethnology The science that analyzes and compares human cultures, as in social structure, language, and religion.

evaporation Change of a solid or liquid into a vapor.

evolution Change over the course of time; specifically, the change in the nature and characteristics of living things through natural processes and selection for survival traits.

existentialism A philosophy that emphasizes the uniqueness and isolation of the individual in a hostile or indifferent universe.

Fahrenheit Of or relating to a temperature scale that registers the freezing point of water as 32°F and the boiling point as 212°F at one atmosphere of pressure.

fauna The animals characteristic to a region, period, or special environment.

fermentation A chemical reaction that splits complex compounds into relatively simple substances, as in the conversion of sugar to carbon dioxide and alcohol by yeast.

Fermi level The dividing line above which energy levels tend to be empty, and below which energy levels tend to be full.

Fermi-Dirac statistics A formulization of statistical mechanics used to describe quantum particles, which applies to fermions.

fermion Any of a class of elementary particles characterized by their angular momentum, or spin.

ferro-magnetism The characteristic of substances such as iron or nickel or various alloys that exhibit magnetic properties.

festering Generating pus, or undergoing decay or rot.

finite differences A branch of mathematics in which a theory of the differences between successive pairs of numbers is developed.

first law of thermodynamics Also known as the law on conservation of energy, which states that the sum of kinetic energy, potential energy, and thermal energy within a closed system remains constant.

fish Any or numerous cold-blooded strictly aquatic vertebrates.

fission The splitting of an atomic nucleus resulting in the release of large amounts of energy.

Flamsteed's Star Catalogue Published as *Historia Coelestis Britannica* in 1725, a catalogue of the fixed stars from the observations of John Flamsteed, which exposed and corrected a large number of errors in contemporary astronomical tables.

flora The plants characteristic to a region, period, or special environment.

fluoride A binary compound of fluorine with another element.

fossil A remnant, impression, or trace of an organism of past geologic ages that has been preserved in or turned into stone.

Fourier series A trigonomic series by means of which discontinuous functions can be expressed as the sum of an infinite series of sines and cosines.

function A mathematical correspondence that assigns exactly one element of one set to each element of the same or another set.

galaxy A large-scale aggregate of stars, dust, and gas, containing an average of 100 billion solar masses and ranging in diameter from 1,500 to 300,000 light years.

gallium A rare metallic element that is liquid near room temperature, expands on solidifying, and is found as a trace element in coal, bauxite, and other minerals. It is used in semiconductor technology as a component of various low-melting alloys.

galvanometer An instrument used to detect or measure small electric currents by means of mechanical effects produced by a coil in a magnetic field.

gamma radiation Electromagnetic radiation emitted by radioactive decay and having energies from ten thousand to ten million electron volts.

gaseous Being in a state of matter distinguished from the solid and liquid states by relatively low density and viscosity, the ability to diffuse readily, and the tendency to become distributed uniformly through any container.

gelatin A transparent brittle protein formed by boiling the specially prepared skin, bones, and connective tissue of animals. Used in foods, drugs, and photographic film.

general theory of relativity Developed by Albert Einstein in 1915 to explain apparent conflict between the laws of relativity and the law of gravity.

genes A specific sequence of nucleotides in DNA or RNA that is located in the germ plasm, specifically the carriers of genetic traits.

genetics A branch of biology that deals with the heredity and variation of organisms.

geodesic The shortest line between two points on any mathematically defined surface.

geodesic dome A domed or vaulted structure of lightweight straight elements that form interlocking polygons.

geology The science or study of the history of the earth and its life, especially as recorded in rocks.

geometry The mathematics of the properties, measurement, and relationships of points, lines, angles, surfaces, and solids.

germ cell An egg or sperm cell.

germanium A brittle, crystalline, gray-white metalloid element, widely used as a semiconductor, as an alloying agent and catalyst, and in certain optical glasses.

glacier A large body of ice moving slowly down a slope or valley or spreading outward on a land surface.

Golden Mean The medium between extremes.

gravity A fundamental physical force that is responsible for interactions that occur because of mass between particles.

hadron Any of a class of subatomic particles, including protons and neutrons, that take part in the strong interaction.

hafnium A metallic element that resembles zirconium in its chemical properties that readily absorbs neutrons.

half-life The time required for half the nuclei in a sample of a specific isotope to undergo radioactive decay.

harmony The science of the structure, relation, and progression of musical chords.

heliocentric Referred to or measured from the sun's center or appearing as if seen from it.

helium Colorless, odorless inert gaseous element occurring in natural gas and radioactive ores.

hemisphere A half of a sphere bounded by a great circle; a half of a symmetrical, approximately spherical object divided by a plane of symmetry.

hemoglobin The iron-containing respiratory pigment in red blood cells.

hertz A unit of frequency equal to one cycle per second.

heterogeneous Consisting of dissimilar elements or parts; completely different.

hierarchy The classification of any group based on a predetermined standard or set of standards, expressed in ordered relation to one another.

holistic A style of medicine that attempts to treat both the body and the mind.

hominids Primates of the family Hominidae, of which *Homo sapiens* is the only extant species.

horticulture The science or art of cultivating fruits, vegetables, flowers, or ornamental plants.

human genome The set of chromosomes characteristic of human beings, with the genes they contain.

hybrid The offspring of genetically dissimilar parents, especially of different varieties or species.

hydrodynamics The branch of science that deals with the dynamics of fluids, especially compressed fluids, in motion.

hydrostatics A branch of physics that deals with the characteristics of fluids at rest, especially with the pressure of an immersed body.

hydrotherapy The external use of water for the treatment of diseases.

hygiene The science of the promotion and preservation of health.

hypnosis An induced sleeplike state in which the subject may experience forgotten or suppressed memories, hallucinations, and heightened suggestibility.

hypothesis An assumption or concession made for the sake of argument.

ice age A cold period marked by episodes of extensive glaciation.

icosahedron A polyhedron, or solid bounded by flat surfaces with each surface bounded by straight lines, consisting of 20 triangular faces.

immunology The branch of medicine dealing with the immune system.

in-vitro (also **in vitro**) In an artificial environment outside the living organism.

incandescent Emitting visible light as a result of being heated.

individuation The act or process of individuating, especially the process by which social individuals become differentiated one from the other.

induction The generation of an electromotive force in a closed circuit by varying magnetic flux through the circuit; the charging of an isolated conducting object by momentarily grounding it while a charged body is nearby.

inertia The tendency of a body to remain at rest or stay in motion unless acted on by an outside force.

influenza An acute viral infection marked by inflammation of the respiratory tract and by fever, chills, and pain.

insulator An object or substance that prevents the passage of heat, electricity, or sound into or out of.

internal combustion engine An engine in which fuel is burned within the engine

intoxicants Chemical agents that stimulate or excite.

Inuit A member of an Eskimo people, especially of Arctic Canada or Greenland.

ion An atom, group of atoms, or molecule having a net electrical charge acquired by gaining or losing one or more electrons from an initially neutral configuration.

isotope Any of two or more species of atoms of a chemical element with the same atomic number and chemical behavior.

kinetic energy The energy possessed by a body because of its motion.

Kinetoscope Developed by Thomas Edison, an early precursor of the motion picture projector.

laser (Light Amplification by Stimulated Emission of Radiation) Acronym for any of several devices that convert electromagnetic radiation of mixed frequencies to one or more discrete frequencies of highly amplified and coherent radiation.

latitude The angular distance north or south of the equator, measured in degrees along the meridian.

lawrencium A short-lived, radioactive synthetic transuranic element produced from californium and having isotopes with mass numbers 255 through 260 and having half-lives of a few seconds to three minutes.

lepton Any family of elementary particles, including the electrons and neutrinos, that take part in the weak interaction.

letheon The name under which William Thomas Green Morton attempted to patent the anesthetic sulpheric ether in 1846

Leyden jar One of the earliest and simplest forms of an electric capacitor, consisting of a stoppered glass jar containing water, with a wire or nail extending through the stopper into the water.

light year The distance light travels in one earth year, used as a measure of distance in astronomy.

limestone A common sedimentary rock consisting mostly of calcium carbonate.

liquid A substance capable of flowing or being poured.

lithium A high reactive metallic element used as a heat transfer medium, in thermonuclear weapons, and in various alloys, ceramics, and optical forms of glass.

logarithmic table A table or chart that contains a function that is the inverse of an exponential function.

logic The science that deals with the study of validity.

longitude Angular distance east or west, measured with respect to the prime meridian at Greenwich, England.

luminiferous Emitting light, especially as in self-generated light.

magnesium A light, silvery-white, moderately hard metallic element that in ribbon or powder form burns with a brilliant white flame.

magnetic monopole A hypothetical particle that has only one pole of magnetic charge instead of the usual two. A magnetic monopole would be a basic unit of magnetic charge.

magnetic poles Either of two limited regions in a magnet at which the magnet's field is most intense, each of which is designated by the approximate geographic direction to which it is attracted.

magnetism The class of phenomena exhibited by a magnetic field.

mammal Any of a class of warm-blooded higher vertebrates that nourish their young with milk secreted from the mammary glands.

marine Native to, inhabiting, or formed by the sea.

mathematics The study of the measurement, properties, and relationships of quantities, using numbers and symbols.

matrix A rectangular array of numeric or algebraic quantities subject to mathematical operations. Something resembling such an array, as in the regular formation of elements into columns and rows.

matter Something that occupies space and can be perceived by one or more senses; a physical body, a physical substance, or the universe as a whole. Something that has mass and exists as a solid, liquid, or gas.

mechanics A branch of physical science that deals with energy and forces.

medulla oblongata The lowermost portion of the vertebrate brain, continuous with the spinal cord, responsible for the control of respiration, circulation, and certain other bodily functions.

meiosis The process of cell division in sexually reproducing organisms that reduces the number of chromosomes in reproductive cells, leading to the production of gametes in animals and spores in plants.

membrane A thin, pliable layer of tissue covering surfaces or separating or connecting regions, structures, or organs of an animal or a plant.

meningitis Inflammation of the meninges of the brain and the spinal cord, most often caused by a bacterial or viral infection and characterized by fever, vomiting, intense headache, and stiff neck.

Mercury The planet of our solar system that is closest to the sun.

mesmerism A strong or spellbinding appeal; fascination. Hypnotic induction believed to involve animal magnetism.

meson Any of a family of subatomic particles that participate in strong interactions, are composed of a quark and an antiquark, and have masses generally intermediate between leptons and baryons.

metallography The study of the structure of metals and alloys, especially by optical and electron microscopy and X-ray diffraction.

metaphysics A division of philosophy that is concerned with the study of reality and being.

metastasis A secondary cancerous growth formed by transmission of cancerous cells from a primary growth located elsewhere in the body.

meteor A bright trail or streak that appears in the sky when a meteoroid is heated to incandescence by friction with the earth's atmosphere.

meteor shower A large number of meteors that appear together and seem to come from the same area in the sky.

meteorology The science that deals with the study of weather.

metric system A decimal system of units based on the meter as a unit length, the kilogram as a unit mass, and the second as a unit time.

microbe A minute life form; a microorganism, especially a bacterium that causes disease.

microorganism An organism of microscopic or submicroscopic size, especially a bacterium or protozoan.

microscope An optical instrument that uses a lens or a combination of lenses to produce magnified images of small objects, especially of objects too small to be seen by the unaided eye.

Milky Way The galaxy containing the solar system, visible as a broad band of faint light in the night sky.

Mimas The satellite of Saturn that is sixth in distance from the planet.

mineralogy The study of minerals, including their distribution, identification, and properties.

Miocene Of, belonging to, or characteristic of the geologic time, rock series, and sedimentary deposits of the fourth epoch of the Tertiary Period, characterized by the development of grasses and grazing mammals.

molecular biology A branch of biology dealing with the ultimate physiochemical organization of living matter.

molecule The smallest particle into which an element or a compound can be divided without changing its chemical and physical properties; a group of like or different atoms held together by chemical forces.

monatomic Having one replaceable atom or radical.

moraine An accumulation of earth and stones carried and deposited by a glacier.

mutation A sudden structural change within a gene or chromosome of an organism resulting in the creation of a new character or trait not found in the parental type.

mycology The branch of biology that deals with the study of fungi.

narcotic An addictive drug, such as opium, that reduces pain, alters mood and behavior, and usually induces sleep or stupor. Natural and synthetic narcotics are used in medicine to control pain.

natural history The study and description of organisms and natural objects, especially their origins, evolution, and interrelationships.

natural selection A natural process that results in the survival and reproductive success of individuals or groups best adjusted to their environment and that leads to the perpetuation of genetic qualities best suited to that particular environment.

naturalist One that advocates and practices the belief that all action, thought, and inclination are based only on natural desires and instincts.

nebula A diffuse mass of interstellar dust or gas or both, visible as luminous patches or areas of darkness depending on the way the mass absorbs or reflects incident radiation.

neon A rare, inert gaseous element occurring in the atmosphere to the extent of 18 parts per million and obtained by fractional distillation of liquid air. It is colorless but glows reddish orange in an electric discharge and is used in display and television tubes.

nervous system The system of cells, tissues, and organs that regulates the body's responses to internal and external stimuli. In vertebrates it consists of the brain, spinal cord, nerves, ganglia, and parts of the receptor and effector organs.

neurologist One who studies the medical science that deals with the nervous system and disorders affecting it.

neutrino Any of three electrically neutral subatomic particles in the lepton family.

neutron An uncharged elementary particle that has a mass nearly equal to that of a proton and is present in all known atomic nuclei except hydrogen.

neutron star A celestial body hypothesized to occur in a terminal stage of stellar evolution, essentially consisting of a superdense mass of neutrons and having a powerful gravitational attraction from which only neutrinos and high-energy photons can escape, thus rendering the body invisible except to X-ray detection.

Newcomen engine A steam engine developed in 1705 by Thomas Newcomen and John Calley.

nitric acid A transparent, colorless to yellowish, fuming corrosive liquid or a highly reactive oxidizing agent used in the production of fertilizers, explosives, and rocket fuels and in a wide variety of industrial metallurgical processes.

nitric oxide A colorless, poisonous gas produced as an intermediate during the manufacture of nitric acid from ammonia or atmospheric nitrogen.

nitroglycerin A thick, pale yellow liquid that is explosive on concussion or exposure to sudden heat. It is used in the production of dynamite and blasting gelatin and as a vasodilator in medicine.

nitrous oxide A colorless, sweet-tasting gas used as a mild anesthetic in dentistry and surgery.

nomenclature The process of naming.

Northern Hemisphere The half of the earth north of the equator.

nuclear Of or relating to the atomic nucleus.

nuclear force Strong interaction.

nucleic acid Any of various acids (such as DNA and RNA) that are composed of nucleotide chains.

nucleon A proton or a neutron, especially as part of an atomic nucleus.

nucleotide Any of several compounds that consist of a sugar joined to a base that are the basic structural units of nucleic acids.

nucleus The positively charged central portion of an atom.

nutrition The process of nourishing or being nourished, especially the process by which a living organism assimilates food and uses it for growth and for replacement of tissues. The science or study that deals with food and nourishment, especially in human beings.

Oberon The moon of Uranus that is fifth in distance from the planet.

oceanography A science that deals with the study of oceans, and includes their physical characteristics, the physics and chemistry of their waters, and marine biology.

octahedron A polyhedron with eight plane surfaces.

ophthalmic Of or relating to the eye; ocular.

ophthalmoscope An instrument for examining the interior structures of the eye, especially the retina, consisting essentially of a mirror that reflects light into the eye and a central hole through which the eye is examined.

optics A science that deals with the nature, properties, and effects of light.

orbit A path followed by one body in its revolution around another.

organelle A differentiated structure within a cell, such as a mitochondrion, vacuole, or chloroplast, that performs a specific function.

oscillate To vary between alternate extremes, usually within a definable period of time.

oxygen A nonmetallic element constituting 21 percent of the atmosphere by volume that occurs as a diatomic gas and in many compounds such as water and iron ore. It combines with most elements, is essential for plant and animal respiration, and is required for nearly all combustion.

paleontology A science dealing with the life of past geological periods as known from fossil remains.

Palladian Of or characteristic of an architectural style of the mid 18th century derived from that of Palladio, especially in Britain.

parabola A plane curve formed by the intersection of a right circular cone and a plane parallel to an element of the cone.

parallax The angular difference in direction of a celestial body as measured from two points on the earth's orbit.

paramagnetism Relating to or being a substance in which an induced magnetic field is parallel and proportional to the intensity of the magnetizing field but is much weaker than in ferromagnetic materials.

parity The concept that an object or system can be the mirror-image equivalent of another object or system.

particle accelerators Devices used to accelerate charged elementary particles or ions to high energies.

partons A hypothetical elementary particle believed to be a constituent of hadrons.

patent A grant made by a government that confers upon the creator of an invention the sole right to make, use, and sell that invention for a set period of time.

Pauli exclusion principle The principle that two particles of a given type, such as electrons, protons, or neutrons, cannot simultaneously occupy a particular quantum state.

pendulum A body suspended from a fixed support so that it swings freely back and forth under the influence of gravity, commonly used to regulate various devices, especially clocks.

penicillin Any of a group of broad-spectrum antibiotic drugs obtained from penicillium molds or produced synthetically, most active against gram-positive bacteria and used in the treatment of various infections and diseases.

peptide Any of various natural or synthetic compounds containing two or more amino acids linked by the carboxyl group of one amino acid and the amino group of another.

perihelion The point nearest the sun in the orbit of a planet or other celestial body.

periodic law The principle that the properties of the elements recur periodically as their atomic numbers increase.

periodic table of elements The arrangement of chemical elements based on the periodic law.

pesticide A chemical solution, used primarily in agriculture, to destroy pests.

petroleum A thick, flammable, yellow-to-black mixture of gaseous, liquid, and solid hydrocarbons that occurs naturally beneath the earth's surface, can be separated into fractions including natural gas, gasoline, naphtha, kerosene, fuel, and lubricating oils, paraffin wax, and asphalt, and is used as raw material for a wide variety of derivative products.

pharmacology The science of drugs, including their composition, uses, and effects.

phenomenon An occurrence, a circumstance, or a fact that is perceptible by the senses.

philosophy Inquiry into the nature of things based on logical reasoning rather than empirical methods.

phlogiston A hypothetical substance formerly thought to be a volatile constituent of all combustible substances released as flame in combustion.

phonograph A machine that reproduces sound by means of a stylus in contact with a grooved rotating disk.

photoelectric effect Ejection of electrons from a substance by incident electromagnetic radiation, especially by visible light.

photon The quantum of electromagnetic energy, generally regarded as a discrete particle having zero mass, no electric charge, and an indefinitely long lifetime.

physics The study or science of matter and energy.

physiology A branch of biology that deals with the functions of living matter.

piston A solid cylinder or disk that fits snugly into a larger cylinder and moves under fluid pressure, as in a reciprocating engine, or displaces or compresses fluids, as in pumps and compressors.

plasma The clear, yellowish fluid portion of blood, lymph, or intramuscular fluid in which cells are suspended.

plate tectonics A theory of global dynamics having to do with the movement of a small number of semirigid sections of the earth's crust, with seismic activity and volcanism occurring primarily at the margins of these sections. This movement has resulted in continental drift and changes in the shape and size of ocean basins and continents.

Pliocene Of, belonging to, or designating the geologic time, rock series, and sedimentary deposits of the last of the five epochs of the Tertiary Period, characterized by the appearance of distinctly modern animals.

polemic A controversial argument, especially one refuting or attacking a specific opinion or doctrine.

pole Either extremity of the main axis of a nucleus, a cell, or an organism.

poliomyelitis A highly infectious viral disease that chiefly affects children and, in its acute forms, causes inflammation of motor neurons of the spinal cord and brainstem, leading to paralysis, muscular atrophy, and often deformity.

politics The study or science of government.

polonium A radioactive metallic element that emits an alpha particle to form an isotope of lead.

polygon A closed plane figure bounded by three or more line segments.

positron (*antielectron*) The antiparticle of the electron.

potassium A soft, silver-white, highly or explosively reactive metallic element that occurs in nature only in compounds. It is obtained by electrolysis of its common hydroxide and found in, or converted to, a wide variety of salts used especially in fertilizers and soaps.

precession The motion of the axis of a spinning body, such as the wobble of a spinning top, when there is an external force acting on the axis.

primate A mammal of the order Primates, which includes the anthropoids and prosimians, characterized by refined development of the hands and feet, a shortened snout, and a large brain.

prism A solid figure whose bases or ends have the same size and shape and are parallel to one another, and each of whose sides is a parallelogram.

prognostic A sign or symptom indicating the future course of a disease.

protein A substance that consists of amino-acid residues joined together by peptide bond. It contains the elements of carbon, hydrogen, nitrogen, oxygen, and usually sulfur.

protozoa Any of a large group of single-celled, usually microscopic, eukaryotic organisms, such as amoebas, ciliates, flagellates, and sporozoans.

psychoanalysis The method of psychiatric therapy originated by Sigmund Freud in which free association, dream interpretation, and analysis of resistance and transference are used to explore repressed or unconscious impulses, anxieties, and internal conflicts.

psychology The study or science of mind and behavior.

Pythagorean The syncretistic philosophy expounded by Pythagoras, distinguished chiefly by its description of reality in terms of arithmetical relationships.

qualitative analysis Chemical analysis designed to identify the components of a substance or mixture.

quantum The smallest amount of a physical quantity that can exist independently, especially a discrete quantity of electromagnetic radiation.

quantum electrodynamics The quantum theory of the properties and behavior of electrons and the electromagnetic field.

quantum mechanics Quantum theory, especially the quantum theory of the structure and behavior of atoms and molecules.

quantum theory A theory in physics, based on the concept of the subdivision of radiant energy into finite quantities and applied to numerous processes involving transference or transformation of energy at an atomic or molecular scale.

quark Any of a group of hypothetical elementary particles having electric charges of magnitude one-third or two-thirds that of the electron, regarded as constituents of all hadrons.

racemic Of or relating to a chemical compound that contains equal quantities of dextrorotatory and levorotatory forms and therefore does not rotate the plane of incident polarized light.

radar A method of detecting distant objects and determining their position, velocity, or other characteristics by analysis of very high frequency radio waves reflected from their surfaces.

radiation Energy radiated or transmitted in the form of rays, waves, or particles.

radius A line segment extending from the center of a circle or sphere to the circumference or surface.

reflexology The study of reflex responses, especially as they affect behavior.

refraction The turning or bending of any wave, such as a light or sound wave, when it passes from one medium into another of different density.

reincarnation Rebirth of the soul in another body.

renormalization Bringing an object into a normal or more normal state once again.

reptile A classification of air-breathing vertebrates that includes alligators, lizards, snakes, and turtles.

rhetoric The science or study of writing or speaking as a means of communication.

rheumatism Any of several pathological conditions of the muscles, tendons, joints, bones, or nerves, characterized by discomfort and disability.

salivate To secrete or produce saliva.

salts A classification of compounds that result from the replacement of part or all of the acid by a base.

satellite A celestial body that orbits a planet; a moon.

Saturn The sixth planet from the sun and the second largest in the solar system.

scandium A silvery-white metallic element found in various rare minerals and separated as a byproduct in the processing of certain uranium ores. An artificially produced radioactive isotope is used as a tracer in studies of oil wells and pipelines.

scientific method The principles and empirical processes of discovery and demonstration considered characteristic of or necessary for scientific investigation, generally involving the observation of phenomena, the formulation of a hypothesis concerning the phenomena, experimentation to demonstrate the truth or falseness of the hypothesis, and a conclusion that validates or modifies the hypothesis.

SCUBA (Self-Contained Underwater Breathing Apparatus) The acronym designating an apparatus that utilizes a portable supply of compressed gas supplied at a regulated pressure, used for breathing underwater.

second law of thermodynamics Physical law that gives a precise definition of a property called entropy. The law states that the entropy of an isolated system can never decrease.

sedimentary Of or relating to rocks formed by the deposition of sediment.

seismic Of, subject to, or caused by an earthquake or earth vibration.

seismograph An instrument for automatically detecting and recording the intensity, direction, and duration of a movement of the ground, especially of an earthquake.

seismology The geophysical science of earthquakes and the mechanical properties of the earth.

selenium A nonmetallic element, red in powder form, black in vitreous form, and metallic gray in crystalline form, resembling sulfur and obtained primarily as a byproduct of electrolytic copper refining.

septicemia A systemic disease caused by pathogenic organisms or their toxins in the bloodstream.

serology The science that deals with the properties and reactions of serums, especially blood serum.

serum The clear yellowish fluid obtained upon separating whole blood into its solid and liquid components.

short-wave An electromagnetic wave with a wavelength of approximately 200 meters or less, especially a radio wave in the 20- to 200-meter range.

silicon A nonmetallic element occurring extensively in the earth's crust in silica and silicates, having both an amorphous and a crystalline allotrope, and used doped or in combination with other materials in glass, semiconducting devices, concrete, brick, refractories, pottery, and silicones.

singularities A point in space-time at which gravitational forces cause matter to have infinite density and infinitesimal volume, and space and time to become infinitely distorted.

skeleton The internal structure composed of bone and cartilage that protects and supports the soft organs, tissues, and other parts of a vertebrate organism.

smallpox An acute, highly infectious, often fatal disease caused by a pox virus and characterized by high fever and aches with subsequent widespread eruption of pimples that blister, produce pus, and form pockmarks.

sodium A soft, light, extremely malleable silver-white metallic element that reacts explosively with water, is naturally abundant in combined forms, especially in common salt, and is used in the production of a wide variety of industrially important compounds.

solar system A sun, together with the group of celestial bodies including planets, asteroids, and comets, that are held by its gravitational force and revolve around it.

sonar A system using transmitted and reflected underwater sound waves to detect and locate submerged objects or measure the distance to the floor of a body of water.

Southern Hemisphere The half of the earth south of the equator.

special theory of relativity The physical theory of space and time developed by Albert Einstein, based on the postulates that all the laws of physics are equally valid in all frames of reference moving at a uniform velocity and that the speed of light from a uniformly moving source is always the same, regardless of how fast or slow the source or its observer is moving. The theory has as consequences the relativistic mass increase of rapidly moving objects, the Lorentz-Fitzgerald contraction, time dilatation, and the principle of mass-energy equivalence.

species A classification or "family" of living things, having common physiological attributes, designated by their similarities.

specific heat The ratio of the amount of heat required to raise the temperature of a unit mass of a substance by one unit of temperature to the amount of heat required to raise the temperature of a similar mass of a reference material, usually water, by the same amount.

spectrum The distribution of energy emitted by a radiant source, as by an incandescent body, arranged in order of wavelengths.

speed of light Defined as the distance that light travels in 1 second (exactly 299,792,458 meters per second, or about 186,000 miles per second).

sphere A three-dimensional surface, all points of which are equidistant from a fixed point.

Sr^{90} Also known as Radiostrontium, similar to Calcium in its chemical behavior, including its deposition in human bone.

staphylococci bacteria A spherical gram-positive parasitic bacterium of the genus *Staphylococcus*, usually occurring in grapelike clusters and causing boils, septicemia, and other infections.

statics Mechanics dealing with the relations of forces that produce equilibrium among material bodies.

steam engine An engine that converts the heat energy of pressurized steam into mechanical energy, especially one in which steam drives a piston in a closed cylinder.

stellar Of or relating to a star or stars.

stellar photometry Measurement of the properties of light, especially luminous intensity of the sun.

strontium A soft, silvery, easily oxidized metallic element that ignites spontaneously in air when finely divided. Strontium is used in pyrotechnic compounds and various alloys.

subatomic Having dimensions or participating in reactions characteristic of the constituents of the atom.

sulfur A pale yellow nonmetallic element occurring widely in nature in several free and combined allotropic forms. It is used in black gunpowder, rubber vulcanization, the manufacture of insecticides and pharmaceuticals, and in the preparation of sulfur compounds such as hydrogen sulfide and sulfuric acid.

sulfuric acid A highly corrosive, dense, oily liquid, colorless to dark brown depending on its purity and used to manufacture a wide variety of chemicals and materials including fertilizers, paints, detergents, and explosives.

summation The process by which multiple or repeated stimuli can produce a response in a nerve, muscle, or other part that one stimulus alone cannot produce.

superfluid A fluid, such as a liquid form of helium, exhibiting a frictionless flow at temperatures close to absolute zero.

surgeon A physician specializing in surgery.

surgery The branch of medicine that deals with the diagnosis and treatment of injury, deformity, and disease by manual and instrumental means.

syllogism A formal argument consisting of a major and a minor premise.

synchrocyclotron A cyclotron that accelerates protons and positive ions by using frequency modulation to synchronize the phase of the accelerating potential with the frequency of the accelerated particles to compensate for relativistic increases in particle mass at high speeds.

syphilis A chronic infectious disease caused by a spirochete (*Treponema pallidum*), either transmitted by direct contact, usually in sexual intercourse, or passed from mother to child in utero, and progressing through three stages characterized respectively by local formation of chancres, ulcerous skin eruptions, and systemic infection leading to general paresis.

syringe A medical instrument used to inject fluids into the body or draw them from it.

systematics The science of classification.

tabes dorsalis A late form of syphilis resulting in a hardening of the dorsal columns of the spinal cord and characterized by shooting pains, emaciation, loss of muscular coordination, and disturbances of sensation and digestion.

tartrate A salt or an ester of tartaric acid.

telegraphy Communication by means of the telegraph.

telescope A tubular optical instrument used for viewing distant, primarily astrological objects, by means of the infraction of light rays through a lens.

terrestrial Of or relating to Earth or its inhabitants.

Tertiary Of or relating to salts of acids containing three replaceable hydrogen atoms or relating to organic compounds in which a group, such as an alcohol or amine, is bound to three nonelementary radicals.

tetanus An acute, often fatal disease characterized by spasmodic contraction of voluntary muscles, especially those of the neck and jaw, and caused by the toxin of the bacillus *Clostridium tetani,* which typically infects the body through a deep wound.

tetrahedron A polyhedron with four faces.

theory The analysis of a set of facts in their relation to one another; in science, a proposal based on study, observation and research given as an explanation for certain phenomena.

therapeutics Medical treatment of disease; the art or science of healing.

thermodynamics A branch of physics that deals with the mechanical action or relations of heat.

Titania A satellite of Uranus.

toxin A poisonous substance, especially a protein, that is produced by living cells or organisms and is capable of causing disease when introduced into the body tissues but is often also capable of inducing neutralizing antibodies or antitoxins.

transmit To send (a signal), as by wire or radio.

transmitter An electronic device that generates and amplifies a carrier wave, modulates it with a meaningful signal derived from speech or other sources, and radiates the resulting signal from an antenna.

transmutation Transformation of one element into another by one or a series of nuclear reactions.

transverse Situated or lying across; crosswise.

tritium A rare radioactive hydrogen isotope with atomic mass 3 and half-life 12.5 years, prepared artificially for use as a tracer and as a constituent of hydrogen bombs.

tuberculosis An infectious disease of human beings and animals caused by the tubercle bacillus and characterized by the formation of tubercles on the lungs and other tissues of the body, often developing long after the initial infection.

unified field theory A physical theory that combines the treatment of two or more types of fields in order to deduce previously unrecognized interrelationships, especially such a theory unifying the theories of nuclear, electromagnetic, and gravitational forces.

uniformitarianism A geological theory stating that existing processes, acting in the same manner as they do at the present, are sufficient to account for all geological change.

uranium A heavy silvery-white metallic element, radioactive and toxic, easily oxidized, and having 14 known isotopes of which U 238 is the most abundant in nature. The element occurs in several minerals, including uraninite and carnotite, from which it is extracted and processed for use in research, nuclear fuels, and nuclear weapons.

uranium 235 A light isotope of uranium with the mass number of 235, that when bombarded with slow neutrons undergoes rapid fission into smaller atoms with the release of neutrons and energy. It is the primary material used in nuclear power plants and atomic bombs.

Uranus The seventh planet from the sun.

vaccine A preparation of a weakened or killed pathogen, such as a bacterium or virus, or of a portion of the pathogen's structure that upon administration stimulates antibody production against the pathogen but is incapable of causing severe infection.

vacuum A space empty of matter.

vapor The gaseous state of a substance that is liquid or solid under ordinary conditions.

Venus The second planet from the sun.

vertebrate A classification of living organisms, defined as those possessing a spinal column.

virus The causative agent of an infective disease.

viscosity The condition or property of being viscous.

viscous Having relatively high resistance to flow.

vitamin Any of various fat-soluble or water-soluble organic substances essential in minute amounts for normal growth and activity of the body and obtained naturally from plant and animal foods.

vivisection The act or practice of cutting into or otherwise injuring living animals, especially for the purpose of scientific research.

volcanoes An opening in the earth's crust through which molten lava, ash, and gases are ejected.

vortex A spiral motion of fluid within a limited area, especially a whirling mass of water or air that sucks everything near it toward its center.

vulcanization To improve the strength, resiliency, and freedom from stickiness and odor of (rubber, for example) by combining with sulfur or other additives in the presence of heat and pressure.

wave equations A partial differential equations whose solutions describe wave phenomena.

wave mechanics A theory that ascribes characteristics of waves to subatomic particles and attempts to interpret physical phenomena on this basis.

weak force A fundamental interaction between elementary particles that is several orders of magnitude weaker than the electromagnetic interaction and is responsible for some particle decay, nuclear beta decay, and neutrino absorption and emission.

X-ray A relatively high-energy photon. A stream of such photons is used for their penetrating power in radiography, radiology, radiotherapy, and scientific research.

Zeeman effect The splitting of single spectral lines of an emission spectrum into three or more polarized components when the radiation source is in a magnetic field.

zenith The point on the celestial sphere that is directly above the observer.

zoology The branch of biology concerned with the classification, properties, and vital phenomena of animals.

Index